Robert E. Powis

The MONEY LAUNDERERS

Lessons From
The Drug Wars -
How Billions Of
Illegal Dollars Are
Washed Through
Banks & Businesses

PROBUS PUBLISHING COMPANY
Chicago, Illinois
Cambridge, England

ISBN 1-55738-262-X

Printed in the United States of America

BB

3 4 5 6 7 8 9 0

To my wife, Elise

And to many people in and out of government who
gave valuable insights and advice.

TABLE OF CONTENTS

FOREWORD

Money laundering has always been used to dispose of the proceeds of a variety of criminal offenses that involve payments for contraband goods or illegal services. However, the explosion of drug use dating back to the late 1970s has made money laundering a familiar topic.

Americans are estimated to spend between $80 billion to $120 billion annually on illegal narcotics and virtually all payments are made with currency. The cash paid for the drugs must be laundered or cleansed so that drug traffickers can create the illusion that the money comes from legitimate sources. To meet this need, an industry of money laundering specialists has developed.

There is a considerable amount of mystique and mystery about money laundering activity. While some of the launderers go through a series of convoluted transactions designed to confuse the average person, the basic concept of money laundering is easily understandable.

This book seeks to shred the mystique of money laundering by detailing the procedures of a number of significant money laundering operations that were ultimately dismantled by federal law enforcement agencies. In view of the proximity of drug dealing to money laundering, the book also discusses some of the successes and shortcomings in the "War on Drugs" waged by the Reagan and Bush Administrations. Finally, the book provides direction to banks and other financial institutions on how to cope with problems associated with money launderers.

PROLOGUE

Money laundering has been defined as the use of money derived from illegal activity by concealing the identity of the individuals who obtained the money and converted it to assets that appear to have come from a legitimate source. A simpler definition is the washing of dirty money to make it appear to be legitimate.

Although money laundering has been around for a long time, it wasn't until 1970 that any meaningful legislation was enacted to deal with it. That legislation, commonly known as the Bank Secrecy Act (BSA), went into effect in 1970. The BSA mandated a series of reporting and recordkeeping requirements designed to help track money laundering activity and to penetrate the veil of secrecy surrounding off-shore bank accounts. The requirements were based on the theory that unusual transactions of currency at domestic financial institutions and unusual shipments of currency into or out of the United States might be related to criminal activity.

The BSA legislation attempted to attack money laundering with a five-pronged system of requirements. The law mandates the following:

- Banks and other financial institutions are required to report currency transactions over $10,000 by or on behalf of the same person on the same business day. The report must be made to the Internal Revenue Service (IRS) on IRS Form 4789, which is known as a Currency Transaction Report (CTR). There are exceptions to the filing requirements for transactions conducted between domestic banks and for transactions conducted by banks with certain retail businesses and government agencies.

- A Customs report must be filed by persons who transport or ship currency or monetary instruments over $10,000 into or out of the United States. The report must be filed on a Customs Form 4790. It is known as a "Report of International Transaction of Currency or Monetary Instruments" and is commonly referred to as a CMIR. There are certain exceptions to this filing requirement for banks.

- Citizens and resident aliens are required to file a report with the IRS if they maintain a financial interest in or signature authority over a foreign bank account with a balance of over $10,000 during a calendar year. The report must be filed on IRS Form 90-22-1. It is known as a "Foreign Bank Account Report" (FBAR).

- The Treasury Department is required to maintain a consolidated database of the information collected on the three reporting forms. The idea is that Treasury can track unusual domestic and international flows of currency and monetary instruments and identify money launderers and drug kingpins.

- Records must be maintained for a wide variety of financial transactions conducted by banks and other financial institutions. Most of the records required are of the type that sound business and accounting principles would dictate in any event. The reason for the recordkeeping requirement is to maintain a paper trail for IRS agents and other federal investigators to be able to follow in tax evasion and other criminal investigations.

Several factors conspired to delay and reduce the effectiveness of BSA requirements. Bankers challenged the constitutionality of the law and that issue was not settled until 1974 when the Supreme Court ruled that the BSA reporting requirements did not violate the search and seizure provisions of the Fourth Amendment. After that issue was settled, there was a period of massive non-compliance by banks and other financial institutions with BSA reporting requirements. The non-compliance problem was aggravated by a lack of concern and interest on the part of bank regulatory agencies toward BSA compliance issues. It was not a priority issue for the regulators and banks were not pushed to comply. Financial institution compliance with the reporting requirements was minimal from 1974 until 1984.

The explosion of drug use in the late 1970s dramatically increased money laundering activity and brought about increased enforcement activity. The Federal Reserve Bank conducted a study that showed there was a $4.3 billion surplus of currency in Florida in 1979 while most other areas of the country were showing currency deficits. A logical conclusion from this study was that a good part of the surplus was from drug money. As a result of the study, Treasury reviewed CTR filings from Miami banks and discovered that approximately $350 million in currency transactions had been reported for some thirty business and individual accounts. Treasury convinced the Justice Department to participate in a multi-agency task force that would investigate the individuals responsible for the currency transactions. The task force, known as Operation Greenback, was formed in Miami in 1980. It was staffed primarily by Customs and IRS agents working together in the same office space along with prosecutors from the Justice Department. Their mission was to investigate the unusual currency deposits in South Florida to determine if BSA violations were occurring and to establish if the money was linked to drug trafficking organizations.

Operation Greenback was very successful. It clearly established that a class of professional money laundering specialists had arisen and that there were strong ties between the money launderers and drug trafficking organizations. A number of major money launderers were successfully prosecuted. Greenback cases developed against launderers such as Isaac Kattan, Beno Ghitis, Hernan Botero, Alberto Barrera and Ramon Milian Rodriguez are detailed in this book.

Enforcement activity against money launderers in the late 1970s and early 1980s identified a number of shortcomings in the BSA. In the years that followed, there were several amendments to the law and the regulations in an effort to stop cash transactions from slipping between the cracks of reporting requirements.

In 1980, the regulations were changed so that banks could no longer exempt non-bank financial institutions and foreign banks (including foreign subsidiaries) from the currency reporting requirements. Other regulatory changes provided for stricter identification for individuals conducting large currency transactions and stricter limitations on the kind of business accounts that banks could exempt from the reporting requirements.

In 1984, the BSA was amended to drastically increase penalties for non-compliance with the currency reporting requirements. Most offenses were raised from the status of misdemeanors, with a maximum jail term of one year, to felonies, with maximum jail terms of up to five years. The Internal Revenue Code was amended by the Tax Reform Act of 1984 to require the filing of reports to the IRS by persons engaged in a trade or

business who received more than $10,000 in currency, in one or more re-
lated transactions, during the conduct of their business. Such reports must
be filed on IRS Form 8300. Information from these reports is fed into the
Treasury Department BSA database.

The most significant piece of legislation ever enacted to deal with
money laundering was the Money Laundering Control Act of 1986. It finally provided federal agents and prosecutors with the necessary tools to
fight money launderers on a level playing field. It established the crime of
money laundering where previously no such crime had existed. It also
made several significant amendments to the BSA, including:

- It became a crime to structure transactions to evade the reporting
  requirements of the BSA.

- Banks were required to obtain statements from accountholders
  whose accounts were to be exempted.

- Civil and criminal penalties were further increased. Persons com-
  mitting willful violations now faced a maximum jail term of 10
  years.

Also included in the Money Laundering Control Act was an amendment to the Right to Financial Privacy Act that made it easier for banks to
furnish suspicious transaction information to federal enforcement agencies
without running the risk of being sued by customers.

The enactment of the Money Laundering Control Act was followed, in
1987, by a host of changes in Treasury regulations that closed many BSA
compliance loopholes.

Additional amendments to the BSA in 1988 were followed by
recordkeeping regulation in 1990 which requires financial institutions to
obtain identification and maintain records of all purchases with currency
of monetary instruments in amounts between $3,000 and $10,000. The
monetary instruments covered include cashier's checks, bank checks and
drafts, traveler's checks and money orders.

EFFORTS TO EVADE

The legislative and regulatory changes that came out of Washington over
the past ten years have certainly provided a new arsenal of weapons in the
battle against money laundering and have made it more difficult for launderers to operate. Professional money laundering specialists have always
been aware of the BSA. With each change in the law and the regulations,

these launderers have reacted with new techniques in an attempt to keep just one step ahead of federal investigators.

For example, the launderers in South Florida in the late 1970s and early 1980s knew that repeated large currency deposits directly into Miami banks did not trigger any government inquiries. However, when Operation Greenback agents began to investigate the large cash deposits, the launderers' tactics changed. Some reacted by dispatching troops around the country to purchase cashier's checks, money orders and similar instruments in amounts under $10,000 to evade BSA reporting requirements in a laundering technique which came to be known as "smurfing." And when banks and federal investigators caught on to that trick, some launderers took their business away from the banking system by smuggling huge amounts of currency directly out of the United States.

The early chapters of this book deal with the well-organized operations of launderers for Colombian cocaine distributors who were involved in the large cash deposits, "smurfing" and transporting currency out of the country. Their operations are contrasted with the somewhat bumbling and rudimentary operations of launderers for a heroin ring in the "Pizza Connection" chapter. The heroin launderers struggled to cleanse millions of dollars while the cocaine launderers were disposing of billions.

When the laws and enforcement activity put the heat on "smurfing" and currency smuggling operations, the launderers started to use otherwise legitimate businesses as a cover for disposing of enormous amounts of cash. The chapter on Operation Polar Cap details the largest single laundering operation ever broken up by the government. A number of jewelry firms used the facade of gold trading as a front for disposing of over $1 billion in currency.

The evasive techniques conjured up by launderers have not only made the job of federal investigators more difficult, but they have also forced financial institutions to adopt new concepts in the way business is done. These concepts are "know your customer," "don't be used by money launderers," "report suspicious transactions," "strictly comply with the BSA" and "know the source of your customer's funds." These are today's watch words of survival for banks and other financial institutions. They replace the old maxim of "see no evil, hear no evil," which seemed so prevalent in the past.

Any banker who doubts this turn of events need only be reminded of the case of the Bank of Credit and Commerce International (BCCI) wherein the bank and a number of senior managers were convicted of money laundering charges in 1990 after an undercover agent wire-transferred millions of dollars of drug money through the bank as part of a massive government sting operation. Chapter six recounts the details of that sting.

The laundering operations described in this book have all been broken up by government enforcement action. Most of the launderers were caught and prosecuted and many of them are serving substantial jail sentences.

Money laundering is a vital and infamous component of international narcotics trafficking. The reverse side of the importation and distribution of drugs is the need for the illicit proceeds to be taken out of the country to pay for still more drugs and to generate still greater profits, all the while concealing the source of these proceeds. The government hopes this need represents a point of vulnerability in the battle against the drug trade. By using the reporting requirements of the BSA, the objective is to choke the flow of drug dollars out of the country and achieve deterrence by making the movement of drug money as risky as trafficking in the drugs themselves. The money laundering statutes, with their Draconian penalties, have substantially increased this risk.

It is far more difficult today for money launderers to ply their trade. As long as there is a drug trade that generates huge volumes of currency, there will be a need to launder that money. Hopefully, through diligent efforts by government investigators and prosecutors, with the assistance of the banking and business communities, the most obvious avenues of money laundering will be cut off, making it even more difficult for drug traffickers and money launderers to prosper from their deeds.

ABOUT THE AUTHOR

Robert E. Powis is an author, consultant and lecturer on money laundering issues and the Bank Secrecy Act. As Deputy Assistant Secretary of the Treasury for Enforcement from 1981 to 1984, he played a key role in overseeing the dismantling of major laundering organizations. This first-hand knowledge of what went on during the early 1980s has been bolstered by literally hundreds of hours of interviews with those involved in the laundering operations detailed, as well as the involved law enforcement personnel, judges and lawyers.

During that period, he coordinated Treasury's effort against money laundering and was heavily involved in the administration of the Bank Secrecy Act. Mr. Powis' book, *Bank Secrecy Act Compliance*, (Chicago: Bankers Publishing Co., 1989), now in its third printing, has been used by thousands of banks in the United States to develop effective compliance programs and to avoid being victimized by money launderers.

Mr. Powis served in the United States Secret Service for 27 years. When he left that organization for Treasury in 1981, he was the Assistant Director for Investigations. He directed all field office investigative operations of the Secret Service.

Since 1984 Mr. Powis has been Chairman of INTERPASS, Ltd., an international security consulting and investigative firm with offices in New York and Washington, D.C. Mr. Powis has provided advice to a number of financial institutions on money laundering issues.

CHAPTER 1

THE PIZZA CONNECTION:
THE HEROIN MONEY LAUNDRY

The "Pizza Connection" was a major heroin distribution ring that operated in parts of the Northeast and Midwest between 1979 and 1984.

The government began investigating the Pizza Connection in 1980 during a Federal Bureau of Investigations (FBI) probe of the activities of individuals in and around New York who appeared to be involved with several homicides. During November 1980, associates of these individuals were observed moving boxes and suitcases full of cash. By early 1981, it became clear that the FBI had stumbled onto a group of Sicilian mobsters who were dealing in heroin. A number of these dealers owned pizza parlors which served as "fronts" for their drug dealing activities.

Like all drug organizations, the Pizza Connection mob needed to launder the cash generated by its heroin sales. But when it came to actually laundering money, this group came away looking like "The Gang That Couldn't Shoot Straight."

Not that the government investigators assigned to the case were much better—their efforts had the flavor of a "Keystone Cops" episode. Investigative efforts were laboriously slow and sporadic. There was little in the way of communication and coordination between FBI offices or the FBI

1

and other federal law enforcement agencies. Indeed, it could be said that the Pizza Connection highlights key shortcomings in the government's attempts to curtail money laundering during the early 1980s.

The methods used by the Pizza Connection launderers involved converting small denomination currencies to 50 and 100 dollar bills, smuggling large amounts of cash directly out of the country, depositing large amounts of currency into accounts at brokerage houses, and structuring bank deposit amounts to evade federal currency reporting requirements.

The launderers, themselves, seemed an unlikely cast of characters. They included Sal Amendolito, a wholesale fish exporter, who turned out to be a bumbling cheater; Frank Castronovo, the owner of an Italian restaurant in Menlo Park, New Jersey; Sal and Filippo Salamone, the owners of two pizza parlors in Bloomsburg, Pennsylvania; Franco Della Torre, a Swiss businessman with close ties to drug dealers in Italy; and Paul Waridel, a Turkish antiquities dealer, who had served three years in an Italian prison for opium smuggling.

The methods used by these individuals to launder money were somewhat crude and unsophisticated. Nevertheless, they were able to launder millions of dollars in heroin proceeds and stay in business for nearly four years.

The government's efforts to combat money laundering, at the time, were hampered by laws and regulations without teeth, by a failure to pursue financial institution compliance with the Bank Secrecy Act, by a lack of coordination, and by shortcomings within individual law enforcement agencies.

THE FISHMONGER TURNED LAUNDERER

One of the early money launderers in the Pizza Connection was Sal Amendolito. He had been in the fish business in Italy, importing fish from the United States and other places. Some years before he had been a partner in a financial consulting business in Milan that specialized in exporting lira to Switzerland on behalf of clients who wanted to evade Italian currency control laws.

Amendolito came to the United States in the late 1970s and set up a fish exporting business, shipping fish back to Italy. By early 1980, the exporting business was in financial trouble.

According to testimony subsequently provided by Amendolito, he was contacted in early 1980 by Sal Miniati, a Milanese businessman, who offered him a new business venture. Miniati had been handling some of Amendolito's fish exports and had been his partner in the financial consulting business. The new venture, Miniati said, involved pizza parlor owners in the New York area who needed to send cash to Switzerland for a Sicilian construction company that was building a resort. The catch: they wanted to move the money without being identified by the Internal Revenue Service. In fact, the cash came from heroin sales.

According to Amendolito's account, Miniati said the pizza people wanted to move $9 million and would be willing to pay Amendolito one percent of that amount for his services.

Upon agreeing to the arrangement, Amendolito was given the name of an Italian contact, Olivero Tognoli, who was described as a wealthy Milanese businessman who would provide the money to the construction company after it arrived in Switzerland. He was also given a telephone number in New Jersey and a nickname. Amendolito called the number, spoke with the man who answered to the nickname, and set up a meeting for early July at the Roma Restaurant in Menlo Park, New Jersey. The meeting took place in early July 1980.

The day after their meeting, the New Jersey contact, Frank Castronovo, gave Amendolito $100,000 in cash, thereby launching Amendolito's career as a money launderer.

After receiving the money, Amendolito visited 12 different banks in New Jersey, opening accounts at each in the name of his business, International Fish Services, with cash deposits in amounts just under $10,000.

By structuring the deposits in amounts under the $10,000, Amendolito could legitimately skirt Bank Secrecy Act reporting requirements and evade government scrutiny. And if anybody asked about the deposits, he would say the money came from his business.

Once the money was on deposit, Amendolito bought bank checks at each of the banks, using the funds on deposit, and kept his one percent commission in each account. Once again, no Currency Transaction Reports were required, because no currency changed hands.

Amendolito then took the 12 bank checks to four international banks in New York—Credit Suisse, Swiss Bank Corporation, Citibank, and the Lavaro Bank—and negotiated three of the bank checks at each bank. The money was then wire transferred to one of three Swiss bank accounts that he had been instructed by Miniati to use. Again, because no cash was involved, no reports were required by the IRS.

When the wire transfers were posted to the Swiss bank account, the laundering operation was complete. The heroin money from Castronovo had been washed by Amendolito to make it appear as though it had been received in the conduct of his fish business. It ended up in a secret, numbered Swiss bank account with no indication that it had been accumulated through heroin sales.

In the days following that first series of transactions, Amendolito was a busy man. But soon, he began wearying of his task. As he handled additional $100,000 packages of currency on behalf of Castronovo, Amendolito found himself racing to each of the 12 New Jersey banks to make deposits of just under $10,000, then racing back to the banks to buy bank checks, and then on to one of the four international banks in Manhattan to wire transfer the funds. Amendolito was exhausted. Making matters worse, Castronovo said he was ready to supply larger amounts of cash.

Amendolito called Miniati in Italy and told him of his problems. Miniati said he would look into an easier way to get the money to Switzerland.

COMIC OPERA

On July 21, 1980, Castronovo gave Amendolito four suitcases containing $550,000 in $5, $10, and $20 bills. Amendolito called Miniati, who assured him that his problem had been solved. Amendolito was told to contact a Mr. Lanfranchi, a public relations representative at Finagest, a Swiss investment firm with offices in midtown Manhattan.

This instruction set off a series of events that had overtones of comic opera. The image of suave, knowledgeable money launderers became forever tarnished as Amendolito, the fishmonger, and Lanfranchi, the PR rep, bungled their way around in the heat of a New York summer trying to dispose of $550,000 in small denomination bills.

Upon receiving the cash, Amendolito telephoned Lanfranchi, told him he had the money, and arranged a meeting for the following day. Lanfranchi, meanwhile, contacted his colleagues at Finagest headquarters, and was told to bring the money to Conti Commodity Services in the World Trade Center in lower Manhattan.

The next day, Amendolito packed the money into four leather bags and drove with it to Manhattan in an old station wagon. He met Lanfranchi in midtown, and the two drove together to Conti's offices in lower Manhattan. Once there, however, they learned that the firm was not equipped to handle that amount of currency, and they were referred to the Chase Manhattan Bank branch on the ground floor. They brought the leather bags with the money into the Chase branch, but once again they were disappointed when they were told that the branch could not handle that volume of small denomination bills.

However, there was a light at the end of the tunnel. Amendolito and Lanfranchi were told to bring the money to Chase Manhattan headquarters, just a few blocks away. They dragged the leather bags back into the station wagon and crawled over to the bank's main office in the typical snarled traffic of lower Manhattan. But when they finally arrived and carried the bags of cash into the bank, it was nearly closing time and the currency counting machines were all tied up. They were told to come back the next morning.

Once again, the two men loaded the bags of cash back into the station wagon and drove off. It had been a day of total frustration. It was amateur hour in the money laundering business.

On the following morning, Amendolito and Lanfranchi returned to Chase Manhattan with the money. Bank staffers accepted and counted the money and recorded it as a cash transaction from Finagest's New York office. At Lanfranchi's direction, it was credited to the account of Finagest at Credit Suisse in Lugano. The date of the transaction was July 23, 1980.

The Bank Secrecy Act regulations had been changed just a few weeks before to require all banks to file reports of currency transactions involving nonbank financial institutions (like Finagest) in amounts exceeding $10,000.

The whole area of Bank Secrecy Act compliance, regulation, and enforcement in 1980 was one of benign neglect. Banks and the federal bank supervisory agencies paid little attention to compliance; and when regulatory changes were made they were poorly communicated.

The first enforcement agency to become aware of the Chase Manhattan/Finagest transaction was the FBI, during questioning of Sal Amendolito in the fall of 1983. However, no referral was made by the FBI to the IRS about the transaction. The transaction first became a matter of public record during the trial of the Pizza Connection case in 1984. Finegest was never penalized for not filing a CTR, which was required by law to report its currency transaction with Amendolito.

The problems Amendolito had disposing of the $550,000 illustrate graphically the difficulties drug organizations and their money launderers have dealing with the proceeds of their operations. Currency (particularly in small denominations) is bulky and difficult to transport. Drug dealers do not want the money connected to them. Frank Castronovo wanted insulation—he did not want money tainted by heroin sales deposited into a bank in his own name. Amendolito took care of that, and he also managed to avoid a paper trail—no reports were filed with the government, and there was no record of Amendolito's name at either Chase Manhattan Bank or Finagest.

The government only learned of the situation by being tipped to the transaction and by making a direct inquiry at Finagest. Of course, the IRS might have stumbled on the transaction in an audit of Finagest records, but there is only a slim possibility that may have occurred.

In handling the first several $100,000 bundles of currency from Castronovo, Amendolito gave himself some cover. By keeping his deposits under $10,000, he was assured that no reports would be filed with the government detailing the transactions. He did, however, leave a paper trail in the twelve banks that could be followed. The checks were negotiated at the four international banks in New York and the proceeds were transferred to numbered Swiss bank accounts, which is where the paper trail ended. His cover: if the deposits and check purchases were ever unearthed, he would maintain that they represented the proceeds of his fish business, and that the wire transfers represented payments on business loans.

OUTBOUND CURRENCY SMUGGLING

After the harrowing experience with the $550,000 cash package, Amendolito realized that he needed a better way to move large sums of currency. The accounts at the 12 New Jersey banks were useful, but he could not personally handle large amounts of money by continually making deposits under $10,000. There simply was not enough time in the day to make all the necessary cash deposits and check purchases. Besides, he knew eventually he would draw attention to himself if he continued depositing cash and purchasing bank checks on a daily basis.

The Finagest fiasco was something Amendolito did not want to go through again. He was aware that money could be taken directly out of the country without using banks, so he decided to experiment. He asked Castronovo for a smaller amount of money and was given $28,000. He purchased $27,000 in bank checks at three of the banks where he had accounts, making the checks payable to himself. He kept $1,000 as his commission, which amounted to slightly more than 3.5%. Amendolito then took the $27,000 in bank checks and chartered a flight to Nassau in the Bahamas.

Amendolito knew if he took more than $5,000 in currency or bearer instruments out of the country a Customs Form 4790, or CMIR, declaring the amount would have to be filed. He deliberately had the bank checks made payable to himself so that they wouldn't be bearer instruments. Therefore, no government form or declaration was required.

Amendolito took the chartered flight to Nassau to observe what would happen. He was encouraged by what he saw: no one asked him what he was carrying. He reasoned that he could probably bring currency on the flight without any questions being asked. He was also encouraged by what happened upon his arrival in Nassau. There was only a perfunctory immigration inquiry into his citizenship, and no one was interested in what he was carrying.

After his arrival in Nassau, Amendolito went to Banca Svizzera Italiana (BSI). One of the three numbered Swiss bank accounts that Miniati had given him was at the BSI branch in Menderisio, Switzerland. Amendolito opened an account at the Nassau branch, deposited the bank checks he brought with him, and then wire transferred most of the money to the numbered account at the BSI branch in Menderisio.

While at the Nassau branch of BSI, Amendolito met the manager, Peter Albisser. He learned from Albisser that there were no restrictions on bringing U.S. currency into the Bahamas, so there was no need to declare any of the money. Albisser said he was willing to accept large amounts of U.S. currency and assured Amendolito that he would personally assist in getting the cash into the bank. Amendolito returned to the United States satisfied that he had found a new way to get the Pizza Connection money to Switzerland.

On July 30, 1980, Miniati telephoned Amendolito to say Tognoli, the contact in Italy, had a new source of funds who would be calling Amendolito within a few days. In the meantime, on July 31, Amendolito picked up $500,000 in currency from Castronovo after getting a telephone call from Miniati. He packed the money in suitcases and chartered a flight to Nassau, where he was met by Albisser.

The trip went off without a hitch. Thanks to Albisser's connections, he was even spared the perfunctory immigration questions. No one was interested in what he was carrying. He was not required to file any forms with Bahamian Customs.

Fresh from his successful trip, Amendolito leased office space at 575 Madison Avenue on August 1 to conduct his money business. The space, a small cubicle, was part of a large block of small offices controlled by World Wide Business Centres. The lease arrangement provided Amendolito with a receptionist, telephone answering, mail, copying, and secretarial services that he shared with a large number of other businesses. He called his new firm Overseas Business Services.

On the very next day, Amendolito received a telephone call from a man who said he was referred by Tognoli. It was the new source of funds. A meeting was arranged for the following afternoon on a street corner in Queens.

At that meeting, Amendolito met Salvatore and Vito Catalano. Salvatore Catalano was a major heroin dealer. The two brothers told Amendolito they would have more than $1 million that needed to be transferred. They gave him a piece of paper with a telephone number and the names Vito and Sal.

After the meeting with Vito and Sal, Amendolito telephoned Miniati and expressed concern that something illegal was going on. Amendolito did not like the idea of the street corner meeting. Miniati assured him that the brothers were okay and that the money was not tainted by criminal activity. He said that the Catalano brothers just wanted to avoid identification by the IRS in transferring this large sum of money.

On the following day, Miniati telephoned Amendolito. He told him that the money was ready and instructed him to contact the Catalano brothers. Amendolito made the call, but neither of the brothers were at the location. Later, Sal Catalano contacted Amendolito and said he and his brother were ready with the "one point five." A meeting was arranged for the following morning at the same Queens street corner where they first met.

Amendolito was concerned. He had successfully moved $500,000 to Nassau on a chartered flight. However, $1.5 million was a different story—it was three times the volume of currency. He would need more suitcases. Questions might be asked. Suppose something went wrong? Amendolito decided to call Albisser, the BSI branch manager. When Albisser heard how much cash was involved, he agreed to come to New York the following day; he had a way to dispose of the money.

Amendolito reserved a room at the Barbizon Plaza on Central Park South. He assumed that the Catalano brothers would want him to count the money, so the room could serve two purposes—he could count the money there with the brothers and then he could use the room to transfer the cash to Albisser.

On the next morning, Amendolito went to the Queens street corner. Only Sal Catalano showed up. Amendolito suggested that the two men go to a hotel to count the money, but Catalano said that wouldn't be necessary. Amendolito backed his station wagon up to the trunk of Catalano's car, took one large and two smaller suitcases into the station wagon, and drove on to Manhattan.

Upon arriving at the Barbizon Plaza, Amendolito had a bellman help him bring the suitcases to his room, where he began the tedious task of counting the cash. The total came to $1,540,000. He set aside $53,900 for himself—his 3.5% commission. Soon after, Albisser came to the room with his deputy manager. Albisser told Amendolito that they were bringing the money to their correspondent bank in New York, which turned out to be the Bank of Boston's New York office.

REGULATORY SHORTCOMINGS

Albisser's deposit of almost $1.5 million in currency at the Bank of Boston was ironic. It completed a chain of transfers of large sums of money where no reports were made to the government. The currency transaction at the Bank of Boston was handled as a deposit from an international bank and no CTR was filed. The irony lies in the fact that the Treasury Department had just changed its Bank Secrecy Act regulations to require reports on cash transactions between domestic banks and foreign banks.

Treasury had long been concerned that money launderers were moving unusually large amounts of currency from foreign to domestic financial institutions. Money launderers were taking advantage of an exemption in currency transaction reporting requirements for bank-to-bank transfers. New regulations that became effective on July 7, 1980 had limited the exemption to transfers between domestic banks. The Albisser deposit at Bank of Boston took place on August 5, 1980.

The level of compliance by banks with strictures of the Bank Secrecy Act in the late 1970s and early 1980s was appalling. The level of scrutiny by the federal bank regulatory agencies for compliance with those requirements was equally appalling. The result was that bankers simply did not pay any attention to the regulations.

The Bank of Boston was no exception. In fact, it was probably the leading example of noncompliance. The bank did not even begin filing CTRs for transactions involving foreign banks until late 1984, when a federal investigation uncovered the fact that it had not been filing the forms. In the interim, thousands of transactions involving hundreds of millions of dollars went unreported. Bank of Boston pled guilty to violating currency reporting rules and was fined $500,000. It was a watershed case. Publicity about criminal charges, guilty pleas, and criminal and civil penalties involving the Bank of Boston marked a turning point in BSA compliance in early 1985. Thousands of banks scrambled to comply. Congressional hearings were held, and the law was changed to impose stricter penalties and fines for noncompliance.

During the firestorm of publicity surrounding the Bank of Boston case, the bank launched a public relations campaign of its own in an attempt to minimize its culpability. Ironically, one of the themes of the campaign was that the thousands of transactions that went unreported were legitimate commercial transfers. While that may have been true in most cases, it was certainly not the case in the Catalano to Amendolito to Albisser to Bank of Boston transfers.

To be fair, it is highly probable that even if the Albisser transaction had been reported on a CTR, nothing would have been done about it at the time. Treasury's ability to review and analyze CTR data in 1980 was not good. Even as late as 1988, despite many improvements in its tracking system, Treasury was unable to pinpoint the flow of over a billion dollars of currency into a number of Los Angeles banks as suspicious.

Also, to be fair to the Bank of Boston, it was not alone in failing to comply with the BSA. Shortly after the Bank of Boston violations were publicized, a number of other big money center banks were penalized for similar violations. Among them: Bank of America, Bank of New England, Manufacturers Hanover, Crocker National, Citibank, and Chemical Bank.

As for Amendolito, on the morning after laundering the $1.5 million deal for Sal Catalano, he received a telephone call from Castronovo, who had another half million. Amendolito went to Castronovo's Roma Restaurant and picked up the money. It was actually $550,000. He telephoned Albisser, who said it would be okay to bring the money down to Nassau that day. He was met by Albisser and the money was transferred smoothly.

In less than one month, Amendolito had moved about $3.5 million in cash out of the United States. No CTRs or CMIRs detailing these transactions were filed with the government. In some cases, there was no paper trail of any transaction. In other cases, there was a limited paper trail— some transactions had been recorded, but the records could only be of value to government investigators if they had information linking the transactions with heroin trafficking.

NO HONOR AMONG THIEVES

In late August 1980, Amendolito flew to Switzerland to talk with Miniati in person. He wanted to get a better percentage for his efforts; 3.5% was no longer a big enough cut. He also wanted to restart his fish business and was hoping to interest Miniati in providing some financial backing.

He met with Miniati in Lugano and told him what he had in mind. Miniati said that they would have to talk to Tognoli about an increased percentage of the currency transactions.

While Amendolito was in Lugano, Miniati introduced him to Franco Della Torre, who was touted as a financial expert who formerly had been with Finagest. Amendolito recalled Finagest with unpleasant memories. The three men talked about the problems of moving cash out of the United States. Della Torre, who had recently opened his own business, offered a solution. He said he knew of some Swiss nationals who would fly to New York, pick up large amounts of American currency, and bring it back to Switzerland. He said he would charge between 6% and 6.5% of the amount brought over on each trip. Amendolito was not interested; he was only getting 3.5% and was looking to increase his slice.

Miniati and Amendolito then flew to Sicily where they spent time with Tognoli. Tognoli said he was pleased with Amendolito's efforts, and after some discussion, he agreed to let Amendolito have 4% of all money handled in the future. While Amendolito was in Sicily, Tognoli introduced him to Leonardo Greco. Tognoli said Greco might be interested in financing Amendolito's fish business. Unbeknownst to Amendolito, Greco was the head of a major Mafia crime family. He was also the kingpin of the drug operation that was moving heroin into the United States. Amendolito was surprised that Greco knew he was moving money for Tognoli. Greco listened to Amendolito's proposition about the fish business. He seemed interested, but nothing ever came of it.

After an extended stay in Europe, Amendolito returned to New York, ready to resume his currency transfer business. In early October, he received a telephone call from Miniati, with instructions for a $619,000 pickup from Castronovo. He was to deliver $290,000 of the money to some Italian furriers staying at the Southgate Hotel in New York, and move the remainder to one of the three Swiss bank accounts.

Amendolito picked up the money at the Roma Restaurant. There were two packages. Castronovo told him that one contained $320,000 and the other $299,000. Amendolito made a terrible mistake. He did not count the money. He removed $9,000 from the package he thought contained $299,000, and drove to New York. At the Southgate Hotel, he delivered what he thought was now the $290,000 package to a designated room. There were four men in the room playing cards; they had been expecting him.

Amendolito then drove to his office at 575 Madison Avenue, where he had installed a currency counting machine. When he counted the remaining package, he discovered, to his horror, that it contained only $220,000 instead of $320,000. He quickly telephoned Castronovo, who told him there had been $399,000 in one package and $220,000 in the other. Castronovo said that Amendolito was mistaken in thinking it was the other way around. Amendolito raced back to the Southgate Hotel, where the furriers still sat, but they claimed they had received only $290,000.

Amendolito felt sick. He quickly telephoned Miniati and told him about the whole incident. He said that he no longer wanted to deal with Castronovo.

A short time later, Amendolito received a call from Tognoli, who said he should not be overly concerned about the loss of money, although he added that Amendolito was responsible for the loss and would have to pay it back. Tognoli also told Amendolito he wanted him to continue dealing with Castronovo.

Amendolito was upset. He was mad at himself for not counting the money in each package, and he was mad at Castronovo. He thought that Castronovo had deliberately deceived him about the amount in each package. He also wondered if Castronovo had held out $100,000 for himself. On the other hand, Tognoli and Miniati suspected Amendolito of pocketing the $100,000. Amendolito didn't realize it at the time, but the $100,000 shortage was the beginning of a series of incidents that would combine to terminate his money laundering activities for the heroin operation.

In a series of telephone conversations with Miniati and Tognoli, Amendolito made it clear that he no longer wanted to pick up money from Castronovo. Instead, he wanted the money brought to him at his Madison Avenue office. The change was finally agreed to and Tognoli picked a courier—a distant cousin of his named Philip Matassa.

Matassa was 25 years old, and had come to the United States from Italy about a year previously. In mid-October, Matassa began making pickups from Castronovo and delivering boxes of money to Amendolito. The two men developed a routine: Matassa would pick up a load of money from Castronovo, usually in one or two cardboard boxes, telephone Amendolito at his office to let him know he was on the way and telephone him again from the lobby of his office building. Amendolito would then come downstairs and help move the cartons of currency into his office. Unbeknownst to Amendolito, Matassa was also making currency deliveries to another location.

Amendolito liked the new arrangement. He didn't have to waste time driving to New Jersey for the money. Instead, he could concentrate on counting the money in his office and making arrangements to move the money out of the country.

There were, however, a few new wrinkles in the way the money was moved. For example, it was proving costly to charter flights all the time, so Amendolito began using commercial flights.

In early November, the flow of cash brought by Amendolito to BSI in Nassau had become so great that Albisser suggested taking some of the money elsewhere. He put Amendolito in touch with a friend in the Bank of Butterfield in Hamilton, Bermuda. From mid-October until late December of 1980, Amendolito laundered and transported about $6.5 million out of the United States. Almost $3 million was deposited in the Bank of Butterfield; the remainder went to Albisser's bank in Nassau. All the money in these accounts eventually was wire transferred to one of the three Swiss accounts controlled by Miniati.

The operative word here is "eventually." Amendolito discovered he could make a little more than his 4% commission by keeping the money in interest-bearing accounts at both banks. Interest on $1 million at six percent came to about $165 a day. If Amendolito could delay wire transfers for 10 days to two weeks or longer, he could pocket an extra $1,650 to $2,500. Actually, the bankers encouraged him to leave the money in as long as possible in return for the services that they provided. The delays in wiring the money to Switzerland, though, eventually got Amendolito in further trouble with Tognoli.

Amendolito mixed up his trips to Bermuda and the Bahamas. Sometimes he would go on commercial carriers and sometimes he would charter flights. He would usually carry between $400,000 and $600,000 on each trip.

On one occasion he showed up at JFK airport in New York with $400,000 in currency stuffed into a carry-on bag. He had a reservation on a flight to Bermuda, but he never made the flight after security personnel discovered the money. The police were called, and so was the Customs Service. Amendolito explained that he was taking the money to Bermuda in connection with his fish business, and was told that he would have to fill out a Customs Form 4790, also known as a CMIR, because he was transporting more than $5,000 in currency or bearer instruments in or out the country. He was given the form and filled it out in the amount of $220,000, but by the time he completed the paperwork he had missed the flight to Bermuda. He went home with the form and the money. A few days later he flew to Bermuda on another commercial flight, but this time he did not carry the money on board with him. Instead, he packed the cash in a suitcase and had the airline load it as checked baggage. He did not have to complete any forms for Customs, was not stopped or questioned, and was reunited with the suitcase in Bermuda. Once in Bermuda, Amendolito deposited the $400,000 in the Bank of Butterfield.

In October 1980, shortly after Amendolito had resumed transporting cash to the BSI Bank in Nassau, Albisser introduced him to a Bahamian political figure named Deighton Edwards. It was intimated that Edwards would be in a position to help if Amendolito ever ran into problems in Nassau with his currency transporting activities. At their first meeting, Edwards indicated that he was having financial difficulties and needed a loan. Amendolito believed that if Edwards didn't get the loan, he might encounter problems with his money shipments. Edwards indicated that $250,000 would be very helpful. After conferring with Miniati and Tognoli, Amendolito gave Edwards $230,000 in cash.

As Amendolito resumed his money laundering activities in October 1980, some events were occurring in law enforcement circles that would eventually bring down the Pizza Connection. The first event occurred in late October when an informant told an FBI agent in White Plains, New York that a group was about to launder $60 million in U.S. currency through a business located in the Horn and Hardart Building at 655 Third Avenue in Manhattan.

A crack FBI surveillance team began watching the building during the last week of October. On November 3, a silver Audi with New Jersey license plates pulled up near the address, and a man holding a black bag stepped out of the car. The man entered the building and delivered the black bag to a firm known as Idea Development Company. The license number on the car was checked and was found to belong to Frank Castronovo. Subsequent investigation identified the driver of the vehicle as the owner of the Roma Restaurant in Menlo Park, New Jersey. Castronovo was a link to the FBI investigation in New York of some Mafia figures who were believed to be connected to several homicides. Castronovo had been observed in the company of several of these individuals by FBI surveillance teams. The FBI also learned that the black bag Castronovo delivered to Idea Development Company contained $200,000 in cash. Amendolito didn't know it, but Castronovo had another outlet for his drug money.

During November, Philip Matassa had been picking up cash from Castronovo and delivering it to Amendolito. About three weeks after the FBI surveillance team spotted Castronovo at 655 Third Avenue, Matassa received unusual instructions from Tognoli. He was to meet two men in a parking lot in Brooklyn and receive two boxes. One was to be delivered to an office at 655 Third Avenue, the other was to go to Amendolito.

Matassa met the men and made the pickup. He delivered the first box to Idea Development Company at 655 Third Avenue, where he was spotted by the FBI surveillance team. Matassa then headed to Amendolito's office, followed by the FBI. The surveillance team watched Matassa enter the lobby of 575 Madison Avenue, make a telephone call, and remove a box from the trunk of his car after being met by Amendolito. The two then took the box into the building and stepped into an elevator, where they were joined by one of the surveillance agents. The agent watched the two men leave the elevator at the 10th floor, and it was determined that the 10th floor was occupied by World Wide Business Centres.

Incredibly, though, no inquiry was made by the FBI team at World Wide Business Centres until one year later, so there was no connection made between Amendolito and Mantassa or Castronova.

Matassa continued to make deliveries to both Idea Development Company and Overseas Business Services. In early December, he delivered a box of cash to Amendolito. As he was driving away en route to Idea Development Company, he noticed a car following him. He was not sure at first. Matassa panicked. He took off at high speed, made a few wild turns and finally lost the car. That was enough for him. He was sure that the police were following him. He was an alien and did not want trouble. He did not make the delivery to Idea Development Company. Instead, he returned the money and told his associates he was through.

Matassa's resignation forced Amendolito to resume making pickups of cash from Castronovo at the Roma Restaurant. He had moved about $3.5 million from October until the time Matassa quit. However, problems were brewing. Amendolito was getting greedy. He was not satisfied with a 4% commission. He started to keep money in his accounts in the Bank of Butterfield and BSI for longer and longer periods before making wire transfers to one of the Swiss accounts. He kept the interest on the money for himself. Tognoli suspected what was happening. In late November, he telephoned Amendolito and accused him of deliberately holding back on the wire transfers so that he could pocket the interest. Amendolito denied the accusation and blamed the delays on the banks that he used in Bermuda and Nassau. He said the banks insisted on keeping the money in noninterest bearing accounts for a period of time so that they could profit from the service they provided in handling the large amounts of currency. Tognoli told Amendolito to speed up the wire transfers. He reminded him that he still owed the $100,000 that he lost in the furrier's transaction. He also told him that he would have to recover the loan that he made to Deighton Edwards.

During December 1980, Amendolito moved an additional $3 million from Castronovo. In early January, Tognoli telephoned Amendolito and arranged a meeting in Montreal. At the meeting Tognoli said that he wanted the $100,000 from the furrier's deal paid off as soon as possible. He also told Amendolito to start collecting money from Edwards to repay the loan. Finally, he said he wanted all the money in the banks in Bermuda and Nassau transferred to the Swiss accounts within 24 hours.

Amendolito returned to New York. On the next day he transferred all the money in the BSI and Bank of Butterfield accounts to the Swiss banks. When the figures were checked, it was discovered that Amendolito was short $140,000. Tognoli telephoned him and said he now owed $470,000. Tognoli told Amendolito to come to Italy to discuss how the debt would be paid. Amendolito was finished as a money launderer. He actually made a trip to Sicily, where he met with Tognoli and Greco. The $100,000 that was lost in the furrier deal was forgiven, and he was told to begin paying off the remaining $370,000.

Amendolito returned to the United States and disappeared. He never made any effort to pay off the debt.

It was not until November 1981, almost one year later, that the White Plains FBI agent went to World Wide Business Centres at 575 Madison Avenue with surveillance photographs of Amendolito and Matassa. Up to this point, the agent still did not know the identity of the individual who was photographed with Matassa one year earlier. The agent was concerned an inquiry would prematurely tip off the money laundering operation.

While there was certainly some basis for caution, there does not seem to be any explanation for such a lengthy delay. If surveillance had continued at 575 Madison Avenue, it would have revealed that the man in the photograph no longer did business there after January 1981. Surveillance of the unknown man in the photograph would have identified him back in November 1980. Despite the long delay, the FBI agent who interviewed the manager of World Wide Business Centres struck a gold mine. The manager immediately identified the man in the photograph as Sal Amendolito, who had skipped out on his lease owing back rent. The manager turned over all of Amendolito's telephone and telex records that were made from World Wide Business Centres, and a list of authorized employees. The manager told the agent how Amendolito kept two safes and a currency counting machine in the small room that his firm, Overseas Business Services, had occupied. He also noted that Amendolito had a burglar alarm installed in the office.

The telephone and telex records revealed that Amendolito had made many telephone calls and sent numerous messages to Frank Castronovo, Sal Miniati, and Olivero Tognoli.

By the time Amendolito was identified in November 1981 as a money conduit for Frank Castronova, the FBI investigation of the Mafia figures connected with the homicides had indicated that some members of the group were involved in heroin distribution. The Amendolito money laundering investigation was coordinated with the drug and homicide investigations.

Among the leaders of the heroin distribution operation were Giuseppe Ganci and Salvatore Catalano. Ganci had been seen with Frank Castronovo on several occasions by FBI surveillance teams. Salvatore Catalano was the individual who had turned over $1.5 million in cash to Sal Amendolito on a Queens street corner in August 1980.

NEW WAYS TO LAUNDER

In January 1981, with Amendolito out of the picture, the Mafia bosses needed to find another conduit for moving U.S. dollars from New York to Switzerland. A number of alternatives were found. Two are noteworthy because of the methods used and the fact that the Mafia chieftains in Italy were not confident that Americans would get their profits to them in Europe.

One of the money moving alternatives involved an Italian banker named Antonio Cavalleri. Cavalleri was the manager of the Credit Suisse office in Breganzona, Italy, a town in the Swiss Alps. Cavalleri was friendly with two Mafia money launderers named Enrico Rossini and Vito Roberto Palazzolo. Rossini had been an investment banker. He and Palazzolo formed a Swiss company known as Traex. Ostensibly, Traex was a legitimate investment firm. In reality, it was a vehicle for moving drug profits and capital used to purchase heroin base for Leonardo Greco's operation. When Amendolito was cut off, Rossini and Palazzolo had a conversation with Cavalleri who had a solution to the problem of moving large quantities of U.S. dollars to Europe. Cavalleri knew a SwissAir employee who he believed might be willing to help. Rossini agreed to open an account for Traex at the Breganzona branch of Credit Suisse. Cavalleri would attempt to recruit the airline employee.

Cavalleri assisted Rossini in opening the Traex account. He also convinced the SwissAir employee that a group of Swiss businessmen wanted to move their profits in cash from the United States to Switzerland with no questions asked. During most of 1981 and for a few months in 1982, the SwissAir employee regularly brought large amounts of currency to Switzerland on SwissAir flights from JFK to Zurich. He transported over $10 million in U.S. currency during that period. The money all went into the Traex account.

In February 1982, the FBI learned of the currency transportation by the SwissAir employee and started to watch him on his trips to New York. On one occasion, they followed him to a parking lot in Brooklyn, where he received a Samsonite suitcase from a man who was driving a vehicle with Pennsylvania license plates. Subsequent investigation determined that the man was Filippo Salamone, the brother of Salvatore Salamone, a major heroin dealer. Each of the brothers owned pizza restaurants in Bloomsburg, Pennsylvania, a sleepy college town in central Pennsylvania.

Sal Salamone devised his own scheme for minimizing the proliferation of small bills from heroin sales. He coaxed waitresses at his pizza restaurant to exchange the small bills at local banks for $50s and $100s. Such exchanges would enable couriers like the SwissAir employee to take a larger haul out of the country.

But by mid-February 1982, the SwissAir employee wanted out of the currency transportation business—he was afraid of getting caught. Money was piling up and it had to be moved.

In February 1982, Franco Della Torre, who had been handling money for the heroin organization in Switzerland and in Italy, moved to New York and set himself up in a suite at the Waldorf Astoria. He took over the void left by the SwissAir courier by moving money through an account at Merrill Lynch, in New York, to Switzerland.

Della Torre had been connected with Finagest in Lugano, Switzerland in early 1980. In fact, he had suggested the use of SwissAir employees to move cash between New York and Switzerland when he met Amendolito in Lugano in September 1980.

Della Torre arrived in New York as a representative of Traex. Traex had an account with Merrill Lynch in Lugano, Switzerland. Before Della Torre went to New York, Traex opened an account at the New York office of Merrill Lynch and designated Della Torre as the person responsible for transactions in this account. As a result, Merrill Lynch officials were under the impression that Della Torre was an official of the firm.

Filippo Salamone supplied Della Torre with large quantities of currency, bringing the cash directly to Della Torre's suite at the Waldorf. On

March 24, 1982, Della Torre brought $1,000,110 in small denomination bills into Merrill Lynch headquarters and deposited it into the Traex account. He expressed some concern to Merrill Lynch officials about the safety of the money. He indicated that he would be bringing in another large amount of currency the following day and asked for assistance.

Merrill Lynch assigned two security officers to go to Della Torre's suite at the Waldorf on the following day. They helped him remove several suitcases from the room, and returned by taxi to Merrill Lynch headquarters. The suitcases were taken to a vault in the commodities office, where the money was counted—$1,310,000 in cash, packed by denomination.

On the next day, March 26, 1982, Della Torre had another load of cash, and security officers were again sent to his hotel to safeguard the money. This time, Merrill Lynch had arranged for the money to be delivered directly to Banker's Trust Company because Merrill Lynch was not capable of continuing to handle the large amounts of cash. Merrill Lynch officials were on hand when Della Torre and the security officers arrived with the money; the count was $689,910 in small bills.

One of the security officers was a former FBI agent who realized there was something highly unusual and suspicious about these large cash transactions. The security officer contacted a former associate who was still in the FBI's New York office and told him what had transpired. He asked if the FBI had anything on Della Torre and/or Traex, but apparently there were no files on either.

The agent submitted a report about the transactions reported by the security officer, but no other federal agency was told of the transactions. Both the IRS and the Customs Service had agents working on money laundering in New York at the time. Della Torre was possibly violating the Bank Secrecy Act since in effect he was acting as a nonbank financial institution and was not filing Currency Transaction Reports identifying the source of the funds.

It is difficult to understand why the FBI's New York office did not know anything about Franco Della Torre by late March 1982. The agent from the White Plains office, who had the money laundering case involving World Wide Business Centres, by then should have come across Della Torre's name and address amidst Amendolito's records. Apparently, though, he had not yet entered Della Torre's name into the FBI's indices by the time the Merrill Lynch security officer made his inquiry.

The Merrill Lynch security officer was so concerned about the Della Torre transactions that he wrote a memorandum to his superiors. The memorandum indicated that Della Torre's transactions were suspicious and that the practice of conducting business in large amounts of cash is questionable. Despite the memorandum, Merrill Lynch assisted Della Torre in two more large cash transactions.

On April 23, 1982, Della Torre deposited $499,960 with Merrill Lynch and on April 29, 1982 he deposited $1,408,455. Both transactions involved small bills. After the April transactions, Merrill Lynch closed out the Traex account in New York. This brought a protest from Merrill Lynch's manager in Lugano, who sent a cable to New York extolling the virtues of Traex. The cable indicated that Franco Della Torre was a valued Traex client. This shocked officials in Merrill Lynch who had assumed that Della Torre was an officer of Traex.

Under Merrill Lynch rules, the firm should not have accepted even a check from Della Torre. By the time the Traex account was closed, a total of $4,908,435 in small bills had been laundered through it. Some of this money was wire transferred to the Traex account with Merrill Lynch in Lugano. The remainder was wire transferred to a Traex account at Union de Banque Suisse.

The Merrill Lynch manager in Lugano was so interested in the Traex account that he flew to New York with Enrico Rossini to argue the case with senior officials for continued cash transactions. During this meeting, Rossini proposed putting $50 million in cash into the Traex account. Merrill Lynch refused to handle further cash transactions.

WHEN E.F. HUTTON TALKS . . .

Even before the Merrill Lynch account was closed out, Della Torre was aware of impending problems. After the three transactions in March, Merrill Lynch expressed concern and raised questions in Lugano about the origin of the money and the reputation of Traex. With this in mind, Della Torre, in early April, opened an account in the name of Traex at the headquarters office of E.F. Hutton. Between April 27, 1982 and July 2, 1982, he made 11 cash deposits into the E.F. Hutton account, totalling $7,432,800.

Della Torre decided there was too much activity in the Traex account. In early July 1982, he opened another account at E.F. Hutton in the name of Acacias Development Company.

Cash deposits to the Acacias account began in earnest on July 6, 1982. In all, Della Torre made 11 cash deposits to that account between July 6, 1982 and September 27, 1982. Total value of the deposits was $8,250,745. The combined total of cash deposited by Della Torre into the Traex and Acacias accounts at E.F. Hutton during the five-month period beginning on April 27, 1982 was $15,683,545.

Prior to Della Torre's cash transactions at E.F. Hutton, a senior vice president at the firm directed an employee to arrange for large cash deposits at Bankers Trust. Della Torre arrived for the first deposit with two gym bags filled with small denomination bills. He then left and returned a short time later with another bag full of money. The first two deposits came to over $1.3 million. Bankers Trust officials became concerned about the source of the money and refused to take any more. Their excuse was that they could not spare employees to count the money.

One Bankers Trust official did tell an E.F. Hutton official of his concerns over the legitimacy of the money. The E.F. Hutton official responded that the brokerage house was making the deposit and that Bankers Trust would not be liable for any wrongdoing. Nevertheless, Bankers Trust stopped taking the cash.

E.F. Hutton officials then arranged for Della Torre's currency deposits to be made at other New York banks. They also furnished security for Della Torre's trips from hotel rooms to the banks on several occasions. E.F. Hutton employees later admitted that the Traex and Acacias transactions were highly unusual. However, their legal department was never contacted even though E.F. Hutton filed CRTs, it never notified any federal enforcement agencies of the highly suspicious nature of these transactions. Greed prevailed over common sense.

In late March 1982, the FBI agent investigating Amendolito gave a list of names from records of Amendolito's telephone calls to a U.S. Customs agent to run through the Treasury Department's Financial Law Enforcement Center's (FLEC) data base. The data base contained the names of all persons listed on Currency Transaction Reports. The list, which included Della Torre's name, had not yet been entered in the FBI's own indices. In early October, the Customs agent reported back to his friend in the FBI that Della Torre's name was listed on a number of CTRs as the person who had conducted more than $15 million in currency transactions at the New York offices of Merrill Lynch and E.F. Hutton. The money had been credited to accounts in the names of Traex and Acacias at the two brokerage firms. Entries into the FLEC data base in 1982 were frequently more than 90 days behind receipt of the forms by the IRS, hence the delay.

The information about Della Torre was a major breakthrough for the FBI investigation. It was the first time that the agents involved in the investigation became aware of the full extent of Della Torre's currency activities. FBI agents in New York served a subpoena to E.F. Hutton on October 5, 1982, demanding all of the records on the Traex and Acacias accounts. It was determined that the Acacias account was still open. E.F. Hutton officials knew Della Torre was out of the country, but he was expected back in New York. The agents requested that they be notified of Della Torre's return. An E.F. Hutton official promised cooperation.

During the entire time that Franco Della Torre was depositing huge amounts of currency with E.F. Hutton, the firm never notified enforcement authorities, even though the transactions were highly unusual and suspicious. E.F. Hutton, however, had no inhibitions about notifying Traex of the FBI's inquiry. Despite promises of cooperation made to FBI agents in New York, E.F. Hutton took a series of actions which resulted in the notification to Vito Roberto Palazzolo of the FBI's interest in the Traex and Acacias accounts.

First, the New York office closed out the Acacias account. Then the Lugano office was notified that the Acacias account had been closed and that the FBI was interested in the account and Franco Della Torre. The Lugano office notified E.F. Hutton headquarters in New York that most of the money that had been received in the Acacias and Traex accounts in Lugano from the New York accounts of these firms had, in turn, been transferred to another account in the name of P.G.K. Holding.

P.G.K. Holding had an office in Zurich. It was listed on E.F. Hutton's books as an importer and exporter of precious gems. The owner of P.G.K. Holding was none other than Vito Roberto Palazzolo. The manager of the Hutton office in Lugano notified Palazzolo on October 7, 1982 of the FBI's inquiries regarding Traex, Acacias, and Della Torre. On October 10, 1982, P.G.K. Holding deregistered itself in Zurich and relocated to Zug, Switzerland. Franco Della Torre never returned to New York. The notification to P.G.K. Holding apparently was ordered by E.F. Hutton's General Counsel, who claimed that he gave the order to protect the safety of his employees.

E.F. Hutton's behavior in the Pizza Connection case was unconscionable. Not only did it allow itself to be used in a heroin money laundering scheme, but it tipped off the bad guys when the government started to close in. Why? It was a combination of greed and the old Swiss banking theory that the source of a customer's funds is not the business of a financial institution. E.F. Hutton skirted on the fringe of illegality in this case, but it did not break any laws. The crime of "money laundering" had not yet been established in federal criminal statutes. However, E.F. Hutton clearly had established a track record of dealing with money launderers.

E.F. Hutton's Providence, Rhode Island, office became involved in a drug-related money laundering operation in 1984. It failed to file a large number of CTRs required by federal law. In 1985, E.F. Hutton pleaded guilty to federal criminal charges and received a substantial fine. E.F. Hutton's actions in the Pizza Connection case had something to do with the decision to prosecute in Providence and also with the severity of the sentence. E.F. Hutton's shortcomings in the Pizza Connection case were cited time after time in Congressional hearings and by the President's Commission on Organized Crime as the basis for the need to establish money laundering as a crime.

Della Torre was able to move large sums of money from the United States to Switzerland, but he was not a very efficient money launderer. He left a clear paper trail from New York to Switzerland with his name all over it. Despite being a bungler of sorts, Sal Amendolito's currency transfers to Bermuda and the Bahamas were more efficient—they left no paper trails.

CTRs filed by Merrill Lynch and E.F. Hutton clearly established millions of dollars of currency transactions by Della Torre. The firms' records indicated that the money was being transferred to accounts in Switzerland. Nevertheless, Della Torre provided insulation for the drug dealers. As long as he didn't identify the source of the cash, the dealers were in the clear.

THE FBI INVESTIGATION TAKES SHAPE

Information about Della Torre's currency deposits at the New York brokerage houses was an important milestone in the FBI investigation of the Pizza Connection. Up until October 1982, the case had been foundering. Surveillance and bits and pieces of informant information had developed some interesting associations between different members of the mob. There was no question that many of the meetings observed were connected with criminal activity. As time wore on, there was little doubt that one of the criminal activities involved heroin distribution, and that some of the large cash movements represented the fruits of heroin sales. But there was no hard evidence.

The FBI did not know what was being said at meetings that were observed. There was no heroin that could be linked to any of the suspects. The full extent of Amendolito's money laundering activities was not yet known.

The Customs information about Della Torre changed many things. In the first place, it produced hard evidence of millions of dollars of cash moving from New York to Switzerland in a manner that suggested the money was from drug sales. Of even greater importance was that the Della Torre information, when pieced together with all the surveillance reports and informant information, provided the basis for the installation of a series of court-ordered wiretaps on the telephones of key players in the Pizza Connection.

When the FBI learned of the CTRs indicating Della Torre had deposited millions of dollars in cash at Merrill Lynch and E.F. Hutton, agents went to the U.S. Attorney's office in the Southern District of New York for subpoenas. There, they dealt with Louis Freeh, a highly competent and aggressive prosecutor who previously had been an FBI agent. Freeh had a reputation as a tiger in pursuing major criminal conspiracy cases.

Freeh assisted in the issuance of subpoenas to the brokerage houses. He became interested in the entire Pizza Connection case. He saw that there was a strong possibility that the FBI had developed enough evidence to obtain wiretaps on the telephones of a number of the prime suspects in the case. He saw the possibility of a major heroin conspiracy case involving Mafia figures and millions of dollars headed to Switzerland.

During November and December 1982, Freeh held dozens of meetings with FBI agents who were working on the Pizza Connection case. At his direction and urging, they pulled together every scrap of information that had been developed during the two-year investigation of the suspects. Their object was a massive affidavit that would support an application to the U.S. District Court for a number of wiretaps of the principal targets. After months of work, court-ordered wiretaps were installed in February 1983 on a number of telephones.

The wiretaps could probably have been in place at least one year earlier if the FBI had pursued the money laundering aspects of the case more aggressively. If inquiries had been made at World Wide Business Centres on a timely basis, Amendolito would have been identified much earlier and he might have been taken into custody while he was still laundering heroin money. The inquiries would have resulted in Della Torre's name being entered into the FBI's indices earlier, so that when the Merrill Lynch security officer told the FBI about Della Torre's cash transactions, the agent who checked the indices would have known that Della Torre was a person frequently telephoned by a suspected heroin money launderer named Salvatore Amendolito.

The FBI was remiss in not sharing apparent money laundering information with other federal agencies. Both Customs and the IRS had jurisdiction over Bank Secrecy Act violations. If the FBI was not in a position to follow up on Amendolito's money laundering activities, or the deposit of several million dollars in currency at Merrill Lynch, Customs and the IRS would have. Both situations were indicative of possible violations of the Bank Secrecy Act. The first time the FBI provided any information to either the IRS or Customs was in March 1982 when the names in Amendolito's telephone book were supplied for a check against Treasury's Bank Secrecy Act database.

The lack of information sharing by the FBI in this case is not atypical. It happens frequently in single agency investigations. What happened is a good argument for multi-agency task force operations in drug and money laundering investigations. Multi-agency task forces, with agents located in common space, frequently result in a great deal of information sharing that would not ordinarily occur. This kind of information sharing invariably leads to greater efficiency.

The wiretaps, which started in February 1983, contributed much to the ultimate successful completion of the investigation and prosecution of the Pizza Connection. But they were not without problems. Many of the conversations were in Sicilian, which necessitated a need for personnel who could interpret what was being said. Complicating the language barrier was the fact that the members of the conspiracy frequently used code words in discussing matters directly related to criminal activity. The code system had to be thoroughly studied before it was understood.

The wiretaps also created fantastic personnel demands. Not only were agents needed to monitor the intercepted conversations, but much more physical surveillance was required. There was not much point in learning of a planned meeting during a telephone intercept if agents could not watch the meeting to see who showed up. The FBI requested and obtained assistance from the Drug Enforcement Administration (DEA) in meeting its additional personnel requirements. Dozens of DEA agents assisted the FBI on monitoring wiretaps and conducting surveillance during 1983 and 1984.

Despite the problems, wiretap information was important to the final outcome of the case. Suspected associations were confirmed. There were some incriminating conversations. There were some indications that the topic of conversation concerned drugs and/or the disposition of drug money. But there was no hard evidence. There was no actual heroin that could be tied to the money movements and the incriminating conversations.

HEROIN ENTERS THE PICTURE

However, a major break came out of a DEA investigation in Philadelphia. A DEA agent had infiltrated a heroin distribution ring in that city. The agent met with a tavern owner named Benny Zito, through whom he ordered a kilo of heroin in April 1983. Zito indicated that his source was in New York. Shortly after the order was placed, agents monitoring the tap on the telephone of Giuseppe Ganci overheard the incoming call from "Benny" in Philadelphia. The caller appeared to be ordering a kilo of heroin, and Ganci was insisting upon payment upon delivery. On the following day, Zito told the DEA agent that he would have to pay $200,000 up front prior to secure delivery of the heroin. DEA decided to put the money up front.

The DEA undercover agent paid Zito $200,000 for the heroin, after which Zito telephoned Ganci and told him he had the money and was on his way to New York. DEA and FBI surveillance teams were actually able to follow Zito to New York and observe his meeting with Ganci. Zito left Ganci's house with a package, which was identical to the one Zito delivered to the undercover agent later the same day. The package contained one kilo of heroin.

The undercover buy from Zito was important to the successful prosecution of the entire Pizza Connection. It established clearly that the mob was in fact dealing heroin. The coded telephone conversations now had more meaning. It was no longer supposition on the part of agents that the suspects were talking about heroin—it was reality. The Ganci-to-Zito-to-DEA agent transfer of the heroin package proved that to be the case.

The wiretaps, and the surveillance conducted in conjunction with them, provided information that, in April 1983, Filippo Salamone was transporting large amounts of currency from the United States to Switzerland. Telephones controlled by both Salamone brothers in Bloomsburg, Pennsylvania, were among those being wiretapped. In April a series of telephone calls indicated that Filippo Salamone was going to take a trip with a large amount of money. Salamone and his wife and children were followed from a home they had in Jackson, New Jersey, to JFK Airport in New York. Salamone went aboard a SwissAir flight to Zurich after checking in two large suitcases as baggage. His wife called him in West Germany a few days later. The number where she reached him was traced to Vito Roberto Palazzolo.

When Della Torre's activities were uncovered in October 1982, Filippo Salamone apparently took over as the conduit of money between U.S. heroin distributors and Palazzolo in Switzerland. Salamone by-passed banks and brokerage houses by taking the money directly to Switzerland.

THE FISHMONGER RETURNS

In July 1983, the FBI investigation of the Pizza Connection received a major boost with the arrest of Amendolito in New Orleans. Amendolito had disappeared from the New York area in December 1982 shortly after being told by Tognoli that he would have to pay back the Deighton Edwards loan of $230,000 and the $140,000 shortage that showed up in the accounts he maintained at banks in Bermuda and Nassau. He had neither the money nor the inclination to pay off these debts.

In the spring and summer of 1983, Amendolito surfaced in New Orleans and became involved in a flim-flam deal designed to swindle some Arab sheiks out of $50 million to $100 million. The sheiks were led to believe they were lending the money to the government of Costa Rica. The FBI office in New Orleans became involved in an investigation of the swindle.

In mid-July, Amendolito was taken into custody in connection with the swindle. The arresting agents determined that he was wanted for questioning by the FBI's New York office in connection with a major heroin money laundering operation. Amendolito was more than happy to cooperate, both with the swindle case and with his currency transactions in New York. He wanted to stay out of jail. He provided full details about his relationship with Sal Miniati, Olivero Tognoli, Philip Matassa, and Frank Castronovo and all the currency transactions with them. This marked the first time the FBI knew the full extent of Amendolito's money laundering activities. He maintained throughout the questioning that he never knew the money he handled came from drug sales. He said Miniati initially told him that some pizza owners in New York and New Jersey wanted to send money to Europe to build a resort in Sicily. He maintained that Miniati told him that the suppliers of the money wanted to avoid IRS scrutiny.

Amendolito said that from time to time he became suspicious of the source of the funds. But, whenever his suspicions were aroused and he raised the issue with Miniati he was always assured that the money had come from legitimate sources. He particularly remembered being uneasy about his meeting with the two brothers, Vito and Sal, on a Queens street corner regarding a cash transfer of $1.5 million. In subsequent questioning, Amendolito identified a photograph of Salvatore Catalano as the brother named Sal who gave him $1.5 million in cash on a Queens street corner in early August 1981. This was extremely important because Salvatore Catalano was the boss of the heroin distribution organization.

Amendolito never wavered from his story about not knowing that the money came from heroin sales, despite repeated interrogation sessions. He testified to the same effect during a grand jury appearance in 1984 and during the trial of the Pizza Connection case in 1985. Amendolito was never indicted for any criminal activity associated with the Pizza Connection or the New Orleans swindle—that was the deal his attorney worked out with government prosecutors in exchange for his testimony.

Amendolito's information and subsequent testimony were very important to the government's case. It tied heroin distributors to a cash flow that went from New York to Switzerland. It provided direct evidence against Salvatore Catalano, the heroin kingpin in New York, and Olivero Tognoli, one of the bosses in Sicily. Amendolito became a protected government witness. It is believed that he is still in the government's witness protection program.

PROSECUTION AT LAST

In the summer of 1983, the Justice Department launched a new investigative and prosecution program designed to destroy major drug trafficking organizations. The program was known as the Organized Crime Drug Enforcement Task Force (OCDETF) program. Task forces were set up in 13 major geographic areas of the country. The program was the brainchild of Rudolph (Rudy) Guiliani, who at the time was Associate Attorney General of the United States.

The task force program was set up to promote joint investigations by agents from DEA, the FBI, the Customs Service, IRS, and the Bureau of Alcohol, Tobacco and Firearms with prosecutors from U.S. Attorneys' offices. The program was modeled after Operation Greenback, a highly successful interagency money laundering task force in Florida. The goals, funding and objectives of the new OCDETF program were much broader in scope.

In December 1983, Rudy Guiliani left the Justice Department to become the U.S. Attorney for the Southern District of New York. He was well aware of the Pizza Connection case in New York. One of his first official acts, on becoming the U.S. Attorney in New York, was to have the Pizza Connection case designated as an OCDETF case under his supervision. This was done over the objections of the FBI and several U.S. Attorney's in other jurisdictions who had pieces of the case. One particular benefit of the jurisdictional switch was that additional agencies were brought into the case. IRS was made aware of Bank Secrecy Act violations, over which it had jurisdiction, for the first time in December 1983. The Customs role was broadened with regard to Bank Secrecy Act violations under its jurisdiction.

By the time Guiliani took over the prosecution, it was well on its way to being wrapped up. Louis Freeh had remained with the case and was preparing an indictment.

The Pizza Connection case was presented to a federal grand jury in Manhattan during early 1984. On April 19, 1984, the grand jury returned an indictment, charging 38 defendants with participating in a major international heroin trafficking and money laundering operation. There were 12 counts in the indictment—11 dealt with drugs and one count charged a conspiracy to violate the Bank Secrecy Act.

The indictment received massive publicity. It was announced by William French Smith, who at the time was the Attorney General. The Bank Secrecy Act conspiracy count charged some of the most prominent players in the Pizza Connection: Frank Castronovo, Franco Della Torre, the Salamone brothers, Salvatore Miniati, Olivero Tognoli, and Salvatore Catalano. The kingpins of the entire operation, Sicilian Mafia leaders Gaetano Badalamenti and Leonardo Greco, were also charged.

After the initial indictment was returned, the case was prepared for trial and additional investigative work was performed by the various agencies that comprised the OCDETF. In the course of this preparation and investigation it became apparent that additional BSA violations had been committed by the defendants—violations that had not been charged in the original indictment. The government went back to the grand jury and presented evidence of these additional offenses, and the grand jury returned a superseding indictment. The new indictment charged the same offenses as the original, plus three additional counts. The new charges included false statements made to Merrill Lynch and E.F. Hutton which caused the firms to file false reports with the IRS. It also charged violations connected with a pattern of illegal activity involving the failure to file CTRs related to the deposit and transfer of more than $28 million over a four-year period. In addition, Vito Roberto Palazzolo was added to the new indictment, making him the 39th defendant charged.

Some of the defendants were fugitives and were not located before the trial began. Salvatore Catalano and another mob member were killed in gangland-style executions. Three of the defendants (Franco Della Torre, Paul Waridel, and Enrico Rossini) were located in Switzerland, but Swiss law did not provide for extradition on the basis of BSA violations.

In the summer of 1985, a team of government prosecutors and defense attorneys traveled to Switzerland and took depositions from the three. The deposition of Paul Waridel was particularly helpful. Waridel, a Turk living in Switzerland, was the intermediary between the Sicilian heroin distributors headed by Leonardo Greco and Yasar Musullulu, the Turkish supplier of heroin base. Waridel dealt with payments for the heroin base. He was the conduit for money going to Yasar Musullulu from Vito Roberto Palazzolo, Enrico Rossini, and Franco Della Torre. The latter three acted on behalf of Leonardo Greco in paying for the drugs supplied by Musullulu.

Two defendants pled guilty to minor charges before the trial commenced. Giuseppe Ganci was not tried because he was dying of lung cancer—he died in the middle of the trial.

The trial of the Pizza Connection organization began September 30, 1985 in Manhattan in the U.S. District Court for the Southern District of New York. There were 22 defendants out of the original 39 who were indicted, and 21 defense attorneys. The government's prosecution team was headed by Louis Freeh. The trial lasted a tortuous 17 months.

The jury reached a verdict on March 2, 1987. Twenty-one of the defendants were found guilty. They included Gaetano Badalamenti, a boss of the Sicilian Mafia. His son, Vito Badalamenti, was the only defendant acquitted. All of the defendants received substantial jail terms.

And what happened to the individuals who actually laundered the money? Sal Amendolito became a key government witness during the trial and was never charged in the case. Franco Della Torre, Paul Waridel, and Enrico Rossini escaped prosecution by remaining in Italy and cooperating with the government. Filippo Salamone fled the United States and is a fugitive.

Vito Roberto Palazzolo also became a fugitive. Several years ago he was caught in a heroin money laundering operation in South Africa and is now serving a jail sentence in that country.

Sal Miniati and Olivero Tognoli were never apprehended. They remain fugitives.

Philip Matassa, Tognoli's cousin, pleaded guilty in a separate case to a Bank Secrecy Act violation. He received probation. It is ironic that none of the heavy money launderers in this case went to jail. However, Philip Matassa, a part-time courier, was convicted and placed on probation. The real launderers either became fugitives or cut deals with the government.

Of course, compared with the Columbian cocaine money launderers who were operating out of Miami during the same period, the heroin launderers were moving small sums of cash. The Pizza Connection launderers dealt in millions of dollars. The cocaine launderers dealt in many hundreds of millions of dollars. The cocaine launderers, with experience as currency exchangers, tended to be more sophisticated and clever in their operations. The Pizza Connection launderers were frequently bumbling and lacking in knowledge about how to move large quantities of cash inconspicuously.

CHAPTER 2

THE EARLY COCAINE MONEY LAUNDERERS:
ISAAC KATTAN AND OTHERS

Money laundering activity reached a fever pitch in South Florida between 1977 and 1981. Most of the action was in Miami, which had become the primary entry point for Colombian narcotics.

Many different money laundering organizations emerged to launder the billions of dollars in cash generated from the sale of marijuana and cocaine. Most were run by Colombians with experience in the black market currency exchange business. Their operations were characterized by large cash deposits (typically in small denomination bills) in accounts established in any number of area banks under fictitious names. The cash was brought to the banks by couriers (typically young Colombian males) in paper bags, boxes, suitcases or anything else they could find. Once the money was deposited into an account, it was moved out quickly using personal checks, cashier's checks, or wire transfers to accounts in other banks, either locally or in offshore tax havens.

The Colombian money launderers took advantage of lax Bank Secrecy Act compliance and enforcement. And they were always on the lookout for corrupt bank officials who could be bribed into ignoring BSA reporting requirements.

It wasn't until 1980 that federal investigators began to pursue violations of the BSA in earnest. That's when a task force known as Operation Greenback was set in motion. By the end of 1981, many of the Colombian money launderers had been arrested; even more had fled to Colombia. The era of huge cash deposits in Miami area banks had come to a close.

ISAAC KATTAN

The most famous of the money launderers of this period was Isaac Kattan-Kassin, better known as Isaac Kattan. Kattan was believed to have laundered $100 million or more a year in Colombian drug money between 1977 and 1981.

Born in Syria in 1935, Kattan was the son of Sephardic Jews who had fled Germany in the early 1930s. Isaac's father became a money exchanger. Much of the money handling in the Middle East is done by private entrepreneurs and not by chartered banking institutions. It is of biblically historical precedent that money exchangers in the region provide a variety of banking and money exchanging services outside of normal banking channels. As Isaac grew up in Syria, he learned the business from his father. In 1955, Kattan's father moved the family again, this time to Cali, Colombia, where father and son found an active demand for their services.

There was a flourishing black market in Colombia at the time for various foreign currencies, particularly U.S. dollars. Colombian businessmen needed dollars to buy raw materials and manufactured products overseas. Wealthy Colombians wanted to convert pesos to hard currencies such as U.S. dollars and waned to invest their savings in more stable foreign markets. The Colombian peso was constantly losing value against the dollar and other hard currencies. Wealthy South Americans from countries with even less stable economies than Colombia came looking for Colombian pesos and hard currencies such as the dollar. Colombian businessmen who exported merchandise frequently understated the value of the merchandise exported to avoid high tariffs imposed by the government on exports and to evade taxes on the profit from the sale of their merchandise. They accepted payment for the undeclared portion of the exports in the currency of the country to which goods were shipped. Colombians living and working in the United States frequently shipped dollars back to their families in Colombia. While dollars were desirable for some Colombians, pesos were a necessity for all purchases of goods, services, and property. And Colombia, like many South American countries, had strict currency control laws that prohibited citizens from holding, importing, or exporting dollars. The only businesses, other than banks, that were legally allowed to deal in dollars were currency exchanges and travel agencies.

The currency exchange house run by the Kattans in Cali serviced the needs of wealthy Colombians and businessmen who needed dollars for overseas investments and purchases. It also provided Colombians who had acquired dollars (through, for example, under the table export payments) with pesos for use in the Colombian economy. The currency exchange houses operated outside of official banking channels and outside the realm of government-imposed exchange rates (which included a tax many Colombians considered confiscatory).

In the early 1960s, Isaac Kattan opened a travel agency business in Bogota, under the name Viajas Pacifica. The new business complemented his father's currency exchange house. Dollars accumulated legally by Viajas Pacifica were made available to the currency exchange and pesos acquired by the currency exchange were turned over to the travel agency. It wasn't long before Viajas Pacifica became a front for a thriving black market in dollars and other foreign currencies in Bogota.

Currencies were traded both in Colombia and overseas. During the 1960s and 1970s, the search for overseas trading opportunities led Isaac Kattan to travel to Central America, Miami, New York, and other South American countries.

By the mid-1970s, Colombian marijuana, known as "Colombian Gold," had become popular in the United States, and as a result, large amounts of U.S. dollars began flowing into Colombia. Estimates by the Colombian central bank, Banco de la Republica, estimated that $400 million in hard currency was brought into the country during 1977 from drug trafficking.

The Colombian bosses of the marijuana trade reached out to black market money exchangers like Isaac Kattan to convert their U.S. dollars to pesos. Kattan first became involved with the marijuana wholesalers in 1976, which was about the same time the Colombians became aware of the potential of cocaine.

Prior to then, the relatively small flow of cocaine that was smuggled into the United States was controlled by a group of Cubans. Their base of operations was Miami. Deals were agreed to there. Payments and deliveries were made there. The Colombians who handled the marijuana trade also worked through Miami. As long as the Cubans handled cocaine and the Colombians handled marijuana, there were no problems.

But then some of the Colombians decided to enter the cocaine business. They purchased cocaine paste and base in Peru and Bolivia and set up laboratories in Medellin, Colombia, where the base and paste were converted into the finished product, cocaine hydrochloride, then packaged and smuggled into the United States, usually in South Florida. By 1979, the demand for cocaine in the United States was incredible and the Colombian traffickers were in full swing. They had only two serious problems during those early years: competition and opposition from the entrenched Cuban dealers, and what to do with the huge piles of U.S. dollars they were accumulating.

DEALING WITH COMPETITION

The first problem was solved by muscle. At that time, the Colombian drug distribution picture did not focus on a monolithic organization; there were a number of drug trafficking organizations. The "Colombian Cowboys," as they were called, came into Miami in a big way in 1978 and slugged it out with the Cubans and each other until 1982. The Cubans were overwhelmed; the Colombians were better organized and better armed. Bloody shootouts in hotels, motels, shopping malls, expressways, and public streets were commonplace. Often, innocent people were wounded or killed by automatic weapons fire intended for rival drug dealers.

The shootouts did not abate until 1982 when the Reagan administration sent several hundred federal agents into the area in a mission known as the South Florida Task Force. The task force succeeded in cutting down on street violence, and it forced the Colombians to disperse their operations to a number of other major cities.

The second major problem—what to do with the cash—posed a whole series of headaches. Dollars are bulky and very heavy, particularly in small denominations. Two million dollars in $20 bills weighs 246 lbs. To store that much cash, a trafficker needed a considerable amount of space and tight security. Millions of dollars in cash presented too great a temptation to holdup men and members of rival drug organizations.

The storage and security headaches accentuated the need for the Colombians to get rid of the cash as quickly as possible. But, what to do with it? The Colombians transacting the drug deals didn't want their names associated with money that came from drug sales. The bosses in Colombia didn't want the dealers in Miami to have any control over the money; besides, the bosses needed pesos, not dollars. Enter Isaac Kattan and a number of other currency exchangers.

What to Do With the Cash?

After doing some money laundering for marijuana distributors in 1976, Kattan went to work full time for several cocaine organizations in 1977.

Kattan's travel agency and the currency exchange business he had taken over from his father in 1975 meshed nicely with the needs of the drug bosses. For years, Kattan had been receiving pesos from businessmen who wanted him to credit their accounts overseas with foreign currencies so that they could buy merchandise or accumulate wealth. Colombia has always had a thriving business community. Coffee, meat products, flowers, and textiles are among a wide range of products Colombians had been exporting for years. Imports included cars, trucks, farm equipment, raw materials, and household products. Over the years, Kattan had to turn away some of the businessmen. They wanted him to handle too many pesos, and he couldn't acquire enough foreign currency (particularly U.S. dollars) to accommodate their needs.

Doing business with the drug bosses changed all that for Isaac Kattan. He had run Viajas Pacifica as a moderately successful travel agency and black market money exchange for a number of years. Now he had hit the big time.

Kattan acquired a partner named Jaime Escobar. Escobar was a financial "wizard." The cocaine bosses needed pesos badly. They had huge amounts of U.S. dollars accumulating both in Colombia and in Miami. The match was perfect. Kattan could now take all the pesos the businessmen could bring to him. These pesos were just what the drug bosses needed. And he could use the dollars the drug bosses had accumulating in Miami to carry out the commercial and personal needs of businessmen and wealthy individuals who supplied him with pesos in Bogota.

The cocaine bosses' need for pesos extended to every facet of their business. They needed to pay suppliers in Peru and Bolivia who provided cocaine paste and cocaine base. They needed to pay the workers who trekked into the jungles of Peru and Bolivia to buy the raw product. They needed to pay pilots who flew the raw cocaine to Colombia. They needed to pay pesos to set up laboratories in Columbia; to pay workers in these laboratories; to pay for the ether and acetone used to convert cocaine paste to cocaine hydrochloride; and to pay pilots to transport the finished product to staging areas on the north coast of Colombia. Last, but far from least, they needed pesos in Colombia to reward themselves for their business success.

The rewards the drug bosses gave themselves included every kind of luxury item imaginable: expensive cars, lavish estates and ranches, horses, yachts, private aircrafts, bodyguards, and servants.

Kattan had to adjust his business operation to accommodate his new clients. He established offices in New York and Miami. He hired two workers in Miami to handle the large amounts of dollars that accumulated from drug sales every day. He personally began to transport to New York large quantities of dollars that he received in Bogota. He initially used a bank account in Miami for large cash deposits. Later, he opened accounts at other banks and financial institutions for cash deposits and used the original account as a clearinghouse into which he moved money from the other banks. The money in the clearing account was then paid out on behalf of the businessmen who supplied him with pesos in Bogota. Kattan's operation was well-planned, well-organized, and ran smoothly.

The clearinghouse bank that Kattan used was the Bank of Miami. As early as 1972, Kattan had opened an account at this bank under the name "Sam Conti" to facilitate his money exchange and travel agency businesses. Long before the drug money started to flow, this account was used by Kattan to move money supplied to him in Cali and Bogota by Colombian businessmen.

Expansion

In 1977, when he started to deal with the Colombian drug bosses, Kattan expanded his operation to better deal with large sums of cash. He and his partner, Escobar, each bought apartments in Villa Regina, a Miami high-rise. Over the next four years, Kattan spent more and more time in Miami, while Escobar ran the business in Colombia.

Kattan also acquired another apartment in the same high-rise that he stayed in; this apartment became the focal point of his money laundering activities. He installed money counting machines, telephones, and computers. All of the money Kattan and his two employees picked up from drug dealers was brought to the apartment to be counted and sorted. It was then stacked by denominations and packaged for delivery to banks.

Bank deposits were usually made shortly after the banks opened in the morning. After the deposits were made, Kattan and his couriers would pick up more currency from drug contacts. Afternoons were spent counting and sorting currency.

Kattan also spent hours on the telephone each day to his offices in Cali and Bogota and to the drug bosses in Colombia. The drug bosses would tell Kattan where and from whom to pick up cash, and he would advise them of the amount of pesos available to them from the previous day's pickups. Kattan's calls to his offices in Colombia would coordinate the flow of pesos to the drug dealers and determine what the businessmen, who supplied the pesos, wanted done with the dollars they had on deposit in U.S. banks.

Initially, Kattan used the Sam Conti account at the Bank of Miami for large cash deposits. But he quickly realized that there was just too much volume going into the account. Within a short time, he opened four more accounts at the bank. One was in his name, the others were in fictitious names. During 1977 and 1978, millions of dollars in cash were deposited into these accounts by Kattan and his employees.

The Bank of Miami routinely filed Currency Transaction Reports, as required by the Bank Secrecy Act, for all deposits over $10,000. The CTRs were sent to the Treasury Department and stored away. Although the theory behind CTRs was to better identify individuals and businesses handling large sums of cash (under the assumption that persons handling large amounts of cash in unusual circumstances would be close to criminal activity, particularly drug trafficking), in reality, hardly anyone in the federal government was paying attention to the information on the CTRs.

Isaac Kattan and a number of other money launderers went about their business with very little interference from government authorities.

Kattan was aware that there was not much enforcement of the BSA when he started handling drug money. If anyone questioned him about his activities, he had a set alibi. He was in the travel agency and currency exchange businesses in Colombia. He received dollars from U.S. tourists which he brought into the United States. He handled flight capital from a number of wealthy clients who had accumulated dollars. Kattan received instructions from Colombian businessmen who sent people to him with large amounts of cash, and he disposed of the money pursuant to their instructions. He wasn't doing anything wrong. He was not violating any laws. He assumed that the cash he received from individuals in Miami came from legitimate sources. He never questioned where the money came from. He did not believe he was required to file any reports for the receipt of this money.

Isaac Kattan both moved and laundered money for the Colombian drug bosses. He insulated them from association with the money from drug sales. He was the only one who could identify them as the source of the cash in Miami, and he never did. He could provide a smoke-screen of business activity to cover his currency transactions. He did not appear to be violating the laws that existed in the late 1970s.

When Kattan first started working for the Colombian marijuana dealers in 1976, the big problem was smuggling U.S. dollars out of Colombia after he exchanged the drug dealers' dollars for pesos. Drug smugglers weren't the only source of U.S. dollars for Kattan's travel agency and currency exchange businesses—U.S. tourists and other black market sources also contributed to his inventory of dollars.

Whenever the volume of cash accumulated became unmanageable, Kattan would personally transport the money to the United States. He brought some money to Miami and deposited it into the Sam Conti account at the Bank of Miami. But most of the dollars accumulated in Colombia were brought to New York and deposited into various accounts that had been established at Deak-Perera, the international money exchange house.

Kattan transported the dollars in suitcases on flights he took to New York or Miami from Bogota. He declared the currency he was carrying by filling out Customs Form 4790, which at the time required declarations whenever currency or bearer instruments worth over $5,000 were transported into or out of the country. Years after he was arrested and convicted, Kattan was questioned about why he openly filed the Customs forms showing the amounts of dollars he was bringing into the United States. His reply was that he was not doing anything wrong by bringing the money into the country and no one could do anything to him for filing a Form 4790. In fact, he noted, he would have been breaking the law if he did not file the form each time that he brought in a large amount of dollars.

Deak-Perera was headquartered in New York, but it had offices throughout the world. Kattan opened and controlled a series of accounts at Deak-Perera's New York office between 1975 and 1977. One was in the fictitious name Jose Vega. The other four were in the names of business associates of Kattan's. Deak-Perera employees in New York knew who Kattan was. They had seen his passport and often did business with him. Nevertheless, Deak-Perera management accepted numerous large cash deposits into Kattan's various accounts. CTRs were completed in the names on the accounts; often, Kattan's name did not even appear on the forms.

TREASURY TAKES NOTICE

In the late 1970s, some officials at the Treasury Department began paying attention to the reporting forms required by the Bank Secrecy Act. By 1977, Customs personnel had noted that the name Isaac Kattan was appearing with some frequency on Form 4790s, which indicated that he had transported several million dollars in U.S. currency into New York from Colombia. Customs advised the Office of the Assistant Secretary (Enforcement and Operations) in the Treasury Department of the discovery.

Soon after, in early 1978, Bob Stankey, a former IRS agent who worked in the Office of the Assistant Secretary (Enforcement and Operations), noticed unusual currency activity involving Deak-Perera's New York office. CTRs filed by that office indicated that unusually large sums of currency were being deposited into a few accounts. Stankey persuaded Assistant Secretary of the Treasury Richard Davis to order an IRS compliance examination of Deak-Perera's New York office.

The examination determined that most of the unusual currency activity during the period January 1, 1977 to June 30, 1978 occurred in the five accounts opened by Isaac Kattan. The examination further determined that Kattan was the real owner of all five accounts. It also revealed that Deak-Perera filed 58 false CTRs in 1978 covering currency deposits in the various Kattan accounts. Examiners identified 53 separate Kattan deposits in 1978 that were split or structured among the five accounts in amounts between $9,000 and $10,000. Kattan deliberately structured the deposits to avoid having CTRs filed. There was nothing wrong in what Kattan did because at that time there was no law that prohibited the act of structuring transactions to evade BSA reporting requirements. Deak-Perera was required by the instructions on the back of the CTR (Form 4789) to report multiple same day transactions by or for the same person totalling more than $10,000, but it did not do so. The total of Kattan's 53 deposits of slightly under $10,000 each amounted to more than $480,000. There were also 27 large cash deposits to the fictitious Jose Vega account.

The information developed during the compliance audit prompted IRS agents to question Isaac Kattan. The interview took place in New York in February 1979. Kattan was businesslike and cooperative. He told the agents that the currency he had been depositing at Deak-Perera was accumulated in his currency exchange and travel agency business in Colombia. He told them that he had brought the currency to New York and had filed Customs Form 4790, known as a CMIR (Currency and Monetary Instrument Report). Kattan acknowledged that he had opened five accounts in names other than his own; he said he did this to facilitate his operations in Colombia. Kattan also admitted that he had split deposits among the five accounts in amounts just under $10,000 in an effort to avoid having CTRs filed. What he did not tell the agents was that a considerable amount of the money came from drug dealers in Colombia. Nor did he tell them that as they were speaking, his employees were busily engaged in depositing millions of dollars worth of drug proceeds into various accounts in Miami banks.

Several years after his arrest and conviction, Kattan stated that he had deposited about $25 million in cash that he brought from Colombia into the accounts at Deak-Perera in New York between 1977 and 1981. He also said he moved most of the money in the Deak-Perera accounts to the Bank of Miami by way of Deak-Perera bank drafts. He did this because Bank of Miami cleared the drafts in five days whereas New York banks took about 20 days to clear the drafts.

IRS agents doubt Kattan's claim of bringing $25 million in currency into the United States. They believe he deliberately overstated amounts on the Customs forms to provide himself a cover for drug currency he collected in the United States and deposited at Deak-Perera and Miami banks.

THE SHELL GAME

Kattan continued moving large volumes of currency deposits into the various Bank of Miami accounts until May 1978, when Bank of Miami officials became concerned about the "exposure" of handling large currency transactions. Bank officials suggested that Kattan move his currency deposits to other banks. Among the banks suggested was Popular Bank and Trust Company and Northside Bank of Miami. Bank of Miami had sold Popular Bank and Trust Company, a Cayman Island corporation with an office in Miami, in February 1978, to a group headed by Andres Rodriguez, a resident alien who lived in Miami and who had been convicted in Guadeloupe of swindling bank customers. At the same time, Rodriguez had also obtained the controlling interest in Northside Bank of Miami.

A Bank of Miami official introduced Kattan to Francisco Bastida who was soliciting business for Popular Bank and Trust Company and for Northside Bank. Bastida, in turn, brought Kattan to Andres Rodriguez and Francisco Navarro, a vice president at the bank. Navarro had previously worked for Bank of Miami as head of international banking. Navarro had also served as an assistant vice president at Popular Bank and Trust Company at the same time that he was working for Bank of Miami.

The four men concocted a scheme to facilitate Kattan's money laundering operation. Kattan opened an account at a Northside Bank branch near his apartment in the name of Jaime Ruiz. He also opened an account at Popular Bank and Trust Company. It was agreed that Kattan would deposit cash into both accounts. No CTRs would be filed for deposits into the Popular Bank, and the money deposited into Popular would be transferred to Popular's account at Northside where it would be transferred to the Jaime Ruiz account.

Beginning in May and continuing through September 1978, Kattan and his couriers deposited about $7 million in currency into the two accounts. Approximately $2.2 million went into the account at Popular Bank and Trust Company, and then moved into the Jaime Ruiz account at Northside, without the filing of CTRs. About $4.8 million in cash was deposited by Kattan directly into the Jaime Ruiz account at Northside. False CTRs were filed for these deposits showing that the transactions were conducted by Jaime Ruiz. Kattan paid a one percent fee to Rodriguez for his help in concealing the true nature of the transactions.

The arrangement at Northside and Popular was very satisfactory to Kattan for a short period of time. Then something happened that ruined it—in August 1978, he began to notice shortages in the account. The missing money came to about $200,000. After several meetings with Rodriguez and Navarro in an effort to reconcile differences, Kattan became convinced that he was being ripped off. It was a classic case of one thief swindling another. Kattan was not in a position to complain to the authorities, but he did stop transacting business at Rodriguez' banks.

Kattan wasn't the only money launderer using these two banks, nor was he the only one swindled by Rodriguez. Law enforcement sources believe Rodriguez stole millions from the money laundering organizations he serviced. Apparently that wasn't enough, though, because Rodriguez went a step further and sold about $5 million in offshore certificates of deposit to wealthy investors, through Popular Bank. The bank then defaulted on paying off $1.5 million of these certificates when they came due, leading the Florida State Comptroller to shut down the bank in 1978, and to force Rodriguez to relinquish control of Northside Bank in April 1979. The new owner of Northside Bank became none other than Bank of Miami. Ultimately, the swindle perpetrated by Rodriguez led to his conviction on racketeering and mail fraud charges.

Undeterred by his problems with the Northside Bank, Kattan found other banks in the Miami area for his currency activities. At various times during 1978 and 1980 he maintained accounts under a variety of names at Continental Bank, Flagship Bank, Southeast Bank, Capital Bank, Republic Bank and other Miami area banks, pouring millions of dollars in cash into each.

KATTAN'S DOWNFALL

Several events occurred in Washington in 1979 and 1980 which led to the downfall of Isaac Kattan and a number of other money launderers in the Miami area. In the summer of 1979, Treasury obtained the cooperation of the Federal Reserve in studying currency flows in the United States. The study showed that while 30 Federal Reserve offices throughout the United States showed net payouts of currency during the period 1970 through 1978, seven offices showed net currency receipts or surpluses. Two of these offices, Jacksonville and Miami, combined, accounted for 77% of the total surplus. The combined total of the Florida cash surplus was $3.2 billion in 1978. The total of the cash deficit of the 30 offices with net payouts of cash was $14.4 billion. The study further indicated a remarkable increase in the growth of the Florida cash surplus beginning in 1977. This increase coincided with the start of the flow of cocaine to South Florida from Colombia. There was no legitimate business reason or other area of criminal activity that could explain the Florida currency surplus; it had to be tied to drug activity.

Another development that hurt the money launderers was a series of hearings conducted by the Senate Permanent Subcommittee on Investigations, beginning in late 1979. The focus of those hearings was illegal drugs and drug money laundering. The data on the South Florida currency surplus was spoon-fed to the subcommittee by mid-level Treasury officials who wanted to see some action taken against the individuals handling the drug money in Florida. The hearings prodded the Treasury Department into a realization that something had to be done about drug money laundering.

Operation Greenback

In 1980, Bill Nickerson, at the time Treasury Deputy Assistant Secretary for Enforcement, came up with the idea of a multi-agency task force based in Miami. It was to concentrate on money launderers by investigating violations of the Bank Secrecy Act and related statutes, using information from CTRs and CMIRs to identify potential suspects. The task force known as "Operation Greenback," became one of the outstanding examples of successful interagency cooperation. Greenback was an amalgam of IRS agents, Customs agents, and Assistant U.S. Attorneys designated specifically to investigate and prosecute cases originated by the agents.

The DEA was invited to participate in Greenback; two agents were assigned but they rarely appeared at Greenback offices. They mostly served in a liaison capacity and rarely participated in joint investigations.

Greenback commenced operations in April 1980, with 12 designated targets. The targets were individuals and businesses in South Florida whose names appeared on CTR and CMIRs for transactions involving hundreds of millions of dollars. Isaac Kattan was one of the targets. His name showed up in connection with millions of dollars of cash transactions at several banks in Miami and millions of dollars of CMIRs for currency transported into the United States from Colombia. Another target was a series of accounts at Northside Bank of Miami that reflected huge cash deposits during 1978 and early 1979. One of these accounts was in the name of Jaime Ruiz.

Agents from Operation Greenback began investigating Isaac Kattan and the Northside Bank accounts in the fall of 1980. The investigations started out separately, but it was quickly determined that the Jaime Ruiz account at the Northside Bank belonged to Isaac Kattan. Much of Kattan's activities at other banks in the Miami area did not readily lend themselves to criminal charges. But his involvement at the Northside and Popular Banks in concert with Andres, Rodriguez, Francisco Navarro, and Francisco Bastida was so blatant that a prosecutable criminal case was quickly developed. By mid-January 1980, Greenback attorneys had prepared a draft indictment charging Kattan and the other three with a number of counts of failure to file CTRs and with the filing of false CTRs. There was some delay as the U.S. Attorney's office deliberated over whether to indict the Northside Bank. Complicating the decision was the fact that the bank had been taken over by the Bank of Miami.

While Operation Greenback personnel were contemplating whether or not to indict Northside Bank, Isaac Kattan continued his currency activities at a feverish pace. He opened an account at the brokerage firm of Donaldson Lufkin Jenrette in Miami during the last week of December. On January 2, 1981, Kattan's employees started to make large currency deposits to the account. The first was $285,000, and the deposits kept getting larger. In three weeks, over $12 million in cash went into the account. By the time the brokerage house closed out the account in February, over $20 million in cash had been deposited into the account. Unlike the bankers who had accepted Kattan's money for four years and did nothing, the manager of the Donaldson Lufkin Jenrette office in Miami was suspicious and did something about his suspicions.

In mid-January, William Tennille, manager of the Donaldson Lufkin Jenrette office in Miami, notified the Miami Police Department, the U.S. Customs Service, and the FBI of his suspicions that Kattan's cash deposits were derived from drug sales. He allowed the deposits to continue for a time, hoping that there would be a quick arrest that would solve the problem. When an arrest did not materialize, Tennille closed out the account, on or about February 6.

The information Tennille furnished to the U.S. Customs Service was passed on to Customs agents assigned to Operation Greenback during the third week of January, at about the same time that Greenback agents were getting ready to arrest Kattan for his involvement in the Northside Bank case. A decision was made to place Kattan under surveillance. During the last week of January, Greenback agents observed Kattan's couriers bringing boxes from the building where Kattan owned an apartment to the Donaldson Lufkin Jenrette office. During the first week of February, Greenback agents noticed another surveillance team watching Kattan—this one from DEA. A conference was hastily arranged to sort out the interests of the two groups.

At the conference, it was learned that one of Tennille's employees at Donaldson Lufkin Jenrette was friendly with a DEA agent and had told the agent about the huge cash deposits being made by Kattan and his courier. DEA had prior information about Kattan. The agency had been informed by Treasury in 1979 that Kattan was one of about 20 individuals whose name appeared repeatedly on CTRs filed by banks in the Miami area in connection with large currency transactions. The new information, coupled with this prior information, had prompted DEA to place Kattan under surveillance. The result of the DEA and Greenback conference was an agreement to conduct a joint investigation. Greenback agents were included on

DEA surveillance teams, and it was agreed that no arrest would be made without the concurrence of both groups.

One of the first things the joint surveillance team observed, beginning on February 6, 1981, was the fact that Kattan and his couriers were making visits to the Great American Bank of Dade County. The couriers were obviously bringing boxes of money into the bank. Kattan decided to do business at Great American Bank just after his account at Donaldson Lufkin Jenrette was closed out. Kattan's choice of Great American Bank was quite a coincidence because Greenback agents had an open investigation on the bank from a separate money laundering case.

Bank Complicity

Greenback's open case on Great American Bank was prompted by a Federal Deposit Insurance Corporation examination in September 1980. Gene Sykes, the examiner who conducted the routine review of bank records, noticed the bank was taking in huge volumes of currency in its installment loan department. This fact in itself was unusual, but Sykes noted other highly suspicious circumstances, like the issuance of large denomination cashier's checks to individuals without any supporting loan documents. Sykes also found 12 CTRs indicating that an employee of the bank brought in large amounts of currency to Great American Bank. Sykes noted millions of dollars of currency deposits to two accounts, one in the name of "Interfil" and one in the name of "Luis Rondon." The examination report indicated highly suspicious currency transactions were being conducted at the bank which suggested the possibility of a money laundering scheme involving bank officials. The information in Sykes' report was referred to Greenback for investigation.

Kattan had heard from another money launderer named Carlos Piedrahita that the Great American Bank was a good place to do business. As a matter of fact, the "Luis Rondon" account identified in Gene Sykes' examination was an account opened and controlled by Piedrahita. Piedrahita introduced Kattan to bank officials Lionel Paytuvi and Carlos Nunez. By the time he met with Nunez and Paytuvi, Kattan had a problem. With the Donaldson Lufkin Jenrette account closed, he had accumulated $3 million in currency. Paytuvi, a vice president in charge of the loan department, and Nunez, a loan officer, agreed to accept the $3 million in cash as payment for the purchase of a number of cashier's checks payable to the names on the accounts which Kattan had at the Bank of Miami. Kattan paid the bankers a $20,000 fee up front to handle the transaction.

After the $3 million purchase of cashier's checks, Kattan spoke to Nunez about future currency deals. Nunez insisted that he open a checking account and deposit currency into the account. Kattan then opened a checking account at Great American Bank in the name of "Currency Exchange Corporation." Nunez agreed not to file CTRs on the cash deposits over $10,000. He also agreed to issue cashier's checks in fictitious names that Kattan would supply. Kattan was to pay 0.8% of each transaction as a fee for this service. Between February 10 and February 26, 1981, Kattan's employees deposited $6 million in currency in the Currency Exchange Corporation account, and Nunez received $47,000 for handling the money.

CLOSING IN

While Kattan was meeting with Great American Bank officials and starting a new laundering operation through that bank, the joint DEA/Operation Greenback surveillance team continued its observations. Kattan was observed leaving his apartment early every morning as he carried out his daily routine of meetings with two employees and with strangers. The meetings took place in restaurants, parking lots, banks, alleys, and on street corners. Kattan carried a beeper, and he was observed receiving numerous messages on the beeper. Usually, he would make a call from a pay phone shortly after receiving a beeper message.

It was later learned that these calls were from the drug bosses in Colombia and from their representatives in Miami. Typically, Kattan would get a telephone call from a drug boss in Colombia calling to advise him of a currency delivery. The drug boss would then mail half of a dollar bill to Kattan in Miami, and within a few days a courier would show up with the other half of the dollar bill. Only if the two halves matched, would Kattan do business with the courier. This individual would then turn over to Kattan a large quantity of small bills, usually ranging from several hundred thousand dollars up to a million dollars.

The meetings with couriers usually involved boxes, bags, or bundles being handed to Kattan or one of his employees. The agents assumed that there was cash inside. The packages would be loaded into the trunks of rented Chevrolets which Kattan and his associates always drove. After a pickup, the rental car would be driven to Villa Regina, the exclusive condominium complex where Kattan owned two apartments. Kattan and his employees were observed moving packages from the trunks of the rental cars to his cash counting apartment, and the following morning they would move the packages out of the apartment and over to Great American Bank. Kattan was a fast and reckless driver. He frequently made U-turns. He always seemed to be in a hurry.

In the middle of the surveillance of Kattan, Greenback agents received a tip from an informant that three officers of the Great American Bank were accepting large currency deposits into an account without filing

CTRs. The tipster identified the officers as Elaine Kemp, Head Teller, Carlos Nunez, Loan Officer, and Lionel Paytuvi, Vice President in charge of the Installment Loan Department. The name on the account was Currency Exchange Corporation. On February 26, 1981, the surveillance team watched Kattan and his couriers meet with two individuals on a Miami street corner and move a large red suitcase from one car to another. The senior DEA agent ordered an arrest despite the prior agreement that no arrest would be made without the concurrence of Greenback agents. Kattan and the other two individuals were arrested. The red suitcase was in the possession of the two strangers. When the suitcase was opened, the agents expected to find money, but to their delight and surprise, they found 20 kilos of cocaine.

Kattan and the two individuals he met, Hector and Orlando Espinosa, were charged with possession of cocaine. Bail was set at $5 million for each man. The Espinosas were determined to be Colombian citizens. Kattan was found to be in possession of $1,400 in cash in his pockets, $16,000 in cash jammed under the front seat of his car, and $385,000 in cashier's checks in his briefcase. There also was a copy of a $1.2 million wire transfer order to a Swiss bank and several financial record books detailing money movements in Switzerland and Colombia.

Greenback agents were upset about the way that the arrest situation was handled. There was a clear understanding that no arrest would be made unless both DEA and Greenback agreed. To make matters worse, DEA supervisors would not let Greenback agents question Kattan prior to his appearance before a magistrate. The agents had a lot of information about Kattan's money laundering activities and felt that they might have obtained some useful information by interviewing him just after his arrest.

Nevertheless, Greenback agents were pleased with the result of the arrest. They were glad to see that Kattan was caught with incriminating evidence.

The day after Kattan's arrest, Greenback and DEA agents cooperated in executing search warrants at the Great American Bank and the Bank of Miami. The search became a media event with heavy newspaper, television, and radio coverage. Records pertaining to Kattan's transactions were seized at both banks. In addition, records pertaining to two other money laundering operations were seized at the Great American Bank. While searching through records at the Great American Bank, agents also found copies of CTRs which had been filled out for a number of large transactions by Kattan's Currency Exchange Corporation. Subsequent investigation determined that the originals of these CTRs were never filed with the IRS, as required by law, and that they in fact had been destroyed.

Search warrants were also executed at Kattan's money counting apartment in the Villa Regina and in other apartments controlled by him. The agents seized a telex machine, several money counting machines, and thousands of financial records. A review of the seized records indicated Kattan used foreign bank accounts in Canada, Peru, the Bahamas, Venezuela, Panama, and Switzerland.

After the execution of the search warrants and the associated media coverage, the two banks went on a counter media blitz of their own. Officials and attorneys representing both banks held press conferences and alleged that the searches were a publicity stunt. They received a lot of coverage with their allegations, but in the end (1983) Great American Bank and three senior officers were convicted of violating the Bank Secrecy Act.

On the day following his arrest, a bail hearing was held for Isaac Kattan, and his bail was reduced to $2 million. He was never able to post bail. During the hearing he identified himself as a money exchanger and estimated his wealth at $5 million. A week later, Kattan and the Espinosas were indicted on cocaine possession charges.

In mid-March, Kattan was indicted for his laundering schemes. This was the indictment that had been drafted in January in connection with the currency deposits at the Northside and Popular banks. Andres Rodriguez, Francisco Navarro, and Francisco Bastido were indicted along with him. The 16-count indictment charged the four with failing to file CTRs in some instances and false filing in others. A decision had been made not to press charges against the Northside Bank.

In April, Kattan faced additional charges. This time he was indicted for his role in getting the Great American Bank and some of its employees to ignore CTR filing requirements. Indicted along with him were the bank itself and bank officers Lionel Paytuvi, Elaine Kemp, and Carlos Nunez. The bank and the three officers were also charged with CTR violations in connection with $9 million that had been deposited in the Luis Rondon account and some $71 million in cash that had been deposited in the Interfil account during 1980. The three bank officers had arrangements with the holders of those accounts for payoffs in return for not filing CTRs.

Trials and Convictions

In early May, Isaac Kattan went to trial on the cocaine possession charge. He testified in his own defense and vehemently denied that he had ever dealt in cocaine or knew that there was cocaine in the red suitcase the Espinosa brothers were carrying at the time of his arrest. The jury deliberated only 20 minutes before finding Kattan guilty on May 7, 1981. Three months later, he was sentenced to 30 years in prison.

In September 1981, Kattan pleaded guilty to the CTR charges stemming from the Great American Bank case, and was sentenced to five years to be served concurrently with his 30 year cocaine possession sentence.

DEA agents in Switzerland located several bank accounts controlled by Kattan. Through the use of the Swiss Mutual Assistance Treaty with the United States, DEA was able to have $3.3 million in these accounts frozen. This money was eventually forfeited to the United States.

Most of the charges in the Northside Bank indictment were dismissed on a technicality by a U.S. District Court Judge in Miami. The government appealed the dismissal, and the 11th Circuit U.S. Court of Appeals over-ruled the lower court's ruling and reinstated all counts of the indictment in January 1983. Isaac Kattan pleaded guilty to one count of this indictment a few months later and received another five-year sentence, to run concurrently with the 30-year drug charge sentence.

Andres Rodriguez was convicted of separate charges of racketeering and mail fraud in 1983 and was sentenced to six years in prison. These charges involved looting accounts at the Northside Bank. In February 1984 he pled guilty to two CTR violations in the money laundering case and was sentenced to 10 years in prison to run concurrently with his six-year fraud and racketeering sentence.

Lionel Paytuvi, Elaine Kemp, and Carlos Nunez were tried and found guilty of CTR violations in March 1984. All three bank officers received jail sentences. The Great American Bank pleaded guilty to four counts involving CTR violations in April 1984. Isaac Kattan cooperated with the government during the trial of the Great American Bank officers, but never was called on to testify.

Despite his cooperation in the Great American case, Kattan has steadfastly refused to identify the drug bosses for whom he laundered money. He believes that his family would be harmed if he put the finger on his employers.

In retrospect, Isaac Kattan was a very successful money launderer. He laundered somewhere around $400 million in cash over the course of four years. Kattan was the best known of a number of money launderers during an era where large amounts of currency were deposited directly into banks and other financial institutions. Despite his efforts to evade identification, though, the sheer volume of the money he handled brought attention to his operation and made him vulnerable to arrest.

Kattan had a cycle of money movement and laundering activity that uniquely satisfied the needs of business clients and drug bosses. These business clients preferred dealing with Kattan both to evade taxes and duty on imports, and because they obtained a better exchange rate for the conversion of pesos to dollars. The bosses found that he was able to convert their dollar profits to pesos in Colombia.

Isaac Kattan, though, was only one of many money launderers who moved money for the Colombia drug bosses in South Florida between 1977 and 1981. Two other notable launderers were Hernan Botero and Bheno Ghitis.

HERNAN BOTERO

Hernan Botero-Moreno opened five accounts in five different names at the West Broward Office of the Landmark First National Bank of Fort Lauderdale on December 31, 1979. The opening of these accounts was to lead to a series of events that included the funnelling of $55 million in cash through the account over the course of the next ten months; the indictment of Botero and his brother, Roberto, on charges of mail fraud and CTR violations; the extradition of Botero from Colombia, under terms of a new treaty; and Hernan Botero's conviction and sentence to 30 years in a federal prison.

Today, Hernan Botero sits in jail proclaiming his innocence and charging that he was framed and railroaded by the government and several associates. Government agents and prosecutors are equally firm in their conviction that Hernan Botero was a major drug money launderer for Colombian drug dealers, that he received a fair trial, and that his jail sentence was appropriate.

Hernan Botero was born in Medellin, Colombia on October 29, 1932 to a businessman father and an aristocratic mother. His mother's father had accumulated one of the largest fortunes ever made in Colombia. Botero graduated from a Jesuit high school in Medellin, and in 1951, moved with his family to New York so that he and his two brothers could be educated in U.S. colleges. Hernan received a degree in civil engineering from Rensselaer Polytechnic Institute in 1955. His brothers, Roberto and Jorge, also received engineering degrees from RPI.

In 1955, Botero's father purchased a chemical company in Medellin, and in 1956, Botero became the president of the firm, known as Sulfacidos, S.A. Under his direction the company expanded and succeeded, and by the late 1960s it had an annual net income of $8 million. While Botero was running the chemical company, his father made other investments, including the purchase of a controlling interest in the Hotel Nutibara in Medellin and substantial amounts of stock in several Colombian companies. In 1961, Hernan Botero bought an interest in a professional soccer team called Atletico Nacional, which became very successful and was known throughout Colombia.

In 1970, the Botero family sold its interest in Sulfacidos and Hernan resigned as president. Botero formed Hernan Botero and Company Ltd., which served as the Colombian agent for foreign shipping companies that bid on the maritime transportation of agricultural products. This business flourished.

At about the same time, Botero became involved in the buying and selling of foreign currency, dealing in the black market rather than through the Colombian banking system. His money exchange business was named Cia Rodnan, S.A.; it was wholly-owned by Botero's wife and sons.

Hernan Botero did some of his currency exchange business with Peinado Navarro. Navarro started out as a desk clerk at the Hotel Nutibara, where he frequently handled foreign currency exchanges. Navarro branched out and started to handle transactions on his own account both for hotel guests and for other individuals who needed to buy and sell foreign currencies. Eventually Navarro became the Comptroller of the Hotel Nutibara, but the currency exchange business became so successful that he resigned his position and devoted all his working time to the business, which was known as Inversiones Peinado Navarro (IPN).

IPN was a licensed currency exchange broker, with an office in Medellin. Hernan Botero's currency exchange activities included doing business with Navarro and IPN. They had a friendly business relationship. This association would eventually lead Hernan into the middle of a multi-million dollar drug money laundering scheme. The government claims Botero was the leader of the operation. He claims that he was an unwitting dupe who was the victim of perjured testimony by two thieving bank officers, and that he was betrayed by his friend, Peinado Navarro, and possibly by his brother, Roberto Botero.

In 1978, Hernan Botero and his second wife, Rosalia Montoya, purchased a palatial home in suburban Miami in an exclusive area of West Broward County known as the Bonaventure Development. The house was purchased in the name of Cia Rodnan, S.A. Botero and his wife came to the United States about four times a year with their two minor children. Shortly after the purchase of the house, Botero opened an account in the name of Cia Rodnan, S.A. at the Landmark First National City Bank of Fort Lauderdale, ostensibly to facilitate his currency exchange business. He deposited checks payable to the firm into the account, and he wrote checks on the account for the purchase of Certificates of Exchange from the Banco de Colombia, a commercial bank. The Certificates of Exchange were issued by the Central Bank of Colombia, the Banco de la Republica and were payable in pesos. Botero would then sell the Certificates of Exchange at a profit and deposit the checks received for the certificates into the Landmark Bank.

During 1979, Botero's business with the Landmark Bank involved only checks, not currency. His dealings at the bank were handled by an employee named Dolores Eirin.

The government's version of Botero's activities was presented in detail during Hernan Botero's trial in 1985. It offers excellent insights into how cash was moved through the Landmark Bank to evade the BSA reporting requirements. The government's version of the case follows.

The Prosecution's Case

The prosecution contended that the money laundering scheme began in October 1979 when Botero asked Dolores Eirin about the possibility of running large amounts of currency through the bank without reporting it to the government. Eirin spoke to bank officer Alan Campbell about her conversation with Botero, and he, in turn, talked to another bank officer, Gary Dodson, about the proposition. The three agreed among themselves that it could be done.

Campbell and Dodson at the time were involved in a complicated fraudulent loan scheme whereby bank loans were made to customers who would not otherwise have qualified, while other loans were being made to fictitious names. This scheme was not uncovered until October 1980, by which time the two had defrauded the bank out of between $700,000 and $1,000,000. Campbell was the assistant cashier and Dodson was a credit analyst.

In December 1979, Botero returned to the West Broward office of the bank, where Eirin introduced him to Campbell and Dodson. Botero told them that he needed to deposit large amounts of cash in the bank without completing CTR forms. Botero told them he had a product that originated in Colombia and was brought to the United States where it was sold for cash. He said that he needed to get the U.S. dollars converted to pesos in Colombian banks as quickly as possible to take advantage of fluctuating currency rates. He also said he needed to deposit about $400,000 worth of currency each day. Botero and the three bankers agreed that he would pay them 0.75% of the gross deposits in return for sorting and counting the currency and for not filing CTRs.

During this meeting, Botero told the bankers that various couriers would bring money to the bank. After the money was processed and counted, 98.5% was to be wire transferred to other accounts per Botero's instructions; 1.5% was to remain in the account, half of which was to go to the bankers. The remainder of the money was to remain as working capital.

Hernan Botero returned to the bank later in December and opened five accounts. The number of accounts was suggested by Gary Dodson and Alan Campbell. All five accounts were opened in Hispanic names provided by Botero. When asked for identifying information for bank records on each accountholder, he made a telephone call, after which he provided

El Salvador passport numbers for each of the five names. The bankers gave the original signature cards to Botero and told him to have them signed and returned for the bank's files. In the meantime, the bank's rules required a temporary signature card to be on file for a new account to be used. Gary Dodson signed the temporary account card with a twist of humor—he signed the name of Juan Valdez, the Colombian coffee grower who appears in television ads. The bankers agreed between themselves on a cover story to explain huge cash deposits. Since the identification numbers on the accounts were purported to be Salvadoran passport numbers, a story was concocted that the accountholders were professional people in El Salvador who were getting their U.S. dollar holdings out of the country because of political unrest.

On December 31, 1979, the first deposit was made to the account. Hernan Botero brought an individual known as Lee Restrepo (later identified as Losardo Restrepo) and introduced him to Eirin, Campbell, and Dodson as someone who would be making currency deposits. Both men left the bank. When Restrepo returned a short time later, he deposited about $400,000 in cash into the Juan Valdez account. Later that day Botero returned to the bank to make sure that everything had gone smoothly, and when he learned that it did, he paid his first fee to the bankers, drawing a $3,000 check on his company account, Cia Rodnan, S.A., payable to cash. He gave the check to Dodson, who brought it to a teller and obtained cash. Dodson brought the $3,000 back to Botero, who, in turn, gave the money to the three bankers. This was the only time that a fee was paid from Botero's business account.

Within a few days after the accounts had been opened, Hernan Botero returned to the bank with signatures executed on each of the signature cards. On the next day, Lee Restrepo brought in approximately $400,000 in currency. Three of the accounts received $100,000 each; deposits of $50,000 and $49,585 were made to the other two accounts. The bankers were given written authority by the accountholders to make transfers between the accounts to keep them in balance. Money was to be transferred out of the accounts on Botero's instructions. After the first deposits were counted and credited to the five accounts, CTRs were prepared. A copy was placed in the bank's files, while the originals, which should have been sent to the IRS, were destroyed.

The currency deposits of the first few days set a pattern for future deposits. Currency was brought into the bank by one of several Hispanic couriers who would go to Dolores Eirin because she spoke Spanish. Eirin would take the courier to Dodson or Campbell, and the courier would be taken into the vault where the cash would be counted by one of two employees and receipts would be issued to the courier. There were between six and ten couriers introduced by Botero. Restrepo brought in about 60%

of the currency. Another courier, Jaime Bustemonte, brought in about 20%. The remaining cash was brought in by the others.

Campbell, Dodson, and Eirin decided to share their fee with two female employees who regularly counted the money. They were each given 10% of the fee to be split evenly among them.

Frequent deposits of about $400,000 continued after the first two deposits. After each deposit, the funds were immediately wire transferred out of the bank on instructions from Hernan Botero. Most of the money was wired to accounts of Colombian banks, particularly to the account of Banco de Trabajadores of Bogota, Colombia at the Pan American Bank in Miami. After about six weeks of almost daily currency deposits, Hernan Botero told Campbell, Dodson, and Eirin that he was returning to Colombia and that all the activity concerning the accounts would be taken over by his brother, Roberto.

Roberto Botero became very involved in the day-to-day operation of the accounts, sometimes telephoning Dodson and Campbell with conflicting and changing instructions and generally making a nuisance of himself. Hernan Botero also telephoned from Colombia about the accounts.

Sometime in March 1980, after about 60 deposits had been made and wired out, the bank's main office in Miami inquired as to the nature of the wire transfer activity. Campbell and Dodson were able to give a satisfactory explanation, but they decided the wire transfers were attracting too much attention. So, they conferred with Roberto Botero and it was agreed that cashier's checks would be used for future transfers out of the accounts. The switch to cashier's checks was made because all three of the bankers had authority to sign cashier's checks and there was no reason for the main office to learn of the transactions on a daily basis.

The cashier's check policy involved the issuance of checks in amounts of about $50,000. The checks were usually made and signed by Campbell because he had the highest signature authority. They were made out mostly for deposit to accounts that certain Colombian banks maintained at U.S. banks, and sent to the banks via Express Mail almost on a daily basis.

Most of the cashier's checks were mailed to the Pan American Bank of Miami and were payable to a specific account number of Banco de Trabajadores of Bogota. However, some were sent to other banks, including Bankers Trust Company International Bank in Miami and to a bank in Pittsburgh. Letters containing the checks usually were addressed to specific officers of the banks under instructions from one of the Botero brothers. Some of the checks were made payable to Miami bank accounts of two other Colombian banks, Banco de Bogota and Banco de Estado. Records later obtained from the Colombian government revealed that almost all of the funds transferred through the Pan American Bank of Miami went into Colombian bank accounts controlled by Inversiones Peinado Navarro.

Sometime in August 1980, Botero's chief courier, Restrepo, started his own independent money laundering operation at the Landmark Bank. For the next two months, Restrepo brought his own currency to the bank on a regular basis, depositing it into three accounts previously opened by another launderer named Carlos Urdaneta, who had stopped making cash deposits. Restrepo was issued cashier's checks for the money in these accounts, payable to names that he furnished to Dodson and Campbell. Restrepo paid a 1% fee for his transactions and insisted that Campbell and Dodson not tell the Boteros' of his personal enterprise.

The two bank officers estimated that Restrepo brought in about $15 million in currency between late August and October 20, 1980—this was over and above currency deposited in the five Botero accounts.

Campbell and Dodson, who testified for the government at Hernan Botero's trial in 1984, claim that neither Hernan nor Roberto Botero ever stated that the cash coming into the bank was from drug sales. However, they recalled several conversations with Lee Restrepo in which he alluded to the drug connection and comments by Urdaneta that suggested the Boteros were involved in the drug trade. They also testified that on one occasion, Restrepo told them that one of Botero's boats had been seized during the Cuban Mariel boatlift with a load of cocaine on board.

All of the activity in the five Botero accounts and in the three Urdaneta accounts stopped on October 20, 1980 when federal bank examiners came to the West Broward Branch. By this time, approximately $55 million in currency had been deposited into the Botero accounts. Over $17 million had been put into the Urdaneta accounts from Urdaneta and Lee Restrepo. The examiners questioned a number of bank employees, but particularly Eirin and Dodson, about the large cash deposits to the Botero and Urdaneta accounts. Dodson and Eirin told them that to the best of their knowledge, the money was coming from El Salvador because the account-holders feared political unrest.

Hernan Botero telephoned Alan Campbell at his residence during the course of the bank examination. He wanted to know if the currency deposits could continue. Campbell told him that he and Dodson and Eirin all felt that the deposits should be stopped because it was not safe to continue. After the telephone call from Hernan Botero, Gary Dodson was contacted by Roberto Botero to arrange a meeting. Roberto was accompanied to the meeting by Augusto Peinado Navarro, who did not speak English. Dodson suggested the possibility of one last huge cash deposit of as much as $5 million. Roberto said that they would think about it. This was the last contact that Dodson had with either of the Botero brothers.

In early November 1980, Alan Campbell was fired by Landmark Bank because of his involvement in the loan fraud scheme. Several days later, Gary Dodson resigned to go into the real estate business. Campbell was questioned by FBI agents on November 10, 1980 with his attorney present. During this interview, he admitted his own involvement in the loan fraud operation and implicated Gary Dodson. He also started to provide details about the money laundering operation. Campbell's attorney stopped the interrogation so he could work out a deal with the U.S. Attorney's office. He was able to get a commitment for a sentence of nine months of unsupervised probation, if Dodson cooperated fully, including testimony before a grand jury and at any trials that might result. Gary Dodson and his attorney struck a similar bargain with the U.S. Attorney's office. All of the information obtained from Dodson and Campbell was turned over to Customs and IRS agents from Operation Greenback in December.

In January 1981, the U.S. Attorney's office began presenting the money laundering case to a federal grand jury in Miami. In the midst of the grand jury investigation, a decision was made to arrest as many of the participants as possible lest they flee to Colombia. On February 10, 1981, Operation Greenback agents arrested Dolores Eirin at the West Broward Branch of the Landmark First National Bank. Roberto Botero and Carlos Urdaneta were arrested that same day. Arrest warrants had been issued for Hernan Botero and Losardo Restrepo, but neither could be found. It was learned that Hernan Botero had departed for Colombia a few days before the arrest warrants were issued. The arrests were accompanied by a great deal of publicity, and very high bonds were set. Eirin's bail was $3.5 million, Roberto Botero's was $5 million, and Urdaneta's was $2.5 million. There was a tremendous amount of publicity in Colombia about the arrests and about the fact that warrants had been issued for Hernan Botero and Losardo Restrepo. Hernan Botero was a nationally-known figure in Colombia.

In the meantime, the grand jury presentations continued, and on February 19, 1981, the grand jury indicted the Botero brothers, Dolores Eirin, Losardo Restrepo, and seven others with a 16-count indictment charging offenses connected with the currency deposits at the Landmark Bank. The charges included mail fraud, BSA violations, and importation of cocaine.

There was no crime of money laundering at the time. The bank employees could be charged under the Bank Secrecy Act for not filing CTRs, but the people who bribed the bank employees not to file CTRs could not be charged with failure to file because they were under no legal obligation to do so. The government got at these individuals by charging them with a combination of charges involving the BSA, conspiracy, and mail fraud. Hernan and Roberto Botero were charged, in effect, with conspiring to cause CTRs not to be filed and with causing cashier's checks with fictitious payee names to be placed in the mail for purposes of defrauding the IRS of its right to receive information about the transactions.

The cocaine importation charge was admitted by all concerned to have been very weak and was dropped from the indictment before the trial of

Roberto Botero and Dolores Eirin. There was no cocaine seized in the case. The cocaine charge was based on hearsay remarks attributed to Losardo Restrepo by Dodson and Campbell.

Hernan Botero remained in Colombia following Roberto's arrest. In March 1981, he sought out an interview with a DEA representative in Medellin during which he vehemently denied any involvement with drugs or with drug money laundering. He said was aware that there was a warrant for his arrest in Miami and that he wanted to return to Miami to clear his name. But he said he would only do so if he received a written commitment from the U.S. judge allowing him to travel back and forth to Colombia until the time of trial, so he could attend to his business interests.

Botero also told the DEA agent, Herbert Williams, that he had heard from his brother, Roberto, that two former employees of the Landmark Bank of Fort Lauderdale had falsely accused him of laundering drug money. He said the bankers were lying to avoid being sent to jail for crimes that they committed at the bank. He denied a story that had just appeared in a Medellin newspaper alleging that he was the head of a Latin drug smuggling group. The story claimed that he was connected to a Colonel Arce of the Bolivian Army and to another person who was the owner of the housing development where he bought his home in the Miami area. Hernan denied knowing these individuals. The newspaper article also indicated that FBI and/or IRS agents would soon travel to Colombia to conduct an investigation, and he offered to make his records available to them. He qualified the offer, though, by saying that he would have to get his attorney's permission.

In the summer of 1981, IRS agents Peter Abalia and Michael J. Mullaney, both assigned to Operation Greenback, travelled to Colombia to work on the Botero case. The trip came about as the result of a May 1981 letter from the Superintendent of Banking in Colombia to the Federal Reserve Bank of Atlanta. The letter indicated that the banking agency had conducted its own investigation of the currency activities of Hernan Botero and others because it appeared that some Colombian currency laws may have been violated. The letter said that about $7 million of the money had been traced from the Pan American International Bank of Miami back to Colombia and that the agency was seeking to cooperate with U.S. authorities in their investigation. When the agents arrived in Colombia, they were well received. With the cooperation of Colombian authorities, they were able to review the records of Inversiones Peinado Navarro and bank records which showed that the funds from the cashier's checks deposited to the accounts of Colombian banks at the Pan American Bank of Miami were eventually credited to Inversiones Peinado Navarro. They also found records of the receipt of U.S. dollars at IPN in the names of about 3,000 persons with Canadian, U.S., Brazilian, and Mexican addresses and passport numbers.

Mullaney and Abalia made two more trips to Colombia, in late 1981 and in 1982, to collect additional evidence. They were able to trace almost all of the $55 million that had been deposited in the Landmark Bank to Colombian banks controlled by IPN. Voluminous records of IPN indicated that all of the U.S. dollars received had come from currency exchanges with thousands of tourists who visited Colombia. A review of the passport numbers of some 300 Americans listed in the IPN records indicated that about 200 were numbers that had never been issued. In all, the agents received copies of some 12,000 pieces of documentary records from IPN and Colombian banks relating to the money in the Landmark accounts.

In 1979, Colombia and the United States entered into a bilateral extradition treaty for cases involving drug offenses. In 1981, both countries ratified the treaty. In 1982, Carlos Lehder, one of the major cocaine distributors in Colombia, was indicted in Jacksonville, Florida on drug smuggling charges. The United States began to press Colombia to extradite Lehder, but Lehder's attorneys opposed extradition on grounds that the treaty was unconstitutional. In September 1983, the Colombian Supreme Court determined that the treaty satisfied constitutional requirements, and a warrant was issued for Lehder's arrest, but he became a fugitive. Subsequent political activity in Colombia resulted in a disinclination on the part of the Colombian government to honor the extradition treaty. In March 1984, the warrant for Lehder's arrest was dismissed.

In April 1984, the cocaine cartel had Lara Bonilla, the Justice Minister of Colombia and a relentless foe, assassinated—an act which prompted a 180 degree turn-around by the Colombian government on the extradition issue. On May 8, 1984, the President signed an extradition order for Carlos Lehder. Lehder once again became a fugitive and some of the major cartel members temporarily relocated to Panama. With the political climate in Colombia turning in favor of the extradition treaty, U.S. officials initiated extradition proceedings against 60 Colombian defendants, including Botero.

One of the first individuals arrested in the aftermath of the Bonilla slaying was Hernan Botero. He did not flee Colombia with the leaders of the cartel. He remained at his home in Medellin trying to reconstruct his business empire and openly protesting his innocence on the drug money laundering charges. The U.S. Embassy in Bogota initially requested Hernan Botero's extradition in an Embassy Note dated May 16, 1984, referring to charges in the indictment dated February 19, 1981. He was arrested on May 28, 1984, and the U.S. Embassy formally requested his extradition in another note dated June 26, 1984. The second note was accompanied by a certified copy of the indictment against Botero and an affidavit of the Prosecutor, Gerald J. Houlihan, in support of the request for extradition. Houlihan's affidavit specifically referred to a count in the indictment which charged Botero and others with the importation of cocaine, despite the fact that the cocaine importation charge had been dropped from the indictment in April 1983.

Prompted by Hernan Botero's arrest, the attorneys for Roberto Botero and Dolores Eirin in June 1984 decided to press for a quick trial. Roberto Botero's attorney, Joel Hirschhorn, was particularly interested in a trial before Hernan Botero's return to the United States because his strategy was to try to show that Hernan was the real culprit and that Roberto didn't know what was going on.

The trial started during the last week of June. Gary Dodson and Alan Campbell testified as the government's main witnesses. The two were not very strong witnesses. In fact, Hirschhorn was able to tear Campbell apart on the stand, detailing hundreds of crimes he had committed while working for Landmark Bank. However, the poor showing of the witnesses was counterbalanced by a great deal of evidence documenting cash deposits which tended to corroborate the former bankers' story. The testimony of Roberto Botero and Dolores Eirin actually bolstered the government's case. Many of their statements were clearly contradicted by other witnesses, like Campbell and Dodson.

Roberto Botero attempted to portray himself as an innocent dupe. He attempted to explain how the accounts were used for legitimate currency exchange activities, but his testimony was not very clear. Also, he was badly hurt on cross-examination by an inability to explain the source of the currency going into the Landmark accounts.

Dolores Eirin's testimony stretched credibility in a number of areas. She denied that Hernan Botero had opened the five accounts, claiming instead that she had opened the accounts for five different residents of El Salvador who had come to the bank in December 1979. She denied receiving money from Campbell and Dodson, and denied telling them that she put the money they gave her into an account she maintained for a nephew. The prosecution was able to prove that she deposited $37,000 into the nephew's account during 1980, and was able to discredit her on other denials she made with respect to Botero's payments.

Roberto Botero and Dolores Eirin were both found guilty. Dolores Eirin was sentenced to two years of imprisonment to be followed by five years of probation. Roberto Botero was sentenced to eight years in prison and a fine of $120,000.

In early January 1985, the Colombian courts ruled in favor of the extradition of Hernan Botero, after the U.S. State Department sent a corrected copy of the indictment to the Colombian government. In deciding in favor of extradition, the Colombian court acknowledged that the charges in the indictment did not spell out a crime under Colombian law. However, the court stated that it had to look behind the actual charges and recognize that the crimes charged were committed to further cover up the real crime of cocaine importation. Hernan Botero was extradited along with three other Colombians, thereby becoming the first Colombian citizens extradited to the United States pursuant to the treaty relating to alleged drug offenses.

None of the four extradited were considered to be "big fish." The big fish, the real cartel bosses, Jorge Ochoa and Pablo Escobar, were hiding out in Panama as guests of General Manuel Noriega.

When Hernan Botero was transported to Miami on January 5, 1985, he was immediately placed in solitary confinement.

Botero's trial began in U.S. District Court in Miami on June 3, 1985. He was represented by a well-known Miami defense attorney named Neal R. Sonnett. Gary Dodson and Alan Campbell provided crucial testimony against Botero. They both stated that he offered them fees for accepting large currency transactions without filing the CTRs required by law. The government introduced records of the cash deposits into the five accounts that Botero opened at Landmark Bank, as well as evidence showing that most of the deposits went from the Landmark Bank to accounts of Colombian banks at the Pan American Bank of Miami by way of wire transfers and cashier's checks. The government then was able to trace the flow of the money in the Colombian bank accounts to the credit of the Medellin money exchange firm of Inversiones Peinado Navarro. The government produced as evidence the names of about 300 persons with U.S. passports and addresses. These names had been obtained by Greenback agents Abalia and Mullaney from IPN records when they went to Colombia in 1981. Testimony established that about 200 of the passport numbers never had been issued. Five individuals whose passport numbers and addresses matched those found in IPN records testified and related similar stories: each had visited Colombia in 1979 or early 1980 and had stayed at the Hotel Nutibara for at least one night, but had never exchanged dollars for pesos at the hotel or IPN. The testimony of these individuals was devastating to Botero's defense.

The picture painted by the prosecution was that IPN had falsified records to show the receipt of millions of U.S. dollars from tourists, and thereby evaded Colombian currency restrictions that prohibited currency exchangers from acquiring more than $20,000 at one time and also prohibited Colombian citizens and businesses from acquiring dollars. The books of IPN were doctored to show that the money came from foreign tourists. IPN would have the Colombian government believe that it obtained millions of U.S. dollars in currency from tourists from many countries and then shipped the currency to the United States where it was deposited in the Landmark Bank. The money was eventually moved from Landmark and was credited to IPN in accounts at Colombian banks. This made the IPN activity appear legitimate to Colombian authorities. The testimony particularly hurt Botero because it appeared that the identities of the tourists were being obtained, in many cases, from the records of the Nutibara Hotel, and Hernan Botero and his family were closely associated with the ownership and management of the hotel. The defense was not able to disassociate Hernan Botero from the activities of IPN.

Neal Sonnett did not put Hernan Botero on the stand during the trial. In not doing so, he gave up any possibility of being able to let the jury hear Hernan's version of what transpired. Sonnett was convinced that the government had not proven its case beyond a reasonable doubt. He thought that the jury would recognize what he believed—that Dodson and Campbell were liars—and would not believe their testimony. He was wrong. The jury on June 18, 1983, found Botero guilty on all counts after one full day of deliberation. On September 13, 1985, Botero was sentenced to 30 years in prison.

Hernan Botero's Version

Hernan Botero is a prisoner in the maximum security Federal Correctional Institution at Marianna, Florida. At age 57, with a variety of physical and emotional ailments, it could be a death sentence. He is depressed and angry, but not broken. He continues to wage a fight to establish his innocence. Indeed, he appears to be firmly convinced that he is innocent. He is bitter against the U.S. system of justice, and against his brother, Roberto, and former friend Peinado Navarro who he believes betrayed him in the case for which he has been sentenced. His trial attorney, Neal Sonnett, is thoroughly convinced that Botero was not guilty of the charges brought against him. The attorney who currently represents him, Edward Canfield of Washington, DC, also believes in his innocence.

Not surprisingly, Botero's version of the facts in his case varies significantly from the government's case. The most critical difference lies in the testimony of Gary Dodson and Alan Campbell, the former employees of the Landmark Bank of Fort Lauderdale. Botero and his attorneys steadfastly maintain that the two bankers perjured themselves and are primarily responsible for the jury's guilty verdict. The defense view is that Hernan Botero never initiated any scheme at the Landmark Bank, and that he never approached Dolores Eirin regarding cash deposits. On the contrary, Eirin first broached the subject to him, the defense claims. She knew that he was in the currency exchange business because he had previously explained the nature of his business to her in connection with insuring that checks that he drew on his existing account at the bank would be paid immediately so that he could quickly change pesos for dollars in Colombia to take advantage of favorable exchange rates. She told him that the bank was interested in handling large currency deposits. This conversation occurred in December 1979, when Botero went to the bank to check on a monthly statement for his account. Botero agreed to inquire of some of his associates in the currency exchange business on behalf of Eirin to see if they were interested in making cash deposits. Eirin introduced Botero to Campbell and Dodson, but other than introductions and small talk, there were no discussions with them about deposits of large amounts of currency, the filing or nonfiling of currency reports, or anything that could remotely be considered to involve criminal or conspiratorial activity. He never had a conversation with them during this meeting or any other time about a "product" that originated in Colombia and was sold in the United States.

After the proposition by Eirin, Botero contacted Augusto Peinado Navarro, the owner of IPN, and told him that Landmark was seeking cash accounts. Navarro said he might be interested if the commission did not exceed 0.75%. He suggested that Botero try to negotiate the commission down by telling the bankers that $400,000 a day would be deposited into the account. Neither Botero nor Navarro saw anything unusual with paying a bank commission; nor did they consider 0.75% an exorbitant fee. In Colombia, banks charge up to 1% for a simple transfer of funds from one city to another, 0.5% for purchases of certificates of deposit, and 1% for arranging bank loans. Navarro told Botero that he wanted the money that went into Landmark Bank to be wire transferred to certain accounts of Colombian banks at Pan American International Bank in Miami. He also said that he wanted 1.5% of each deposit to remain in Landmark Bank, and that half that amount was to be used to pay the bank's commission.

Botero returned to Landmark Bank with Navarro's proposal, whereupon it was accepted by the three bankers. During the discussion, Botero made notations on a legal pad about the amount of commissions the bank would make on the deposits. He relayed Navarro's instructions regarding the wire transfers and the amount of funds which should remain in the account. Botero claims he never had any discussion with the bankers about currency reporting requirements or whether or not reports would be filed. At all times, he believed that commissions would go to the bank for counting, processing, and wire transferring funds. At no time did he ask or suggest to the bankers that the account be handled in any other way than legitimately. Hernan knew that IPN was a licensed currency exchange house and he believed that IPN would deal in legitimate business transactions.

Hernan Botero acknowledges that he made some money on the currency deposits. Peinado Navarro asked him to assist him in checking on the amount of the deposits and the wire transfers to other banks because he spent time in the Fort Lauderdale area, lived near the bank and had an account there, and knew the bank officials. Navarro agreed to pay Botero a commission for his services. Part of the commission was reflected in funds which were transferred from the five accounts into Botero's CIA Rodnan account; the rest was paid in Colombia. The total amount of his commissions was 1%. This was the full amount of his profit from the IPN transactions. Botero had no ownership interest in IPN and no ownership interest in the currency that was deposited in the Landmark Bank. He never had any connection with the actual purchasing or acquisition of the currency that was deposited into the accounts.

Botero's only role was to verify the amounts of the deposits that had been made and to relay Navarro's instructions regarding the accounts to which funds were to be transferred. Navarro handled all of the details regarding the purchase of U.S. currency. Botero never had any dealings with the sellers or couriers of the U.S. currency.

Contrary to Campbell's testimony, Botero said he never brought any couriers into the bank. He never introduced Losardo Restrepo or any of the other couriers to Campbell, Dodson, or Eirin. He never even met Restrepo until March 1981 at a soccer game in Medellin. He did furnish the bankers with the names of the couriers who would be bringing money into the bank. He obtained these names from Navarro.

When Hernan Botero went to the Landmark Bank to convey Navarro's willingness to make currency deposits, he assumed he would be opening one account in the name of IPN. Dolores Eirin explained that the bank preferred to open five separate accounts in the names of five individuals, rather than one corporate account. She said that since it would really be IPN's accounts, it didn't matter what names were used. Botero called Navarro from the bank and explained the situation to him. He requested Navarro to designate five separate names for the accounts. Eirin suggested the story of Salvadoran nationalities. Navarro supplied both the names and passport numbers for the accounts. Botero denies that he supplied the names of the accountholders. He maintains that the establishment of bank accounts in fictitious names is a common occurrence in Colombia. He claims that he did not become aware of American currency reporting requirements until November 1980.

After the initial currency deposit, Campbell asked Botero to write a check payable to cash from his own account in the amount of $3,000 for the first commission. Botero complied. Botero and his attorneys maintain that this is an indication that he thought the commission was being paid directly to the bank and is a further indication of his innocence. If he thought that the commission was being paid as a bribe, the money could have been drawn directly in cash from funds brought to the bank, thereby obliterating any paper trail.

After the initial commission payment, Botero told Dolores Eirin that if the 0.75% fee was a bank commission, it should be charged by means of a debit memo to the affected account. Eirin agreed and the commission payments were subsequently handled in that manner. The debit memo commission procedure is, according to Botero, a strong indication that he believed the commissions were legitimate bank charges.

A major issue raised by Botero and his attorney centers on whether Botero was ever knowingly involved with drugs, drug trafficking, or drug money laundering. The thrust of the government's case was that Hernan Botero knowingly laundered drug monies. The government used testimony by Campbell and Dodson recounting statements by Losardo Restrepo to suggest to the jury that Botero was directly involved in drug trafficking. The statements attributed to Restrepo were that Botero lost a boat loaded with drugs during the Mariel boatlift. The jury apparently bought this testimony.

Even worse from the defense point of view was that the probation officer was persuaded by this testimony to conclude in his presentence report that Botero must have been part of a massive drug smuggling operation and thus represented a serious and immediate danger to the welfare of the community. He recommended a substantial period of incarceration, both to prevent Botero from continuing illegal activities and to discourage others who might be disposed to commit similar crimes. The conclusions and recommendations of the probation officer led directly to Hernan's 30-year sentence.

The defense claims that Botero was never involved or connected in any way with drug trafficking. The government did not present any evidence of trafficking on his part. Botero never even met Restrepo until 1981, almost a year after the statements were allegedly made. No boat owned or controlled by Botero was ever seized during the Mariel boatlift. Botero and his attorneys believe that Restrepo never made the comments about the Cuban boatlift to Campbell and Dodson.

Botero denies ever telling the bankers that he dealt in a "product" from Colombia which was sold in the United States for cash. The defense points out that IRS agent, Mullaney, investigated Botero both in the United States and in Colombia and that his investigation yielded no information that linked him to drug trafficking. The defense established from Mullaney, on cross-examination, that he had found dozens of telexes of ship movements in Botero's home when it was searched, that he investigated every boat mentioned in the telexes, and that he was unable to connect any of them with actual drug seizures or with reports of suspected drug smuggling activity.

The defense also points to the testimony of DEA agent Herbert Williams, who interviewed Botero in Medellin. Williams said that Hernan Botero was known to be a legitimate Colombian businessman.

The defense produced a number of character witnesses during the trial who testified to Botero's well-known reputation for honesty and integrity. The defense also produced dozens of letters, prior to sentencing, from Colombians who knew Botero, attesting to the fact that Hernan was an honest businessman who was never suspected of dealing in drugs.

Botero and his attorneys take exception to the conclusion that just because $55 million in currency went into the Landmark accounts, the money had to be from drug proceeds. They claim that such a conclusion fails to recognize and understand the realities of the Colombian currency exchange business and the enormity of the nondrug black market in Colombia. Harsh restrictions by the Colombian government against the possession of U.S. dollars by Colombians and restrictions against the exchange of dollars for pesos has created a huge black market. When these restrictions are coupled with high duties and taxes on the import and export of legitimate products, the black market runs into the multibillion dollar range—a market run through licensed currency exchanges like IPN. The defense concedes that many drug dealers availed themselves of the services of the money exchangers to get their drug profits back to Colombia, but points out that the black market in nondrug capital was at least as substantial, and could just as easily have been the source of the funds deposited into the five Landmark accounts.

In a sentencing letter to the judge, dated November 20, 1985, Neal Sonnett cites Congressional testimony that suggests the amount of currency handled in the Colombian black market from the underdeclaration of legitimate products exported to the United States was $2 to $3 billion annually in the early 1980s. Sonnett's letter points out that although people in South Florida may have equated large cash deposits with drug money, Colombian Nationals knowledgeable of the currency exchange business knew very well that nondrug black market exports and other circumstances (like flight capital) could, and did, easily account for deposits in the amounts involved in this case. This is what Hernan Botero knew and believed.

Botero and his attorneys contend that there was no evidence introduced at the trial indicating where the cash being deposited actually came from. In view of that fact, they argue, it is incorrect to assume that the funds represented drug proceeds. The attorneys contend that Botero did not know the source of the funds, that he had no responsibility for the deposit of the funds into the accounts, and had no reason to believe that

Navarro and IPN were conducting anything other than a lawful currency exchange business.

Because Hernan Botero did not testify in his own defense at the trial, his version of what went on was not fully explained to the jury. It is obvious by their guilty verdict that the jury believed the uncontroverted testimony of the two bankers, Campbell and Dodson.

To make matters worse for Botero, Neal Sonnett advised him not to provide his version of the case to the probation officer who prepared the presentence report. While Botero was able to furnish the probation officer with details of his finances, family history and personal life, he did not provide key elements of his version of what happened. As a result, the probation officer's presentence report to the judge was based on the prosecution's version. The probation officer accepted the prosecution's version of the case and recommended a severe sentencing category because, in his view, the offense involved the laundering of approximately $55 million in drug proceeds.

The first time that the sentencing judge received a full explanation of the defense version of the case was in Neal Sonnett's lengthy letter. It was too late. Judge Spellman sentenced Hernan Botero to 30 years in a federal prison.

DIVERGENT VIEWS

Ed Canfield is the feisty and aggressive senior partner of the small, but prestigious, Washington, DC law firm of Casey, Hogan and Canfield. The firm specializes in appellate matters. Both Canfield and his firm have unimpeachable reputations for integrity. Canfield was retained by Hernan Botero to explore avenues of appeal after Neal Sonnett was unsuccessful at both the U.S. Court of Appeals and Supreme Court levels—the District Court conviction was upheld in both forums.

Canfield attempted to get Hernan's sentence reduced. On March 10, 1989, he appealed to the 11th Circuit Court of Appeals with a motion under Section 2255 of the Federal Rules of Criminal Procedure to vacate, set aside, or correct a sentence imposed on a person in federal custody. The Court of Appeals denied the appeal in December 1989.

In February 1990, Canfield assisted Botero in writing a letter to the Chief U.S. Probation Officer in Miami requesting a review of the original presentence probation report because it contained numerous errors in making a recommendation for 100-plus months of imprisonment. The letter was given to Judge Spellman, who ordered a review of the presentence report. In the summer of 1990, the judge ruled that there were no errors in the presentence report that would warrant a recommendation for a lesser sentence.

Ed Canfield feels that a grave injustice has been inflicted on Hernan Botero. To begin with, he is convinced, from reading the trial record and interviewing Botero, that his client was not guilty of the offenses charged. He believes that the bankers, Dodson and Campbell, perjured themselves to avoid jail sentences. He further believes that statements in the probation officer's presentence report, which indicate Botero must have been part of a large drug smuggling operation and that the money that passed through the accounts in the Landmark Bank was drug money, are not supported by the trial record. Canfield believes that these statements influenced Judge Spellman to impose a sentence that far exceeds what should have been meted out for the crimes charged.

Finally, Canfield believes that former Assistant U.S. Attorney Gerald Houlihan seriously erred in the affidavit he sent to the Colombian government in support of the U.S. government's extradition request for Botero. The affidavit specifically stated that Botero was charged with the importation of cocaine into the United States, despite the fact that the importation charge had been dismissed more than a year before.

Canfield also takes issue with a statement in the affidavit that the allegations in the indictment against Botero charged that the cash he handled was derived from narcotics transactions. There is not one mention in the indictment that the cash involved at the Landmark Bank was derived from narcotics transactions, Canfield notes. Without these statements in the affidavit, Ed Canfield believes that Botero would not have been extradited by Colombia.

The error in the indictment was brought to the attention of the Colombian courts by Botero's Colombian attorney and was repaired within a few months when Houlihan sent a corrected indictment. But the damage had been done. The seed had been planted. Hernan was labeled as a drug dealer. Even after it was known that the drug smuggling charge was dropped, there was still that statement in Houlihan's affidavit that the cash was derived from narcotics transactions. The Colombian court that finally ordered Botero's extradition conceded that the offenses charged in the indictment were not crimes under Colombian law, but the court stated that it looked behind the offenses to the fact that they involved a criminal activity related to drug trafficking.

Ed Canfield is deeply disturbed by Houlihan's actions in the extradition process. He says he hates to think that a fellow attorney, much less a former federal prosecutor, would stoop to deception and falsehood to accomplish what he might perceive to be a desirable goal. Yet, he claims this is his inescapable conclusion. He says he has tried on several occasions to reach Houlihan, who is now in private practice in Miami, to talk to him about the situation. But Houlihan has declined to discuss the case. This refusal also disturbs Ed Canfield. He says he realizes that Houlihan is under no obligation to talk to him about his actions as a prosecutor. But he says it raises some concerns about the former prosecutor's motivation in doing the things he did.

For his part, Gerald J. Houlihan says there is no question in his mind about the guilt of both Roberto and Hernan Botero. He believes the government produced an overwhelming amount of evidence in both cases and established guilt well beyond a reasonable doubt. He acknowledges that the government's case against Hernan Botero hinged on the testimony of Campbell and Dodson, but he notes that there was a great deal of corroboration for their testimony. He believes their story about their contacts with Hernan Botero. He said they never wavered in the accounts they gave from the time they started to cooperate with the government.

With respect to the affidavit in support of a request for extradition, Houlihan insists that when he forwarded the copy of the indictment to Colombia he was not aware that the importation of cocaine charge had been dropped against Hernan Botero. He said that he had a practice of not dropping any charges against a person who was a fugitive. The cocaine charge against Roberto Botero and Dolores Eirin had been dropped at a time when the case was being prepared for trial. He says that he did not realize that the charge had also been dropped against Hernan Botero. The copy of the indictment in his file at the time the affidavit was prepared still contained the importation count. He contends there was absolutely nothing sinister or intentional with regard to this issue—it was an honest mistake on his part.

As for his statement in the affidavit that Botero transported cash derived from narcotics transactions, Houlihan argues that there was underlying information in the investigation that the currency had, in fact, come from cocaine sales. He notes that he was precluded from entering some of this information during the trial because it was barred by the rules of evidence. He says that Neal Sonnett brought up the issue of drugs in his summation to the jury at Botero's trial. Houlihan does not believe that his statements in the affidavit in support of extradition had any effect on the Colombian government's decision to extradite. He insists that the Colombian Court that decided this issue fully understood that there was not a drug charge pending against Hernan Botero.

Houlihan is proud of his role as the vigorous prosecutor of the Botero brothers. He points with pride to his presentencing memorandum to the judge in the Hernan Botero case.

"Money laundering is a vital and infamous component of international narcotics trafficking," the memorandum explains. "The 'flip side' of the importation and distribution of drugs is the need for the illicit proceeds to be gotten out of the country to pay for still more drugs to generate still greater profits, all the while concealing the source of these proceeds. The government hopes this need represents another point of vulnerability in our battle against the drug trade. By using the reporting requirements of the Bank Secrecy Act, our objective is to choke the flow of narcotics dollars out of the country and achieve deterrence by making the movement of narcotics money as risky as trafficking in the drugs themselves."

That memorandum was written five years ago. Today, as an attorney representing banks, Houlihan has different views. For one thing, he now believes that the reporting requirements are unnecessary because they serve no useful purpose. He has also become a defender of Latin American "flight capital."

His new sentiments were expressed clearly in a 1989 address he made before the International Symposium on Money Laundering. Speaking of "the time honored practice of receiving deposits of 'flight capital'," Houlihan said: "As we know, these deposits are generated from legitimate foreign investors who deposit U.S. dollars as protection from the political and economic instability of their country. Although these deposits are generally from countries with foreign currency controls, this practice is encouraged by our State Department and Congress. Moreover, it had been an acceptable tradition long before drugs became a problem. Although the process can be abused by drug dealers, there is no calculable benefit to prosecute these legitimate investors who seek the economic shelter of the United States. However, these 'innocents' have been targeted as accomplices of the drug trade. That is unrealistic, wrong and misleading. In short, the devastation to banks and foreign investors of 'flight capital' prosecutions may be the misleading 'body count' of this war."

It is ironic that four years after convicting Hernan Botero, Gerry Houlihan ends up championing the cause of Latin American flight capitalists. It was precisely this kind of legitimate investor that Hernan Botero claims to have worked for by purchasing dollars in the Colombian "parallel market" or "black market" and then sending the money to the United States for deposit.

Houlihan concedes he and other prosecutors were shocked by the sentence Hernan Botero received. He says he would not have been surprised by a 10- or 15-year sentence, but the 30-year term astounded him. He notes that Judge Spellman had a reputation as a relatively light sentencer. He also points out that Spellman respects Neal Sonnett. He is aware that Sonnett truly believes Hernan is innocent and says he totally disagrees with him.

Hernan Botero remains in the Marianna Federal Correctional Institution. He maintains a voluminous file regarding his case. It appears that he spends almost all of his time going over the details of his extradition, trial, and sentencing. He frequently writes letters proclaiming his innocence. He maintains contact with Ed Canfield, both by letter and telephone.

Hernan is particularly bitter against his brother, Roberto. In May 1984, after he was arrested in Colombia on the extradition warrant, Roberto's attorney, Joel Hirschhorn, came to see him in jail in Colombia. Hirschhorn told him that he was pushing for a quick trial for Roberto because he thought he could beat the case if he made Hernan look like the kingpin of the whole operation. Hernan Botero says that he begged Hirschhorn not to pursue this course of action, but it was to no avail. Hernan Botero says he is also angry with his brother for becoming involved in the accounts at Landmark Bank. He claims he never asked Roberto to do so, and that he never told Dodson and Campbell that Roberto would be in charge of the accounts while he was in Colombia. Botero claims that while he was in Colombia he made regular calls to the bank to check on the accounts and provide transfer information. He reported regularly to Peinado Navarro and received all of his instructions from Navarro, he claims. Botero notes that he continued to collect his 1% commission from Navarro for looking after the accounts during the time that he was in Colombia. He maintains that anything that Roberto was doing with the accounts had to be as the result of some agreement with Navarro—an agreement that neither ever told him about.

Hernan Botero says he is suspicious of his brother's involvement and wonders if he knew something about the source of the currency.

Hernan Botero has a favorite statement that seems to best express his situation: "I was extradited for one crime, convicted of something else, and sentenced for neither." To make matters worse, in his view he was guilty of nothing. He points out that he was extradited for conspiracy to falsify public and private documents and for helping to conceal the object or proceeds of a crime; that he was convicted of a conspiracy to conceal material facts and for mail fraud; and that he was sentenced for money laundering and drugs.

Botero explains that he had been involved in the currency exchange business for a number of years, during which time he frequently dealt with Peinado Navarro and his company, IPN. He knew him to be a legitimate currency exchange operator. IPN was fully licensed to exchange currency in Colombia. His own dealings with Navarro always involved checks. They dealt in the black market, or parallel market, on behalf of investors and businessmen who wanted to accumulate dollars in the United States, despite Colombian currency control laws. Hernan Botero believes that Peinado Navarro betrayed him. When Dolores Eirin told him that Landmark Bank was interested in accepting U.S. currency, he was not personally interested. However, he knew that Navarro needed dollars. When he agreed to help Navarro manage the accounts, it never occurred to him that the money would be coming from illegal sources. On one or two occasions, he recalls that he became concerned about the amount of the money being deposited, but adds that Navarro assured him that the money was from legitimate sources.

Botero now realizes that Navarro must have known that the money came from drug sales, if that is indeed where it came from. And if this was the case, he believes he was used by Navarro as an unwitting dupe. He concedes that today, looking back on what happened in 1979 and 1980, he should have made greater strides to determine the source of the money. However, he does not feel that he should have been convicted for not making such inquiries.

Hernan says he is also bothered by the fact that the Colombian government extradited him while not holding Peinado Navarro personally responsible for any wrongdoing by IPN. The Colombian government investigated the activities of IPN concerning false statements over the receipt of U.S. dollars from foreign tourists. Peinado Navarro was found not to have any personal responsibility for these statements. The company was charged with offenses and eventually paid a small fine after pleading "no contest" to the charges.

Hernan Botero says he had no indication that IPN was making false statements on its receipts of U.S. dollars. He adds that he does not understand why so much was made of this issue at his trial because it was a matter over which he had no control. If false entries were made, he notes, they had to have been made either by Navarro or by his employees.

Hernan Botero goes to great lengths explaining his business dealing in the so-called "dollar black market" or "parallel market." In the simplest of terms, he explains, he would buy Certificates of Exchange through a Colombian bank, paying for the certificates with a check drawn on the Cia Rodnan account at Landmark Bank. Usually, he says, he would order the certificates through the Banco de Colombia and would pay for it with the Cia Rodnan check. Banco de Colombia would then order a Certificate of Exchange from the Colombian Central Bank, Banco de la Republica, and it would be delivered to him on the next day. The Certificate of Exchange was issued in the amount he had purchased it for at the rate of exchange on that day. It was a promise to pay pesos at the official exchange rate in 120 days. Since the value of the peso was almost always diminishing against the dollar, it could be held for 120 days and the holder would receive more pesos. But the purchaser had another option, he noted: selling the certificate to a brokerage house or commercial bank within a few days and obtaining slightly more pesos than the value on the date of purchase. Such a sale would be at the official rate of exchange which was at a price per dollar higher than the black market price. He would obtain a check in pesos for an amount greater than what he would have obtained in the black market. Hernan explains that he would take his pesos check to a black market exchange house, such as IPN, where he would buy a check in dollars. Since the black market price was lower than the official rate, he would be able to buy more dollars with his peso check than he had originally spent for the pesos. The profit was small, but it could become substantial if a high volume of checks and certificates of exchange could be transferred in a short period of time. The dollar check that he obtained from IPN would then be shipped overnight to the Landmark Bank for deposit to the Cia Rodnan account.

With each run of the cycle, Hernan Botero made more profit. The profit was dependent on the fact that the peso kept going down in value against the dollar. It was also dependent on a high rate of check turnover. Finally, it was dependent on the necessity that the checks that Botero deposited in the Cia Rodnan account be treated as cash so that the money in the account could be used immediately to buy more Certificates of Exchange. A five-day delay for a check to clear would have brought this whole cycle to a standstill, Botero notes. It also would have prevented him from taking advantage of minute fluctuations in the value of the dollar.

Botero claims to have explained his business to Dolores Eirin, and she seemed to have realized the need for his checks to be handled as cash. Botero says he conducted his check business with Eirin in the Landmark Bank account of Cia Rodnan for almost a year before she told him that the bank was interested in currency deposits.

Hernan Botero asserts that there is nothing illegal with the check activity which he conducted in the black market or parallel market. Likewise, he believes there was nothing illegal with what he did for Peinado Navarro with regard to currency deposits.

The bottom line for Hernan Botero in his trial was the testimony of Campbell and Dodson. He maintains they committed perjury when they claimed that he asked them not to file CTRs for deposits into the account. He says the issue of CTRs never came up in his discussions with them, and that at that time he didn't even know that CTRs were required on the deposits.

Hernan Botero maintains that he was never involved in any drug deals and never associated with known drug dealers. Sources close to the investigation and prosecution of the Botero case advised that Hernan Botero's name had never surfaced in government agency files as a suspect drug dealer or money launderer prior to the Landmark Bank situation; he was not even an original target of Operation Greenback. It was, as one investigator put it, "a case that was dumped in their laps."

While Hernan Botero's name was not known to government agents, Losardo Restrepo's name was. Restrepo's name had appeared in DEA files as early as 1978 as a suspect drug dealer and money launderer for the

Ochoa family, which ran a large cocaine distribution operation in Colombia.

Research uncovered information that ties Losardo Restrepo to conduits for the disposition of drug money similar to those used by Isaac Kattan. Sometime in 1984, the Swiss government became interested in an account in a Swiss bank which had been used for money laundering. A number of checks were deposited in the Swiss account from the Capital Bank and Landmark Bank. The U.S. Department of Justice was asked to investigate the origin of these checks. Under the terms of a treaty between the United States and Switzerland, Charles Saphos, the attorney in charge of Operation Greenback, was appointed as the Swiss representative in the United States in charge of the inquiry. The investigation revealed that the checks from the Capital Bank came from an account that was controlled by Isaac Kattan, and the checks from the Landmark Bank came from the three accounts opened by Carlos Urdaneta at the time when Losardo Restrepo was making currency deposits to those accounts.

Isaac Kattan was questioned by Greenback agents about the transactions in 1984. He said the money he deposited in the Capital account came from one of four or five Colombian drug distributors for whom he worked in 1980.

The discovery that Losardo Restrepo was a rather significant money launderer with ties to the Ochoas certainly leads one to wonder if Navarro and Restrepo used Hernan Botero as an unwitting dupe in the opening of the Landmark accounts and the movement of the money out of the accounts to Colombia. It should be recalled that Restrepo was believed to have made 60% of all currency deposits to the Botero/Navarro accounts, and at the same time was depositing an additional $17 million into the Urdaneta accounts.

Where does the truth lie in the case of Hernan Botero? Should he have been extradited? Should he have been sentenced to 30 years in jail? And was he guilty or innocent of the crimes charged?

A case certainly can be made for the fact that Botero might not have been extradited, if Gerald Houlihan's affidavit did not refer to a nonexistent drug smuggling charge and a statement that the cash that went into the Landmark Bank was derived from drug sales. These statements, plus a strong desire by the Colombian government in the wake of the assassination of Lara Bonilla to prove that it was serious about cracking down on the cocaine drug lords, were what led to Botero's arrest and extradition. There is also the issue of whether or not the Colombian court erred in interpreting the U.S. statutes involved in the charges against Botero. Certainly, Hernan Botero was in the wrong place at the wrong time.

A strong argument can be made that Botero's sentence was excessive. There was no direct evidence at the trial that tied him to drug trafficking or to the proposition that the money in the case came from drug sales. At best, there was the hearsay testimony of Campbell and Dodson about what Restrepo allegedly told them about Botero's involvement with drugs. But Botero's case at sentencing was severely damaged by Neal Sonnett's advice not to discuss his version of the case with the probation officer who prepared the presentence report.

Whether or not Hernan Botero was guilty of the charges filed against him, only he really knows. He had a trial that was fair by American standards of justice. The jury obviously believed the testimony of Campbell and Dodson. Obviously the bankers were out to save their own skins. Could they have been lying about Hernan's involvement? Of course! Could they have been telling the truth about his involvement? Of course!

Ed Canfield has not been successful in any of his appeal efforts on Botero's behalf. He is not so naive as to think that some of the $55 million in the Landmark accounts was not drug money. What he does believe is that Hernan did not know that drug money was involved. He believes that if there was drug money involved, the people who knew about it were Peinado Navarro, Losardo Restrepo, Carlos Urdaneta, and possibly even Roberto Botero. Canfield also firmly believes that, whether or not the cash came from drugs, Hernan did not commit any crime.

In support of the government's side of the case, it is difficult to understand how a person in the currency exchange business would not have known about U.S. laws regarding the reporting of currency transactions above $10,000. Isaac Kattan and other contemporary Colombian currency exchangers were very well aware of the U.S. laws on currency. It is also difficult to understand how Botero could have been constantly checking on amounts deposited and where the money should be sent without knowing more about the source of the funds.

Also, from the government's perspective, there was the belief that Campbell and Dodson were telling the truth about Hernan's involvement.

So what happened to the other people in the case? Alan Campbell and Gary Dodson pleaded guilty to conspiracy charges and received nine months of unsupervised probation. Losardo Restrepo is a fugitive, presumably living in Colombia. Carlos Urdaneta was sentenced to three months in prison. Dolores Eirin was sentenced to two years in jail. Roberto Botero was sentenced to eight years in jail.

In similar cases, Salvatore Amendolito, one of the main money launderers in the Pizza Connection case, struck a bargain with the government and, in return for his cooperation and testimony, was not charged with any criminal offenses. Beno Ghitis, the next subject of this book, was convicted of laundering more than $250 million in drug monies and was sentenced to six years in prison.

The Ghitis conviction was overturned on appeal after he had served two years of his sentence. He subsequently entered into a plea bargain agreement with the government, pleaded guilty to a conspiracy charge, and was sentenced to time served. Today, Ghitis is a free man.

Andres Rodriguez, the crooked banker who swindled customers and allowed Isaac Kattan and others to use his bank for money laundering, received sentences of six years and ten years to be served concurrently. These sentences were imposed in Miami in 1984.

In view of all this, it may be that the sentence imposed on Hernan Botero was somewhat excessive.

BENO GHITIS AND SONAL

Beno Ghitis came from an influential and respected family in Cali, Colombia. In 1980, at the age of 32, he was operating a family-owned travel agency in Cali, known as Viajes Atlas, and a currency exchange business. Both businesses were founded by his father, Alter Ghitis, and had been in operation for 20 years. Beno had degrees in chemical engineering and political science. He was bright and articulate.

In March 1980, Beno Ghitis opened a business checking account in the name of Sonal at the downtown Miami branch of Capital Bank. The individuals who had signature authority on the account were Ghitis, his wife, Sonia, and his father, Alter Ghitis.

Between March and early May 1980, a series of large currency deposits were made into the account by young Hispanic men. The deposits were in small denomination bills and ranged in amounts up to $1 million. The money was brought into the bank in boxes, suitcases, flight bags, and paper bags, two to three times a week. The money was counted by bank employees in the presence of the couriers.

In early May 1980, Victor Eisenstein introduced himself to Rolando Pozo-Illas, the manager of Capital's downtown Miami branch. He explained that he worked for Beno Ghitis and that he would be handling the deposits into the Sonal account from that point on. Pozo checked with Ghitis and verified that he had hired Eisenstein.

Victor Eisenstein operated out of a small office located near the bank under the business name American Overseas Enterprises. Eisenstein started to make regular currency deposits into the Sonal account. From the very beginning of the cash deposits, the bank charged a service fee of 0.125% for counting and processing the currency.

In late May 1980, Rolando Pozo told Eisenstein he would no longer accept cash deposits. Eisenstein notified Ghitis, who immediately flew to Miami and met with Pozo, but he could not persuade him to change his mind. A meeting was quickly arranged with Abel Holtz, the president of Capital Bank. At this meeting, an agreement was reached for the resumption of the currency deposits. However, the service fee was to be increased substantially, from 0.125% to 0.5%. Ghitis also agreed to provide the bank with a counting machine to speed the deposit process.

Cash deposits into the Sonal account were resumed by Eisenstein. Deposits on the order of $1 million to $2 million were being made to the account at a rate of two or three times a week. Eisenstein usually delivered the currency in suitcases, duffle bags, and flight bags.

In late July 1980, the bank notified Eisenstein that it wanted the cash deposits switched to its North Bay Village branch. In August, Eisenstein moved into an office in the building that housed the North Bay Village Branch of Capital Bank. At this location, he received currency deliveries from a number of couriers and deposited them into the Sonal account. Eisenstein brought the money to a room used by the bank for counting purposes, where it was counted by bank employees using the money counting machine that had been provided by Ghitis.

In March 1981, Eisenstein became concerned about the origin of the cash he was receiving and depositing into the Sonal account and expressed his concern to Ghitis. Ghitis assured him that the money was from legitimate sources. In a March 7 letter to Eisenstein from Cali he stated: "The monies received by us in the United States are in connection with exchange transactions from (as far as we know) the exporting and importing of agricultural products, raw materials, etc., sales commissions and other categories, received abroad by private individuals who are primarily from our country." He added: "Even though some of these transactions involve the handling of cash, they do not give rise to mistaken associations with illegal operations which are so fashionable these days in Florida."

The time frame and the nature of the comments are both very interesting in light of the fact that the Kattan and Botero arrests and indictments had been widely publicized in Miami during February 1981. The similarity of the Sonal situation to the Kattan and Botero cases undoubtedly prompted Eisenstein to express his concerns to Ghitis. News coverage at the time also playedup the role of Operation Greenback in investigating drug money launderers.

The actions of the Capital Bank with respect to currency reporting requirements were also very interesting. From March 1980, when the account was opened, until April 1981, Capital Bank filed CTRs for all the currency deposits into the Sonal account, as required under the law and the regulations of the time. However, in April 1981, the bank ceased filing CTRs and began filing Customs Forms 4790, which at that time, were required of individuals who transported or shipped currency or monetary instruments in amounts over $5,000 into or out of the United States. The form was also required of bank officials handling currency in excess of $5,000 who had reason to believe the money had been transported from outside the United States and that a Form 4790 had not already been filed.

The precise reason why Capital Bank changed its procedures is not known. The bank would later attribute the switch to confusion over what the law required. Bank officials claimed they had reason to believe that the cash was brought in from Colombia and that no one had filed Form 4790. They said they believed that if they filed the Form 4790 there was no need to file a CTR for the same transaction. The regulations actually required that both forms be filed under the circumstances alleged by the bank.

In any event, the Forms 4790 filed by the bank for the Sonal deposits were incomplete, and instead of being filed with the U.S. Customs Service, the forms were sent to the IRS in Ogden, Utah, which was where CTRs were sent. IRS forwarded the forms to the U.S. Customs Service in Miami, which sent them on to Operation Greenback because of the high dollar values involved.

Information on the forms indicated that Victor Eisenstein was bringing the money into the United States from Colombia. At about the same time, the Treasury Department forwarded information on Sonal and Eisenstein to Greenback because of the high dollar volume of CTRs that were filed by Capital Bank in 1980 and early 1981. An investigation was begun.

Between January 1 and August 21, 1981, Victor Eisenstein deposited $242,238,739 in the Sonal account. At nearly a quarter of a billion dollars, the amount of currency handled made Isaac Kattan and Hernan Botero look like small-time operators. Additional millions of dollars in cash passed through the Sonal account in 1980.

Because of the high dollar volume of CTRs and CMIRs filed by Capital Bank in the name of the Sonal account, both Treasury and the Customs Service targeted the bank and Sonal for investigation in connection with possible money laundering activities. The case was referred to Operation Greenback for investigation.

The investigation began in April 1981. Greenback agents from Customs and IRS identified Beno Ghitis and Victor Eisenstein as the principal players in Sonal. Sporadic surveillance of Eisenstein's office in the Capital Bank Building in North Bay Village revealed that a number of Hispanic males visited on a daily basis and delivered suitcases, cardboard boxes, duffel bags, paper bags, and flight bags. Eisenstein was observed bringing the containers from his office to a special room in the Capital Bank branch in the same building.

At about this time, Abel Holtz, the bank's president, was getting nervous about the amount of currency being deposited in his bank. He sent for Ghitis. The two men met at the bank some time during June 1981 and discussed the origin of the cash going into the Sonal account. Holtz said he was suspicious that such large amounts of cash could only be generated by drug transactions. He noted that Colombia was a source country for drugs, and he expressed concern about his bank's exposure if the money came from drugs. Ghitis assured Holtz he was not a drug dealer and that he never did business with anyone he suspected was in the drug business. He said that the major portion of the monies he obtained were purchased from other money exchangers who were not in the drug business. Ghitis told Holtz that he could not guarantee that all of the money came from non-drug sources.

Either Beno Ghitis was very convincing or Abel Holtz was greedy, because the aftermath of the conversation was that Capital Bank increased the cash handling fees on the Sonal account from 0.5% to a flat $300,000 a month, retroactive to May 1, 1981. At the time the fee was increased, about $30 million a month was moving through the Sonal account. The fee, therefore, amounted to about 1% a month. Had the fee arrangement been continued for a full year, Capital Bank would have collected $3.6 million from Sonal.

The Operation Greenback investigation of Sonal and Capital Bank proceeded slowly during the summer of 1981 because of limited personnel resources and the concurrent investigation of a number of other major money laundering operations, including the Isaac Kattan and Hernan Botero cases. However, by mid-August, Customs and IRS agents were ready to proceed. Victor Eisenstein's name had been entered into Customs' computerized watch list of suspicious persons. Customs inspectors check incoming individuals against this list at all border points. On August 16, Eisenstein was questioned by Greenback agents when he arrived at Miami International Airport from a trip to Colombia. The agents were successful in persuading Eisenstein to cooperate with the government.

An undercover agent was introduced into Eisenstein's office in the Capital Bank building in North Bay Village. The agent was allowed to listen in on several telephone conversations between Eisenstein and Beno Ghitis.

During the days of August 19 and 20, 1981, the undercover agent observed the delivery of $7,012,799 in currency, consisting mostly of small and medium denomination bills, to Eisenstein's office. The couriers who delivered the currency would not accept receipts. Of the total amount delivered on the two days, $4,781,799 was delivered by "Alberto Rodriguez" and "Hector Gomez" on behalf of Carlos Molina. A delivery of $844,000 was made by a "Brigette Edelman." "Alberto Rodriguez" delivered over $2.5 million in cash on August 19. When he came into the office, he was introduced to the undercover agent by Eisenstein. The agent helped him remove the money from his car and bring it up to Eisenstein's office. Surveillance agents outside the building had observed the make and license of the car Rodriguez drove.

On August 19, Eisenstein made a deposit of $2,157,000 into the Sonal account at Capital Bank. The deposit consisted of the Edelman delivery plus $1,313,000 of the cash delivered by Alberto Rodriguez. A large amount of cash was left overnight in Eisenstein's office that night, despite the fact that there was literally no security for the office.

When Alberto Rodriguez departed Eisenstein's office on August 19, he was followed by Greenback agents and was observed purchasing an Avianca Airline ticket. When agents approached Avianca personnel after Rodriguez left the ticket counter, they learned that he had purchased a one-way ticket from Miami to Colombia for September 2, 1981. The ticket was issued in the name of Carlos Toro, the same name assigned the license on the car "Rodriguez" was driving. It was determined that a Florida operator's license had been issued to a Carlos Toro at the same address used for the car registration. There was no such address. The photograph on the operator's license was one of Alberto Rodriguez.

On August 20, Rodriguez returned to Eisenstein's office, accompanied by an individual named Hector Gomez. They delivered over $2 million in currency. At Eisenstein's request, they both showed Colombian identification. When they left the office, they were followed to an Avianca Airline ticket office where they appeared to buy tickets. Surveillance continued after they left the Avianca office. Rodriguez was observed making telephone calls from several different pay phones. The two were eventually followed to a location in Miami Beach. They parked in an illegal parking space and departed on foot.

Early on the evening of August 20, Eisenstein received a telephone call from Beno Ghitis in Colombia. The call was monitored by the undercover agent. Ghitis told Eisenstein that "Alberto" knew that Eisenstein had been talking to Customs, and instructed Eisenstein not to make any more deposits into the Sonal account. Ghitis also told Eisenstein to put whatever cash he had in the office in a safe deposit box until things cleared up. Shortly after the telephone call, Greenback agents seized all the currency that was in Eisenstein's office—$3,686,639. Also seized were various containers including duffel bags, a suitcase, a hand travel bag, a flight bag and cardboard boxes. Eisenstein turned over all of Sonal's records. Among the boxes of cash delivered by Gonzalez on August 20 was a copy of a Colombian newspaper.

At the same time the cash was being seized, Greenback agents in Miami Beach notified the local police of the vehicle illegally parked by Rodriguez. The vehicle was impounded. Two Avianca Airline tickets were found in the glove compartment of the car, both had been purchased on August 18, 1981 for one-way flights from Miami to Medellin on August 29.

The tickets were in the names of "Hector Gomez" and "Gilberto Rua." The car was found to contain a large, steel-reinforced, secret compartment behind the rear seat which could be opened by a switch hidden beneath the driver's seat. A Customs narcotics scent dog was used to examine the secret compartment, and the dog alerted positively to the scent of narcotics. Another Customs narcotics dog examined the currency and containers which had been seized from Eisenstein's office and alerted positively to the residual scent of narcotics.

On August 21, Greenback agents obtained a seizure warrant from a U.S. Magistrate in Miami for the monies on deposit in the Sonal account at Capital Bank. The amount in the account when the warrant was executed was $4,255,625.39.

Records seized from Sonal and the Capital Bank revealed that during the eight-month period from January 1 until August 20, 1981, Eisenstein received $242,238,739 from 37 different couriers. All of the money was deposited into the Sonal account. The records showed that over $191 million of the total was delivered by Alberto Rodriguez or couriers working for him. The records purported to show that Beno Ghitis purchased the $191 million from Carlos Molina. Rodriguez made the deliveries for Molina. Carlos Molina was Luis Carlos Molina, a money exchanger who resided and conducted business in Colombia. He was a major money launderer for a number of Colombian cocaine kingpins. The remainder of the money deposited to the Sonal account came from 28 different individuals, all of whom were Colombians who did not work or reside in the United States.

Most of the 37 couriers who delivered money to Eisenstein were only known by nicknames or Hispanic first names. Sonal records also revealed the existence of an account in the name of Sonal at Bank Leumi in New York City, with a balance of $453,731.95. The records also showed the currency deposited to the Capital Bank was quickly moved out by checks payable to individuals in Colombia who had delivered pesos to Ghitis. They had purchased dollars from Ghitis' currency exchange by paying in pesos. Ghitis delivered the dollars in the form of checks drawn on the Sonal accounts in Miami and in New York. The checks were payable in U.S. currency upon presentation to U.S. banks.

On August 24, 1981, the Treasury Department, at the request of Operation Greenback attorneys and agents, assessed a civil penalty of $10 million against Sonal for violations of the Bank Secrecy Act. A copy was immediately provided to an Assistant U.S. Attorney in the Southern District of New York, who obtained a temporary restraining order directing the attachment of the money in Sonal's Bank Leumi account. The theory behind the civil penalty was that Sonal was a non-bank financial institution which had not filed CTRs for the monies received in Eisenstein's office. Another theory was that Sonal had not filed CMIRs (Customs Form 4790s) indicat-

it had transported the money in the Sonal accounts into the United States. Indeed, the records of the IRS and the Customs Service failed to show any filings of CTRs or CMIRs by Sonal and/or Ghitis and Eisenstein during the entire period that currency deposits were being made into the Capital Bank.

Beno Ghitis' attorneys challenged the seizure of the cash in Eisenstein's office and in the Sonal account at Capital Bank. Over a year went by before the case went to trial. Beno Ghitis remained in Colombia. Victor Eisenstein continued to live in the Miami area. Alberto Rodriguez, alias Carlos Toro, and Hector Gomez disappeared. Presumably, they fled to Colombia. The Avianca Airline ticket purchased by Alberto Rodriguez for the September 2 flight to Colombia on September 2 was not used. The names of Alberto Rodriguez, Carlos Toro, and Hector Gomez were not on the manifest or passenger list for the flight.

The forfeiture of the cash seized in Eisenstein's office and the money on deposit at the Sonal account in the Capital Bank was adjudicated in a civil trial in federal court in Miami during September 1982. It was a non-jury trial before U.S. District Court Judge Peter Beer. The government's case consisted of testimony by Greenback agents who had worked on the case and voluminous records of Sonal and Capital Bank. Victor Eisenstein was in the courtroom and presumably was going to testify for the defense in opposition to the forfeiture. Beno Ghitis flew in from Colombia and was a spectator at the trial. He wanted to assist in opposing the forfeiture. Greenback attorneys and agents had been planning for some time to file formal charges against him, but Ghitis was in Colombia and the Colombian government at the time was not honoring the extradition treaty it had with the United States. Now, Ghitis was in their midst.

The trial continued on every working day from September 20 through September 27. It was obvious that the trial would terminate on September 27. Early that morning, Greenback agents obtained arrest warrants for both Ghitis and Eisenstein. The trial ended that day as expected. Judge Beer confirmed the Magistrate's finding of probable cause, which formed the basis for the seizure of the cash in Eisenstein's office and the money on deposit in the Sonal account. At the conclusion of the trial he ordered written briefs to be filed by attorneys for both sides. Ghitis and Eisenstein departed the courtroom and shortly thereafter were taken into custody by Greenback agents. The two were formally charged and held on hefty bails. One week later they were indicted on one count each of conspiracy to defraud the United States and two counts each of failure to report currency transactions. Ghitis and Eisenstein were tried on the charges in the U.S. District Court in Miami in mid-November 1982. Both were found guilty of all charges.

In the meantime, the civil case, involving the seizure of the Sonal monies, proceeded forward. Judge Beer received written briefs from government and defense attorneys. On October 29, 1982, he heard oral arguments from attorneys representing both sides. On December 3, Judge Beer issued a final judgment in favor of the government. He ordered the money seized in the Sonal account at the Capital Bank and in Eisenstein's office to be forfeited to the United States.

Judge Beer issued an 18-page written opinion of Findings of Fact and Conclusions of Law in conjunction with his final judgment. This opinion contains some very interesting comments about the case and about drug money laundering in the Miami area in the early 1980s. Portions of the decision are quoted as follows:

> Thus, I conclude that Ghitis acting in behalf of Sonal, failed to take such reasonable precautions as should have been taken to determine that the currency—purchased in the course of his negotiations in Colombia—was untainted by narcotics transactions. Specifically, I conclude that every principal actor in this drama— Ghitis, Holtz, Eisenstein and Molina—knew or reasonably should have known that the cash that is the subject matter of the seizures we here deal with was drug tainted. . . I conclude that Ghitis, as operator of Sonal, did not engage in personal involvement in drug transactions. Even so, I am convinced that the cash came from drug sales and, in large measure at least, found its way to Colombia-based drug operators who, thereupon, sought to launder the cash by "passing it through" a reasonably reputable money exchange house - here, Sonal via Molina.

> I conclude that the great bulk of the cash that we are here concerned with followed this basic route:

> 1. A street transaction for drugs.
> 2. Into the hands of a drug dealer in the United States.
> 3. Into the hands of a drug producer in Colombia.
> 4. "Sold" at a discount by the Colombian drug producer to, for example, Molina who, in return for getting the cash at least part of the way back into the quasi-legitimate mainstream, "discounts" at a rate based upon what the traffic will bear.
> 5. "Sold" at a more stable discount rate by Molina to Sonal with the obligation to make the physical delivery to Sonal's Miami "office" (Eisenstein).

6. Deposited by Sonal in its account but earmarked as funds of Molina so that Sonal checks could be drawn at Molina's instructions to them.

Thus, Molina—the real crossover contact—could, with impunity, direct Sonal checks to receivers. Those checks could arrive anywhere in the world in any amount and be fully accepted due to Sonal's so-called good name. That's what it looks like to me.

In his conclusions of law, Judge Beer showed excellent insight into what really went on in drug money laundering business.

Dade County and environs do not exist in a vacuum. It would be both unrealistic and a derogation of the common experience consideration that I am obligated to bring to my deliberations here if I did not take into account that Miami and environs have become a currency center for drug activities. At times pertinent, various laundering operations were the order of the day among those embarked upon far reaching drug activities. Indeed, an essential element of big time or big money drug operations is a reasonably dependable system of getting street drug dollars into usable bank accounts. What better way than via money exchange operations with some aura of legitimacy? Indeed, with only a little softening of traditional concepts of business morality and the violation of a few somewhat obscure federal statutes, a couple of not-too-cautious money exchange houses and a "fee"-hungry bank could be (and in this case became) an ideal laundry system. No one needed to get really involved. It would only be necessary that no one be too inquisitive. Elaborate hopes could become almost immediate realities if "fees" could be charged commensurate with the need to have huge amounts of small denomination "dirty" cash laundered into neat, clean checking accounts able to be dispatched—with impunity —across the world.

But the parties (I conclude) overloaded the scheme, and it shorted out in the process. They went too far too fast and leaks sprung up which led eventually to the seizure with which we are here concerned. . . . But I'm sufficiently convinced that the great bulk of the funds did come to Miami in spite of Sonal's protestations to the effect that U.S. cash in large amounts and small denominations is a desirable commodity in Colombia.

Judge Beer's written opinion was refreshing. Greenback attorneys and agents loved the decision although they did not agree with all of the rationale in his findings. Mike McDonald, who was the IRS supervisor, and Chuck Saphos, the lead attorney, both believed the judge had the laundering operation well figured out, with one exception—they do not believe that most of the money that came into Eisenstein's office came directly from Colombia. They agree that some of it did because they are aware that some drug proceeds were being shipped directly to Colombia during that period. However, they believe most of the cash, perhaps as much as 80%, came directly from drug sales consummated in the U.S.

McDonald and Saphos argue that the attractiveness of an operation like Sonal to the drug lords in Colombia was that the tortuous process of smuggling cash out of the United States to Colombia and then smuggling it back in could be avoided. Why go through that process when a major distributor could have his representatives deliver currency to Molina's couriers in Miami? The couriers would then deliver the money to Victor Eisenstein for deposit in the Sonal account. Cashier's checks drawn on the Sonal account would be used to move the money into correspondent accounts maintained by Colombian banks at international banks in Miami. The money would then be used in exchange for pesos furnished by Colombian businessmen seeking dollars. The pesos went to the cocaine bosses.

McDonald and Saphos believe that the cash flow in the Sonal case was similar to that in the Isaac Kattan case. The difference was that Kattan used multiple banks and multiple accounts. They also believe that the Hernan Botero operation at the Landmark Bank worked pretty much the same way.

After the defeat in the civil forfeiture case, Ghitis and Eisenstein faced sentencing on their criminal convictions. Sentencing was imposed in the U.S. District Court in Miami on January 25, 1983. Beno Ghitis was sentenced to six years imprisonment and was fined $610,000; Victor Eisenstein was sentenced to four years in prison and was fined $210,000. Both men appealed their convictions.

EDUCATING CONGRESS

During early 1983, the Senate Permanent Subcommittee on Investigations held a series of hearings on "Crime and Secrecy: The Use of Offshore Banks and Companies." The panel became interested in the Sonal case as an example of the use of an offshore currency exchange company in drug money laundering. A number of government witnesses testified.

Beno Ghitis, who had begun to serve his prison sentence, agreed to appear as a witness before the subcommittee. His testimony provided some excellent insights into the workings of the black market in U.S. dollars in Colombia and other South American countries. Of course, his testimony minimized the role of drug money in black market operations, and it was flavored toward his own innocence in the case for which he was serving a six-year sentence. He insisted that he never intended to violate U.S. law.

Ghitis testified that his currency exchange business performed two kinds of transactions. One was the sale and the other the purchase of foreign currencies. He pointed out that for the Colombian, the dollar is not only a foreign currency, but is a commodity. He said that, generally, his currency exchange business bought dollars from Colombians in the United States and Colombia and paid out money in Colombian pesos. A purchase of dollars was done when his exchange house acquired dollars from a customer, paying him in pesos. A sale of dollars was done when his exchange house delivered dollars (or a check denominated in dollars) to a customer, receiving pesos in return. Ghitis testified that his sale transactions were limited to Colombia. He said he sold dollars in cash, or as checks drawn against accounts in the United States. Purchase transactions were more elastic, he said, in that dollars were either delivered to his office in Colombia or to accounts in other countries, especially the United States. The payment, however, with pesos, was always done in Colombia.

Ghitis said that his currency exchange house in Colombia, known as Sonal, was one of the largest in South America. Licensed by the Colombian government to trade dollars, the business was previously known as Viajes Altas.

Prior to his appearance before the subcommittee, Beno Ghitis submitted a prepared statement. That statement indicated that by the beginning of 1980 the business was averaging about $50 million a month in currency transactions. However, when he testified, he revised this statement to indicate that by the middle of 1981 the business had grown to the point that it was averaging $35 million a month.

During his testimony Ghitis proudly proclaimed that under his management Sonal's business doubled in volume each year. Perhaps he revised his original statement because he realized that not even good management could account for an increase in volume of 100 times in just 18 months. The only thing that could account for such phenomenal growth was drug money.

Ghitis attributed the growth of the black market in dollars to a number of factors. One was the tight restrictions imposed by the Colombian government on the exchange of foreign currencies. These restrictions centralized all transactions through the Banco de la Republica, the central bank. Drastic changes in the international situation during the 1970s demanded corresponding changes in these restrictive policies, Ghitis argued. However, the government limited itself to the adoption of superficial measures which caused the diversion of huge amounts of dollars to the private or black market.

Ghitis brought the house down with laughter when he testified that another reason for the growth of the black market is the fact that the national sport in Colombia is to cheat the Colombian government. He cited estimates from official sources that as much as 50% of the Colombian economy is underground. Only about 10% of the population has bank accounts, he noted, either because they are illiterate or because they don't trust banks and checks. Ghitis explained that the handling of substantial amounts of currency outside the banking system is part of the Colombian way of life.

Beno Ghitis also explained how his currency exchange was able to prosper. He said that his rates of exchange were in between those of the Banco de la Republica and the official rate. The central bank adopted a policy in the 1970s of discounting 7% to 11% on the exchange of dollars to pesos. This was done as an anti-inflationary measure. He gave an example: If the official exchange rate was 45 pesos to the dollar, the Banco de la Republica would buy at 42 to the dollar, Sonal would offer 43 pesos for a dollar; the central bank would charge 45 pesos for the sale of dollars, the official rate, and Sonal would sell at 44 pesos to the dollar. Sonal always offered better rates than the central bank at both ends of the transactions, he said, regardless of the official rate.

Ghitis testified that there was a large increase of dollars in the black market in Colombia in 1979. He said that the central bank moved to absorb dollars from the black market and profit from the large difference between buying and selling prices. The central bank did this by opening a window which allowed anyone to sell dollars without limitation as to amounts and without presenting any identification. This became known as the "sinister window" of the Banco de la Republica. Ghitis said this did not affect Sonal because his rates were always better and because the central bank only bought dollars physically located in Colombia, whereas Sonal could buy dollars in the United States.

Ghitis did not testify as to the reason for the increase in dollars in the black market in 1979. Perhaps that was because he knew that it was due to the burgeoning U.S. market for Colombian cocaine.

As for the sale of dollars in Colombia, Ghitis testified that Colombian businesses needed dollars to purchase merchandise outside the country, and that Sonal sold dollars mostly to businesses that needed to import goods to Colombia. The dollars were sold in checks drawn on Sonal accounts in the United States, which were payable in dollars when presented. Ghitis noted that the Colombian Mercedes Benz dealer must pay for his imports in dollars; Mercedes Benz will not accept Colombian pesos in payment for automobiles. Therefore, the Colombian dealer bought checks in dollars from Sonal and paid with pesos. Sonal offered a better rate than did the central bank.

Additionally, some importers dealt with Sonal because they did not bother to get a license from the government to import goods. These companies were seeking to evade duties on imported goods and taxes on the profits realized from the sale of these goods. Without an import license, the businessmen could not buy dollars from the central bank. Therefore, they purchased dollars from currency exchange houses like Sonal.

Beno Ghitis' testimony regarding sales of dollars in Colombia accurately describes the conditions that existed during the time Sonal maintained an account at Capital Bank. His testimony with regard to the purchase of dollars, however, minimized the importance of cocaine trafficking and overemphasized other sources.

Ghitis identified four sources from which a money exchange house can purchase dollars. He said that one of these sources was drug smuggling, and observed that this was the only source the U.S. government was apparently able to understand. This reference to drug smuggling was contained in one sentence and was the only reference to drugs as a source of dollars in his prepared statement.

The other sources of dollars detailed in Ghitis' prepared statement included money from U.S.-based Colombians to their families back home; the transfer of international capital to Colombia (so-called flight capital) by investors who sought to take advantage of the relatively stable Colombian peso, which, coupled to high bank interest, returned a net interest of 20% or more in dollars; and the illegal or undeclared exportation of conventional products from Colombia.

As for the transfer of dollars between U.S.-based Colombians and their families in Colombia, Ghitis indicated that most of these monies had formerly been sent as currency or checks through the mail. However, many small one-person currency exchange businesses had sprung up in Colombian communities in the United States, and by 1981 most of the money headed for relatives in Colombia was delivered to these currency exchangers. The local currency exchanger would then order his agent or office in Colombia to pay pesos to the intended relative. The small exchanges then sold their dollars to larger exchange houses in the United States.

Ghitis, in his testimony, did not quantify how much flight capital flowed through Colombia. But experts believe the sum was insignificant. Most flight capital from South America is believed to flow to Europe and the United States.

Much of Ghitis' testimony about the operation of the Colombian black market in dollars was interesting, informative, and accurate. However, his attempts to minimize the amount of dollars generated by narcotics sales and his attempts to portray illegal or improper business export practices as the main source of the dollars that his business handled did not wash. There were no claims by Ghitis or anyone else that exports from Colombia to the United States increased significantly in 1979, 1980, and 1981. Yet there were significant increases in dollar surpluses in both Colombia and Miami during this period.

The one export from Colombia that did increase significantly during this time was cocaine. Cocaine sales for dollars was the only logical and rational explanation for the cash surpluses. Likewise, drug sales were the only logical and rational explanation for the tremendous increase in Beno Ghitis' currency exchange business.

The senators on this Committee weren't fooled. Judge Beers wasn't fooled. Neither was the jury that convicted Ghitis.

Beno Ghitis started to serve his six-year prison sentence immediately upon his conviction in November 1981. Both he and Eisenstein filed appeals based on a decision by the trial judge not to allow an attorney to testify on Ghitis' behalf. Ghitis maintained, during the trial, that he had consulted with an attorney named Joaquin Fernandez, who advised him that he was not required by law to file Currency Transaction Reports for the cash deposits to the Sonal account at the Capital Bank. Ghitis' trial attorney, Joel Hirschhorn, attempted to call Fernandez as a defense witness. [Hirschhorn was the same attorney who represented Roberto Botero.] Chuck Saphos, the attorney in charge of Operation Greenback who was trying the case for the government, objected to Fernandez' testimony. The trial judge upheld Saphos' objection and disallowed the testimony.

On appeal, Ghitis' attorney argued that Fernandez should have been allowed to testify. The appeal process took over two years. Finally, in 1985, the Fifth Circuit Court of Appeals ruled in Ghitis' favor. The conviction was set aside. Ghitis and Eisenstein had already served more than two years.

The government was prepared to retry the two. However, a series of conferences between government attorneys and the attorneys for Ghitis and Eisenstein resulted in a plea bargain. By the terms of this agreement, Ghitis and Eisenstein each pleaded guilty to all counts of the three-count indictment and were sentenced to time already served. Based on the agreement, both men were freed after their guilty pleas and resentencing.

Ghitis made out very well compared to Hernan Botero—a quarter of a billion dollars laundered in exchange for two plus years in jail.

In an ironic twist, Joaquin Fernandez, the attorney who allegedly told Ghitis that he did not have to file CTRs, was convicted of a money laundering charge in 1989 and served a year in prison.

And what about our greedy banker, Abel Holtz? What ever happened to him? Well, Abel Holtz is still active in the banking business, and there is even a street named after him in downtown Miami, Abel Holtz Boulevard.

His operations continue in Miami, but they now extend to both Washington, DC and Los Angeles. He runs banks in both of these cities.

Holtz managed to escape prosecution in the Sonal case. The U.S. Attorney's office in Miami considered the possibility of prosecution for a long time. There was pressure from IRS and Customs agents in Operation Greenback to prosecute Holtz and the Capital Bank. The problem was what to charge him with. The crime of money laundering had not yet been placed on the books. There was the possibility of a BSA charge for failure to file CTRs between April and August 1981. But there were problems with such a charge because the bank did file CMIRs for all of the cash deposits into the Sonal account. While the CMIR was not the correct form to file, Holtz and Capital Bank argued that the CMIR filings represented a good faith effort to comply with the law and the regulations because they had been told by the customer that the cash had come from overseas. Under the regulations and interpretations that existed at the time, Capital Bank should have filed both CTRs and CMIRs for each transaction if the money came from overseas and the bank had reason to believe that its customer had not already filed a CMIR. The problem was that the regulations and interpretations were not that clear.

Had the case against Holtz and Capital Bank been strong and clear-cut, it would have been prosecuted forthwith. Because the case was weak, it languished for several years. It was reassigned from one assistant U.S. Attorney to another. Finally in 1984, the case was reassigned to Greg Baldwin. Baldwin was a veteran prosecutor who had been assigned to Operation Greenback since early 1981. He had a reputation for being hardworking, dedicated, effective, and fair-minded.

In the end, Baldwin decided that there was no chance of convicting Abel Holtz and the Capital Bank. He believed there was sufficient evidence to have them indicted. However, he did not believe that the government should seek indictments unless there is sufficient evidence to obtain a conviction. His recommendation was approved by U.S. Attorney Leon Kellner. The decision against prosecution was unpopular with some enforcement agents and prosecutors. There were rumors of "improper political influence." These rumors persist until the present day.

Greg Baldwin is now a successful attorney with the prestigious Miami law firm of Holand and Knight. He left the U.S. Attorney's office in 1986 after prosecuting criminal cases for 10 years. He bristles at rumors over the Holtz case. He is emphatic in stating that there was absolutely no political influence of any kind brought to bear on him in making a recommendation as to whether or not to proceed with the Holtz case. He states that both U.S. Attorney Stanley Marcus and his successor, Leon Kellner, emphasized that they wanted an honest evaluation of the case as to the chances of a successful prosecution. He says that Edward Bennett Williams, Holtz's attorney, never indicated anything but that he would defend a prosecution on the merits of the facts and the law. Greg Baldwin is very positive and forceful in stating that, whatever he may have thought of Abel Holtz and Capital Bank, the case just wasn't there. He has no second thoughts. He feels as strongly now as he did in 1984 that the government could not have convicted Holtz on the available evidence.

THE END OF AN ERA

The seizure of almost $8 million from Eisenstein's office and the Sonal account at the Capital Bank in August 1981 marked the end of an era for the kind of cocaine money laundering operations that had been prevalent in the Miami area since 1977. This era was marked by large currency deposits directly into bank accounts. It was the era of bank accounts in fictitious names; fees paid to bankers for not filing CTRs; and of young Hispanic males lugging millions of dollars in small bills into banks in paper bags and cardboard boxes.

Banks had been lax in complying with the BSA reporting requirements. Federal bank examiners had not been checking on compliance in this area.

Miami was awash with drug money. But things started to change as the result of Operation Greenback. It wasn't just the arrests and the widespread publicity stemming from charges against banks and bankers. Greenback ran educational programs for bankers on BSA compliance. Agents got into the banks on investigative matters and advised management on the reporting requirements. Everybody in the banking community in Miami became aware of what most bankers already knew — that large quantities of currency being brought into banks in small bills by people unconnected with retail business operations probably came from drug sales.

Banks became aware of the possibility of criminal charges and negative publicity. They started to comply with the reporting requirements of the Bank Secrecy Act. They started to turn down large cash deposits not connected with legitimate retail business. Bankers started to tip off Operation Greenback to suspicious transactions involving large currency deposits. The money launderers came to the realization that they would have to find new ways to ply their trade.

The large cash deposit era enabled Colombian drug bosses to launder billions of dollars through Miami. There were many more launderers than Kattan, Botero, and Ghitis. Felix Gateno, Fabio Jarmillo, Arturo Fernandez, and Antonio Ruiz were all major launderers who fled to Colombia when they became aware of Greenback inquiries. They are all fugitives.

The Greenback investigation of the Arturo Fernandez organization in 1981 determined that over $32 million in currency had been deposited by that organization in just the Continental Bank. Other banks were also involved.

The investigation of the Felix Gateno organization in 1981 involved the filing of 377 CTRs by a number of banks showing currency deposits into business accounts of a company named Viomar. The total amount of these deposits exceeded $56 million. Gateno had also filed CMIRs indicating that he had transported $16 million in currency from Colombia to the United States.

There were at least a dozen other organizations handling multimillion dollar quantities of cash on an annual basis. The size, scope, and finesse of the various Colombian drug money laundering operations of the late 1970s and early 1980s made the money laundering arm of the Mafia Pizza Connection heroin organization look like a disorganized small-time business.

But by the early 1980s, the era of large currency deposits had ended. The launderers had to find new ways to clean their money. Drug sales continued and cash piled up. One of the new methods that developed in South Florida in late 1981 and 1982 was to structure cash transactions into multiple deposits under $10,000 so that CTRs would not be filed.

CHAPTER 3

"SMURFING":
IN MIAMI AND ELSEWHERE

One of the tactics the money launderers turned to when they realized that they could no longer move large quantities of cash through banks without risking investigation was to structure transactions. With structuring, large sums of currency are broken down into amounts under $10,000 for purposes of conducting transactions at banks and other financial institutions.

Structuring was not really a new concept; people had been doing it on and off ever since the Bank Secrecy Act was enacted. But it became a major trend among drug launderers in late 1981 and lasted for a number of years.

The concept was simple. John Smith has $20,000 in cash that he wants to deposit to his bank account without letting the IRS know about it. To evade transaction reporting requirements, he breaks down his $20,000 into three separate bundles and makes two separate cash deposits of $7,000 each and one $6,000 cash deposit. In other words, he structures his deposit to evade BSA requirements for filing CTRs.

Sal Amendolito in the Pizza Connection had done some structuring. Isaac Kattan had done some structuring. Both found it to be labor-intensive and cumbersome. As long as they could dispose of large amounts of cash at one time, there was no need to structure transactions. They abandoned the process in favor of large deposits. But once the banks in and around Miami began shutting down large currency operations in 1982, many money launderers were forced to turn to structuring.

The launderers used many different methods to structure their transactions. One involved numerous cash deposits into bank accounts in amounts under $10,000. Another relied on cash purchases of bank checks and cashier's checks in amounts under $10,000. Yet another involved cash purchases of traveler's checks and money orders. Drug money launderers used these tactics around the country. With Miami as the cocaine dealing capital of the United States, however, there was more cash there than anywhere else.

The Colombian money launderers developed structuring into an art form—the art form that became known as "smurfing."

Smurfing involved organizations, usually consisting of five to 15 people, that laundered drug monies through a series of structured transactions. Large quantities of cash would be given to small groups within the smurfing organization, which would then travel around to various cities where individual members would go to a number of banks and buy cashier's checks and money orders in amounts under $10,000. Continuous purchases would be made until the group had disposed of all its currency. The cashier's checks and money orders would then be shipped back to Miami and deposited into bank accounts.

Smurfing evaded BSA reporting requirements on the purchase side of the transactions by sticking to amounts of less than $10,000. Back in Miami, when the checks were deposited, there was no need to file CTRs because the forms were required only for currency transactions.

Smurfing was expensive, time-consuming, and labor-intensive, but it worked for some organizations and it still is used today.

Agents assigned to Operation Greenback became aware of the existence of organized structuring groups operating out of Miami in late 1981. By the middle of 1982 they had identified about 20 different groups that were handling large sums of cash. They seemed to be all over the place. Not only were these groups operating throughout Florida, but reports started to filter in of structuring activities all over the country, and a number of the reports indicated a connection with Miami. The groups seemed to be so active in so many places that Greenback agents started to call the individuals buying cashier's checks and money orders "Smurfs," after the blue cherubs made famous in television cartoons. The name stuck. "Smurfs" were the people transacting business at the banks, and the process of laundering cash through the organized purchase of monetary instruments became known as "smurfing."

Operation Greenback did not work on many smurfing cases. The proliferation of money laundering operations in the Miami area was so great that the task force restricted its targets to organizations that had laundered a total of at least $100 million. Generally, the known smurfing organizations were not dealing in amounts that large. The smaller smurfing organizations were investigated by IRS and Customs agents assigned to routine criminal investigations. Greenback did, however, investigate several large smurfing organizations. The largest of these, and the one that perhaps best illustrates smurfing, was a group headed by Alberto Barrera.

ALBERTO BARRERA, ALIAS "PAPA SMURF"

In early 1983, Greenback agents began receiving information about a large smurfing organization based in Miami and headed by one Alberto Barrera. Agents dubbed Barrera "Papa Smurf."

Information from several sources indicated that Papa Smurf had about a dozen people working for him. Informants reported the group was buying cashier's checks at banks all over the country. The press of work on larger cases and the fact that there was only general information about the Barrera operation (including the names of a few smurfs) restrained Greenback agents from concentrating on the case.

In September 1983, a tip from a bank in Phoenix led to a concentrated multistate investigation which resulted in the break-up of Papa Smurf's organization and a good look at how the group operated. The tip came on September 21, 1983. A teller in a Phoenix bank was handling the purchase of a $5,000 cashier's check with cash. She recalled that the man purchasing the check had been in the bank the previous day making a similar cash purchase. She thought that it was unusual and somewhat suspicious, so she watched the man leave the bank and took down the license number of the car he was driving. The bank then reported the incident to the Phoenix Police Department, which determined that the car was a rental. After checking with the rental agency the police determined that the car had been rented on September 14 to Jorge Obando, who had a Florida driver's license with an address in Miami, and was staying at the Ramada Hotel while in Phoenix.

The Phoenix police officers contacted local Customs Agent John V. Adams, who ran Obando's name through the Customs TECS system, a computerized criminal information system. Adams found that Obando was a suspect in a money laundering case in Miami. Adams then telephoned Customs in Miami and learned that Operation Greenback had information that Jorge Obando was a member of the Alberto Barrera smurfing organization. Greenback agents asked Adams to investigate what Obando was up to in Phoenix.

Adams and Phoenix police officers went to the Ramada Hotel on the afternoon of September 21 and observed the car that Obando had rented. On the following morning, Customs agents and police officers set up a surveillance at the hotel. Obando was observed leaving during the mid-morning. Over the course of the next few hours Obando was observed entering and leaving eight different banks in the Phoenix area. Inquiries made at each bank immediately after he left determined that he had used cash to buy a $5,000 cashier's check at each. While Obando was going from bank to bank, officers back at the Ramada Hotel learned that he had checked out. Searching through the trash in his room the officers found a piece of paper with notations of expenditures for five individuals: J. Mantilla; C. Villalta; O. Mantilla; Maritza Neira; and J. Obando.

After Obando finished purchasing cashier's checks, he drove to the Phoenix Airport and returned the rental car. He was then followed to an airline ticket counter where he appeared to be booking a flight. Shortly after he left the counter, officers inquired and learned that Obando had booked a flight to Denver that was due to leave in 30 minutes. Agent Adams telephoned the Customs office in Denver and requested a surveillance be conducted on Obando when he arrived there.

When Obando's aircraft arrived at the airport in Denver, a team of Customs agents was waiting. A man answering Obando's description was observed getting off the aircraft and meeting with four or five other people. All appeared to be of Hispanic origin, and there was at least one woman in the group. The group got into one car and drove to the Rodeway Inn. Several people got out of the car and went into the hotel. The car was then followed to the Stapleton Plaza Hotel.

The vehicle was determined to be a rental car that had been rented by Ovidio Mantilla-Ortiz. His Florida driver's license showed a Miami address.

Customs agents made inquiries at both hotels that evening, September 22. They determined that four individuals with Miami addresses were registered in the Rodeway: Louis Hector Neira, Lucia Maritza Neira, Ovidio Mantilla-Ortiz, and Jorge Enrique Obando. The first three had checked in September 20; Obando had just checked in. The agents who checked out the Stapleton Plaza Hotel came up with a real bonanza. They found that there were two people with Miami addresses registered in the hotel: Alberto Barrera and Margarita Mejia. What a break! Papa Smurf himself was on the scene to dole out money and oversee the operation. Barrera and Mejia had checked into the Stapleton on September 20.

Things were starting to fall into place. Operation Greenback was advised of the names on the hotel registers. The name of Louis Neira had previously been reported to Greenback as being a member of the Barrera organization. The names of Lucia Maritza Neira and Ovidio Mantilla-Ortiz matched with two of the names on the expense sheet found in Obando's room at the Ramada Hotel in Phoenix.

On the next day, September 23, 1983, Customs agents followed two members of the group as they went to nine banks in the Denver area. It was later determined that the two had bought cashier's checks or money orders in each bank and had paid with cash. On the following day, September 24, agents were able to follow one member of the group as he went to eight different banks and used currency to purchase cashier's checks for amounts under $10,000.

Customs agents were not able to follow one of Barrera's smurfs, Ovidio Mantilla-Ortiz, that day. What happened to him was a great assist to the overall investigation. Mantilla-Oritz drove a rental car to the World Savings Bank in Arvada, Colorado, a suburb of Denver. He went into the bank and purchased two money orders in the amount of $2,600 each, tendering $5,200 in cash as payment. As the teller was counting the money, she noticed that one of the bills was really a $1.00 note that had been altered to make it look like $10.00. The teller notified her supervisor, who called police. The police arrived and arrested Mantilla-Oritz. He was charged with first degree forgery. A search of his car uncovered, among other things, $46,010.77 in U.S. currency, a road map of the Denver area (marked with dots indicating the location of banks), and numerous white envelopes.

Ovidio Mantilla-Oritz insisted he was unaware of the altered $1.00 bill. He declined to answer questions about the source of the $46,000. Mantilla-Oritz was held in jail overnight and released. The cash was seized, but the seizure was never contested. It was obvious that Mantilla-Oritz was expected to dispose of the $46,000 before returning to the hotel. If he had not been arrested, he would have used the money to purchase cashier's checks and money orders from banks all over the Denver area.

Ovidio Mantilla-Ortiz' arrest disrupted Papa Smurf's plans to unload cash in the Denver area. The entire troupe left Denver on September 27. Jorge Obando flew to Omaha, Nebraska; the others all returned to Miami. Customs agents went through the trash left in each of the rooms occupied by the Smurfs at the Roadway and Stapleton Plaza Hotels. In Alberto Barrera's trash they found a garment bag with Margarita Mejia's name and address attached. Envelopes were also recovered that bore the letterhead of First Bank of Wheatridge, Colorado, and handwritten numerical dollar figures. Subsequent investigation determined that a cashier's check in the amount of $5,000 had been purchased at that bank by one member of the group.

While the Smurfs were busy in Denver, Customs agents were just as busy back in Phoenix canvassing banks about unusual cash purchases of cashier's checks and money orders. A surprising number of tellers recalled such transactions over the previous two weeks and some were able to identify several photographs of the Smurfs as purchasers.

Wherever there was a recollection of an incident and an identification of one of the Smurfs, efforts were made to tie the recollection to a particular transaction involving cashier's check sales. A number of transactions were identified, and in some cases, the checks already had been negotiated and returned. The checks all were deposited to an account at the Irving Trust International Bank in Miami in the name of Banco Santander, a Colombian bank. This was a breakthrough! One of the accounts used by the Barrera smurfing organization had been identified.

Greenback agents inquired about the account at Irving Trust. Subpoenaed records indicated there had been deposits to the account on September 14, 19, and 23, 1983. The deposit on September 14 was $190,000 and consisted of cashier's checks and money orders that had been purchased from Phoenix banks between September 6 and September 10. On September 19, $513,000 was deposited to the account, all in cashier's checks and money orders purchased from Phoenix banks during the period of September 13 through September 17. On September 23, there were two deposits of $158,000 and $129,000 respectively. Again, the deposits were in the form of cashier's checks and money orders purchased from Phoenix banks; these purchases were made between September 20 and September 22. All of the cashier's checks and money orders involved in these deposits were in amounts under $10,000.

Customs agents continued their inquiries at Phoenix banks. They found that some of the cashier's checks associated with the Smurfs had been deposited to an account at Bank Leumi Le-Israel, B.M., Miami. The account was in the name of the Panama Branch of Bank Leumi Le-Israel, B.M. Records of the Miami branch of the bank revealed a deposit of $104,880 on September 20 consisting of money orders and traveler's checks in amounts less than $10,000 purchased at banks in Phoenix between September 13 and September 17, 1983. All told, Barrera's Smurfs had bought over 200 cashier's checks and money orders totaling more than $1 million during the course of two weeks and two days in Phoenix.

Records of the Panama branch of Bank Leumi's account at the Miami branch of Bank Leumi showed a $505,700 deposit on September 23 which consisted entirely of cashier's checks and money orders in amounts under $10,000. About $350,000 worth were purchased at Denver banks between September 20 and September 22; the remainder were purchased in the Miami area on September 22. This then indicated that Barrera had some Smurfs operating in the Miami area while others were on the road. The agents dubbed the group on the road as the "traveling circus."

When Jorge Obando arrived in Omaha on September 27, 1983, he met Carlos Villalta. Both rented cars and checked into the Ramada Central

Hotel. At the request of Customs agents in Denver, Omaha police kept the two under surveillance. During the next three days, the two men were observed going into more than 30 banks in Omaha and Lincoln. Inquiries at each bank revealed that in every case cashier's checks or money orders were purchased with currency. The average purchase was about $5,000. Numerous bank tellers identified photographs of Obando and Villalta as the individuals who purchased the instruments. The two Smurfs left Omaha on October 1 and returned to Miami.

Greenback agents learned that a deposit of $765,000 had been made to the Bank Leumi Panama account at the Miami branch of Bank Leumi on October 5, 1983. The deposit include 60 cashier's checks and money orders, totalling approximately $300,000, that had been purchased by Obando and Villalta during their trip to Omaha. The remainder of the deposit was also in monetary instruments in amounts under $10,000 that had been purchased in Denver and in the Miami area.

Greenback agents received information that Carlos Villalta, Louis Neira, and Jorge Mantilla-Ortiz were flying to Portland, Oregon on October 10, 1983. Customs agents in Portland were notified and asked to keep tabs on the trio. On October 11 and 12, the three Smurfs were observed visiting various banks in the Portland area. Inquiry at the banks determined that cashier's checks and money orders were being purchased with currency in amounts under $10,000. On October 13, Carlos Villalta was observed in the company of a fourth man at the Sheraton Inn, where the three were staying. Police officers on the surveillance team recognized the fourth man as a local resident named Juan Martinez who had been arrested two years earlier on charges involving two kilos of cocaine. Villalta was questioned by FBI agents and Portland Police the next day about his association with Martinez, he denied knowing him. Villalta was released after being questioned, and a short time later, he, Neira, and Jorge Mantilla-Ortiz checked out of the hotel and flew back to Miami.

The records of Bank Leumi Le-Israel in Miami showed that a deposit of $299,580 was made to the account of Bank Leumi, Panama on October 1983. The deposit consisted of 55 cashier's checks and money orders that had been purchased at banks in Portland during the period that the three Smurfs were there.

After the Portland trip and the questioning by police, Papa Smurf's laundering organization began concentrating its efforts in South Florida.

In November, Greenback agents obtained a court order authorizing a pen register and trap and trace on the home telephone of Alberto Barrera. A pen register is a device placed on a telephone line which identifies all numbers dialed from the telephone as well as the telephone numbers from which incoming calls originate. When the pen register initially went into operation, agents were dismayed to learn that a "Blue Box" was being used at the residence to complete long distance calls. A "Blue Box" is an illegal device used to circumvent long distance toll charges and eliminate telephone company records which otherwise would list the long distance telephone numbers called.

It appeared that the investigators would be stymied in obtaining information on long distance calls made from "Papa Smurf's" home telephone. However, the agents received a bonus when they checked with Southern Bell Telephone Company to advise of the use of the Blue Box. The telephone company was already aware of the Blue Box in Barrera's residence, and as part of their own security procedures, they had been tracking its use since September 1, 1983. The company had records of all calls made through the device, listing numerous calls to hotels, pay telephones, and residences in Phoenix, Denver, Omaha, Portland, Morgan Hill, California, and Colombia.

Southern Bell's records showed 95 calls to numbers in Phoenix between September 6 and September 19, including many to the Ramada Hotel and the Sheraton Airport Inn. Jorge Mantilla-Ortiz had stayed at the Ramada between September 6 and September 12, and Jorge Obando had stayed there between September 14 and September 22. There were also numerous calls to pay telephones in the Phoenix area.

The telephone company records revealed 26 long distance calls to the Denver area between September 19 and September 28, including a number of calls to the Rodeway Inn, where three of the Smurfs had stayed while in Denver. One call was made to the Denver City Jail on September 25, when Ovidio Mantilla-Ortiz was in custody for passing bogus currency, and another was made to the attorney who represented him.

Southern Bell records showed that between September 26 and September 30, the Blue Box was used to make 23 calls to the Omaha, Nebraska area from Barrera's residence. Six of the calls were made to the Ramada Inn Central where Carlos Villalta was staying; others were made to pay telephones in the Omaha and Lincoln area. There were also records of 47 calls to the Portland, Oregon area between September 25 and October 14, including calls to hotels used by the Smurfs.

Smurfing, as carried out by "Papa Smurf's" organization, was an expensive way to launder money. Airline tickets, rental cars, meal charges, and hotel bills for the Smurfs added to the cost of doing business. It was clear, however, that Alberto Barrera was out to save money on long distance telephone calls. The Blue Box allowed him to save money and to keep in close contact with his "traveling circus."

Apparently alarmed by the questioning in Portland and the arrest of Ovidio Mantilla-Ortiz, the Papa Smurf organization slowed down its operations in November and December. The Irving Trust account of Banco Santander was closed out in early November. Activity in the Bank Leumi account trailed off significantly. Most of the deposits consisted of cashier's checks and money orders purchased in banks throughout South Florida. Alberto Barrera and a number of his Smurfs apparently had gone to Colombia before Christmas to visit relatives. They did not return until late January.

In February and March 1984, the Blue Box at Alberto Barrera's residence started to reflect a large number of telephone calls to California. There had always been some calls to a telephone in Morgan Hill, California and to San Jose, California. But now the calls to those numbers and to others in San Francisco and Los Angeles started to show a marked increase. The number telephoned in Morgan Hill was listed to Betty Montoya at the residence of Juan Montoya. The number in San Jose was listed to William Roldan, who, it was determined lived with his son, William Roldan, Jr. The Roldans and Montoyas soon were identified as active Smurfs working for Alberto Barrera.

In late March, surveillance was begun on Barrera and some of his Smurfs. On March 26, Greenback agents observed a Federal Express truck arrive at Louis Hector Neira's Miami residence. The driver delivered a large envelope to a male who answered the door. Immediately after the delivery, the driver was questioned by agents, who learned that the shipper listed on the air bill was Juan Montoya, at an address in Sunnyvale, California. The individual who signed for the package gave his name as Guillermo Rodriguez. This was determined to be an alias used by Louis Hector Neira. The driver told the agents that he had made four similar deliveries in the prior two weeks. He recalled that all of the packages had come from California, and that the earlier deliveries had been signed for by Maritza Neira. It was later learned that Louis Neira and his wife, Maritza, were the only individuals living at that address.

Shortly after the Federal Express delivery, Louis Neira left the house and drove to a Miami office building. He entered a suite that had been leased by Alberto Barrera. A short time later, he departed with Barrera and they drove to the offices of Security Pacific International Bank.

After the pair left the building, agents questioned personnel at the bank. The questioning provided a major breakthrough in the investigation. It was learned that Louis Neira had just made a deposit of $46,500, consisting of 14 cashier's checks, each in amounts of $5,000 or less. The checks were all purchased in the San Jose, California area on March 23. The account to which the checks were deposited was in the name of Banco De Occidente, Panama Branch. Banco De Occidente was a Colombian Bank, the Panama branch of which had, over time, become a frequent conduit for drug money laundering. Some of this activity was linked to General Manuel Noriega, the former Dictator of Panama.

The Security Pacific account had been opened in February 1984, and since that time had taken in about $2 million. Not surprisingly, the deposits always consisted of cashier's checks and money orders in amounts under $10,000, and were usually made by Alberto Barrera or Margarita Mejia. However, it was determined that Louis Neira had made another deposit on March 23 in the amount of $79,070 consisting of 38 cashier's checks and money orders in amounts of $4,000 or less. Each had been purchased in the San Jose area on March 19. Greenback agents sent photocopies of the deposited instruments to the IRS Criminal Investigations Office in San Jose with a request that an investigation be conducted.

The San Jose investigation determined that the cashier's checks and money orders in the deposits of March 23 and March 26 to the Banco De Occidente account at Security Pacific had all been purchased by Juan Montoya, Alex Montoya, and Guillermo Arrango at banks in San Jose, Palo Alto, and San Mateo. In a number of instances, tellers who became suspicious about the transactions turned on bank surveillance cameras and obtained photographs of the purchasers, who were later identified as being the three suspects. Other times, tellers were able to identify photographs of one of the three Smurfs as the purchaser of a particular instrument. The three Smurfs used fictitious names in each of the purchases.

On March 29, Greenback agents learned from the Security Pacific Bank that 60 cashier's checks and money orders totalling $229,700 had been deposited to the Banco De Occidente account by Margarita Mejia. Each had been purchased from banks in San Jose and San Francisco on March 26 and March 27. The name William Roldan appeared as the payee on five of the cashier's checks. A second deposit was made to the same account on that day by Alberto Barrera. It totalled $194,020 and consisted of checks and money orders purchased at banks in and around San Jose.

On April 1, Louis and Maritza Neira moved to a new residence they had purchased in Miami. The next day, Greenback agents retrieved two bags of garbage that had been left outside at the old address. Inside one of the bags, agents found carbon copies of three money orders that had been purchased at Naples Federal Savings and Loan Association in Naples, Florida on March 30. The original of these money orders had been part of a deposit of 17 money orders totalling $50,000 that had been made by Louis Hector Neira on March 30. All 17 money orders had been purchased at banks in the Naples area on March 29 and 30; Louis Hector Neira was identified by bank personnel as the purchaser of three of the instruments.

IRS agent Fred Meyers, who had been assigned to Operation Greenback since its inception in 1980, was in charge of the Alberto Barrera investigation. When Meyers learned of the identification of the Smurfs in the

San Jose area and of their connection with Alberto Barrera, he went to San Jose to develop first-hand information about that operation. He flew there on April 2, 1984, and on April 3, he joined IRS agents from San Jose in a surveillance at the home of Juan Montoya. Montoya left his residence early in the morning and was followed to the Roldan residence, where he was observed a short time later leaving with the younger Roldan. Over the next few hours the two were followed to eight different financial institutions in Menlo Park. In each instance, Roldan remained in the car while Montoya went into the bank and purchased either cashier's checks or money orders with currency. Records at the eight institutions showed that the value of the instruments purchased totalled over $40,000. Montoya used fictitious names for each instrument purchased.

On April 5, the cashier's checks and money orders Montoya purchased in Menlo Park were deposited into the Banco De Occidente account at Security Pacific International Bank. They were part of a much larger deposit of 86 instruments totalling $249,470. The deposit was made by Louis Hector Neira.

Surveillance at Juan Montoya's residence in Morgan Hill on April 5 revealed that William Roldan, Jr. went into the house in mid-morning. A short time later, a car driven by Guillermo Arrango left the driveway; Arrango was accompanied by Alex Montoya, a brother of Juan Montoya. The car was followed to the Bank of America branch in Morgan Hill, where Arrango made a cash deposit of $1,800 into his personal account.

While the California wing of Papa Smurf's organization was laundering money in San Jose and environs, things were humming in Miami. Greenback agents setup surveillance at Security Pacific International Bank on April 10, where Margarita Mejia was observed leaving the bank and meeting Alberto Barrera. They left the area in Barrera's car. While at the bank, it was learned, Mejia deposited $390,000 worth of cashier's checks and money orders. The checks had been purchased in the greater Miami area and in Naples, Florida. One money order in the amount of $1,000 was purchased at the Hollywood, Florida branch of the Home Savings and Loan Association. Included among the cash used to pay for the check was a counterfeit $100 bill.

When asked for identification, the purchaser of the check produced a Florida driver's license with the name Luis Villota, and a Miami address. Investigation determined that Villota actually resided at this address. Among the other items in the April 10 deposit by Mejia were cashier's checks and money orders purchased at banks in Naples, Florida. Surveillance photographs taken by suspicious tellers established that Jorge Obando was the individual who bought many of the checks.

Legal Problems

Despite the fact that the Smurfs were obviously out to break the intent of law by laundering huge sums of money through the purchase and deposit of relatively low value cashier's checks and money orders, there was no easy way to snag them. At the time all this was going on, there was no crime on the books that prohibited the structuring of deposits to evade BSA reporting requirements. Consequently, the government had to devise a method from existing law to make a case against Smurfs.

Clearly, smurfing organizations were scheming to evade the filing of CTRs on their cash transactions. Prosecutors decided to use a combination of statutes and some convoluted legal theory against smurfing organizations. Their rationale was that a smurfing operation was a conspiracy to deny the IRS information to which it is entitled to under the Bank Secrecy Act. The following statutes were combined in filing charges against the Smurfs: Section 371 (conspiracy), Section 1001 (covering up and concealing material facts), and 31 USC 5313 (failure to file reports of currency transactions).

The theory behind this type of case building is known in legal jargon as a "Kleine Conspiracy," named for a case where a similar approach was used. To make it all work, agents had to establish that there was a scheme or conspiracy; they had to identify the other participants in the scheme; and they had to be able to prove that the scheme was designed to conceal, or cover up, the various transactions to evade the filing of CTRs.

By building its case in this manner, the government also had a better chance of identifying and arresting more members of the Barrera organization. Furthermore, Greenback agents wanted to make sure that they could develop a case against Papa Smurf (Barrera) that would stick. Barrera stayed behind the scenes. He did not actually buy cashier's checks. He was usually not around when the Smurfs were doing business in the banks where instruments were purchased.

Meanwhile, back in Miami, activity by the Barrera organization was picking up steam. On April 11, agents watching the Security Pacific International Bank saw Alberto Barrera go into the bank. After he departed, it was determined that he had deposited $87,000 in cashier's checks and money orders to the Banco De Occidente account. One of the items deposited was a $3,000 cashier's check purchased April 10 at the Miller Square office of the Florida National Bank in Miami. A photograph of Luis Villota was identified by bank employees as the purchaser. Another item in the deposit was an $8,000 cashier's check that had been purchased at the Sunset Office of the Florida National Bank in Miami that same day by a man identified as Villota. In each instance, Villota used a fictitious name.

When Barrera left the Security Pacific Bank on April 10, he drove off in a rental car. It was later determined that this car had been rented both in his name and that of Daisy Villota, the wife of Luis Villota.

On April 12, Alberto Barrera was observed entering the Security Pacific Bank, where he deposited $492,000 in money orders and cashier's checks into the Banco De Occidente account. All of the instruments had been purchased in banks in Miami, Fort Lauderdale, West Palm Beach, Tampa, St. Petersburg and other Florida cities. Investigation at the various banks determined that many of the instruments had been purchased by Luis Villota, Jorge Obando, Jorge Mantilla-Ortiz and Ovidio Mantilla-Ortiz.

On the afternoon of April 12, two Greenback agents were in Naples, Florida interviewing personnel at banks where cashier's checks had previously been purchased. As they left the bank, they saw Jorge Mantilla-Ortiz drive up. They watched Jorge Mantilla-Ortiz enter the bank, where he purchased a cashier's checks with $3,000. He then went to three more banks and purchased cashier's checks. As he left the last bank, he was arrested. A search was conducted of his car; agents found 34 cashier's checks totalling $100,000. The checks had all been purchased in Naples earlier that day. The agents also found $101,000 in currency, a Rand McNally map of the Tampa-St. Petersburg area with the locations of banks and shopping centers marked, and an address book. Among the entries in the address book was the name "Luis," with a telephone number for Louis Hector Neira. There was also an entry for "J. Alb.," with the telephone number for Alberto Barrera. There was a notation, "24 horas" with a telephone number that matched that of an answering service for A.M. Investments.

Jorge Mantilla-Ortiz was charged with aiding and abetting the cover-up and concealment of the filing of Currency Transactions Reports required under the Bank Secrecy Act. He was held in $125,000 bail.

The search of Jorge Mantilla-Ortiz' car turned up other interesting item: a CMIR form which purported to show that William Roldan had transported $250,000 in cash into the United States from Colombia on November 25, 1983.

Several hours after Jorge Mantilla-Ortiz was arrested, Operation Greenback received a telephone call from a bank in Cape Coral, Florida. A bank official said an Hispanic male had purchased four $1,000 money orders that day and had also purchased additional money orders at a second branch of the bank in the same town. The purchaser was observed leaving the bank, and bank personnel took down the make and license of the car he was driving. Greenback agents drove by the home of Louis Hector Neira at 10:50 p.m. that evening, where they observed the car parked, as well as the car that had been rented by Daisy Villota and Alberto Barrera. Two vehicles normally driven by Louis Neira were also parked outside

Neira's home. It appeared that some kind of emergency meeting was taking place, prompted by the arrest of Jorge Mantilla-Ortiz. It appeared his arrest may have "spooked" the Papa Smurf organization.

On April 13, 1984, a deposit of $552,000 in cashier's checks and money orders in amounts under $10,000 was made to the Banco De Occidente account at Security Pacific Bank. The deposit was made by a Smurf known only as "Cojo." Agents watching the bank saw Cojo depart and get into a car driven by Luis Villota.

On April 14, IRS agents in San Jose picked up garbage from the residence of David Herrera. The Blue Box monitor from Barrera's residence had picked up 20 long distance calls to Herrera's home. Buried in Herrera's garbage were photocopies of two money orders in the amount of $750 each and one cashier's check for $1,000. The items had been purchased from banks in the San Jose area on March 26, and were part of the deposit of $194,020 that had been made to the Banco De Occidente account on March 29. Also found in Herrera's garbage was a scrap of paper containing the telephone number of Juan Montoya.

Back in Miami, a deposit of $343,484 was made to the Banco De Occidente account by "Cojo" on April 16. He delivered the checks in an envelope with the name of a bank in Cocoa Beach, Florida. The envelope had the name "Alex" written on it and was turned over to Greenback agents by the Security Pacific teller who handled the transaction. The cashier's checks in the deposit had been purchased from banks in northeastern Florida and Atlanta—this was the first indication that the Barrera organization operated in Atlanta.

Over the next few days, Greenback agents made inquiries at banks in Cocoa Beach, Daytona Beach, and Ormand Beach where a number of the cashier's checks had been purchased. The inquiries led to the identification of Alex Montoya as the purchaser of four of the checks. In each instance, a suspicious teller had taken bank surveillance photographs of Montoya as he purchased the checks with cash. Montoya, a California Smurf, had relocated to Florida.

SMURFS EVERYWHERE

On April 18, Fred Meyers, the Greenback agent in charge of the Barrera case, went to Atlanta to investigate the large number of cashier's checks and money orders that had been purchased there on April 12 and 13. He brought photographs of all the known members of the Barrera organization. Meyers wanted to tie up a case against the group as soon as possible. What happened on his trip illustrates the pervasive nature of smurfing activity at that time.

Working with a local IRS agent, Meyers displayed photographs of the known Smurfs, but none of the tellers could identify them. In several cases, suspicious tellers had taken surveillance photographs of the purchasers. Upon examining the photos, Meyers realized they were dealing with two new members of the Barrera organization. While Meyers and his partner were in one of the banks, two Hispanic males entered and each proceeded to buy a $9,000 cashier's check with currency. A teller was told to make sure bank surveillance photographs were taken. In looking at the men, Meyers and the other agent determined they were neither of the two suspects in the existing surveillance photographs.

The two agents positioned themselves outside the bank, and when the two suspects departed, they followed them on foot to another bank. When the suspects left the second bank, the agents watched them get into a car with Florida license plates; they noted the tag number as the suspects drove away. Meyers then checked the license number and learned that the car had been rented in Miami. A Greenback agent in Miami determined the name of the person who had rented the car and telephoned the information back to Meyers in Atlanta. He was a known suspect in yet another smurfing organization.

Meyers began to telephone downtown hotels, looking for the person who had rented the car. He was lucky on the fourth call; a person by that name was registered in the hotel and was not due to check out until the next day.

Early the next morning, Fred Meyers, along with several IRS agents and Atlanta detectives, set up surveillance on the hotel. Shortly after 9:00 a.m., the two Smurfs departed, and were followed to three different banks. In each bank, the two men used cash to purchase $9,000 cashier's checks.

Shortly after the Smurfs left the third bank they were taken into custody for conspiring to evade the reporting requirements of the Bank Secrecy Act. A search warrant was obtained for their vehicle and hotel room. The car yielded $140,000 in cash and cashier's checks in the amount of $160,000. The hotel room was empty. It turned out that the two men were Mexican nationals who had nothing to do with the Papa Smurf organization; they worked for an entirely different smurfing organization, also based in Miami. It was all in a day's work for Fred Meyers.

BACK TO PAPA SMURF

On April 23, Margarita Mejia made a deposit of $37,000 to the Banco De Occidente account. The deposit consisted of cashier's checks that had been purchased in Macon, Georgia on April 19 and 20. Tellers at two different banks in Macon had become suspicious when two Hispanic males purchased cashier's checks with currency in amounts under $10,000. In each location the men were seen getting into a car with a Florida license. Investigation determined the car had been rented by Hernando Prada in Miami. At the time the car was rented, Prada showed a Florida driver's license with a Miami address. The rental car was returned in Atlanta on April 21.

Prada's name was already in Greenback files. He had been observed in a lengthy conversation with Barrera in February; he shared an apartment with Carlos Jiminez. Photographs of Prada and Jiminez were obtained from their Florida driver's licenses. When Meyers saw the photographs he immediately recognized them as the same two men in the surveillance pictures taken by the Atlanta banks a few weeks before. Subsequently, several tellers at banks in Macon identified photographs of Prada and Jiminez as purchasers of some of the cashier's checks on April 19 and 20.

On April 24, Hernando Prada was arrested at a bank in Columbus, Georgia while attempting to buy a $5,000 cashier's check. The teller handling the transaction became suspicious, notified a supervisor and the police were called. After Prada was in custody, a warrant for his arrest was obtained in Miami for conspiring to conceal and cover up Currency Transaction Reports. The car that he was driving was searched, and a number of cashier's checks totaling $185,000, all in amounts under $10,000, were found. Also found was $8,000 in currency, and an address book containing telephone numbers and addresses for about half the members of the Papa Smurf organization.

On April 25, Carlos Jiminez was arrested in Miami, on charges similar to those brought against Prada, in connection with purchases of cashier's checks in Macon, Georgia on April 19 and 20.

While Prada and Jiminez were being arrested in Georgia and Florida, the West Coast wing of the Papa Smurf organization continued to operate. On April 24, IRS agents in San Jose followed Juan Montoya when he left his residence at 8:30 a.m. They watched him as he went to 14 banks in the California towns of Dublin, Danville, and San Ramon, purchasing money orders at each.

On April 26, IRS and Customs agents maintained surveillance on Juan Montoya's residence. Just before 9:00 a.m., Montoya left the house with Guillermo Arrango. The two were followed to a bank in Lafayette, where each purchased cashier's checks. After the first set of purchases, the two men split up. Each was followed. The two were observed going into 17 other banking institutions in Lafayette, Walnut Creek, and Oakland, where they purchased cashier's checks or money orders with currency in amounts under $4,000. Surveillance agents went into each bank after the Smurfs departed and requested that the cash used to buy the instruments be segregated and held until the next day. The agents returned to each bank the next day with a trained Customs Service narcotics detection dog.

The dog reacted positively, indicating the presence of narcotics residue on all of the currency used by the Smurfs to buy the checks.

On April 26, Greenback agents retrieved trash placed outside Barrera's home. There was a small brown paper bag among the normal household garbage. The bag contained several pieces of paper that provided evidence of the extent of the smurfing operation run by Barrera. One was a copy of a letter dated in March 1984 to Banco De Occidente in Panama, authorizing the bearer to withdraw $100,000 from an open account in the name of Jorge Barrera Duran and/or Nancy Velasco. Another item was an envelope with the name and logo of the First Georgia Bank, Atlanta. Checks purchased at that bank had been deposited in the Banco De Occidente account at Security Pacific International Bank on April 16 and 18. There was also a reconciliation sheet with a number of entries for the period April 7 through April 15. The sheet indicated the receipt of $3,100,000 and disbursements of over $4,000,000 during the period.

On April 27, the IRS office in Birmingham, Alabama was contacted by Lt. Butch Mims of the Birmingham Police Narcotics and Vice Unit. He advised that he had received calls from several banks in the Birmingham area that two Latin males were buying cashier's checks in amounts under $10,000, with currency. Lt. Mims had determined that the individuals had stayed at the Ramada Inn in Birmingham from April 24 through April 26, and had registered in the names of Jorge Obando and Gerago Chahin, of Miami. Mims obtained a copy of Obando's Florida driver's license with a photograph from the Florida Department of Motor Vehicles. The photograph was identified by tellers at a number of banks as one of the two men who had purchased the cashier's checks.

On April 30, IRS agents from San Jose picked up garbage that had been left outside the residence of Juan Montoya. The garbage yielded a treasure trove of evidence that tied Montoya into the Alberto Barrera smurfing organization and into deposits at the Banco De Occidente account at Security Pacific International Bank in Miami. Photocopies of cashier's checks and money orders in the amount of $91,684 that had been purchased in California banks on April 12 and 13 were recovered. The originals of the photocopies were part of the $552,000 deposit into the Banco De Occidente account on April 16. Another group of photocopies from the garbage depicted 19 cashier's checks and money orders totaling $54,240. These checks, purchased at banks in the San Jose area on March 15 (and all for amounts under $10,000), were deposited to the Banco De Occidente account on March 20. The deposit total matched precisely the total amount depicted by the photocopies.

Another batch of photocopies in the garbage consisted of 56 cashier's checks and money orders totaling $112,000. The originals were all purchased in the San Jose and San Francisco areas on March 9 and 12 and were deposited to the Banco De Occidente account on March 13 and March 14. Still another batch of photocopies in the April 30 garbage pickup detailed $157,770 in cashier's checks and money orders purchased from banks in the San Jose area on March 19. These items were deposited in the Banco De Occidente account on March 21 and March 22.

One of the items had been purchased at the Glendale Federal Savings and Loan Association office in San Mateo. Two men were together when the purchase was made. A surveillance photograph taken by a suspicious bank teller led IRS agents to identify the pair of Smurfs as Juan Montoya and Guillermo Arrango.

William Roldan moved to a new address in San Jose during the first week of May. On May 11, agents picked up garbage left outside the new residence. In the garbage they found a business card with the name of William Roldan, and the title Assistant Manager of MJM Building Maintenance, with a Sunnyvale, California address. Investigation determined that Juan Montoya was the president and owner of MJM. Also found in the garbage was a sheet of paper with MJM letterhead. Entries on the paper reflected amounts, percentages of profits, and notations of "Willie," "Alex" and Banco De Occidente.

It was clear that the amounts and percentages represented expenses and profits for exchanging cash into cashier's checks. "Alex" referred to Alex Montoya and "Willie" referred to William Roldan, Jr.

The Papa Smurf Family Picture

The investigation had been going on for months. The full dimension of Papa Smurf's organization had been identified. The West Coast operation was headed by Juan Montoya. The Smurfs who worked for him were Guillermo Arrango, William Roldan, Sr., William Roldan, Jr., David Herrera and Juan's son, Alex Montoya. In Miami, Alberto Barrera had two key lieutenants, Louis Hector Neira and Jorge Obando, and a trusted companion and assistant, Margarita Mejia. The traveling circus Smurfs included Carlos Villalta, Ovidio Mantilla-Ortiz, Luis Villota, "Cojo," and Gerago Chahin. Jorge Isaac Mantilla-Ortiz, Hernando E. Prada, and Carlos Jiminez were Smurfs who had been arrested during the course of the investigation.

The smurfing operation continued to roll into mid-May. It was getting time to take the operation down. First, it was decided to gather sufficient background information on Alberto Barrera to clearly demonstrate that he was the head of the organization.

Investigation revealed that Barrera had no visible means of support. He usually remained in his residence during working hours. The Blue Box records of Southern Bell, the pen register and the trap and trace device indicated that Barrera placed and received about 50 telephone calls a day from his residential telephone. Most of the calls were made to or from locations in other cities where his Smurfs were buying monetary instruments from banks. Barrera maintained an office in the name of A.M. Investments in Miami, but he rarely went to this office during the daylight hours. He occasionally went into the office at night. The lease for the office space indicated that Barrera was the President of A.M. Investments. A.M. Investments was not registered as a Florida corporation, nor was it registered with the state of Florida as a foreign corporation. The firm also was not licensed to do business in Dade County. Surveillance on a number of occasions determined that no business was being conducted at A.M. Investments. In effect, it was a sham, or "paper" company.

Despite the fact that he was not employed and had no visible means of support, Alberto Barrera lived very well. He lived with his wife in a house valued at over $400,000, he supported his girlfriend, Margarita Mejia, and he owned six cars (including a Porsche, a Mercedes Benz, an Audi, and a BMW).

In checking on the amount of money being spent by Barrera, agents subpoenaed the records of the American Express Company. They found that he had an American Express card and that he made purchases with the card that averaged about $5,000 a month all through 1982 and 1983. Greenback agents did not realize it at the time but in subpoenaing the American Express records they sent a signal that caused Barrera to flee the country before he could be arrested. An attorney for the American Express Company decided that Barrera should be notified of the fact that the company had furnished copies of his account records to the government. There was no actual legal requirement for the notification, but, within a day of learning of the subpoena, Barrera left the United States in the company of Magarita Mejia.

On May 31, 1984, arrest warrants were issued for 13 members of the Papa Smurf organization. Search warrants were issued and executed at Barrera's residence and office. To their chagrin, Greenback agents found that both places had been cleared of any usable evidence. There was no currency, no cashier's checks, no money orders, and no records indicating the disposition of currency, checks, or payments to Smurfs. Worse than that, the agents discovered that Barrera and Margarita Mejia had flown the coop. Nine arrests were made. Jorge Obando and William Roldan, Sr. also escaped the dragnet. They became fugitives along with Barrera and Mejia.

The arrested Smurfs were all indicted along with the fugitives. Over the next six months, the cases of all the arrested defendants were disposed of. Several pled guilty. The remainder went to trial and were convicted. Juan Montoya and Louis Hector Neira each received four-year prison sentences. The remaining Smurfs received sentences from 18 months to two years.

Questioning of the Smurfs at the time of their arrests and interviews conducted with some of the them in the following months developed some interesting information about how they operated. It was learned, for instance, that the Smurfs were very concerned about their appearance when going into banks. They sought to be neatly dressed and to attempt to blend in with the appearance of people in the community they were in. In large cities, they wore shirts and ties. In Nebraska they bought jeans to match what people wore when they went into banks. The Smurfs had strict orders from Papa Smurf to stay out of trouble while on the road. There was to be no drinking and no drug use. They were instructed not to mix with or hang out with drug dealers, and to stay in good hotels with good security.

One individual was always in charge when a group of Smurfs took a trip to buy checks and money orders. His job was to carry and control the money, to obtain rental cars, and to get hotel reservations. This individual maintained records of the amounts given to each Smurf. He collected checks and money orders that the smurfs bought and he paid them commissions based on the amount of instruments they were able to buy. He would send the cashier's checks and money orders by Federal Express to Alberto Barrera.

A Smurf could dispose of between $50,000 and $100,000 in cash each day, and typically be paid between 0.5% and 1.5%, depending upon his experience and ability. A Smurf who disposed of $100,000 would be paid somewhere between $500 and $1,000 for a day's work. The individual in charge of a road trip would get about 1.5% of all the money laundered. In addition, he would get 0.5% of all currency that he personally laundered at banks.

When the traveling circus arrived in a town for smurfing activity, they would obtain a street map of the city and look in the yellow pages for banks. Then they would plot out bank locations and decide which banks individual Smurfs would go to. They would decide beforehand on the fictitious names to be used as remitters and on the dollar value of the instrument to be purchased. Each Smurf would count out the exact amount of currency that would be needed, sorting out bills that appeared to be counterfeit or that were badly worn or torn. They wanted to avoid any situation that would call special attention to their transactions. The Smurfs found that most banks did not ask for any identification. If identification was requested, they would leave the bank without conducting the transaction.

The Papa Smurf organization was finally broken up. In one month, between mid-March and mid-April, the group had laundered about $3.5 million. Between September 1983 and May 1984 they laundered over $12 million.

There were at least 20 large smurfing organizations operating in Miami in 1983 and 1984, and hundreds of smurfing groups operating in other areas of the country. The smurfing heyday ran from 1982 until 1985. Part of the reason that it was successful was that there was no law that specifically forbade the structuring of transactions to evade the reporting requirements of the Bank Secrecy Act.

Enforcement efforts against smurfing organizations increased substantially during 1983 and 1984. Many arrests were made and many groups were broken up. Banks started to become more sophisticated about smurfing operations. They became aware that these operations were connected to drug money laundering. Some banks refused to sell cashier's checks and other monetary instruments to noncustomers. In many instances, banks notified federal and local enforcement agencies of suspicious transactions involving cash purchases of cashier's checks and money orders.

Smurfing received a considerable amount of publicity from a series of Congressional hearings that took place during 1985. Smurfing operations were highlighted as a means of demonstrating the need for legislation that would make it a crime to structure transactions. The sought after statute was enacted late in 1986.

Enforcement efforts, actions by banks, and publicity from Congressional hearings all took their toll on smurfing by big-time drug organizations. Aside from these factors, smurfing was very expensive. Papa Smurf, for example, received 15% of the money he laundered for his Colombian drug connections. The net result of all of these factors was that smurfing started to decline in 1985. Large drug organizations sought other methods to launder their drug proceeds.

Smurfing, though, did not go away completely. It is still a problem today. However, it is no longer a major way of laundering drug money and it does not involve the frenzied kind of activity that took place between 1982 and 1985. A considerable amount of smurfing activity has moved out of banks and into post offices, convenience stores, travel agencies, and other outlets where money orders and traveler's checks are sold. BSA amendments and regulations adopted in 1988 and 1990 have made it even more difficult for smurfing organizations to operate. Financial institutions must now obtain identification for and maintain records of cash purchases of monetary instruments for amounts between $3,000 and $10,000.

Alberto Barrera was never apprehended by federal authorities. Reliable information indicates he was hacked to death with a machete by drug dealers in Colombia during late 1989. William Roldan, Sr. was arrested in Miami in 1989 and is now serving a jail sentence. Jorge Obando and Margarita Mejia remain fugitives. They are presumed to be living in Colombia.

CHAPTER 4

RAMON MILIAN RODRIGUEZ:
THE FULL SERVICE MONEY LAUNDERER

The era of large cash deposits directly into Miami bank accounts ended in 1982 and was followed by a frenzy of "smurfing" activity in Miami and nationwide. The smurfing era peaked in 1983 and then receded, but it never completely went away; much of the activity simply moved from banks to nonbank financial institutions that sell money orders and traveler's checks.

At about the same time smurfing emerged, some launderers began moving huge loads of currency directly out of the country, thereby by-passing the domestic banking system. This method of laundering was not new; it had been used by some Colombian drug trafficking organizations as early as 1976. It was one of the methods used by some of the launderers in the Pizza Connection mob. What differentiated the activity in 1982 from prior efforts was the sheer volume of the cash being transported, and in some cases, the use of private aircrafts.

113

LEARNING THE BUSINESS

The best example of these latter-day massive currency transporters was the operation run by Ramon Milian Rodriguez between June 1982 and May 1983.

Ramon Milian Rodriguez went far beyond just moving money out of the country; he provided a full-service laundering operation that catered both to U.S. drug dealers and members of the Colombian drug cartel. He not only placed enormous amounts of U.S. currency directly into Panamanian banks, but he would move the money anywhere in the world in a manner that was difficult to trace back to his clients.

Ramon Milian Rodriguez was born in Havana, Cuba in 1951. He came to the United States with his parents in 1959, settling in California. His parents had considerable wealth in Cuba; the family was involved in banking, meat packing, and construction businesses.

Ramon received a B.S. degree in Commerce from Santa Clara University, after which he went to work as an accountant for a Miami accounting firm run by John Haralambibes. Soon after, he became a Certified Pubic Accountant licensed in Florida.

In the course of his duties at Haralambibes' CPA firm, Ramon became acquainted with a client named Dr. Manuel Artime, a hero among Cubans who sought to overthrow Fidel Castro. Dr. Artime had been involved in the ill-fated "Bay of Pigs" operation as a political adviser and was involved in various other covert operations aimed at promoting the overthrow of Castro.

Over time, Ramon became a trusted money handler for Dr. Artime, learning to move money so that it did not leave a paper trail. He learned about bank secrecy laws in various countries and he learned how to incorporate companies in countries that had strict bank secrecy laws. He made covert cash payments for Dr. Artime and he opened accounts in foreign countries in the names of companies that served as vehicles for the movement of money. In the course of his work for Dr. Artime, Ramon made cash payments to the families of some of the Cubans involved in the Watergate case and he moved money to some bank accounts in Nicaragua that had been set up for the benefit of Watergate operatives. In short, Ramon Rodriguez learned how to launder money.

While working for Haralambibes, Ramon also handled accounts for a number of Cuban fishing boat captains who lived in Miami, some of whom were cohorts of Dr. Artime in the anti-Castro movement. Fishing lost much of its financial allure after 1975, when the Bahamas closed off its waters to foreign fishermen. So, many fishermen turned to drug smuggling, and Ramon became their money launderer.

Key to his laundering activities was the fact that he continued to file tax forms on behalf of the fishermen. He would prepare returns showing fishing income as a small percentage of their overall profits. Of course, the drug profits went unreported.

Dr. Artime did not approve of drug smuggling, but he was in poor health and was not in a position to do anything about it. He died in 1976. Ramon continued building his laundering business, and in 1978, he left the Haralambibes firm and opened his own CPA business, taking with him many of his drug smuggler clients.

Ramon Rodriguez began transporting cash in 1976, taking the smuggler's U.S. dollars to Panama. He traveled on commercial flights and declared the money on Customs CMIR forms. Once in Panama, he deposited the dollars into local banks. Over the years his business flourished.

He was more than just a money mover, though. Once he placed money into secret Panamanian bank accounts in the names of paper companies registered in Panama, he could do literally anything a client wanted—pay suppliers for drugs, invest, and stash money in other countries like Switzerland.

Money laundering enabled Ramon to live the good life—he bought expensive cars and a lavish home, ate in all the finest restaurants and joined the prestigious Miami Rowing Club. He even raised campaign money for a Miami mayoral candidate. In 1981, he divorced his first wife and married his bookkeeper.

In 1982, Ramon Rodriguez was contacted by high-level members of Colombian cocaine organizations, including Luis Carlos Molina, chief money handler for the Medellin cartel. The contact came just after enforcement efforts had led South Florida banks to refuse large currency transactions. Although many Colombians had, for years, been transporting U.S. dollars out of the United States and into Colombia, there were limits to how much cash individuals could carry and how much of the cash could be disposed of in Colombia. Ramon, on the other hand, could move large quantities of cash out of the United States and into Panama, where it was easy to dispose of drug dollars.

Although Ramon agreed to work for the Colombians, he had his own problem with how much cash he could physically transport on commercial flights. To solve his problem, he bought a Lear jet and hired two pilots. This greatly expanded his ability to handle increasingly larger quantities of cash. He would fly frequently to San Francisco and New Jersey to make cash pick-ups from clients, then fly the cash to Miami, where it would be counted and packaged. It would then be flown to Panama. With the jet, Ramon could move $5 to $7 million in cash at a clip.

Beginning in December and through the first five months of 1983, Ramon's jet made regular trips to Panama, shuttling millions of dollars in currency with each.

HEADING FOR A FALL

Three things happened in 1983 that led to Ramon's demise. The first was a Federal Reserve study indicating a huge surplus of U.S. dollars coming out of Panama. The surplus amount was far greater than Panama required for its legitimate commercial needs. Roughly, $90 million in U.S. dollars was shipped to Panama's central bank for normal commercial use. Federal Reserve records showed that $1.5 billion in U.S. currency came back to the United States from Panama during 1982, alone. Only one logical conclusion could be drawn: the money had to be tied to drug sales.

Secondly, the Federal Reserve Bank reported its findings to the Treasury Department, which, in turn, asked Customs to review CMIR and CTR filings for a trail of the money. The Customs review showed that Ramon Milian Rodriguez started to file CMIRs in the fall of 1982 for currency shipments from Miami to Panama. The amount claimed on each ranged between $400,000 and $700,000. Customs agents also found that Ramon and his company, Cambios Monetarios International, had filed CTRs between 1980 to 1982 showing the receipt of millions of dollars in currency from a variety of sources, and that the CTR filings stopped at about the same time the CMIR filings began. Operation Greenback was called upon to investigate.

It wasn't the first referral Greenback had received on Ramon Rodriguez. IRS tax examiners had already referred information suggesting Ramon, acting as a CPA, was laundering drug cash through Panama on behalf of his clients. With the information supplied by the IRS and Customs, Greenback opened an investigation on Ramon Milian Rodriguez in late February 1983.

The third nail in the Ramon coffin came shortly after the Greenback investigation began. A DEA agent named Jim Bramble, who was assigned Panama, received information from a confidential source that Ramon Milian Rodriguez of Miami, Florida, was flying millions of dollars in U.S. currency into Panama on a regular basis. With the help of his informant, Bramble was able to observe Ramon's aircraft arrive at Panama City Airport on several occasions during March and April on the military side of the airport. Each time, it was met by an armored car, whereupon boxes would be taken from the plane and loaded into the armored car. The armored car then would deliver the boxes to one of several banks in Panama City.

Surveillance of Ramon in Miami began in March 1983. Greenback agents found him to be a busy man. They learned that he drove a Mercedes-Benz and a Maserati. He made frequent trips in his private plane to San Francisco, New Jersey, and Panama. Each time he returned from a trip to a U.S. city, Ramon and his father would unload boxes into a beat up station wagon, drive to his office, and unload the boxes. Then, before each trip to Panama, the two would reverse the procedure. Coupled with Bramble's observations in Panama, the obvious conclusion was that Ramon was picking up cash in San Francisco and New Jersey and delivering it to banks in Panama.

The conclusion may have been obvious, but the course of action to be taken was not. At the time, there was no crime of money laundering. As for reporting the movement of cash, Ramon's father usually would file a CMIR when a shipment of cash was taken from the United States to Panama, though the dollar values claimed seemed low given the size and number of boxes involved. Complicating matters, Ramon took great pains to cover himself in his movement of currency.

The situation was frustrating. It was clear to the Greenback agents that Ramon was involved in a large money laundering operation, but there was no basis on which to file criminal charges and there was no basis to obtain a search warrant. Eventually, the agents decided to stop Ramon's aircraft the next time that it was loaded for a trip to Panama. The object would be to effect a civil forfeiture of any money found. If it was a substantial sum, a case could be made for a court-ordered wiretap.

Beginning about the end of April 1983, surveillance was conducted on a daily basis in anticipation of the next trip to Panama. All the pieces began to fall in place on May 3. Ramon's pilots were observed preparing his plane for a flight. His father was observed driving a station wagon filled with boxes to the airport, and the boxes were observed being loaded on the plane. The agents were ready to strike, but the plane didn't move. After a considerable delay, the occupants were observed removing the boxes and reloading them into the station wagon. According to the Federal Aviation Commission, the flight was canceled because the plane didn't receive clearance to land in Panama. It was a national holiday in Panama. A new flight plan was filed on the following day for a trip from Fort Lauderdale to Panama.

The payoff finally came for Greenback on May 4. Agents observed activity around the aircraft early in the morning. The two pilots arrived and appeared to be getting the plane ready for departure. Ramon arrived in the company of two men; his father arrived with a station wagon full of boxes. Agents following the father on the way to the airport were amazed to see him stop at a 7-Eleven and get coffee. The boxes in the back of the station wagon remained unattended while he went into the store. The agents felt certain that there was money inside, but they didn't know how much.

After the boxes were loaded on the plane, Ramon's father drove off. Agents followed him. He drove straight home without filing a CMIR.

At the airport, five men boarded the plane: Ramon, the two pilots, and the two men who arrived with Ramon.

Chuck Saphos, the senior Justice Department attorney assigned to Operation Greenback, positioned himself in the FAA Tower at Fort Lauderdale Airport. He wanted to be certain that the intention of the occupants of the plane was to depart the United States and fly directly to Panama. If there was currency on the aircraft, it would be seized because it was being transported out of the country without the filing of a Customs CMIR form. Saphos did not want the people on the aircraft to be able to say they were not headed to a foreign country.

The jet taxied away from the hangar area and requested take-off instructions. The tower asked the aircraft's destination. The reply was "Panama." The tower then directed the plane to the foot of the take-off runway. At this point, Saphos was satisfied that there was a clear intention to fly the aircraft and its contents to Panama. By pre-arrangement, the tower directed the jet to shut off its engines and announced the shut-down of the airport for a brief emergency. Several vehicles filled with agents raced up to the jet. Agents moved toward the plane with guns drawn. The tower instructed the occupants of the aircraft to open the door for a Customs inspection. (Customs is authorized to conduct warrantless border searches for contraband on all movements of individuals and cargo to and from the United States.) Two Customs agents boarded the plane and asked Ramon if there was more than $5,000 in currency on board. Ramon said no. A Customs agent opened one of the boxes and found it filled with currency. That was enough evidence to order the plane and its occupants back to the hangar area for a full Customs border search.

The search uncovered large amounts of currency in every box. While the search was going on, the two men who got on the plane were identified as brothers whose last name was Lara. They were Panamanian attorneys who specialized in registering companies in Panama. It was learned that Ramon Rodriguez had used their services to form Panamanian companies for his clients.

Ramon had a small office at the jet hangar. It bore the name Consolidated Courier and was used to handle the business use of his aircraft. The office was primarily used by the pilots. Ramon Rodriguez consented to a request to search the office and asked to speak to the agent in charge of the investigation.

RAMON COOPERATES

Ramon Rodriguez was interviewed in the Consolidated Courier office. The interview was both interesting and amazing, particularly in view of some outlandish statements and claims that Ramon would later make to a Congressional committee.

The interview began at 9:05 a.m. Those present included Chuck Saphos, the lead attorney for Operation Greenback, Dennis Fagan, the Customs supervisor at Greenback, and Arthur Sumrall, the Greenback agent to whom the case was assigned. Fagan gave Ramon his Miranda warnings. Ramon said he understood his rights and waived them. Ramon was told that he was not under arrest and that he was free to leave or terminate the interview at any time that he wanted. He said that he understood this but that he wanted to talk to those present.

Ramon started by telling the agents they did not fully appreciate who they were talking to. He claimed to be the most sophisticated person any of them had ever dealt with and that at no time in the past had federal agents ever had the opportunity to do so much as they would be able to do with him. He offered to cooperate fully with the government, provided no charges be filed against him, that his cooperation not be disclosed, and that the $4.3 million that he had in the aircraft be returned and he be allowed to continue his operation. It is interesting to note that when the money was later counted, the actual amount came to $5.4 million.

Ramon said it was important that he be allowed to continue transporting the money removed from the aircraft or he would lose credibility with his customers. He said he could forestall his departure with the funds for no more than 24 hours.

Ramon maintained that he had always filed currency forms with Customs, and that he suspected the filing of these forms would generate interest in him and would lead investigators to interview him. When asked why he had not come forward to federal authorities, he did not answer. He said he knew about Operation Greenback, but claimed he was unable to contact the office because it had an unlisted telephone number.

Ramon was again told that he was not under arrest and that he was free to leave, and he again stated a willingness to cooperate. It was obvious to the group in the interview that Ramon had a monumental ego. Among other things, he boasted being the most sophisticated person ever to operate a money laundering business and having an IQ of 150.

Ramon was then asked to accompany the agents to Greenback offices to further discuss his proposed cooperation. Once there, he was again advised that he was free to leave at any time. He said that he understood and that he wanted to stay. He was asked what he would do if his offer was not accepted. He said that it would not be possible for him to continue life

as it had been. He said that he had lived a full life and had done everything he wanted to do. He added that his family was provided for, with
assets hidden such that the government would never be able to touch
them. He claimed to have a $2 million life insurance policy and indicated
that he would consider suicide.

Ramon then proceeded to tell all. He told the agents that he had been
laundering narcotics money for about seven years, and that his clients represented a virtual "Who's Who" of the drug smuggling business. He said
he began laundering while working for Dr. Manuel Artime, whom he described as a leader for the Bay of Pigs invasion.

It was his reputation for honesty that brought the drug traffickers to
him, Ramon claimed. He then provided a list of those traffickers he currently serviced, or for whom he had transported currency in the past. Included on the list were: William Diaz; Bernardo Callejo; Jose Fernandez;
Ubaldo Fernandez; Carlos Soto; Luis Rodriguez; Roberto Rodriguez; Luis
Fuentez; Gilberto Martinez; Mario Castellanos, an accountant who used
Ramon to transport money for clients; Roberto Garcia Esquerdo and Oscar
Rodriguez, lawyers who used Ramon to transport currency on behalf of
clients; and Michael Saber, a Miami businessman for whom Ramon transported currency.

All but Saber were of Cuban ancestry, Ramon noted, and all but Saber,
Esquerdo, and Castellanos were narcotics traffickers.

Ramon also provided a list of Colombian traffickers for whom he had
transported or was currently transporting currency out of the country. The
Colombian clients included: Luis Carlos Molina, Gilberto Rodriguez, Maria
Restrepo, Jorge Gomez, Luca Gomez, Salvador Otero Ospina (who was be-
lieved to be associated with Wackenhut of Colombia), Gustavo Gavaria,
Pablo Correa, Orlando Franco, and Margarita Herrera de Umana.

The money that had been seized from his aircraft, Ramon claimed,
was being transported for Luis Carlos Molina, Gilberto Rodriguez, and
Margarita Herrera de Umana. He said that Molina was one of his biggest
customers, and that Molina came to him after Operation Greenback broke
up the Beno Ghitis laundering operation.

Ramon Rodriguez bragged that he had been laundering money since
1975, and that he had been earning about $1 million a year for the past five
or six years.

When handling large currency shipments, he said, his fee was one-half
of one percent, but when handling smaller amounts (typically for his
Cuban clients) the fee was about 10%.

Ramon said that he received currency in the Miami area at his office in
Coral Gables from designated Colombian couriers, who rotated through
the United States every three to four months. The delivery process included various security features. For example, if the driveway gate was

open, it was a signal that something was wrong and the courier was not to make his delivery. The money delivered by the couriers was not counted at his office, Ramon said. Only the bundles were counted; the actual counts were verified at the banks in Panama where he delivered the money.

Ramon admitted to picking up currency in San Francisco and at Teterboro Airport in New Jersey, as well as from Miami. In San Francisco, he said he used the Butler Aviation facilities and that currency deliveries were made by a courier named "Evon." He said he was making trips to San Francisco about every two to three weeks, transporting currency on behalf of Luis Carlos Molina.

Ramon said he had not picked up money from Teterboro Airport in New Jersey for about six weeks, since the arrest of a courier for Gilberto Rodriguez, his client there. The courier had narcotics and money in his possession at the time of his arrest, as well as telephone numbers for all the other couriers in the New York area. He added, though, that a Miami courier named "Gino" was reorganizing the New York operation.

Ramon Rodriguez claimed that when he flew currency to Panama, his aircraft would go to the military side of Panama City Airport—an arrangement made through contacts with Panamanian military authorities—and would be met by a Brink's armored car. The money would be transferred into the armored car and a guard would sign a receipt book for the amount which Ramon claimed to have delivered. Agent Sumrall had already recovered the Brink's receipt book from the plane, in Ramon's briefcase. A review of the entries in the book revealed receipts for $151 million in currency from November 1982 through the end of April 1983.

According to Ramon, all of the money that was picked up by the Brink's truck was transported to Banco Consolidado in Panama City, and then was deposited to other banks or picked up, depending upon which drug trafficker the money was being transported for. From that point it was disbursed as follows: A person named Jario Casteneda, who was an agent for Luis Carlos Molina, came to the bank and picked up those boxes which belonged to Molina. The currency belonging to Gilberto Rodriguez was taken to Interamericas Bank. Ramon said that Gilberto Rodriguez owned this bank. The currency owned by Margarita Herrera de Umana was deposited to an account at Banco Consolidado. Ramon said that before he acquired the lear jet he would transport currency to Panama for the Cuban drug traffickers in suitcases and would fly on commercial flights. He said that he usually used Air Panama.

Ramon Rodriguez explained that he formed Cambios Monetarios International on May 31, 1979 in Panama as a currency exchange house. He listed himself as the registered agent. The original address was at his former home in Coral Gables. Thereafter, he used a post office box in Panama. "I am Cambios Monetarios International," he said, adding that others on the corporate charter were merely figureheads. The corporate charter, he said, was drawn up by Rafael Fernandez Lara, a Panamanian attorney who was one of the two men on the aircraft earlier that day when it was stopped.

Ramon said he used profits from money laundering to purchase the Lear Jet and expensive cars. He said that his fee was separated from the currency before it was transported to Panama, as opposed to being paid after delivery. Cash in the amount of $6,000 was found in his briefcase—he said that represented the payment Cambios Monetarios International was to make to Consolidated Courier for the trip to Panama. He owned both companies but maintained separate books for each.

Ramon claimed he didn't like transporting large sums of currency; the risks were too great and the profit margins too slim. But he said he got into high volume transports because a personal friend asked him to. He identified the friend as Gabriel Jaime Acevedo, the attorney for Luis Carlos Molina.

Ramon Rodriguez said he had a partner in Panama named "Henry Ford," who made the arrangements for armored cars to be on hand when he arrived with a load of currency. He also identified his employees as Lydia, his wife and the person who took care of his personal finances; Oscar Mateu, his valet; Clement, his father; Rene, his wife's cousin and secretary for the office; and Yebra, a bodyguard who formerly worked for one of his clients.

Ramon bragged of knowing federal judges who "could be bought." He refused to name them, noting that this was a "bargaining point." He would provide details if the deal that he proposed was accepted by the government. He also said that he could provide information about how he structured offshore corporations, if and when the government agreed to a deal.

Ramon claimed to have spent well over $700,000 buying and customizing his Lear Jet, which was owned by Consolidated Courier and chartered to Cambios Monetarios International. He said he was trying to build up Consolidated and believed there to be great growth potential in moving currency.

The agents noted that there had been a $500,000 judgment entered against Cambios Monetarios. Ramon explained that he had allowed the suit and the judgment to be completed because he needed a tax write-off for that year.

Ramon said that he could not cover the loss if the $4.3 million taken from the plane was seized because he was not that liquid, and he would not jeopardize the financial security of his family.

Ramon Rodriguez was questioned about his knowledge of currency reporting requirements for secondary, or nonbank financial institutions.

He said he was aware of Treasury Department legal interpretations that individuals or organizations that regularly handled currency and other financial transactions were, in fact, nonbank financial institutions subject to BSA reporting requirements. He said that he had consulted with his friend and attorney, Joel Hirschhorn, but that Hirschhorn would not advise him on this issue. (Hirschhorn was the attorney who represented Roberto Botero and Beno Ghitis.) He said he then made his own decision not to file reports, since he believed he was not conducting transactions in the United States, but only in Panama.

Ramon was asked if he had records of his money laundering activities. He said that he maintained records, but they were destroyed once both parties were satisfied with the amounts. He then removed a group of monthly ledgers from his briefcase, covering the period from November 1982 through April 1983. The month of December was missing. A notation at the top of each ledger sheet contained the numbers 2 to 4, which Ramon said represented his gross percentages for transactions handled. He said he personally cleared about 0.5% of each transaction after expenses.

Ramon Rodriguez next removed from his briefcase a detailed receipt record for April, as well as what he claimed to be a courier's itemization for April. The receipts detailed all cash received by Cambios Monetarios International for April 1983. He said that he knew someday he was going to need the records, so he carried them along on trips.

Ramon was questioned about Gabriel Jaime Velez-Mejia, an individual who had accompanied him on his jet on a previous trip to Panama. He identified him as an employee of Luis Carlos Molina's company in Panama, which was named "Confirmesa."

Ramon Rodriguez signed a consent for agents to search his office in Coral Gables. He accompanied Greenback agents to his business office and volunteered that he had additional files on Cambios Monetarios International, which he offered to collect and turn over. The agents arrived at the office with Ramon at 6:30 p.m. He collected his records and turned over to Agent Sumrall a number of folders and loose papers which he said consisted of all the files he had on Cambios Monetarios International.

In response to inquiries about the size of his operation, Ramon said he deliberately kept it small, not allowing it to grow beyond his family and his bodyguard. He said he had reached the point where he was handling between $25 million and $30 million in cash a month, and was unable to handle any additional cash. To expand in order to handle greater sums, he observed, would render him vulnerable to detection. He said he had seen other organizations grow large and then falter because there were too many people who could inform on them. Ramon estimated that 20 other organizations were handling about as much money as his group. These admissions become more significant in light of preposterous claims made by Ramon four years later in testimony before a Senate committee about the size and scope of his money laundering operation.

Greenback agents searched Ramon's office. At one point, they found a locked door, which Ramon said led to a closet. He said the key was on a keyring in his briefcase, which had been left back at the Greenback office. While the search continued, Ramon was told that he was free to go at any time. He did so at 10:30 p.m. He was then picked up by his father.

Much earlier in the day, Ramon's father was questioned at his home shortly after large quantities of currency had been found on the aircraft. During the course of the questioning he turned over a completed Customs CMIR form. The form showed a transportation of $430,000 in currency by Ramon Ramon Rodriguez from Fort Lauderdale to Panama on May 4, 1983. He said that he intended to file this form later in the day at the Customs office at Miami International Airport. It should be noted that the amount claimed on the form was exactly 10 percent of the amount that Ramon claimed was on board the Lear Jet. This amount became significant when a review of the entries in the Brinks receipt book, as against the CMIRs that had been filed by Ramon dating back to November 1982, showed that the CMIR amounts claimed on each shipment were exactly 10% of the amount shown to have been received by Brinks in Panama.

The two Lara brothers and the two pilots were released at the Walker Cay hangar area shortly after they had been identified.

ALL BETS ARE OFF

When Ramon told agents that the key to the closet in his office was back at the Greenback office, one of the agents called the office and requested that the briefcase containing the key ring be brought to Cambios Monetarios. An agent arrived with Ramon's briefcase at about 11:00 p.m., 40 minutes after Ramon left. What the agents found in the closet changed everything, as far as any "understandings" with Ramon were concerned. Inside the closet were 62 pounds of cocaine, $14,000 in counterfeit money, and five weapons.

Prior to discovering the cocaine, Greenback agents and attorneys had been inclined to go along with Ramon's proposition that he go to work for them. They had a tentative arrangement with him when he left the office for home. But the cocaine changed their thinking; they now had to charge him. He was arrested at his home at 3:30 a.m., May 5, 1983.

When asked about the cocaine, Ramon said it belonged to his father, and that he had forgotten about it when queried by the agents. He claimed the counterfeit money had been recognized by him and removed from currency shipments before being moved to Panama. Ramon consented to a search of his residence, during which time an additional $5,000 in counterfeit money, six weapons, approximately $35,000 in unregistered bearer bonds, and $35,000 in legitimate currency were located.

Ramon had been using the bonds as collateral for loans arranged for his drug dealer clients. In each situation, the loan was actually made with the client's own funds.

Ramon Rodriguez was placed under arrest and transported to the Greenback office. He became quiet and reflective, and said he did not want to answer any further questions without an attorney present. On the following morning he was formally charged with possession of cocaine. Bail was set at $5 million.

Ramon Rodriguez retained a local Miami attorney. In the days and weeks that followed, attempts were made to get additional information from Ramon through his attorney, but it was fruitless. Ramon had decided to stonewall the government.

His bail was reduced to $2 million. He was able to post bond and was released. He was indicted on a number of charges that included possession of cocaine, failure to file CTRs and CMIRs, and racketeering.

In the days following Ramon's arrest, Greenback agents were very busy, writing up the information supplied by him and providing copies to other federal law enforcement agencies, including DEA.

They reviewed the list of his clients. They were aware of many of them. A few were not previously known. Among the Colombians, the name of Luis Carlos Molina had surfaced many times as a significant money launderer. He was a suspect in the Beno Ghitis case. Gilberto Rodriguez, Salvador Otero Ospina, Gustavo Gavaria, and Pablo Correa were all well known as either drug distributors or money launderers.

Most of the Cuban clients were recognized as active traffickers in the Miami area. One of them, Jose Fernandez, was a major importer and distributor of marijuana, and the subject of an active investigation that was stalled. The information supplied by Ramon and information contained in his records provided the ammunition needed to obtain court ordered electronic surveillance bugging devices. The electronic surveillance paid off and a major case was made against Fernandez.

Greenback agents poured over Ramon's records. Between what was there and what he told them, they realized that he was much more than a transporter of drug money. For the Cubans, he moved the currency out of the country and into accounts in Panamanian banks. The accounts were in the names of Panamanian corporations which were governed by strict secrecy laws. And once the money was in a Panamanian corporate account, Ramon moved it wherever his clients wanted it to go, including to U.S. bank accounts.

The money was moved so that it did not appear to be income to the client. One way was to draw up documents showing a loan from the Panamanian corporation to an American company by way of a wire transfer of funds from the Panamanian corporation's bank account to the bank account of the U.S. company in Florida. The loan documents made the transfer appear legitimate. In reality, the client's own money was being wired to his own U.S. company. In some cases, the records reflected cash payments to the Panamanian corporation in satisfaction of the loan. The payments included amounts for interest due.

Ramon also prepared his clients' tax returns. In some situations, he would deduct interest payments to the Panamanian corporation from the adjusted gross income of a client.

Another way to shield the client from tax liability was to prepare documents showing that wire transfers from the Panamanian corporate bank account were to pay for merchandise shipped by the American company.

Ramon Rodriguez performed similar services for his Colombian clients. He moved their money through a series of corporate accounts to banks throughout the world. In many instances he made investments for them. A favorite investment was certificates of deposit from New York banks.

Ramon Rodriguez was truly a full-service money launderer. His ability to take large amounts of currency directly out of the country completely circumvented the U.S. banking system and obliterated any semblance of a paper trail. His ability to utilize the Panamanian banking and corporate formation system enabled him to continue to mask the paper trail. His use of wire transfers to the accounts of companies in other countries enabled his clients to end up with thoroughly washed money that could not be traced to drug deals and that in many instances was not taxable.

Ramon's tax machinations were nothing short of miraculous. In one case, a drug dealer who was probably earning $1 million per year was portrayed as a carpenter with an adjusted gross income of $20,000 per year.

Greenback agents had a dilemma. Ramon's records contained a tremendous amount of information about drug dealers—information that was shared with other agencies. However, without cooperation and testimony by him, the information was of limited value in making drug cases. The dilemma was solved by turning his records over to IRS Examination Division for the pursuit of tax evasion cases.

Over the next few years a number of successful tax evasion cases were made against the clients and millions of dollars of taxes were assessed.

In 1984, the government filed a second indictment against Ramon Rodriguez, charging him with preparing false tax returns for one of his clients. It also charged him with fraud and obstruction of justice. After the government overcame all of the motions to suppress evidence obtained from the searches of his office and residence, the racketeering, drug trafficking, and BSA charges were ready for trial.

The trial began in November 1985. Ramon testified in his own defense, repudiating most of the information he originally had furnished to Greenback agents. His testimony completely exonerated himself of any involvement with drugs or money laundering. Ramon's father also testified in his defense.

The jury saw through the perjury of both men and found Ramon Rodriguez guilty of all the charges against him. In early 1986, he was sentenced to 35 years in prison. Later in 1986, he pled guilty to the tax fraud and obstruction charges and received an additional sentence of 16 years imprisonment, eight years of which were to run concurrent and eight years of which were to run consecutive to his 35-year sentence. His total sentence then became 43 years in prison.

"A CHANGE OF HEART"

After the sentences were imposed, Ramon Rodriguez contacted the U.S. Attorney's office in Miami several times, offering to cooperate. He offered to provide testimony against major drug figures, typically at times when they became the subject of media attention. At one point, for example, when there was considerable media coverage of the Medellin cocaine cartel, he claimed to have been chief financial officer for the cartel and offered information and testimony against the kingpins. He claimed to have moved billions of dollars of drug money to Panama for the cartel. At another point, when there was considerable press coverage of General Manuel Noriega's involvement in drugs and money laundering, Ramon claimed to have made payments to Noriega in connection with Colombian drug activities.

The U.S. Attorney's office rejected Ramon's offers of cooperation. Prosecutors felt he was not trustworthy, considering, among other things, that he had perjured himself during his own trial. What's more, they noted that he had never made any similar claims during the 10-hour period when he spoke to agents on May 4, 1983. He told the agents that he only used a small number of people in his operation, and that he had moved $151 million to Panama during the seven months prior to his arrest. All of his records were consistent with this amount. No records indicated that more was handled. The list of names given to the agents on May 4 also coincided with information in his money movement and tax records. Ramon never mentioned General Noriega or any of the top cartel members when he was arrested, even when he was attempting to convince Greenback agents of his importance, during the initial interview. The prosecutors believed that he realized, at the time of his arrest, that information that he furnished would have to be corroborated, and he knew that links to the big names could not be substantiated. They believed Ramon would perjure himself just to get out from under a 43-year prison sentence.

GULLIBLE SENATORS

Ramon Rodriguez started to serve his 43-year sentence in 1986. In 1987 he contacted the staff of Senator John F. Kerry, Democrat of Massachusetts, offering to provide information about General Noriega and the Colombian cocaine cartel. What happened over the course of the next year is an incredible story of how two U.S. Senators and the staff of a Senate subcommittee were hoodwinked by a con man par excellence.

In the course of being hoodwinked, however, some nasty things happened. The Reagan Administration's anti-drug efforts were ridiculed in the media; prosecutors and federal agents were held up to scorn for what was portrayed as the inept handling of the Ramon Rodriguez case. An individual named Felix Rodriguez was slandered in news stories after Ramon said he had provided him with couriers for drug money, Ramon Rodriguez became a media star and two Senators with political axes to grind—Kerry and Alphonse D'Amato—went for his preposterous claims hook, line and sinker.

What happened during those Senate hearings should put Americans on guard when they read or hear about sensational testimony before Congressional committees.

Senator John F. Kerry is the Chairman of the Senate Foreign Relations Subcommittee on Terrorism, Narcotics and International Operations. In May 1987, the panel commenced a series of public hearings on Drugs, Law Enforcement and Foreign Policy. Senator Kerry, a Democrat, had an ax to grind with the Reagan Administration's handling of the situation in Panama, with the events that transpired during the Iran-Contra affair, and with the "War on Drugs." When Ramon contacted Kerry's staff with word that he had big-time information regarding all three subjects, he had a receptive audience. Subcommittee staff members met with him in prison and he regaled them with stories of making payoffs to General Noriega on behalf of the Colombia drug cartel, of laundering billions of dollars for the cartel, and of supplying drug money to the Contras.

It is unclear how much the staffers did by way of checking out his stories. What is known, though, is that they did not check thoroughly enough because they were roundly deceived by Ramon.

In the spring and summer of 1987, Ramon testified on three occasions at closed door sessions before the subcommittee. Somehow, some of his testimony leaked to the press, and the *Miami Herald* on July 29 published a story headlined "Contras Got Drug Cash, Colombian Says." The gist of the story was that Ramon Rodriguez, appearing at a closed session of the Kerry subcommittee, testified that he passed drug money to Contra couriers selected by Felix I. Rodriguez, a CIA operative.

In February 1988, Ramon Rodriguez testified at public hearings before the Kerry subcommittee. By this time, Senator D'Amato, a Republican from New York, had become an enthusiastic member of Senator Kerry's crusade, and he joined the hearings at Kerry's invitation even though he was not a member of the subcommittee.

Like Kerry, D'Amato was upset over the administration's handling of General Noriega and believed the administration was not doing enough about the war on drugs. Both men were so blinded by their desire to embarrass the Reagan Administration on these issues that they lost sight of reality when Ramon Rodriguez testified. And they were not helped by the fact that the subcommittee staff did not do a thorough investigation to verify Ramon's testimony.

Ramon became an instant television star at his first public appearance before the subcommittee on February 11, 1988. He portrayed himself as the master money launderer. He testified that he was in the minor leagues of money laundering between 1976 and 1979 when he was moving tens of millions of dollars from the United States to Panama, but that he climbed into the big leagues in 1979 when he met with the major figures of the Colombian drug cartel. The names he dropped included Pablo Escobar, the Ochoa brothers, and Carlos Lehder.

During their initial meetings, Ramon said the Colombians asked him to move between $50 million and $100 million in cash a month. He said he realized that he would need Panamanian government support to bring these amounts into Panama. He claimed that the cartel members arranged for him to meet then Colonel Noriega, which was in late 1979. He said that he made three demands of Noriega and received approval for each: that complete security be provided for all the money once it reached Panama; that immediate credit be given for cash delivered to Panamanian banks; and that he gain access to Panamanian assets such as the use of diplomatic passports, diplomatic pouches, and information. In return, Noriega was to get about 1% of all monies delivered, Ramon claimed.

After the agreement was made, Ramon said he set up a vast money laundering organization consisting of Colombian nationals located in safe houses in Miami, New York, Chicago, San Francisco, Los Angeles, Dallas, Houston, and New Orleans. The number of safe houses varied over time from 10 to 20, he said. He testified that huge quantities of currency were shipped via air freight to Panama, mostly on Eastern Airlines. Toward the end of his career, in 1983, Ramon claimed he was laundering about $200 million a month out of the United States. He claimed to have had 40 to 50 aircrafts available to him, and that his organization had six helicopters and a fleet of used cars for couriers.

In response to a question about why he was personally flying $5.4 million to Panama at a time when he was moving hundreds of millions of dollars a month, Ramon said the money that he personally took to Panama was to make payoffs. He testified that he was earning $2 to 3 million a month for himself in 1983. Asked if he had ever told this to any government investigators prior to testifying before the subcommittee, he said he had told Customs Agent Arthur Sumrall and Justice Department attorney Charles Sathos (his recollection) on the day he was stopped with $5.4 million in cash on his plane.

Had the Senate staffers checked with the arresting agencies, agents, and the Justice Department, they would have found detailed information about Ramon's 10-hours of conversations with Sumrall on May 4, 1983, much of which contradicted what Ramon was telling them. Included with that information would have been a list of clients, none of whom included Escobar, the Ochoa brothers, Carlos Lehder, or Noriega. They would have also learned that two sets of records obtained from Ramon showed that he moved $151 million in currency to Panama between November 1982 and May 1983, and that there was nothing in his detailed records that indicated the ownership or control of 40 to 50 airplanes, a fleet of cars, or six helicopters.

Clearly, Ramon had the greatest incentive to divulge his ties to Noriega and the Medellin cartel when he was caught red handed and offering to cooperate. If Senator Kerry had his staff thoroughly examine the details of Ramon's arrest and conviction, he would have seen the contradictions and it may have caused him to pause before regaling the media with Ramon's preposterous claims. But, he didn't. The hearings went on. Ramon was only warming up, and so were Kerry and D'Amato.

Ramon testified that he was probably paying off General Noriega at the rate of $10 million a month; that the payments started in late 1979 and continued until he was arrested. Some of the payments were made on the instructions of the cartel. He estimated that he paid Noriega between $320 million and $350 million during the period, and that during his last two years of laundering he funnelled $2.5 billion a year through Panamanian banks. He claimed that in 1983 he controlled $11 billion of assets in the United States, and that he invested this money for the cartel in the United States. He said that all money that gets laundered returns to the United States. He said U.S. banks courted his business, and he claimed to have dealt with the likes of Citicorp, Bank of America, and First National Bank of Boston. He claimed to have personally placed $100 million to $200 million in CDs with banks in New York. He also claimed to own armored cars.

Ramon testified that he helped put together a private army of 2,000 individuals with $7 million supplied by the cartel to fight the M-19 Marxist-Leninist revolutionaries in Colombia. He said that he was brought in as an advisor on terrorism and training to fight terrorism. He said he helped procure weapons. He said that the cartel army defeated the M-19 and a deal was worked out so that the M-19 could begin to deal in narcotics. Ramon claimed that the M-19 representative who attended the meeting where this deal was worked out came wired as a human bomb. He said he counseled the cartel against entering into an agreement with M-19 because he could not accept dealing with communists.

Ramon testified that General Noriega used him to furnish law enforcement intelligence information to the cartel. The kind of information furnished, he said, included the identities of U.S. agents working abroad, radio frequencies, and Coast Guard and Navy schedules. He said that the request for information would come to him from the cartel, and he would relay it to an intermediary in Panama who would then pass the request on to Noriega. According to Ramon's account, the cartel had the name and identification of every DEA agent in Medellin in 1982.

Ramon claimed that one motivation for his testimony was a personal vendetta against General Noriega. He said that he believed Noriega set him up for his arrest in 1983; he stated that a telex was sent from Panama to the South Florida Vice Presidential Task Force identifying him as a major money launderer about two months prior to his arrest. He claimed, in his testimony, that no one knew who he was up until that time.

He was wrong, of course. He had been identified previously by Customs after filing a large number of CMIRs showing the transportation of significant amounts of currency from the United States to Panama. He had also been identified by IRS as a tax accountant who was arranging loans for his clients under suspicious circumstances.

Ramon Rodriguez claimed that Noriega tipped off U.S. agents because of his opposition to the agreement worked out between the cartel and M-19.

Ramon Rodriguez testified that all the documents and records associated with the transfer of the hundreds of millions of dollars to Panama, the investments made with this money, the paying of bills, etc., were kept in two places—one was in the cartel's office in Panama, the other had been in his computer in Miami. He claimed that his computer records were destroyed accidentally by the agents who arrested him. He claimed that the computer had a hard disk that should have been removed before the machine was moved, but that the agents were unaware of this and moved it like any other piece of furniture, thereby destroying the information in it.

This was a clever piece of testimony from a man who claimed an IQ of 150, and who wanted to cover his tracks in outlandish testimony before the committee. Greenback agents counter that Ramon did indeed have a computer, and that they brought in computer experts from the IRS to move it. The experts were unable to bring anything up on the computer. They found that much of the computer accessory equipment had never been removed from the boxes that it was shipped in. The agents speculate that the computer was new and that Ramon had never made an entry into it. They concede that it is possible that the disk drive may have been damaged in shipment. But if it was, and if there had been entries made, they feel very strongly that the information would not have differed from that detailed in the thousands of records that were seized. These records contained detailed receipts, information on investments made and tax returns on hundreds of clients. The records detailed the shipment of $151 million in currency to Panama between November 1982 and May 1983, and no more than that. The records did not contain the names of any of the big-time cartel leaders or of Manuel Noriega.

The fact that Senators Kerry and D'Amato were completely taken up with Ramon Rodriguez' testimony can be seen from an exchange of remarks made by them during the hearing.

Senator Kerry: "Let us add one thing to that. Our staff has checked out a great number of the things you have said and obviously you have corroborated other witnesses significantly, and they have corroborated you both by having seen you in Panama, knowing that you were engaged in this and knowing of the details."

"Also, you have given us privately an extraordinary number of names, actual corporations and so forth which have checked out."

"So, this committee obviously has been comfortable in putting you on, but I want the public to understand that I think after the recess we should revisit it."

Mr. Rodriguez: "Sure."

Senator Kerry: "Senator D'Amato."

Senator D'Amato: "Mr. Chairman, for a long time I have maintained that people just really do not have simply any idea of the scope and the magnitude of the dollars involved here, and I think Mr. Rodriguez begins to put this in perspective."

"He was the man who set up this money laundering enterprise which the cartel turned to. Even in spite of his youth at the time, it is obvious from his testimony one can see that this is a man who has extraordinary ability in this area . . ."

How completely Kerry and D'Amato were hornswoggled by Ramon Rodriguez is illustrated further by these quotes from the hearing record of February 11, 1988.

Senator D'Amato: "You go to the man who beat the system to find out how to shore up the system. It's one of the things I suggested with Senator Kerry. I may be criticized for saying this, but it seems to me that you've been in prison a number of years now already, but it's rather incredible that there has not been an effort made by our law enforcement people, recognizing your knowledge of the system, et cetera, to attempt to utilize you, not in terms of exposing people because the safe houses have been changed, the corporations have been changed, but as it relates to dealing with this whole system, and at least to get your knowledge and your expertise in an attempt to utilize them."

"And notwithstanding that you may have been interviewed on several occasions, it's just that kind of lack of commitment that just gets this Senator, and I think some others like Senator Kerry and Senator [Dennis] DeConcini, so riled up when we hear about this war on drugs."

"It is absolutely—if it weren't so serious, it would be laughable. I don't have words sufficient to express to you the contempt that I have for those who should know better, who really carry this on and try to beguile the Congress and the people, et cetera, about a meaningful effort and a meaningful war."

"Here you have the person who ran the money operation for the cartel for years, who hasn't had - has not been utilized in terms of the information. Were it not for Senator Kerry and his committee, et cetera, who has brought this to the fore, you would still be languishing there and we would be without your information."

"I don't mean to put a medal on you. My gosh, we should be able to draw on your experience."

Mr. Rodriguez: "I would like to be fair at all times, because I find that life works out for me better that way. In all fairness, the things that we're discussing today, after having some corroboration and so forth, in 1983 sounded pretty foolish to these people, because it put them in the position that they had to admit that they were totally out of control and totally foolish."

Senator Kerry: "The fact is that you told them in 1983. They didn't want to listen; isn't that accurate?"

Mr. Rodriguez: "Precisely."

Senator Kerry: "Because they made their own judgments."

Mr. Rodriguez: "Well, like I said, they would have to - it's a pretty mind-boggling thing to hear, and it's even more mind-boggling that it was getting by them, and it's still getting by them."

Senator Kerry: "Well, it's sure coming out now. And I think there's a lot more of it to come out. . ."

These appalling exchanges and Ramon Rodriguez' testimony received wide media attention. The impression widely portrayed to the American public was of inept and bumbling investigators and a badly flawed Executive Branch effort in the war on drugs. Nothing could have been further from the truth! Two U.S. Senators, blinded by their own political agendas and very sloppy staff work, were being hoodwinked by a convicted felon, a perjurer, and a man totally without credibility. It was bad enough that they were conned, but it was even worse that they used this con man to launch a vicious attack against competent law enforcement officials.

The Operation Greenback agents and attorneys knew exactly what they had when they arrested Ramon Rodriguez. They realized that they had a significant money launderer whose admissions indicated, and whose records confirmed, that he had laundered $151 million in six months. He was of a stature comparable to Beno Ghitis, whose operation had laundered $242 million in eight months. They realized that he was working for important drug dealers, a number of whom they knew when he provided them with a list of names of his clients. In fact, they recognized one of his clients, Luis Carlos Molina, as the individual who had supplied much of the currency Beno Ghitis laundered. The agents knew Molina was an important launderer for Colombian cocaine kingpins. They were willing to make a deal with Ramon, until they caught him lying about 62 pounds of cocaine that was hidden away in the closet of his office.

Greenback agents and attorneys relied on their instincts and experience in deciding not to proceed with a deal. There is a cardinal rule of good law enforcement that says, don't trust a potential cooperating defendant witness when you catch him in a lie. There was no hesitation when the cocaine was found. Everyone was in agreement. The deal was off.

Ramon Rodriguez could have chosen to cooperate any time after his arrest. He chose not to. His repeated perjury during his own trial and the fact that he induced other witnesses to perjure themselves confirmed that the decision to cancel the deal was the correct one.

Senators Kerry and D'Amato and the staff of the subcommittee were more interested in creating sensational headlines to further their own political causes than in probing why Greenback did not accept Ramon's offer of a deal.

As an aside, it should be noted that all of the major Colombian cocaine traffickers named by Ramon at the subcommittee hearings were indicted by the government in cases made without any assistance from him. Likewise, General Noriega was indicted without any assistance from him.

Ramon Rodriguez again testified in an open hearing before Senator Kerry's subcommittee on April 6, 1988, providing more of the same information. He repeated that by 1983 he was laundering more than $2 billion a year and that he controlled assets of $11 billion. During this testimony, he acknowledged that he had occasionally bought $200 million or $300 million CDs, but there were some new twists. By now, Ramon had become an expert on many topics, and he drew charts for the subcommittee on such topics as the flow of cocaine from the raw leaf to the finished product, the drug industry hierarchy and distribution of profits, and the flow of narco-dollars.

Senators Kerry and D'Amato questioned Ramon on each of these topics and listened in rapt attention as the self-proclaimed expert lectured. Along the way, he rolled out some new information. He claimed to have bribed military and elected officials in many countries, including Mexico, Guatemala, Honduras, Nicaragua, Costa Rica, the Bahamas, Jamaica, and the Cayman Islands. The bribes were supposedly made on behalf of the cartel to keep cocaine flowing.

The Senators used the hearing to again castigate U.S. enforcement agencies. Senator Kerry lamented the fact that no one from DEA or from Treasury had come to debrief Ramon, especially since the committee had found "significant corroboration" for many parts of his testimony. Ramon's advice was sought on how the government could cope with the money laundering problem, and the suggestion was made that the government should seek his advice.

Both Senators were highly critical of the Justice Department for not conducting a grand jury investigation of the information that had been supplied by Ramon. They expressed the hope that the hearings had lit a few fires under Justice and Treasury to undertake a careful, comprehensive review of all the facts provided by Ramon. Senator D'Amato even went so far as to suggest that perhaps the reason government officials had not debriefed Ramon was that there was a reluctance to offer him some form of gratitude for his cooperation in terms of a reduction of sentence. Senator D'Amato had finally taken Ramon's bait.

The bait was a grossly exaggerated account of his own activities with drugs and money laundering and the catch was someone like Senator D'Amato to go to bat for him for reduction of his 43-year sentence.

There is a saying that "truth will out in the end." After the truth had been obscured for some time with regard to Ramon Rodriguez, some of it started to come out in another series of hearings before the subcommittee between July 11 and July 14, 1988. That it did was no thanks to Senator Kerry. Another member of the subcommittee, Senator Mitch McConnell, a Republican from Kentucky, was upset at what he believed to be the partisan nature of the hearings. He had not been present at prior public testimony of Ramon Rodriguez. His staff had heard from enforcement sources in Treasury and Justice that Ramon was totally unreliable. Senator McConnell had also been approached by Felix Rodriguez, who complained that Senator Kerry's staff was keeping him from providing testimony that contradicted Ramon.

Felix Rodriguez had been accused by Ramon of receiving $10 million of drug proceeds for use by the Contras. Though the testimony was given during a closed door session of the panel, it had somehow leaked to the media in June 1987. As soon as Felix Rodriguez heard about a story in the *Miami Herald* which accused him of supplying couriers to pick up drug money from Ramon, he contacted Senator Kerry's staff to deny it and to offer to testify publicly or privately to refute the claims. Felix Rodriguez testified at a closed session of the subcommittee on August 6, 1987, indicating that Ramon had lied in alleging wrongdoing by him. Prior to the hearing, Felix Rodriguez said that he wanted his testimony to be in an open session, but Jack Blum from Senator Kerry's staff insisted the hearing be closed. After the closed session hearing, Felix Rodriguez kept pressing for his testimony to be given in public session. It was clear that Senator Kerry's staff was giving him the run around. Apparently they did not want their star witness to be besmirched.

Senator McConnell was instrumental in getting Felix Rodriguez to testify publicly in the July session. However, before he did, the subcommittee took testimony from Richard D. Gregorie, Chief Assistant U.S. Attorney for the Southern District of Florida.

Dick Gregorie was a highly competent and aggressive prosecutor. He had been prosecuting cases for the Justice Department for 16 years in places like New Jersey, Boston, Connecticut, and Rhode Island. He came to the U.S. Attorney's office in Miami in 1982 as the Chief of the Narcotics Section. After three years he became the Chief of the Criminal Division. He was promoted to Chief Assistant U.S. Attorney in 1987.

Gregorie testified at some length under questioning from Senator Kerry about problems in prosecuting international drug traffickers. He complained about not getting enough help from the State Department in extraditing major drug figures from foreign countries, and he pointed to the inability of the United States to extradite Colombian cocaine cartel member Jorge Ochoa from Spain in 1984. Gregorie had recommended that the government do away with multiple entry visas because they were being abused by drug traffickers.

Gregorie also testified about problems with other government agencies in seeking the indictment of General Manuel Noriega. Gregorie was the prosecutor who developed the case against Noriega.

When Senator Kerry had finished his questioning, Senator McConnell took over. He asked several questions about his previous testimony. Then, out of the blue, Senator McConnell asked Gregorie if he was familiar with Ramon Milian Rodriguez. The Senator knew that Gregorie had supervised the prosecution of Ramon Rodriguez in 1983 when he was Chief of the Narcotics Section. The following exchange is quoted directly from the hearing record.

Senator McConnell: "Is he a credible witness in your opinion?"

Mr. Gregorie: "I would have to say 'No.'" If you asked me would I use him as a witness in any case that I had, as an ethical prosecutor I couldn't put him on the witness stand because I don't believe him."

Senator Kerry: "You don't believe all he says or you don't believe some things he says?"

Mr. Gregorie: "I don't believe a lot of what he says."

"I think he is telling you about 30%-40% of the truth, and the other—the rest of it is things he has made up."

"You have to remember that we arrested him in 1983 with $5 million being flown to Panama. He then began to talk to us because he didn't want to lose his $5 million and he didn't want to go to jail. The things he is saying now he never told the agents in their debriefing. And as time went on and the prosecution continued, whatever became headline news he would come in and say 'I can tell you about that.'"

"We have looked at what he said. We've carefully analyzed it. The IRS has gone through it. The DEA has gone through it and the IRS agent, who is as competent an investigator as I know, say that some of what he now is telling us is physically impossible. He couldn't have laundered the kinds of money in the ways in which he said and been in all the places he says he was in."

"The man has a 150 IQ. He's a brilliant guy, but he has used it in the wrong ways. So, some of what he is saying is truthful, but a majority of what he says I could not believe, and I could not as an ethical prosecutor put him on the witness stand."

Senator McConnell: "Another issue we have been sort of kicking around this morning is not directly within your area of jurisdiction, but I am curious if you have an opinion about whether or not. . ."

Senator Kerry: "Could I just interrupt one second?"

Senator McConnell: "Yes."

Senator Kerry: "Let me come back to that, Dick, because we have talked through our offices about Ramon Rodriguez, et cetera. We have tried to be very careful here. I want to reiterate that before the committee."

"One of the reasons that we have taken so long with respect to any testimony of his in certain parts is that we don't have corroboration of it. And I've tried to be very careful about—you know, that's why I asked you is there some truthfulness because we were able to corroborate through four or five sources the Noriega portions, the connections, the money laundering, the fundamentals of his association to which he testified publicly. Those things which we have questioned that we are not yet thoroughly convinced about, we have also reserved judgment on and kept his testimony from happening. So, I just want people to understand that the committee has been very careful about only putting publicly those portions that we think we can corroborate."

Senator McConnell: "Let me just say I think the committee has not been careful at all with Ramon Milian Rodriguez. This committee has made a television star out of Ramon Milian Rodriguez. And we have yet another person today, in addition to the person who was engaged directly in the prosecution of this convict, who say that he is without credibility. So, with all due respect to you, Mr. Chairman, I don't think we have been careful about Ramon Milian Rodriguez at all."

Senator Kerry: "Well, let's examine that carefully, Senator, because I think it's really important."

Senator McConnell: "It certainly is."

Senator Kerry: "What the U.S. attorney has said is that 35, 40 percent, whatever—you have said that there is credibility to his being a money launderer. Correct? He is. Is that accurate?"

Mr. Gregorie: "Well, we convicted him, Senator, of being a money launderer. He is serving 40+ years in jail as a result of our convictions. So, there is no question he was a money launderer."

Senator Kerry: "So, there's no question about it. Right?"

Mr. Gregorie: "That's correct."

Senator Kerry: "No question about his contacts with Noriega. Correct?"

Mr. Gregorie: "I do have questions about that. There is no question he was laundering money through Panama, that he was bringing huge amounts of money there. As to who his contact was to approve it, we know that he had approval at the airport to put the money on a Brinks truck, that there was a military officer there who assisted him in doing it. Beyond that, I can't say that I know for sure what his contacts were."

After this exchange, Senator Kerry tried to show that Ramon Rodriguez had some credibility because a person named Luis Rodriguez had been indicted based on information that Ramon provided at the time of his arrest. Dick Gregorie disagreed and tried to point out that numerous people had been indicted based on Ramon's records which indicated that he was laundering money for them. The questioning led to the following exchange.

Senator Kerry: "So, he certainly got some credibility."

Mr. Gregorie: "No. He was a money launderer whose records we seized, and following up on those records, we were able to indict individuals. As to his credibility, Senator, I have to disagree with you, and I do that most respectfully."

Senator McConnell then introduced into the record an affidavit prepared by Steve Schlessinger, the Assistant U.S. Attorney who had prosecuted Ramon Rodriguez. He summarized Schlessinger's affidavit by saying ". . . whose view is that this fellow [Ramon Rodriguez] is not in any way reliable."

Two days later, on July 14, 1988, Felix Rodriguez finally got his chance to testify before the subcommittee in public. Felix Rodriguez was a Cuban who had dedicated his life to fighting communism. He served in the U.S. Army in Vietnam. He had risked his life fighting against Fidel Castro. At the time of the hearing he described his situation as being involved in antiguerrilla operations in Central America. He had a great deal of experience on the use of helicopters to transport troops in combat. He was a no nonsense, straightforward individual who had a reputation for personal integrity. He had previously testified before Senate and House committees looking into the Iran Contra affair. He had testified without an attorney and had never invoked the Fifth Amendment. He appeared without an attorney before Senator Kerry's subcommittee.

Senator McConnell started the questioning of Felix Rodriguez, which covered several areas. He related an account of the only time in his life that he ever met Ramon Rodriguez, in January 1985. He completely denied that he had furnished couriers who picked up drug money from Ramon Rodriguez to be used by the Contras. He denied that he had ever met with General Manuel Noriega.

Felix Rodriguez' account of his only meeting with Ramon Rodriguez gives some further insights into the character and reliability of Ramon and further portrays him as a cunning schemer. According to Felix, Ramon sought him out. The meeting was arranged by a friend of Felix' who was a former law enforcement officer. The friend told Felix that Ramon had knowledge of facts which incriminated the Sandinista government in a proposed drug money laundering operation to be established in Panama. The friend further stated that Ramon wanted to pass this information on to someone in authority to negotiate a deal as he was indicted and free on bond.

Felix said he reluctantly agreed to a meeting and that it took place in his friend's office on January 18, 1985. Ramon repeated the information that had previously been furnished by Felix' friend. In addition, he claimed that his organization had passed $600 million to General Manuel Noriega. Ramon boasted that after his arrest he had made one telephone call to his organization and that 60 couriers left the United States within 24 hours. He said that he would compromise the Sandinista government but would never give up on members of the drug cartel. Ramon claimed that he had defused an order for his assassination because he controlled over $300 million in Florida real estate belonging to the cartel—investments that would be lost if he were killed. He said that the cartel had become convinced that he would not turn them in. Ramon said that he was indicted on a technicality and foresaw a sentence of about five years. He said that he didn't want to serve time because of his son.

Felix Rodriguez testified that he turned over the information provided to both the FBI and the CIA. (In fact, the subcommittee heard testimony in closed session in 1987 that corroborated the fact that Felix Rodriguez had provided details of his meeting to the FBI on January 20, 1985.)

Felix Rodriguez' testimony led to a series of exchanges between him, Senator McConnell, and Senator Kerry which, perhaps, best dispose of the issue of Ramon's credibility.

> **Senator McConnell:** "I just mean to complete him before we move on. Is there anything else you have to say about Ramon Milian Rodriguez in terms of your —"

Felix Rodriguez: "Yes, sir. I think he's a liar, and I strongly believe that this committee should pursue who is telling the truth in here. I passed along an affidavit in a letter that I sent to Senator Kerry not too long ago when I asked to testify here openly."

Senator McConnell: "On the issue of Ramon Milian Rodriguez and whether he is a liar, Mr. Rodriguez, you might be interested to know that earlier this week an assistant prosecutor named Gregorie testified before this committee and said that Rodriguez was—that Ramon Rodriguez was completely without credibility."

Senator Kerry: "No, no, no. Now let us be fair. I really want to be fair here."

Senator McConnell: "Well, why don't we just let the record speak for itself? I will not interpret."

Senator Kerry: "But he did not say 'completely.' He said he as a prosecutor would not use him."

Senator McConnell: "I will not interpret what Mr. Gregorie said, Senator Kerry. Just let the record speak for itself."

Senator Kerry: "I am happier that way."

Senator McConnell: "I have an affidavit by the man who prosecuted the Ramon Rodriguez case, a man named Stephen Schlessinger, which I would like to ask be included in its entirety."

"And at this point I would like to read into the record for the benefit of those who remain at this late hour, this was an affidavit of Stephen Schlessinger, who prosecuted the defendant, Ramon Milian Rodriguez. The affidavit is dated June 8, 1988. And this is what Mr. Schlessinger, who prosecuted that case, had to say about Ramon, beginning on page 7. This is among many other things."

"This is an 8 1/2-page memorandum with 18 paragraphs, all devoted to the credibility of Ramon Rodriguez."

"He says, on page 7, paragraph 15:

Any claims Ramon Rodriguez has made that his money smuggling activities were far more extensive than that indicated in his records is also belied by the evidence obtained in the investigation which has led to his conviction. Thus, the evidence reveals that Ramon Rodriguez operated a modest organization in which he played the paramount role. Ramon Rodriguez himself flew to various cities where he personally collected the cash destined for Panama. Likewise, he issued the necessary paperwork and maintained the necessary books and records. Such activity occupied the vast majority of Ramon Rodriguez' time and effort. In order to have transported significantly greater amounts of cash, Ramon Rodriguez would have had to have employed numerous additional persons and, of necessity, he would have needed to greatly expand his capacity to pick up, store, and transport cash. There is no evidence that he did so.

"Paragraph 16:

Likewise, no documentary or tangible evidence was found supporting such claims. Money laundering is an activity which invariable generates considerable paperwork. Obviously, records of the delivery and disposition of huge amounts of cash much [sic] be maintained. Extensive searches were conducted of Ramon Rodriguez' various business and personal premises by Federal agents following his interception on the morning of May 4, 1983.

His person, automobile, airport office, business office, personal residence and warehouse he leased were all searched. No records revealing money-laundering activities magnitudes greater than that for which Ramon Rodriguez was convicted were discovered at any of these sites. Likewise, no addresses, telephone numbers, letters, or other bits of communication between Ramon Rodriguez and any numbers of the Medellin cartel, General Noriega, or persons involved with Contra funding were discovered.

For the reasons set forth above, Ramon Rodriguez is not regarded by this office as a credible witness, and this office has declined to base any court proceedings upon his testimony.

Senator McConnell: "Suffice it to say that there is substantial evidence in addition to your statement, Mr. Rodriguez, that Ramon Rodriguez is completely without credibility."

Felix Rodriguez: "I know that, sir."

Senator McConnell: "Unfortunately, though, he has become something of a television star. We have seen him on network television making wild and unsubstantiated claims about high-ranking officials in this country, and the man is obviously a total liar, and it is a very frustrating experience for those against whom those claims are made, such as yourself."

Felix Rodriguez: "Yes, sir."

Senator McConnell: "The direct quote from Dick Gregorie, the U.S. attorney who testified before this committee two days ago, was this: 'As an ethical prosecutor, I could not put Ramon Milian Rodriguez on the witness stand.'"

Senator Kerry: "That is what I said. I thought we were going to let the record speak for itself."

Senator McConnell: "I just thought I would quote from the record, since we have it.

The Senator then proceeded to read additional excerpts from the memorandum in which Schlessinger laid waste to Ramon Rodriguez' credibility.

"In other words," McConnell said in a parting shot at Kerry, "Everybody, with the possible exception of the chairman, knows that Ramon Rodriguez is devoid of credibility."

Prior to his public testimony, Felix Rodriguez submitted his prepared statement in the form of an affidavit to the subcommittee. He ended his affidavit with the following statement: "It is obvious to me, as it should be to Senator Kerry and members of his subcommittee, that either Ramon Milian Rodriguez, a convicted felon whose credibility was challenged by U.S. Attorney Leon Kellner, who prosecuted him, is lying or I am lying and I urge the subcommittee to find out who is telling the truth and to prosecute the other one for perjury to the full extent of the law. I feel at this time, and for a long time before this, there is enough evidence to reach a conclusion that will serve the cause of truth and not Senator Kerry's political needs."

The fact is that Senator Kerry has never recommended that Ramon Rodriguez be charged for lying to Congress. In fact, he appears to be incarcerated in the witness protection program. He was placed in there by the Justice Department at the request of Senator Kerry and over the objections of several key Justice officials.

There are two other interesting pieces of information about Ramon Rodriguez. In 1987, his father was caught in the middle of a 600 kilo cocaine shipment from Colombia. He was arrested, indicted, and convicted and is now serving a 12-year sentence in a federal prison. The other item is that in November 1990, Ramon Rodriguez filed a civil suit against 20 people alleging that his civil rights were violated because he was denied the right to a fair trial. He alleges damages in the amount of $150 million. Included among the defendants are some of the agents and prosecutors who questioned him on May 4, 1983. Ramon Rodriguez is acting as his own attorney in this suit.

CHAPTER 5

OPERATION POLAR CAP

Operation Polar Cap was the code name given the largest single money laundering operation ever broken up by the United States government. The operation is credited with laundering $1.2 billion in currency taken in by the Colombian cocaine cartel in slightly over two years.

In one phase of Polar Cap, currency from cocaine sales in New York, Houston, and Los Angeles was "washed" through several gold and jewelry businesses into bank accounts in Los Angeles. Funds were then transferred from the Los Angeles accounts to banks in New York and moved to cartel accounts in banks in Panama and Montevideo, Uruguay. The transfers of money to the New York and foreign accounts appeared to be for legitimate purchases and sales of gold by refiners, brokers, and jewelers. Cartel members referred to the Los Angeles, New York, and Houston phase of the operation as "La Mina."

Polar Cap was a classic example of greed and tunnel vision on the part of bankers. Only one bank out of 10 tipped the government to the fact that suspicious transactions involving huge quantities of currency were being conducted by businesses not prone to generating that much cash. Polar Cap also illustrated how businesses could be used to make drug money appear as the proceeds of legitimate business activity. The investigation exposed weaknesses in the system designed by law to provide the government with information about unusual currency transactions so that this activity could be analyzed and investigated. It also exposed weaknesses in the effectiveness of the vaunted federal judicial system. And, perhaps more than anything, it demonstrated the gargantuan amounts of currency that were being realized by Colombian wholesalers from U.S. cocaine sales.

Polar Cap was set against the backdrop of explosive cocaine use among Americans. This surge was precipitated by the advent of crack cocaine, a lower cost derivative that effectively introduced the drug to all classes of society. Crack, which is highly addictive, became particularly popular among young people and inner city populations.

Crack first appeared in Miami and Los Angeles as early as 1983. By 1985, it had spread to inner-city areas in Chicago, New York, Detroit, and Houston. By 1986, it was a national problem— use of crack was spreading like wildfire. The demand for crack required the smuggling of much larger quantities of cocaine into the United States, and hence, the need to launder greater amounts of money.

Simultaneous with the crack explosion, members of the Colombian cocaine cartel were seeking new ways to launder the proceeds of their trade. The era of huge currency deposits by people with shopping bags full of cash had long since passed. Smurfing had been successful for a while, but it had substantial drawbacks. Members of the cartel continued to smuggle large quantities of currency directly out of the United States, but there were physical limitations on how many dollars could be transported and on how much could be absorbed by destination countries. Panama, one of the prime countries, was coming under increased scrutiny by U.S. enforcement agencies and by the Congress.

Enforcement activity in Miami in the early 1980s forced various Colombian cocaine organizations to disperse their activities to other cities. Miami remained an important hub for deal-making, but by 1986, cities like New York, Los Angeles, Houston, and Atlanta had become significant distribution and money laundering centers for many of the cartel organizations.

THE EARLY STAGES—PLANNING AND RECRUITING

It was against this backdrop that representatives of the Medellin cocaine cartel, in early 1986, approached a Uruguayan businessman named Raul Vivas. The Colombians were seeking new outlets to launder dollars from cocaine sales in Los Angeles and other U.S. cities, and approached Vivas through two of his business associates, Celio Merkin and Ricardo Jadue, who had already laundered cash for the cartel. The cartel representatives asked Vivas to establish an organization that could move up to $500 million a year in drug profits from the United States to foreign banks accessible to cartel leaders. His cut would be 5% of all money moved.

Raul Vivas was an Argentinean by birth, who was then living in Montevideo. He had been a successful jewelry and precious metals dealer and had operated a gold refinery. Vivas had traveled extensively throughout the United States and South America and was quite adept at handling foreign currencies. Perhaps most importantly, Vivas had all the markings of a respectable businessman. He was in his early forties, thin, well-dressed and wore glasses.

Merkin and Jadue estimated that Vivas' overhead on the money laundering operation would probably eat up about 3.5% to 4% of the 5% he would be paid; the remainder represented his profit. Thus, by laundering $500 million a year, Vivas could generate a profit of between $5 million and $7.5 million. Even if he only handled $100 million, his profit potential would be in the range of $1 million to $1.5 million a year. Vivas decided to pursue the proposal.

Since he had been dealing in gold for a number of years, Vivas decided to use gold purchases as his front for moving currency on behalf of the cartel. To carry out the plan, he and three associates—Jorge Masihy, Mauricio Mezia, and Pedro Martinez—formed a holding company in Montevideo, Uruguay, known as Letra, S.A., through which they purchased a money exchange business known as Cambio Italia. Ostensibly, the business was a legitimate currency exchange. In reality, it was opened for the purpose of laundering money. They hired Ruben Priscolin, an acquaintance of Vivas, to run Cambio Italia in Montevideo. Another acquaintance of Vivas, Sergio Hochman, who had done some money laundering in the Los Angeles area, was hired to assist the operation in the United States.

In March 1986, Raul Vivas traveled to Los Angeles and set up a money laundering operation, with an office in the heart of the Los Angeles jewelry district. He hired two individuals from Montevideo to help him—Tomas Iglesias and Claudio Fernandez. Iglesias had prior experience as a launderer and knew some Colombian cartel representatives. The office, which operated under the name of R.A.O.F., Inc., was used to count and bundle drug money delivered by customers and to refine gold purchased with drug money.

The R.A.O.F. office was located in a commercial building known as the West Coast Jewelry Center. The building was part of the Los Angeles jewelry district. Some 2,000 jewelry businesses are located in a two-block area on South Hill Street, South Broadway, and West Fifth Street. These businesses are located in suites of large office buildings and in storefronts along the street. A significant portion of the businesses are run by members of an Armenian immigrant community who manufacture gold chains and ornamental jewelry both for wholesale distribution and retail sale. A number of these businesses handled currency from wholesale and retail sales.

The original Vivas money laundering operation ran in the following way. Vivas and Iglesias carried pagers. They would receive telephone messages from customers most of whom were Colombian. The customers would leave a telephone number, usually at a pay phone. Either Vivas or Iglesias would return the call and a meeting would be arranged. At the meeting, the Colombians would turn over a quantity of currency from drug sales. The amounts in those days ranged between $20,000 and $300,000. Vivas or Iglesias would then bring the currency to the R.A.O.F. office, where it would be counted and bundled.

Vivas then used the money to buy scrap gold, gold bars, or gold shot from one of several dealers in the jewelry market area as part of an elaborate scheme to cover up the laundering activity. His earliest purchases were made from Astro Jewelers and S&K Sales. Both businesses were owned by Armenian immigrants. He paid a premium for the gold over market price as a reward for the dealers moving currency through their business bank accounts. He then needed to sell the gold quickly so he could get the money to the Medellin cartel clients. However, it wouldn't make any business or economic sense for a small jewelry business in Los Angeles to be selling large quantities of gold for a price equal to or lower than he could buy it for. A wholesale gold dealer would have quickly sensed that there was something wrong with these sales. Vivas had a way to get around the problem. He took steps to make the gold appear to have been purchased in South America.

South American gold invariably was of lower quality than that traded in the United States Vivas melted the gold he bought and added silver to approximate the quality of typical South American gold. In addition, Letra, S.A. shipped lead-plated gold bars to R.A.O.F. from Montevideo. The shipments were marked as gold and were documented to show that Letra was selling gold to R.A.O.F. Customs documentation for these shipments was shown to buyers of the gold that Vivas had diluted with silver as proof that it had been bought in South America. Vivas then shipped the silver-diluted gold to an associate, Jorge Gallina, in New York. Gallina regularly sold the gold to one of two banks and to a large gold dealer in New York. Gallina instructed the buyers to credit the purchase price to an account set up in the name of Letra, S.A. Within 24 hours after a payment had been credited in this manner, fax instructions would arrive from Cambio Italia in Montevideo, acting on behalf of Letra, to wire transfer the funds to one of several bank accounts in either Panama or Montevideo. When the funds arrived in these accounts, they were transferred to cartel representatives.

The laundering cycle was now complete. Currency from drug sales in Los Angeles moved into the banking system in payment for purchases of gold. The gold was then made to appear as if it had been bought in South America. It was sold in New York and the proceeds ended up in the hands of Medellin cartel members. The funds received by the cartel appeared to be clean money. The dirty currency from cocaine sales had been cleansed by what appeared to be a series of legitimate gold transactions to make it appear to be the fruits of legitimate commercial business. Along the way, Vivas siphoned off 5% of the original amount of currency received as his cut of this laundering activity.

Cambio Italia played an important role in the operation. They were the intermediaries between cartel representatives in Colombia and the Vivas operation in Los Angeles. On a daily basis, information was received from R.A.O.F. on the exact count of each package of currency received. This information was relayed to cartel representatives. Gold plated lead bars were regularly shipped to R.A.O.F. by Cambio Italia. The currency exchange provided wire transfer instructions to the gold buyers in New York to move funds credited to Letra to specific accounts in Panama and Uruguay. Finally, the funds were moved to accounts controlled by the Medellin cartel.

In late April 1986, Raul Vivas sent for Sergio Hochman. Hochman arrived in Los Angeles and initially went to work as a money counter at the R.A.O.F. office at 610 South Broadway. He stayed at Vivas' residence in a Los Angeles suburb. Within a few months, Hochman was also assisting in currency pickups from Colombians. Hochman was initially paid $1,200 per month plus living expenses. Within a few months, his pay went up to $1,600 per month.

GROWING PAINS

By September 1988, Raul Vivas was taking in more money than could be handled by the two jewelers he was using. Furthermore, the quantity of gold being bought was too great for R.A.O.F. facilities to process in its office space. Complicating matters, the Medellin cartel wanted Vivas to take over laundering operations in New York and Houston—operations which held the potential for vast sums of additional currency.

Vivas took a number of steps to cope with these growing pains. First, he recruited a third jewelry firm to sell gold for currency. The firm, known as Ropex Corporation, was owned by Wanis Koyomejian, also known as Joseph Koyomejian. Koyomejian also operated a business known as JSK

Bullion. Both Ropex and JSK Bullion operated in adjoining suites in the same building at 550 South Hill Street in the Los Angeles jewelry district. A third business run by Koyomejian, Rafco Refining, was located on another floor of the same building. Koyomejian and his firms would become major players in Polar Cap.

To solve his gold problem, Vivas solicited the assistance of an old acquaintance, Carlos Desoretz, who was employed by a large gold refinery, Ronel Refining, located in Hollywood, Florida.

Accompanied by Jorge Masihy (who also knew Desoretz), Vivas visited Ronel in September 1986, and offered to sell Desoretz gold at a price slightly under the daily market fix. To sweeten the deal, the two promised a 50-cent kickback to Desoretz for each ounce of gold purchased. Desoretz jumped at the offer, and with the approval of his boss, Richard Ferris, opened a customer account in the name of Orafe, a company that Vivas said he controlled in Buenos Aires. They worked out arrangements for receiving and paying for the gold. Vivas advised them he was living in Los Angeles and that he would be shipping gold from that location. They worked out a payment arrangement whereby payment for gold received would be credited to Orafe at Ronel. Desoretz would then telephone Cambio Italia in Montevideo and advise them the amount of the credit. He would receive instructions to wire transfer the amount of the credit to accounts in Panama, at either Bank of Credit and Commerce International or Banco Occidente. The funds would be transferred from Ronel's account at Chase Manhattan in New York City.

During the fall of 1986, Ronel received gold shipments from Vivas in the range of six to ten kilos several times a week; the arrangement went off without a hitch.

Another step that Vivas took to resolve his problem of mounting currency was to acquire larger office space and hire additional personnel. He moved R.A.O.F. to the building that housed Ropex and Koyomejian's other businesses in November 1986. At about the same time, he hired Juan Carlos Seresi and Ruben Saini, Argentineans who were involved in the jewelry business in Los Angeles. The two were hired to help with currency pickups and to move currency and gold between R.A.O.F. and the Los Angeles jewelry firms that were selling gold for cash. By this time, a fourth jeweler, Rose Marie, Inc., had been recruited to sell gold for cash.

NEW YORK AND HOUSTON

In January 1987, Raul Vivas told Sergio Hochman that he wanted him to go to New York to begin currency operations. Hochman was to operate from office space that had been used by Jorge Gallina when he was receiving gold shipments from Vivas. He was to collect currency from Colombians and then deliver it to Simon Koyomejian, son of Wanis Koyomejian. Simon had a jewelry business in New York and arrangements had been made with Wanis for his son to ship the currency to Ropex in Los Angeles.

Sergio Hochman moved to New York and started a money laundering operation, known as S&H Imports, in space at Jorge Gallina's business. His beeper number was supplied to representatives of the Medellin cartel by Vivas. Shortly after establishing himself at S&H Imports, he started to receive messages on the beeper. He would call back the person and establish a time to make a delivery to the S&H office. The deliveries were made by Colombians. They would give a "La Mina" code which indicated the identity of the person to whom the delivery was to be credited. Money was never counted in the presence of the Colombians and receipts were not given.

After the delivery was made, Hochman and two employees of Gallina would count it in the presence of Simon Koyomejian. Simon would then carry the money to his jewelry business, Orosimo Corporation, located at 580 Fifth Avenue. He would package it and ship it via Loomis or Brinks to Ropex in Los Angeles. Hochman would fax a message to Ruben Priscolin at Cambio Italia in Montevideo giving the "La Mina" code, the date, and the amount. The "La Mina" codes were numbered, such as "La Mina" 14, 15, or 30. The code would indicate to the cartel who the money was coming from. Hochman's salary in New York went up to $4,000 per month, plus all living expenses.

Vivas handled the Houston operation by sending Celio Merkin to that city to run a currency pick-up operation. Merkin established the operation with two office sites. One was for accepting deliveries from Colombians. The other was for counting, packing, and shipping the currency to Ropex in Los Angeles.

The currency shipments from New York and Houston were always labeled as either scrap gold or jewelry. The carriers were never told that the packages contained currency. Each package shipped had a declared insurance value. The launderers saw to it that the declared value of the package always matched the amount of currency being shipped.

THE CURRENCY FLOW GROWS

In mid-November 1986, the Vivas money laundering operation in Los Angeles ground to a halt because of summer holidays in Uruguay. It started up again in January 1987, and by that time currency was starting to flow in from New York. Although the cash from New York dribbled in slowly during the first six months of 1987, it grew dramatically during the second half of the year. The same was true with Celio Merkin's Houston laundry—it started slowly in February, but by the end of the year, it was shipping $5 million a month to Ropex.

All currency collected in New York and Houston went to Ropex. Currency picked up in Los Angeles went to R.A.O.F.

By early 1987 it was clear that the amount of money flowing in the system would require much more gold than the Los Angeles jewelry outlets could supply. So, in February 1987, Vivas recruited a large gold and jewelry dealer, Nazareth Andonian, into the operation. Nazareth and his brother, Vahe, ran two businesses in adjoining suites located in the Los Angeles jewelry market area. The businesses were Andonian Brothers Manufacturing Company, Inc., d/b/a Nazareth Jewelers and VNA Gold Exchange. Vivas began the relationship by buying gold from Andonian Brothers for cash. However, the Andonians' role in the operation grew rapidly and they soon became major players along with Ropex.

During the spring of 1987, Raul Vivas persuaded the owners of Rose Marie, Inc., to substantially increase gold purchases on behalf of R.A.O.F.—to between 30 and 50 kilograms a week. The gold was sold to R.A.O.F. by delivering it to a depository account at a precious metals security company named Prosegur Security with instructions to credit it to the R.A.O.F. account at Ronel Refining in Florida. Rose Marie was paid in cash by R.A.O.F. The cash was passed on to jewelry dealers from whom the gold was purchased, who, in turn, deposited it into their business accounts at local banks.

In the fall of 1987, all currency collections in the Los Angeles area started to go to the Andonian Brothers rather than to R.A.O.F. Even before the switch occurred, most of the money collected by R.A.O.F. had gone to the Andonians for the purchase of gold.

By the end of 1987, Ropex and the Andonian Brothers had become the main players in the Vivas money laundering operation, with most of the currency from cocaine sales in New York, Houston, and Los Angeles going to these two businesses for counting. At the direction of Raul Vivas, the two firms purchased gold in a variety of ways designed to make the currency appear to be the result of legitimate business activity. The currency ended up in Ropex or Andonian bank accounts or in the accounts of several satellite jewelry businesses that were selling gold for cash. Funds in the Ropex and Andonian accounts were wire transferred to pay for gold purchases.

In November 1987, at the direction of Raul Vivas, Sergio Hochman stopped turning over currency to Simon Koyomejian and began shipping the cash he collected directly to the Andonian Brothers in Los Angeles. At the same time, Simon Koyomejian began his own money collection operation, shipping the cash he collected to Ropex in Los Angeles.

Greed is the only explanation as to why Wanis Koyomejian and Nazareth Andonian would have become involved in the money laundering scheme. Neither had a prior criminal background. Both were Armenians who had emigrated to the United States from the Mid-East. Both men were married with children and operated respectable and modestly successful businesses.

During the first six months of 1987, over $19 million in currency was moved through Ropex and related jewelry businesses into banks in Los Angeles. During the same period, over $17 million moved through Andonian Brothers and two related jewelry businesses. The currency from Ropex was deposited through five businesses, using six different accounts at four banks. The currency from the Andonian Brothers went into three business accounts at three different banks.

During the second half of 1987 the money moving activity increased dramatically—about three times as much money was laundered than during the first half of the year. In November alone, the combined total of currency deposits from the Raul Vivas operation amounted to over $30 million.

The "La Mina" phase of Polar Cap really moved into high gear in 1988. During most of that year, the Ropex and Andonian operations and associated jewelry businesses were pushing an average $50 million in cash a month through 10 Los Angeles banks. In June 1988 alone, over $70 million was deposited by the combined operation. Gold purchasing schemes to cover the activity became more sophisticated. Pool accounts and paper purchases and sales replaced the purchase and sale of "physical" gold.

While the amount of money being laundered was remarkable, what was even more incredible was that the government did not have any hard information about the operation until January 1988 and did not begin working to close it down until March 1988. By the time the operation was finally smashed, in February 1989, over $560 million in cocaine money had been laundered by the Raul Vivas operation.

LAW ENFORCEMENT ACTIVITY

The first information that any federal law enforcement agency obtained about the Raul Vivas money laundering operation came in January 1988, when the FBI in New York received information from an official of Loomis Armored Car Service. He reported that Orosimo Corporation, located at 580 Fifth Avenue in New York City, might be shipping millions of dollars in currency to Ropex Corporation in Los Angeles. He advised that Orosimo and Ropex were owned by members of the same family. The Loomis official based his information about the amount of money that might be involved on an event that occurred in mid-December 1987 and a review of his firm's records. A Loomis supervisor in Los Angeles observed a hole in a box that was being shipped from Orosimo to Ropex. He looked into the box and saw that it was filled with currency. The supervisor was aware that Ropex regularly received packages from Orosimo in New York. He also knew that the packages were quite heavy and that the contents were always marked as scrap gold or jewelry. He asked a Ropex employee about the contents of the box. He was told that cash was being sent to Los Angeles by investors who wanted to take advantage of gold prices. The story did not sound right. A review of Loomis records revealed that they had been handling shipments from Orosimo to Ropex since June 1987, that the shipments all claimed to be scrap gold or jewelry, and that the declared value of the packages for insurance purposes was usually between $300,000 and $500,000. On this basis, he surmised that if the packages all contained currency, the amount shipped would be in the millions.

The FBI commenced investigations on Orosimo in New York and on Ropex in Los Angeles. Early inquiries established that Wanis Koyomejian ran Ropex, that a number of relatives worked for him in Los Angeles, and that other relatives, including one of his sons, ran Orosimo in New York. It was also determined that Koyomejian had emigrated from Syria in 1979 and that he did not have a prior criminal record.

Within days after the FBI started to investigate Orosimo and Ropex, federal agents received another piece of vital information. Wells Fargo Bank, headquartered in San Francisco, had a policy of closely monitoring large currency activity to make sure that it was in compliance with the Bank Secrecy Act and to ensure that the bank was not being used by money launderers. The Bank Secrecy Act required financial institutions to report currency transactions over $10,000 on an IRS form, known as a CTR. The Treasury Department had been encouraging banks to avoid being used by money launderers and to report suspicious transactions. Wells Fargo, under the direction of Don Reid, its corporate compliance officer, was light years ahead of other banks in monitoring currency transactions and reporting suspicious activity. The bank's monitoring system had detected the fact that an account at its branch at 610 West Sixth Street in Los Angeles had been generating large currency deposits during November and December 1987. The branch was in the heart of the jewelry district in Los Angeles. The account was in the name of Andonian Brothers Manufacturing Company, a wholesale and retail gold and jewelry dealer located in suites 300 and 313 of the building at 220 West Fifth Street. The account had been opened in September 1987. Early activity in the account was routine. However, in November, ten currency deposits totaling over $3 million were made. Currency activity increased in December. There were 31 deposits totaling $6.4 million. On one day alone, December 7, 1987, there were four currency deposits in the total amount of $1.4 million. The bank had been reporting the currency transactions over $10,000 to the IRS on CTR forms, as required by law. Don Reid and his staff took a hard look at the situation. What they saw was a new account that had $9.4 million in currency deposit activity within a two-month period. They also saw a business that should not have generated that volume of currency transactions from legitimate activity. Reid decided that the activity was suspicious and reported it to the IRS in San Francisco.

The Wells Fargo report, together with the tip from Loomis, generated investigative activity that would lead to the ultimate demise of the Raul Vivas money laundering operation. Wells Fargo is to be congratulated for its action in reporting the suspicious currency activity of the Andonian Brothers. Where were the other banks? Nine other banks in the jewelry district had taken in over $100 million in currency from the accounts of five jewelers during 1987. While they filed CTRs for deposits over $10,000, as required by the Bank Secrecy Act, none of them had reported the activity as suspicious.

The IRS Criminal Investigation Division in San Francisco referred the Wells Fargo information to its Los Angeles office, which commenced a background investigation of Andonian Brothers Manufacturing Company. It was learned that the firm was a jewelry wholesaler and retailer that also dealt in gold and silver. The principals in the business were Nazareth Andonian and his brother, Vahe. IRS agents shared their information with the FBI in Los Angeles. The FBI received additional information from Loomis that there was another customer besides Orosimo that was shipping suspicious packages from New York to Los Angeles. That customer used two business names—Andonian Brothers and S&H Imports. Shipments from the office of these companies were sent to Andonian Brothers Manufacturing Company.

THE BANK SECRECY ACT DATABASE

While the background investigation of Andonian Brothers was continuing, the IRS agents in Los Angeles contacted the Financial Law Enforcement Center (FLEC) at Customs and reviewed their own CTR database in Detroit to see if more information was available about the business. FLEC was the Treasury Department database containing information from all reports required by the Bank Secrecy Act. The maintenance of the Bank Secrecy Act database and the analytical review of the data collected was entrusted to the U.S. Custom Service in 1979.

The IRS inquiry revealed that in 1987 CTRs had been filed by three other banks in the Los Angeles jewelry district showing currency deposits by Andonian Brothers of about $30 million. Over $21 million had been deposited in a Bank of America branch, another $6.4 million was deposited in an account at American International Bank, and $1.9 million went into the Tokai bank. Intrigued by the amount of currency that Andonian Brothers had deposited in the Bank of America and American International Bank accounts, a computer run was conducted on other currency reports filed by these bank branches. Agents were astonished to find that both bank branches together had reported an additional $56 million in currency transactions for three other customers—Ropex Corporation (which deposited a total of $34 million in currency during 1987), MOS Financing - Ropex (which deposited over $17 million in an account it had at American International Bank) and Atayan and Sons Inc. (which deposited about $5 million in an account it maintained at American International Bank). Additional computer runs on several other bank branches in the Los Angeles jewelry district identified well over $150 million in currency deposits by jewelry businesses that appeared to have some relationship with Andonian Brothers and Ropex Corporation.

The information obtained represented both a great failure and a great success of the reporting system required by the BSA. The success was in the ability of the Treasury database to respond to law enforcement inquiries and to provide detailed information about the currency transactions of individuals, businesses, and financial institutions. The failure was in the way that the analytical process of the system was managed. The FLEC was supposed to have the personnel and the software to spot unusual currency trends and to identify individuals, businesses, and financial institutions that were handling suspiciously large amounts of currency. The fact that the FLEC had not been able to identify the movement of over $150 million in currency through 11 accounts in 10 banks in a limited geographic area was a major failure in the ability of the system to proactively identify money laundering targets and refer them for investigation.

In 1984, Treasury had considered moving the Bank Secrecy Act database out of Customs and into an independent organization within the department. There had been some complaints that an insufficient number of money laundering targets were being identified and that other law enforcement agencies were having difficulty getting information from the FLEC. The Customs Service made a strong pitch to retain the database, vowing to add personnel and software to enhance the analytical capability of the FLEC. Customs had told Treasury, in 1984, that it would install an artificial intelligence system that would, in effect, set off bells and whistles when specific accounts and financial institutions started to show large currency transactions. There must have been a short circuit in the system during 1987. Partly as a result of FLEC's failure to proactively identify currency movements in Operation Polar Cap, Treasury, in April 1990, moved the BSA database from Customs to a new independent agency known as the Financial Crimes Enforcement Network (FINCEN).

THE INVESTIGATION CONTINUES

In February 1988, while the FBI and IRS were pursuing investigations of the Ropex and Andonian Brothers, DEA agents in New York received valuable information. An informant who had been a cocaine dealer revealed that he had been introduced to a major money laundering organization in New York City in late 1987, Andonian Brothers, Inc. The dealer/informant was told the business was a money collection and laundering operation that worked for a Colombian-based organization involved in the importation and distribution of cocaine and that he should make cash payments for the cocaine he had received to the Andonian Brothers location. He was instructed that, after the money was dropped off at Andonian's, he was to call certain telephone numbers in Colombia and advise the parties answering of a code name and the exact amount of the money he had delivered. The informant said that he followed this procedure on a number of occasions between November 1987 and February 1988.

At the time that information was being developed about Ropex and Andonian Brothers, DEA had a very important drug money laundering investigation in progress. It involved a major money launderer for the Medellin cartel named Eduardo Martinez. In October 1987, a DEA confidential informant met with Martinez in Medellin and offered to launder large sums of currency for him through the United States and into Panama. During this meeting, Martinez told the informant he was already using the services of "La Mina," and he displayed a ledger which purported to show that "La Mina" had processed $12 million cash during a single month.

Nevertheless, in November 1987, Martinez agreed to use the DEA undercover money laundering operation. During the latter part of November and extending until the end of January, the informant and DEA agents received $12 million in currency from cartel representatives in the United States. The currency was deposited in undercover bank accounts in Atlanta and wire transferred to accounts at the Bank of Credit and Commerce International (BCCI) and Banco Occidente in Panama. Martinez was unhappy with the operation for a number of reasons: a cartel courier had been arrested in Los Angeles, the $1 million in cash he was carrying was seized by the police, and there was a delay of up to five days between the time of the currency deliveries and the receipt of funds in Panamanian bank accounts. Martinez demanded to meet with those in charge of the laundering operation before he did any further business.

Two DEA undercover agents met with Martinez and one of his associates in Aruba in March 1988. During a five-hour recorded conversation, Martinez made several references to a competitor money laundering organization known as "La Mina," noting that it operated in New York, Miami, Houston and Los Angeles. He stated that "La Mina" was in the gold business and exported gold to the United States from mines in Uruguay. He indicated that the system used jewelry businesses to place money into banks. He advised them that the operation had closed down from the beginning of December until January 24 and that was why he had been using their services. He noted that "La Mina" had started up again at the end of January and in one month had laundered $28 million. According to Martinez, "La Mina" was able to get money from the United States into Panamanian banks in one or two days.

DEA considered the Martinez case to be of major significance. They believed he was laundering for major cartel leaders, including Pablo Escobar, Gustavo Gaviria Gacha, and Geraldo Moncada. They did not want anything to interfere with the successful completion of the investigation. They were concerned about any information leaking out of their own organization that could possibly compromise the investigation, the undercover agents, and the confidential informant.

By late March, the FBI, IRS, and DEA were continuing to pursue leads on the Andonian and Ropex investigation. The FBI learned in February from Loomis that some shipments of "scrap gold and/or jewelry" were being made from the Orosimo location with Ropex Corporation listed as the shipper. At about the same time, Loomis advised the FBI that Ropex was making shipments from Houston to its office in Los Angeles.

FBI agents had observed Brinks trucks also making pickups at Orosimo in New York, and an inquiry with Brinks revealed a similar pattern of shipments from Orosimo's New York office to Ropex in Los Angeles. Meanwhile, Loomis advised the FBI that another customer, Andonian Brothers in New York, was also making frequent shipments of "scrap gold and jewelry" to an Andonian Brothers' office in Los Angeles.

During the month of March, Brinks and Loomis records showed that 17 shipments were made from Andonian Brothers in New York to Andonian's Los Angeles offices; the combined declared value of which came to over $15 million. Brinks and Loomis records also showed that there were a combined total of 32 shipments from Ropex and/or Orosimo in New York and from Ropex in Houston to Ropex in Los Angeles in March with declared values totalling more $12 million.

IRS agents maintained contact with the Wells Fargo branch in the Los Angeles jewelry district and learned the Andonian Brothers had deposited over $5 million in currency in January. Wells Fargo also noted that the Ropex Corporation had opened an account at the bank in January and had begun making large cash deposits—more than $4 million were made in February and March, combined. According to the bank, the money deposited to both the Andonian and Ropex accounts was being wire transferred to the same account at the Chase Manhattan Bank in New York.

OCDETF TAKES OVER

By the end of March, IRS and FBI agents realized they were dealing with a money laundering operation that was handling hundreds of millions of dollars a year. They decided to make their information available to the Los Angeles Crime Drug Enforcement Task Force (OCDETF). The OCDETF was an innovation of the Reagan Administration's "War on Drugs." It involved the formation of multi-agency task forces in 13 core cities to concentrate on major drug trafficking organizations. The task forces consisted of agents from DEA, FBI, Customs, IRS, the Bureau of Alcohol, Tobacco and Firearms, and the Immigration and Naturalization Service. A supervisory Assistant U.S. Attorney (AUSA) was placed in charge of the task force in each location and assigned a staff of prosecutors to work on cases developed by task force agents. The theory behind the OCDETF program was to encourage the free exchange of information among federal law enforcement agencies and thereby overcome agency turf battles.

OCDETF attorneys were quick to recognize the potential of the currency deposit information developed by the FBI and IRS. They also learned that DEA was investigating Andonian Brothers. The case seemed made to order for a joint coordinated investigation under the auspices of OCDETF. Because of their concerns about the Martinez case, DEA agents pressed to become the lead agency for the OCDETF investigation. The FBI also pushed for lead agency status in the case. These issues were resolved in Los Angeles when Russell Hayman, the AUSA OCDETF coordinator, decided that DEA would take the lead role in the Andonian investigation and that the FBI would lead the Ropex investigation.

The New York end of the Andonian and Ropex operations was also designated as an OCDETF case, as was the Atlanta-based DEA undercover operation against Eduardo Martinez. Not only was there some interagency bickering, but there were also some indications that the OCDETF core city districts might have some disagreements.

In an effort to resolve these problems, a special coordinating committee was established in Washington. The committee was chaired by Chuck Saphos, the former Greenback Chief, who by this time had become the head of the Justice Department's Narcotics Section. Tough, aggressive, and a vigorous prosecutor, Saphos was the ideal person to knock heads and to push forward with the investigation.

Senior officials from the FBI, DEA, IRS, Customs and the Treasury Department served on the coordinating committee. The purpose of the group was to coordinate investigative and prosecutorial matters and to resolve disputes between agencies and the OCDETF programs in New York, Atlanta, and Los Angeles. The "Saphos Committee" met regularly during the course of the investigation, resolving disputes and ensuring there was full information sharing among all agencies.

It was at this time that the name "Operation Polar Cap" was given to the investigation. The rationale for the name was that it applied to no other ongoing case and had no meaning as far as the investigation was concerned. Thus, if the name ever got out, it would have no meaning.

Resources were a problem all through the Polar Cap investigation. Personnel demands were staggering. Large numbers of agents were required to conduct surveillances, retrieve discarded trash and later on, to monitor audio and video intercept devices. Complicating the situation was the fact that the suspects spoke a variety of languages including Armenian, Turkish and Spanish. The need for agents with unique language capability was at an absolute premium.

TRASH RETRIEVAL

Two of the earliest investigative measures taken in the Polar Cap case was the surveillance of individuals going in and out of the Ropex and Andonian offices, and sifting through trash discarded by each of these businesses to see if any important evidence was being discarded. Neither task was easy. The Ropex and Andonian offices were located in multistory office buildings in the center of the Los Angeles jewelry district. Some 2,000 dealers filled more than a dozen large buildings along the surrounding streets. The Ropex offices were located on the ninth floor of the International Jewelry Center, a new 16-story structure. They had two suites consisting of a showroom and a number of workrooms. The front doors of the Ropex suites were usually locked, and the offices were protected by a building-wide security system that included an alarm system, closed circuit TV cameras, and security officers.

The Andonian Brothers' operation was similarly situated nearby. During the weekday, jewelry dealers moved in and out of the wholesale and retail offices. Retail customers, private couriers and armored car personnel added to the flow of dealer traffic. There was an international flavor to the jewelry district. It was dominated by merchants who had emigrated from Japan, India, Hong Kong, Armenia, Seria, South America and other locations. It was no simple task to watch people entering and leaving either business, nor was it easy to collect discarded trash. Security in the Ropex building particularly complicated matters.

To cope with the conditions that existed, the agencies involved in the investigation reached out for a variety of agents with ethnic and racial backgrounds that could blend in with the types of people who moved on the streets and in the buildings that made up the jewelry districts in New York and Los Angeles. Assistance was requested and received from the Los Angeles Police Department. Surveillance and trash retrieval teams were established. Many of the agents and police officers on these teams were blacks, Hispanics, Asians, and Mid-Easterners, who dressed to appear as cleaning people, couriers, jewelry merchants, delivery men, and homeless people.

Trash retrieval operations started in mid-April and were conducted in the vicinity of both the Ropex and Andonian Brothers' offices. The investigators obtained warrants from the Federal District Court in Los Angeles which authorized them to seize and remove trash left outside the premises of the two firms. Despite many obstacles, a number of trash pickups were made by agents from hallways near the Ropex and Andonian Brothers offices.

The trash retrieval operation yielded a considerable amount of valuable evidence and investigative information. Among the items recovered were:

- Large numbers of invoices from Ropex which appeared to represent cash sales of gold to individuals with addresses in Canada and Mexico. The invoices were the customer's copies and the amounts invoiced ranged between $50,000 and $200,000. Investigation in Canada determined that most of the addresses were fictitious and that the alleged purchasers were probably nonexistent persons. These recoveries were significant because they established that Ropex was prepared to claim that some of the currency being deposited came from gold sales to cash customers.

- A scrap of paper from Ropex trash with the handwritten notations "April 12, 1988 AIB - $670,000 Prosegur - $1,452,122," which appeared to correspond with transactions facilitated by Loomis on April 12 involving a Ropex account at American International Bank (AIB) and a gold bullion dealer named Prosegur used by Ropex and Andonian to cover transfers of funds from their bank accounts to a Ronel Refining account.

- A copy of a canceled check drawn on the account of Ronel Refining Company at Chase Manhattan Bank in New York and payable to Andonian Brothers. (By this time, investigators had already deciphered the complex web of transactions used to cover the flow of cocaine cash.)

On one day, alone, August 12, the following items were found in Andonian Brothers' trash: a piece of paper with the notation "1,000,000 L.A. 34,000 L.A. Inv under Ronel's"; an adding machine tape totaling 1,034,000 with the notation "SPNB 8-10-88 Cash deposits"; and two Andonian Brothers' invoices indicating "Sold to Ronel Ref., 2801 Greene St., Hollywood, Florida" with a combined total value of $1,034,000.

The adding machine tape with the SPNB notation unquestionably referred to Security Pacific National Bank, where Andonian Brothers had an account. The bank filed a CTR showing that Andonian Brothers had deposited $1,034,005 in currency into its account on August 10, 1988. On August 11, 1988, there was a wire transfer of $1,034,000 from that account to the Ronel Refining account at Chase Manhattan in New York.

Trash retrieval operations at Ropex and Andonian continued until September 1988, when both firms obtained shredders and stopped throwing away valuable information. During the period of the retrieval, dozens of scraps of paper were found with written cash denominations and dates. Frequently, the totals would match Loomis and Brinks deliveries on the same days of purported shipments of "jewelry or scrap gold," and both amounts often matched deposit amounts on those days to bank accounts held by Ropex and Andonian. It became very clear that the "scrap gold and jewelry" declared in the armored car shipments from New York and Houston was indeed currency.

PHYSICAL SURVEILLANCE

In addition to trash retrievals and the monitoring of armored car company records, physical surveillance was conducted at the Ropex and Andonian offices in Los Angeles. People were observed entering and leaving these offices and often were followed.

Beginning in April, hundreds of surveillances were conducted on people leaving both premises. Many of the observations mirrored documentary evidence that came from CTRs filed by banks in the Los Angeles jewelry district for currency deposits by Ropex and Andonian. For example, one of the employees of Ropex was Ohanes Khawaloujian. On May 3, LAPD officers observed Khawaloujian and Wanis Koyomejian leaving the Ropex offices, each carrying a heavy briefcase. They were followed to Independence Bank, which later filed a CTR indicating a $640,000 currency deposit to the Ropex account by Wanis Koyomejian.

It was very difficult to conduct direct observations of the doors leading to the Ropex and Andonian offices, but in June agents obtained court orders enabling them to install closed circuit television cameras in the public hallways at both locations. Cameras were installed and focused on all entrances to both offices; agents monitored the cameras, and all comings and goings were recorded on video cassette tapes.

The surveillance observations were very useful in developing evidence against the money laundering operation. Employees and regular visitors of both firms were identified, and a pattern of activity was established. Loomis and Brinks personnel were observed making almost daily deliveries of packages to both offices. Several hours after these deliveries, Ropex employees would carry heavy briefcases or catalogue cases to local banks. In most instances, the bank visited would file a CTR indicating a currency deposit to the Ropex account.

The pattern of activity was slightly different at Andonian Brothers. Andonian would receive the Brinks and Loomis shipments similar to Ropex. However, rather than carrying the money to a local bank, Andonian would have Loomis or Brinks pickup cash within hours for delivery to the Federal Reserve office in Los Angeles, to be credited to the account of Andonian Brothers at one of several local banks. In most instances, the amount of currency in the pickup was very close to the declared value of the armored car deliveries of "scrap gold and jewelry."

Surveillance operations also established a pattern of activity that indicated currency was being delivered to both Andonian and Ropex by persons collecting from sources in the Los Angeles area. Juan Carlos Seresi and Ruben Saini were frequently observed bringing briefcases and packages into Andonian Brothers. Eddie Ortiz and Pedro Fuentes were often observed bringing packages into Ropex. (Ortiz and Fuentes had been hired by Raul Vivas to expand his Los Angeles collection capability.) Currency deposits to local banks would usually be made within hours after these visits.

Surveillance observations also indicated a pattern of visits between Ropex and Andonian and a number of other jewelry outlets in the jewelry district. The pattern of activity indicated currency was being moved from Ropex to other jewelers who then made currency deposits. In some cases, the observations indicated Andonian was receiving currency from other jewelers and then making deposits to its own bank accounts. Finally, surveillance established that both Andonian and Ropex conducted some retail jewelry business on their premises. However, the number of retail business visitors was minuscule compared to the amount of currency being deposited by both firms.

LOOMIS AND BRINKS RECORDS

During the period of trash retrieval and physical surveillance in Los Angeles, the Brinks and Loomis records were constantly being checked to monitor activity. This monitoring reflected some interesting developments. For example, the records showed that in April 1988, Andonian Brothers moved from midtown to lower Manhattan. At about the same time, Ropex started to make shipments from a new office named Rafco, Inc., in the middle of the New York jewelry exchange. Rafco was named after Wanis Koyomejian's son, Raffi. Rafco Refining, Inc., was also a business located in the same building that Ropex occupied in Los Angeles. There was a great deal of traffic between Ropex and Rafco Refining. Beginning in March 1988, Rafco Refining, in Los Angeles, started making large currency deposits to its account at American International Bank.

It wasn't until almost a year later, after arrests had been made and several defendants started to cooperate, that investigators learned of the humorous circumstances that caused the office relocations. One day in late April, Sergio Hochman and two assistants were busy counting a large amount of currency in their midtown New York offices when, suddenly, there was a loud knock at the front door. Hochman saw, through a closed circuit television monitor, two men standing at the door who appeared to be police detectives. Hochman and his assistants panicked. They ran out the back door of the office leaving $2,143,000 behind. Hochman was convinced he was going to be arrested. He collected his family and personal belongings and fled to Montevideo. Raul Vivas maintained contact on the telephone with one of the other employees. The man was terrified. He would not go back into the office.

Vivas then held a series of meetings with Nazareth Andonian and other top players in the Los Angeles operation. It was finally decided that Tomas Iglesias and Vahe Andonian would go to New York and try to recover the money. Three days after the knock at the door, Vahe Andonian and Tomas Iglesias stealthily entered the rear door of the penthouse office suite and found everything intact, except for about $150,000 which appeared to have mysteriously disappeared. Vivas decided it was time to move the collection offices in New York to new locations.

In August 1988, Andonian Brothers started to receive shipments of "scrap gold and jewelry" from Z&G Gold in New York City. This office became the primary shipping point for currency going from New York to Andonian Brothers in Los Angeles. Investigators later learned that the switch was made because the Colombian currency handlers objected to traveling to the office in lower Manhattan; they preferred a midtown drop-off point. Another change in August involved the fact that some shipments from Z&G Gold started to go to Joyce Jewelers in Los Angeles. Joyce Jewelers was located just across the hall from Andonian Brothers; surveillance revealed that Loomis and Brinks shipments to Joyce Jewelers were quickly moved across the hall to Andonian Brothers.

NEW SOURCES OF INFORMATION AND NEW STRATEGY

By early August 1988, the OCDETF agents and attorneys had come to appreciate the broad scope of the Polar Cap operation. Brinks and Loomis records for the four-month period of March 1988 through June 1988 showed that approximately $145 million worth of "scrap gold and jewelry" had been shipped from New York and Houston to Andonian and Ropex in Los Angeles. During the same period, CTRs filed by eight Los Angeles banks showed currency deposits of over $200 million made by Ropex, Andonian, and a number of other associated jewelry businesses. Thus, it was deduced that about $55 million in currency had been collected from sources in the Los Angeles area during the four-month period.

Eduardo Martinez stopped using the DEA undercover money laundering operation in Atlanta in January 1988 because "La Mina" was working so well. However, associates of Martinez in the cartel maintained contact with the undercover agents because they were discussing the possibility of smuggling 14,000 kilos of cocaine into the United States through Mexico. One of the negotiations for that deal took place in Los Angeles in early August. During the course of meetings, a Colombian intermediary pointed out a downtown Los Angeles business building and identified it as "La Mina." The address was that of Ropex.

Two new sources of information proved valuable to the OCDETF investigation. In July, the FBI in New York arrested an individual in connection with the sale and distribution of 52 kilos of cocaine. This individual told FBI agents that on six or seven occasions he had delivered currency, via courier, to an individual named "Paolo" to pay for cocaine purchases. Paolo was identified as Sergio Hochman. He said he had been told by associates in Colombia to contact Paolo by beeper and to identify himself as "La Mina 14" prior to currency deliveries.

In August, a DEA agent assigned to the Los Angeles OCDETF operation went to Montevideo, Uruguay, and interviewed a confidential source who had knowledge of a money laundering operation in Los Angeles, Miami, and New York established in 1986 by Colombian drug traffickers. His description of the operation matched that of "La Mina" including the use of gold transactions to conceal the laundering of cocaine sales. He named two individuals who controlled the operation in the United States as Raul Vivas and Sergio Hochman.

During the summer of 1988, OCDETF agents started to review wire transfer activity from Los Angeles bank accounts to accounts in a number of New York banks. There were a particularly large number of transfers to one account at the Chase Manhattan Bank in New York; the account holder was Ronel Refining of Hollywood, Florida. It was also learned from Chase that, shortly after funds were received in the account from Los Angeles banks, there would be a wire transfer of almost the same amount from Ronel to accounts in banks in Panama and Montevideo.

In August 1988, the ad hoc "Saphos Committee" traveled to Los Angeles and met with OCDETF prosecutors and agents from New York, Atlanta, and Los Angeles. Although it was determined that progress was being made, it was seriously lacking in evidence that could sustain a money laundering or drug conspiracy charge. What was needed was to prove the currency came from drug sales and that the suspects knew it came from some form of criminal activity.

It was clear the needed information was not going to be obtained from any of the routine investigative measures employed to date. So, court ordered electronic surveillances were requested for the premises and telephones of Ropex and Andonian Brothers offices both in Los Angeles and New York. DEA was to apply for and run the Andonian surveillance and the FBI would handle the Ropex phase.

A U.S. District Court Judge in New York approved electronic surveillance at the Rafco, Inc. office and at the Andonian Brothers' office on August 23, 1988. The Los Angeles surveillance request was approved for Ropex offices on September 9, but the request covering the Andonian Brothers' office was held up until November 1.

The court approvals allowed OCDETF investigators to monitor conversations on certain telephones in the offices and to place listening devices in each office that would enable them to hear what was going on even when telephones were not being used. The approvals also allowed the OCDETF agents to place closed circuit television cameras in each office. Electronic surveillance began at Ropex on September 18 and at Andonian Brothers on November 2.

While electronic surveillance applications were being prepared by agents and prosecutors, there were developments involving the money launderers. In the spring of 1988, Celio Merkin left Houston and Raul Vivas sent Ruben Saini to run the Houston currency collection operation. In the summer of 1988, Raul Vivas received a tip from a Los Angeles bank that the IRS had served a subpoena on one of his business accounts. This information, plus the Hochman experience in New York, spooked Vivas. He decided to go back to Montevideo and run the money laundering operation from there. He left Tomas Iglesias in charge of money being channeled from New York to Los Angeles. Juan Carlos Seresi was placed in charge of Los Angeles and Houston collections. Seresi formed a business he called J.C. Jewelers in Los Angeles from which he collected cash prior to delivering it to Andonian Brothers.

ELECTRONIC SURVEILLANCE ACTIVITY

Once the listening and viewing devices were in place and operating, investigators obtained an amazing inside view of how the laundering business operated. Brinks and Loomis shipments from New York were delivered in the morning, whereupon employees would sort the cash by denomination and count it using high speed money counting machines. When the count was completed, the currency was repackaged and prepared for deposit. One dollar bills were not counted. If shipments on a particular day contained an unusually high amount of cash, five-dollar bills were not counted either.

When repackaged money was ready for deposit, Brinks or Loomis employees would come in and remove the packages for delivery to the Federal Reserve under an arrangement where the total amount of the package would be credited to the shipper's account at a particular bank. In some cases, cash that had been repackaged and counted was moved to satellite jewelry businesses, which then deposited the money into their own bank accounts.

Currency was also delivered to Ropex by Eddie Ortiz and Pedro Fuentes, representing the proceeds of cocaine sales in the Los Angeles area. This money was also counted, packaged, and deposited into accounts at Los Angeles banks.

Once currency was deposited into the Andonian Brothers and Ropex accounts, telephone calls would be made by employees of the two firms to their banks, and wire transfer instructions were issued. Underlying all of the currency movements and the wire transfers of funds was a system involving the purchase and sale of gold to cover the fact that the money originated from cocaine sales. Numerous intercepted telephone conversations related to gold transactions.

The electronic intercepts went on for almost five months. In all, some 3,000 reels of audio and video tape were recorded. The suspects in the case spoke in five languages, including two Armenian dialects.

One of the first things OCDEFT agents learned when they started to monitor Ropex in September was that there was trouble with the Houston operation. Ruben Saini had been overseeing the Houston collection office. It turned out that the Customs Service had a money laundering investigation underway on a different group of launderers in Houston. Surveillance of one of the drug dealers who was bringing money to launderers in the Customs investigation resulted in the agents seeing him meet Ruben Saini. They decided to watch Saini. They were not initially aware that he was part of the OCDETF Ropex investigation. Saini became aware of the fact that he was being followed. A series of meetings and telephone conversations were recorded at the Ropex offices during the last week of September in which it was learned that the Ropex office in Houston would be shut down and that future currency collections there would be processed in hotel rooms and delivered directly to the Loomis office for shipment to Ropex in Los Angeles.

Pedro Fuentes and another employee of Juan Carlos Seresi named Jimmy Contreras were sent to Houston to restructure the operation. Wanis Koyomejian was overheard making arrangements for two of his employees to fly to Houston to meet with Fuentes and Contreras. Agents observed Koyomejian's employees board an airplane in Los Angeles headed for Houston on September 27. OCDETF agents in Houston followed the men after they arrived there and observed them meeting with Pedro Fuentes and Jimmy Contreras at the Westin Galleria Hotel. On the next day, Koyomejian's employees delivered three packages labeled "scrap gold" to the Loomis office in Houston. It was valued at $643,000 and was to be shipped to Ropex in Los Angeles. On the following day, agents observed that the packages contained currency which counted out to $643,000.

In late September, Wanis Koyomejian was overheard telling an unknown male telephone caller he was so busy that ones and fives could not be counted. He said they could only count 10s, 20s, 50s and 100s because there was not enough time to count the smaller bills. This conversation graphically illustrated the classic problem all money launderers have processing and counting large volumes of small bills. He also said he gave his employees lie detector tests every six months to make sure they weren't stealing, that there was $3 million in currency in his office as they were speaking, and that his operation had plenty of security and protection. Little did he realize he was under the watchful eyes and ears of the U.S. government.

GREEDY BANKERS

In 1982, William Von Raab, the Commissioner of Customs, made a speech to a group of bankers in South Florida in which he referred to them as "sleazy bankers" for handling large quantities of drug currency. His comment caused an uproar. Bankers were outraged and made their feelings known to the media and politicians.

Von Raab was off the wall in characterizing all bankers as "sleazy." The fact is that most bankers are well meaning, honest business people. However, there were certainly some sleazy bankers in Florida at the time and some went to jail for their actions. Von Raab's mistake was in characterizing all bankers as sleazy.

In the Polar Cap operation in Los Angeles, there were some greedy, if not sleazy, bankers involved. It is remarkable that only one bank, Wells Fargo, came forward to the government to report suspicious cash deposit activity. Ten other banks accepted millions of dollars in currency deposits from businesses that should not have been generating that much currency in the customary conduct of their lawful businesses. These banks did *what was required of them by law*—they filed CTRs for the large currency transactions they were handling—but they did not take the step Wells Fargo did by going to a government agency and drawing its attention to *suspicious activity*. There can be only one explanation for this: greed. Ten banks, in essence, decided they wanted the business, they wanted the profits generated by such transactions, and they decided to turn a blind eye to the fact that the currency could not have come from legitimate sources.

Not only did these banks accept huge volumes of cash from money launderers, but they treated them as favored customers. Dozens of wiretap interceptions reveal that Ropex and Andonian were able to telephone high level people in the banks and get special attention to their needs. Numerous calls were made to get currency account balances and to find out exactly when wire transfers had been sent. The information sought was always quickly supplied to the caller.

Nowhere is the greed element better exhibited than in an intercepted telephone conversation between Arnold Coggeshall, the President of First Los Angeles Bank, and Zepur Morayan, an employee of Andonian Brothers. During conversation, which took place on November 9, Coggeshall asked, "How much are you shipping today?" Zepur replied, "How much? I don't know. I have no idea." Coggeshall replied, "Ship me all you got." Zepur said, "Okay, everything's yours anyway." Here was a bank president with a New England family name that traces its origins back to pre-Revolutionary times exhibiting as much or more greed than the money launderers who were willing to dispose of the money made from the sale of the insidious white powder, cocaine. CTRs filed by First Los Angeles Bank for the months of September and October 1988 reported over $12 million currency deposits into the Andonian Brothers account at the bank. Surely, Arnold Coggeshall didn't honestly believe this cash came from the sale of gold chains and jewelry.

Another indication of the extent to which First Los Angeles Bank pandered to the launderers came from a call placed by Coggeshall to Andonian Brothers on January 17, 1989. At some time previously, Coggeshall had told the Andonians that he would try to get their account exempted from the currency reporting requirements. During the phone conversation, Vahe Andonian inquired as to whether the bank was still working on the exemption, and Coggeshall assured him he was doing all he could.

Banks are permitted to unilaterally exempt the accounts of certain legitimate retail business customers from reports of currency transactions over $10,000, provided the larger sums can be shown to be commensurate with the customary conduct of a lawful retail business. Andonian Brothers was both a wholesaler and retailer of gold and gold jewelry, so to get a unilateral exemption, First Bank of Los Angeles would have had to determine that more than 50% of Andonian's gross sales came from retail transactions. If the wholesale side of the business predominated, the bank would have had to write to the Treasury Department for a special exemption. In this case, it really didn't matter whether the wholesale or retail business predominated. No banker in his right mind could have concluded that $12 million in currency deposits over a two-month period was commensurate with the conduct of a lawful retail or wholesale jewelry business.

In February 1989, when the Polar Cap operation was broken up and arrests were made, attorneys for some of the arrested jewelers claimed that much of the jewelry business in Los Angeles was done in cash. The head of a jewelry association in Los Angeles was widely quoted in the print and electronic media as saying that virtually every legitimate wholesale transaction was conducted through bank checks rather than cash and bankers should have suspected something was amiss when gold and jewelry firms deposited such large amounts of currency.

It wasn't that some of the bankers didn't have suspicions. City National Bank accepted $22.9 million in cash deposits from a jewelry business named Unica Gold and Silver Exchange in 1988. In early November, the bank asked Unica about the high volume of its currency transactions, and the firm responded that it was buying gold from Andonian Brothers and selling it to people who paid cash to take advantage of swings in price in the spot gold market. City National Bank apparently decided to do some checking on Andonian Brothers and to discuss the matter with them. On November 21, 1988, a wiretap recording was made of a telephone call placed by Patrick Bishop of City National Bank to Andonian Brothers concerning the firm's financial condition. Bishop observed that the Dun & Bradstreet report for Andonian Brothers did not jive with what was on the firm's tax returns, nor did the company's sales figures. The company could not explain the differences. It was obvious from this call that City National Bank was getting nervous. At the time of the call, the bank was also receiving large currency deposits from two other jewelry businesses, S&K Sales and Atayan & Sons, Inc., which were both outlets for drug money that was being handled by Ropex. In November alone, the bank received $2.4 million in currency from S&K and $1.2 million from Atayan. The bank, from the nature of the telephone call, was obviously suspicious of the origin of the funds. However, it took no action to communicate its suspicions to any enforcement agency.

City National Bank was not alone. Bank of America received $21 million in currency deposits from Andonian Brothers in 1987 and over $34 million in 1988. All of these deposits went into one account. Bank of America also took in over $9 million in cash deposits from Ropex in 1987 and 1988, and $17 million from Universal Gold Exchange in 1988.

Even more significant were currency deposits into American International Bank (AIB) and Security Pacific National Bank. During 1987 and 1988. AIB processed $118 million in currency from seven different jewelry accounts, including accounts for Ropex, Andonian Brothers, and several other satellite jewelers controlled by Andonian and Ropex. Security Pacific accepted over $160 million in currency deposits into a single account of the Andonian Brothers during the two-year period.

The bankers in the Los Angeles jewelry district, with the exception of Wells Fargo, operated under a "see no evil, hear no evil" philosophy. They were not concerned about the origin of their customer's funds. They technically complied with the Bank Secrecy Act by filing CTRs for currency transactions over $10,000, but they never reported the activity as suspicious. It was this operational philosophy in the Polar Cap case that led the Treasury Department to propose legislation in March 1991 that would legally require financial institutions to file reports on all suspicious transactions.

THE OPERATION BEGINS TO CRUMBLE

In October 1988, Ropex laundering scheme was set back by arrests in a separate laundering investigations.

Customs had been operating a large undercover money laundering sting operation in several major cities. Customs agents, posing as money launderers, had succeeded in enlisting a number of drug dealers in Detroit, Houston, New York, and several other cities as clients. The Customs sting was known as "Operation C Chase." Customs agents picked up currency from drug dealers, placed it into banks in the United States, and then wire transferred the funds to Panama and other offshore locations where Colombian cocaine cartel bosses could use it. Customs agents and federal prosecutors decided to shut down C Chase in early October 1988, and when they did they seized money ledgers in the New York City area indicating the receipt and distribution of over $35 million in "La Mina" accounts between April and early October 1988.

The arrests and seizures associated with the case had a chilling effect on the Ropex operation. Offices were shuffled and currency shipments were throttled.

There was definitely a panic atmosphere at Ropex as a result of the C Chase arrests and publicity. Several intercepted telephone conversations and conferences in the weeks after the arrest bear this out. On October 20, Wanis Koyomejian had a meeting in his office with his accountant. The meeting was videotaped and the conversation recorded. The accountant recommended that Ropex and JSK be closed down without any remaining assets. Wanis suggested the names of the businesses be changed to make them appear to be real estate or investment firms. The accountant said this would only be a "white wash." He wanted to be able to show that Wanis had moved to a new location and that his businesses were totally new entities. At the end of the conversation, they agreed that both Ropex and JSK had to stop operating.

On October 21, Wanis Koyomejian was overheard in a telephone conversation with Richard Ferris, the president of Ronel Refining. Both parties expressed concern over the arrests that had been publicized in the Custom's C Chase operation and recent arrest at a BCCI office in Tampa. They discussed the impact these arrests would have on their operation. Ferris told Koyomejian he and Carlos Desoretz were scared, and he mentioned that the owners of Ronel were growing suspicious.

When the shipments of currency from New York trailed off in October and November, OCDETF agents working on Ropex began to notice a different trend—currency collections in the Los Angeles area started to increase. Electronic and physical surveillance indicated that Eddie Ortiz and Pedro Fuentes, a/k/a "Pepe," became much more frequent visitors to the Ropex offices. Both men worked for Juan Carlos Seresi, who was in charge of the Los Angeles money laundering operation. Agents followed both men on several occasions as they went to J.C. Jewelers, Seresi's office, with some frequency. The surveillances began to pay off when, on November 21, Eddie Ortiz was followed to Costa Mesa, California, about 35 miles outside Los Angeles in Orange County, where he met a man who handed him what appeared to be a cardboard box or shopping bag. The man was subsequently identified as Gilberto Sanchez. When the meeting broke up, several agents followed Ortiz back to the Ropex offices in Los Angeles. Other agents followed Sanchez to a house in El Toro, about 10 miles away, to what turned out to be Sanchez' residence. When Eddie Ortiz went back to the Ropex offices, he was observed on the video monitor unloading and counting currency which he removed from a package similar to the one given to him by Sanchez.

A State of California, Bureau of Narcotics Enforcement (BNE) agent, assigned to the OCDETF investigation, was involved in the Ortiz surveillance, and he referred the information about Gilberto Sanchez to the BNE for a follow-up investigation. BNE agents conducted extensive surveillance on Sanchez during the period of December 1 through December 5, as he toted gym bags, suitcases, boxes, and other containers in and out of his residence. On December 5, the agents saw a woman known to them as Maria Otilla Villada deliver a large black suitcase to the Sanchez residence. They followed her to her residence in Costa Mesa where she dropped off a white trash bag. She left her house and was followed to a parking lot where she was observed meeting with another drug trafficking suspect named Ivan Mendez. Mendez was followed to a parking lot in Santa Ana where he met William Lee Downing. When Mendez was observed transferring a cardboard box from his car to Downing's truck, BNE agents moved in and arrested both men for the sale and possession of cocaine. Ten kilos of cocaine were recovered from the box Mendez placed in Downing's truck. Another ten kilos were recovered from Mendez' car.

Shortly after these arrests, a series of search warrants were executed at the residences of Downing, Villada, and Sanchez. One kilo of cocaine was found at Downing's residence. Ninety-one kilos were recovered from Villada's home and a mother lode haul of 180 kilos was found at the Sanchez residence. In addition, a total of $60,000 in currency was seized.

This was the break OCDETF agents and prosecutors had been waiting for. At last, there was a direct link between cocaine sales and the money being delivered to Ropex.

The arrests and cocaine seizures had a big impact at Ropex and Andonian Brothers. There were a series of telephone calls and internal conversations during the next few days that clearly demonstrated the concern of key players in the organization.

THE GOLD CONNECTION

The "La Mina" phase of the Polar Cap money laundering operation involved a series of gold transactions designed to make it look as though the money from cocaine sales actually came from gold trading. Most of this activity involved Ronel Refining of Hollywood, Florida. In essence, Ronel Refining allowed the Raul Vivas laundering organization to wire transfer drug proceeds through Ronel's corporate bank accounts at Chase Manhattan Bank and Bank of New York. All of the transfers appeared to reflect gold trading activity.

Loren Industries was, in 1986 and for a number of years prior to that time, a publicly-traded company based in Hollywood, Florida. Its shares were traded on the New York Stock Exchange. It was a precious metals dealer specializing in gold and silver. In the mid-1970s, it formed Ronel Refining as a subsidiary, to buy and sell gold and to supply Loren's casting operation with the precious metal. Ronel purchased a variety of different kinds of gold. It bought scraps, "jeweler's sweeps," pawnbrokers' gold, gold bullion dealers' gold, South American dealers' gold (also known as smugglers' gold), dentists' gold, and several other forms of the metal. Gold purchased by Ronel was refined into fine gold bars and resold. Gold sales were made to traders, brokers and wholesale jewelry suppliers. Ronel Refining became the "gold connection" for the Polar Cap money laundering operation.

Richard Ferris was the president of Ronel Refining. He had been with Loren Industries for a number of years and was knowledgeable about the gold business. He ran an almost autonomous operation. Carlos Desoretz was a salesman and bullion trader for Ronel. He had been in the gold business for many years and he knew the business inside out. He and Ferris were close friends. Desoretz' ability to produce customers was an important part of Ronel's business success. Up until 1986, Ronel was doing about $100 million in gross sales annually and showing a net profit of about $500,000. In 1987, revenues shot up to $245 million with a net profit of $1 million. In 1988, Ronel's sales soared to $500 million. Most of the increased volume was due to purchases and sales involving new customers named Letra, Orafe, A-Mark, Ropex and Andonian Brothers.

The Physical Gold Trading Phase

As previously indicated, Raul Vivas and Jorge Masihy worked out a deal with Carlos Desoretz for Ronel to purchase gold from them, and the shipments began in the fall of 1986. The initial shipments posed no problems for Ronel. The company was able to sell the gold to regular customers and make a profit. As agreed, the gold purchased was credited to the account of Orafe. Ronel would receive instructions from Cambio Italia in Montevideo to make payments for the gold by wire transferring funds to specific accounts in Panamanian banks.

In January 1987, Vivas instructed Ronel to credit the shipments to Letra S.A. instead of Orafe. Simultaneous with these instructions, there was a dramatic increase in the amount of gold being shipped. Over a period of time, the amount went up to as much as 70-80 kilos a day. This caused problems for Ronel; it was becoming difficult to find buyers on the open market. In late 1986, Richard Ferris went to the International Precious Metals Institute convention in Nevada, where he met Randy Leshay, an official of A-Mark Trading Company, a large gold broker in Los Angeles. Leshay was looking to buy refined gold and the two entered into an agreement that A-Mark would buy gold from Ronel at a price greater than the market price. Ronel was now able to dispose of the gold it was getting from Letra. It bought gold from Letra below market price and sold it to A-Mark above market price.

The mechanics of the money laundering scheme at that time looked something like this. The Vivas organization accumulated currency from cocaine sales. It used the currency to buy gold from jewelers and small gold dealers in Los Angeles such as Ropex, Andonian Brothers, Astro, and S&K. These firms deposited the currency in their bank accounts. Vivas, using the business name of either Orafe or Letra, then sold the gold to Ronel. Ronel would pay for the gold by transferring funds to accounts in Panamanian banks which were controlled by Vivas. His organization moved the funds in these accounts to the bosses of the Medellin cocaine cartel. Ronel then sold the gold either on the open market or to A-Mark. The Vivas organization lost money on every gold purchase and sale. However, this was a cost of conducting a money laundering operation. It was part of the price that cartel members were willing to pay for getting their drug profits out of the United States in a manner that made the money seem legitimate.

This phase of gold trading in "La Mina" was known as the physical gold trading phase. Actual physical gold was delivered to Ronel by Loomis after having been shipped by Vivas. When Ronel sold gold to A-Mark, it was shipped by Loomis and delivered to A-Mark's premises in Los Angeles. It wasn't long before the players in the gold scheme, (Ronel, Vivas, and A-Mark) began to realize that the same gold was being shipped back and forth across the country and that Loomis was getting rich at their expense. It became clear that the Los Angeles jewelers who sold gold to Vivas were buying that gold from A-Mark. A circular exchange of gold bullion was occurring among Ronel, A-Mark, the jewelers, and Vivas. Richard Ferris marked some gold bars that were shipped to A-Mark and observed that these same bars were later received in a shipment from Vivas.

Depository Account Phase

To reduce the cost of shipping gold back and forth across the country, the parties to the money laundering scheme worked out a depository account transfer arrangement which permitted all gold transactions to take place in Los Angeles. The new arrangement was engineered by Richard Ferris in conjunction with Prosegur Security Agency. Prosegur was an international transport company that had depository account services at its office in Los Angeles. The depository account service allowed customers to store precious metals in Prosegur's vaults. Ronel opened a depository account at Prosegur. A-Mark already had an account there. Gold suppliers to Vivas, such as Ropex and Andonian Brothers, would deliver the gold to Prosegur with instructions to credit it to the Ronel account in favor of Orafe or Letra. Prosegur would send a fax message to Ronel detailing the credit. The Orafe or Letra account at Ronel would then be credited with the value of the gold and Ronel would fax a message back to Prosegur advising that the same gold had been sold to A-Mark and that it should be transferred to A-Mark's depository account.

In this operation, gold arriving at Prosegur from Ropex or Andonian was first placed on a shelf in the Prosegur vault reserved for Ronel. Later, usually on the same day, when the gold was sold to A-Mark, it was simply transferred to another shelf in the same vault that was reserved for A-Mark. The result was a speedy, cost effective method of laundering large amounts of money. The currency would go from Vivas to the gold suppliers (Ropex, Andonian, Astro, S&K, and others), who would use the money to buy more gold from brokers such as A-Mark. Payment for the gold would be by check or wire transfer. When A-Mark bought gold from Ronel, it would wire transfer the payment to Ronel's account at Chase Manhattan Bank in New York. When Ronel credited the Orafe or Letra accounts with the value of the gold, it would receive instructions from Cambio Italia to wire transfer equivalent amounts of money to accounts in Panama. Once again, everybody made a profit except Orafe or Letra, and their loss was a cost of doing business as a money launderer.

The depository account worked well for a number of months during the first half of 1987. An average of 250 to 300 kilos of gold was bought and sold each week to launder currency provided by Raul Vivas during this time. However, in the summer of 1987, a problem developed that necessitated another change—A-Mark tested some gold that it had purchased from Ronel in the Prosegur depository account and found that 10% of it was gold-plated silver. For a short period of time, Ronel insisted on testing all gold that it bought before selling it to A-Mark, which slowed the laundering process considerably.

The A-Mark Pool Account

To cope with the problem of doctored, or sham gold, a new scheme was devised to mask the laundering of drug money with the appearance of gold trading. This scheme involved a gold pool account at A-Mark. With the pool account, Ropex and Andonian would receive currency that belonged to Vivas and use the money to secure a purchase order of gold from A-Mark. They would not actually receive the gold. They would pay Prosegur for the purchase order either with currency or with checks after currency had been deposited into one of their bank accounts. Then they would instruct A-Mark to credit the gold that had been purchased to Ronel's account and send a fax advice to Ronel requesting the gold be credited to the Letra account. Ronel would then sell the gold back to A-Mark, and the Letra account would have a cash value equal to the value of the gold sold. The funds in the account would then be wire transferred to a Panamanian account based on instructions from Cambio Italia.

This method assured A-Mark that the gold bought from Ronel was not tampered with. No real physical gold was even involved. It insured the rapid movement of funds out of Los Angeles and ultimately out of the United States. Ronel and A-Mark made money each time the gold was bought and sold. Vivas, Ropex, and Andonian saved the cost of shipping physical gold to Ronel in Florida. The only delay occurred when Prosegur had problems in counting the large sums of money being delivered by Ropex, Andonian, and other gold suppliers. With the pool account, the amount of gold transactions rose to a value of over $5 million a week.

The weekly volume of gold being transacted and of money being laundered continued to rise until the end of 1987, when the Vivas operation shut down for a vacation in mid-December. The amount of money that had passed through Ronel's bank account to the accounts controlled by Vivas in Panama was $250 million. During 1987, Carlos Desoretz continued to receive a 50-cent kickback for each ounce of gold sold by Ronel. He made $300,000 from this agreement that year. In January 1988, when the money laundering and gold trading activity resumed, Vivas reduced by 45-cents an ounce the price he was willing to pay to Ronel for gold. Instead, he paid a kickback of 45-cents an ounce to Ferris and Desoretz. They split it evenly. Desoretz now received 72.5 cents for every ounce purchased by Ronel, while Ferris received 22.5 cents. Ferris was not aware that Desoretz had been getting a 50-cent-per-ounce kickback since the operation began in 1986.

In early 1988, A-Mark started to become nervous about the whole gold trading scheme. The owners began worrying about their own possible criminal liability if, as they began to suspect, the entire gold trading operation was part of a money laundering scheme. In the spring of 1988, A-Mark notified all parties concerned that it would no longer participate in the A-Mark gold pool arrangement. For a period of time after the announcement, A-Mark continued to sell physical gold to Andonian and Ropex. The volume of these sales caused a serious shortage of physical gold in the Los Angeles area. In May 1988, A-Mark raised its gold price to Andonian and Ropex so far above market prices that they could no longer afford to buy it and they began to seek other sources.

The Ronel Pool Account

The shutdown of the A-Mark pool account and A-Mark's reluctance to deal with Ropex and Andonian brought about a new phase of gold trading activity in the "La Mina" money laundering scheme. It involved the creation of a gold pool at Ronel. In this pool arrangement, the Vivas organization would supply currency to Ropex and Andonian. These firms would then place orders for corresponding amounts of gold from Ronel. Ropex and Andonian would deposit the currency in their bank accounts and, on the next day, would wire transfer sufficient funds to Ronel's New York bank to cover the price of the gold that had been bought. When Ronel received the transfer, it would create a sales invoice documenting the gold sale. Ropex or Andonian, would then fax a message to Ronel with instructions to transfer the gold to the Letra account. Letra would then resell the gold to Ronel, which would appear to pay for it by wire transferring funds from its New York bank to Panamanian accounts designated by Cambio Italia in Montevideo.

Ronel made a profit on every sale. No physical gold ever changed hands. In fact, physical gold did not even have to exist. This scheme was used for several months in the summer of 1988. However, it became clear to Richard Ferris that this operation exposed Ronel to considerable risk—anyone who scrutinized the transactions would see it for the sham it was. Ronel stopped this so-called "Ronel pool account" operation in September.

During the weeks that followed, physical gold trading resumed. Ronel began to see gold shipments from a variety of gold brokers around the country, sent by Andonian and Ropex for credit to the Letra account at Ronel. Letra then sold the gold to Ronel and Ronel paid for it by wire transferring funds to accounts in Panama and Uruguay as instructed by Cambio Italia. But Ronel was not comfortable with this arrangement either.

London Gold Phase

In October, Carlos Desoretz proposed to Raul Vivas a procedure for trading gold on the London market. Vivas liked the idea and asked Desoretz to initiate the procedure with Nazareth Andonian. He said he did not want Wanis Koyomejian involved in the London trading because Koyomejian was dealing with competitor money laundering organizations.

In late October, Ferris and Desoretz went to Los Angeles and met with Nazareth and Vahe Andonian and set up a procedure to trade gold through a London depository account. Trading under this process went on for several months with the Andonian Brothers; all the while Ropex continued laundering by shipping physical gold to Ronel.

The London depository account worked as follows. Andonian Brothers received currency from the Vivas collection organization, and after counting the cash would place an order with an international gold broker named Cargill for an equivalent amount of gold (less the Andonian commission). The Andonian account was handled by a Cargill executive named Greg Alessandra. Andonian would then send a fax message to Cargill instructing that the gold be credited to the Ronel account at Phillip Brothers in London, England. Andonian would then send a fax message to Ronel furnishing all the details of the transaction with instructions that the gold be credited to Letra. Andonian would deposit the money in one of its bank accounts and wire transfer funds to Cargill to pay for the gold. When Cargill received the funds, it would instruct its London broker to transfer the amount of gold that had been purchased to the Ronel account at Phillip Brothers. Ronel would have previously sent a fax message to Phillip Brothers notifying them to expect delivery of a quantity of gold to be credited to the Ronel account. Once the gold was credited to Ronel, it would be sold back to Phillip Brothers or any one of a number of international gold brokers, which converted the value of the gold to funds which would be wire transferred to a Letra controlled bank account in Panama or Montevideo.

Gold Trading Problems Overheard

The gold trading problems that the Polar Cap money launderers encountered were detailed in conversations that were intercepted and recorded after the federal courts authorized electronic interceptions at Ropex and Andonian. The intercepted conversations established very clearly what OCDETF agents had long suspected: that the gold transactions involving Ronel, Andonian Brothers, and Ropex were only conducted to cover the movement of large sums of cocaine profits from the United States to accounts controlled by money launderers for the cocaine cartel in Uruguay and Panama.

On December 12, Nazareth Andonian received a telephone from Ferris of Ronel. Ferris told Nazareth to cut down on the frequency of his dealings with Cargill, and that in the future he should use Cargill only a couple of days a week. In overheard telephone conversations, agents had learned that Alessandra had called both Nazareth Andonian and Richard Ferris, asking each for an explanation of all the gold activity. In comparing notes, both men realized that they had given Alessandra different explanations and they were afraid he was becoming suspicious. Ferris further instructed that he should be sent faxes confirming all transactions.

In mid-December, Cargill stopped doing business with Andonian Brothers. The firm was obviously concerned with the legitimacy of the gold transactions. Other gold trading firms were used over the next few weeks. Nazareth Andonian continued to buy gold for the account of Ronel at Phillips Brothers in London.

THE BEGINNING OF THE END

On January 24, Nazareth Andonian received a telephone call that led to the unraveling of the entire Polar Cap money laundering operation in New York and Los Angeles.

The call came from "Lito" at Z&G Gold in New York. Lito said to Nazareth, "You don't remember Carlos?" Nazareth responded, "Yes, yes." Lito then stated, "I am going to send you a few boxes tomorrow." Nazareth asked, "You are going to start today?" Lito said, "Yes, we started yesterday." Lito advised Nazareth that he sent 14 boxes to VNA and the number is 4-8-6-9. Lito added that he sent 16 boxes for "George" and that is two kilos. Lito clarified, "OK, so you have 4-8-6-9." Nazareth confirmed, "Four kilos eight six nine." Lito replied, "Yes." Nazareth reconfirmed the four kilos eight sixty-nine and Lito agreed. Lito then said, "Don't mix it, OK?" and added, "tell me which one, you know?" Nazareth replied, "Yes, sure... which one is what?" Lito said, "Yes, VNA and George . . . you know?"

The OCDETF agents in Los Angeles who listened to the conversation were aware of the codes used by the money launderers. They interpreted the reference to "four kilos 869" to mean $4,869,000. This was almost $5 million. It was one of the largest single cash shipments ever made. It was obvious that Nazareth Andonian couldn't believe his ears. He deliberately asked "Lito" to repeat the amount twice. The reference to boxes being sent to George was interpreted to mean that they would be shipped to Joyce Jewelers in Los Angeles. VNA was another business name used by Andonian Brothers. It was co-located in Andonians' offices.

In New York, DEA agents had been monitoring a pen register on a telephone number that was subscribed to by Z&G Gold. Z&G Gold and Janed Jewelry had become the primary collection points in New York for currency being shipped to Andonian Brothers. DEA agents on the OCDETF task force in Los Angeles contacted the DEA surveillance team in New York. The pen register in New York showed that at exactly 1:21 p.m., New York time, a call had been initiated from the Z&G Gold telephone to a number registered to Andonian Brothers in Los Angeles. The agents discussed the nature of the conversation. On hearing the details, the New York DEA agents agreed with the meaning of what was about to happen. Lito was getting ready to ship almost $5 million in currency to Andonian in Los Angeles. During the telephone conversation, one of the New York DEA agents mentioned the possibility of seizing the money in New York and closing down the entire operation.

This remark set off a flurry of activity over the next few hours in Los Angeles, Washington, and New York. Los Angeles OCDETF agents conferred with their task force prosecutors; they wanted the case to proceed further, believing more evidence was needed. They also wanted to be able to arrest major players such as Raul Vivas and Sergio Hochman, whose whereabouts were unknown at the time. Perhaps more importantly, the Los Angeles task force wanted to be able to simultaneously execute a large number of search warrants and have arrest warrants ready for all participants when the operation was to be shut down; there would be no time to prepare all the required documentation on such short notice.

The Los Angeles OCDETF communicated with Chuck Saphos at the Justice Department in Washington, who quickly convened a meeting of the Polar Cap coordinating group with representatives from each agency involved in the investigation. There was unanimous agreement that it was premature for the Polar Cap operation to be shut down. They also agreed that the $5 million shipment should not be seized in New York. The decision was communicated to the New York OCDETF and to the DEA managers in New York. There was no disagreement with the decision.

The decision-making process had taken several hours, and the DEA agents working the case on the street in New York had been busy in the interim. They had set up additional surveillance teams to observe both Z&G Gold and Janed Jewelry. They had contacted Loomis officials and advised them of their interest in a shipment that might be made from one of the two jewelers. At about 4:30 p.m., the surveillance agents observed a Loomis van pull up to the location, and watched as the driver entered Janed's and removed a large number of boxes to the van. The van was followed to Kennedy Airport.

The agents consulted with Loomis representatives. The shipment consisted of 30 boxes, for delivery to VNA and Joyce Jewelers. The total declared value of the shipment, which was labeled "jewelry" was set at $4,869,000. The DEA supervisor on the site decided to seize the package.

By the time the DEA's New York office heard of the decision from Washington not to seize the money, the agents on the surveillance team were already at Kennedy Airport. The office in New York was not able to reach the agents at the airport. When communications were finally established, the boxes in the shipment had been put aside in a United Parcel air freight storage area reserved for Loomis. The aircraft that was to transport them to Los Angeles had left. There would be a one-day delay before the next aircraft departed. The boxes had not yet been opened.

A series of telephone calls were made between New York, Washington, and Los Angeles. It was decided not to try to delay the delivery to Los Angeles for a full day. A Customs narcotics detection dog was brought to the area where the boxes were, and the dog alerted to the boxes indicating the possibility that they contained drugs. The boxes were opened and found to be packed with currency. What the dog had alerted to was cocaine residue on the money. The contents of the boxes were seized. A subsequent count determined that the boxes contained approximately $4,869,000 in currency.

A decision had to be made. Should the investigation be terminated and arrests made or should it be allowed to proceed? The decision was to continue the investigation and not to make the arrests at that point. There was a concern that the seizure of the money would compromise the electronic surveillance system. In an effort to avoid this possibility, it was decided to send several Customs agents to Janed on the following morning. They would ask questions about the contents of the shipment and would indicate that it had been seized after narcotics dogs had reacted positively to the boxes. It was believed that the wiretaps would produce some very interesting conversations once the money launderers realized that the money had been seized.

On the morning of January 25, Customs agents arrived at the offices of Janed Jewelry at about 10:00. Employees indicated that they did not know anything about the shipment. Khazad Teirakian, vice president of the firm, told the agents he believed the packages contained jewelry polishing powder, that he knew nothing about money in the packages. He said that the packages were to go to Andonian in Los Angeles.

In Los Angeles, Nazareth Andonian was still expecting to receive almost $5 million that morning. He came into the office early and placed a call to Loomis. The call was recorded. He spoke to the Loomis manager, George Rosenfeld, noting that he was expecting a large number of packages from New York. Rosenfeld said that he was not aware of any shipment, but assured Nazareth that it would be delivered promptly as soon as he received it. At 8:53 a.m., Pacific Time, Nazareth received a telephone call from George Rosenfeld informing him that the morning shipment had come in and there was no package for him.

Nazareth immediately smelled trouble. Telephone calls made by himself and others over the next few hours confirmed his worst fears. He learned that the $5 million was not coming and that Customs agents in New York had precise information as to the actual contents of the boxes shipped to Andonian.

January 25 finally ended for Nazareth Andonian. His operation had lost almost $5 million. The Vivas laundering operation was in a state of panic and confusion. Raul Vivas and Juan Carlos Seresi were in Montevideo. They initially believed that Tomas Iglesias had tipped off enforcement authorities to their activities. Vivas and Iglesias had a falling out in the summer of 1988 and, at that time, Iglesias threatened to expose him to the police if Vivas did not pay him $1 million. Later, Vivas speculated that the Andonian brothers may have stolen the money.

The Andonian phase of the money laundering operation came to a complete standstill. The Colombian customers of Raul Vivas wanted their money. There was over $4 million in a Letra pool account at Ronel. On instructions from Cambio Italia, the account was closed and the money was transferred to accounts in Panama and Montevideo. The Colombians were paid off. No one filed a claim for the $4.8 million that had been seized at Kennedy Airport. The money was eventually forfeited to the United States government.

THE ARRESTS AND PROSECUTION

After the currency seizure, OCDETF agents and prosecutors worked feverishly preparing arrest warrants and search warrants as they prepared to close down Operation Polar Cap. Their efforts doubled when telephone conversations were overheard indicating that some of the launderers were making travel plans. By mid-February, most of the paperwork had been completed. Raul Vivas' whereabouts were known—he was in Montevideo. Uruguayan police were cooperating with OCDETF agents. Sergio Hochman was out of pocket. Agents and prosecutors wanted to be in a position to make simultaneous arrests of as many of the conspirators as possible once they decided to move in. They particularly wanted to arrest the kingpins.

Out of the blue, Sergio Hochman showed up in Los Angeles on February 21, and visited Andonian Brothers. OCDETF supervisors agreed that it was time to move in. Paperwork was completed. Warrants were obtained for the arrest of 35 individuals, 28 of whom were residents of Los Angeles. Search warrants were issued for 17 business locations and 28 residences in the Los Angeles area. Teams of agents and police officers were formed to make arrests and execute the searches. The total complement of enforcement personnel involved came to 140. The teams moved out in the early morning hours of February 22. They swept into the downtown jewelry district just as many merchants were opening their shops. Search warrants were executed at 10 jewelers, including Ropex and Andonian Brothers. Nazareth Andonian was arrested in his office. Wanis Koyomejian was arrested at Ropex offices. A number of employees were arrested at each of these offices.

The scene on the streets of the jewelry district was chaotic. Enforcement vehicles started to move in at the beginning of the rush hour, blocking off some heavily traveled streets. Hundreds of people gathered to see what was going on. They watched with interest as 20 people were led away in handcuffs.

While the arrests were taking place in Los Angeles, five conspirators were being arrested at Janed Jewelry and Z&G Gold in New York City. Richard Ferris and Carlos Desoretz were arrested in their offices in Ronel

Refining in Hollywood, Florida. Raul Vivas was arrested in Montevideo, Uruguay on a warrant issued in Los Angeles. Extradition proceedings were immediately commenced to have him removed to the United States.

Several of the Los Angeles defendants, including Wanis Koyomejian, Sergio Hochman, and Nazareth Andonian were held without bail. Most of the others were held on very high bail ranging up to $500,000. The arrests and searches received massive publicity on the radio, television, and in the print media. Following the arrests, the entire case was presented to a Federal Grand Jury.

On March 8, the Grand Jury handed up two indictments charging 32 individuals and Ronel Refining, Inc., with money laundering, cocaine possession, and conspiracy violations. There were actually two separate indictments, one involving the Ropex aspect of the operation and the other involving the Andonian Brothers operation. Raul Vivas, Sergio Hochman, Richard Ferris, Carlos Desoretz and Ronel Refining were common defendants in each indictment. The two indictments marked a decision by prosecutors to try the Ropex and Andonian cases separately, rather than to attempt one massive trial.

Following the arrests of Polar Cap defendants in Los Angeles and New York, there were two interesting developments in money laundering activity by Colombian cocaine distributors. Several days after the arrests, Eduardo Martinez, the Colombian money launderer who stopped dealing with DEA undercover agents in the summer of 1988, contacted the agents and made arrangements to start supplying them with currency. The second development involved a change in policy by a major Colombian cocaine distribution network in New York. In the summer of 1989, this organization decided to stop all money laundering through U.S. banks, and instead physically transport all currency from cocaine profits back to Colombia where it could be shipped to a number of countries to satisfy the then growing worldwide demand for U.S. dollars. This decision was a direct result of the Polar Cap arrests.

Once the indictments were returned, a new phase of judicial proceedings came into play—the deal-making, the legal positioning, and the eventual trial of those defendants who did not plead guilty. It is a phase that, in this case, highlights some of the problems with and failures of our judicial system.

Throughout the summer and fall of 1989, negotiations ensued between prosecution and defense attorneys. There were also endless motions by defense attorneys to suppress evidence which the government had gathered. In December 1989, Judge William T. Keller, who was handling the Andonian part of the indictment, dismissed all defense motions to suppress evidence and set a trial date in April 1990.

On December 8, 1989, after lengthy judicial proceedings, Raul Vivas was extradited from Uruguay. He was flown from Montevideo to Los Angeles. He pleaded not guilty to the indictment and was held without bail.

By February 1990, negotiations between attorneys resulted in agreements whereby six of the defendants in the two indictments had entered guilty pleas. The six were: Sergio Hochman, Richard Ferris, Carlos Desoretz, Eddie Ortiz, Pedro Fuentes, and Manouk Demirjian.

The most important of these guilty pleas came from Sergio Hochman. As part of a plea agreement, Hochman agreed to cooperate with the government and testify in any trials as a government witness. When Hochman began to cooperate, the government learned from him that Celio Merkin was one of the originators of the money laundering scheme along with Raul Vivas. He told them that Merkin had put up money for the purchase of Cambio Italia, the currency exchange business in Montevideo which controlled the money laundering operation.

While progress was being made in the prosecution of the Andonian indictment, serious delays and problems were being encountered with the prosecution of the Ropex case. The Ropex case was being handled by U.S. District Judge Consuelo B. Marshall, who moved very slowly in handling defense motions to suppress evidence. Wanis Koyomejian's attorney made a motion to suppress all video surveillance tapes that the government had made of activities at Ropex. He argued that there was no statutory authority for videotaped surveillance and that such surveillance was an indiscriminate invasion of privacy and unconstitutional. Technically, the argument about a lack of statutory authority was correct. A federal statute specifically approved listening interceptions such as wiretaps and bugging devices; no statute specifically authorizes video surveillance. However, federal enforcement agencies had been using video surveillance for years. This type of surveillance was usually conducted after an application to a court, similar to a search warrant application, seeking authority to install video devices. This type of surveillance had been tested in the courts on dozens of occasions. Three appeals had been taken to U.S. Courts of Appeals in three different circuits and all had ruled that court-approved video surveillance did not constitute an unwarranted invasion of privacy and all three upheld the government's right to use evidence obtained from such surveillance.

Normally, an issue that had been decided by three different Circuit Courts of Appeals would be considered to be controlling. Judge Marshall viewed the video surveillance at Ropex as being overly intrusive and an invasion of privacy. She attempted to distinguish the Ropex surveillance from the Circuit Court of Appeals cases by finding that it was indiscriminate and not directed toward specific individuals, locations, or events. She also relied on the fact that there was no specific statute that authorized video surveillance. Judge Marshall issued an opinion on March 28, 1990, in which she ruled that the video surveillance in the Ropex investigation was unconstitutional and ordered that none of the evidence gathered from it could be used at the trial.

Judge Marshall's decision set off a bombshell in Los Angeles and Washington. In Los Angeles, a great deal of the evidence collected in the Ropex case was jeopardized. Indeed, defense attorneys immediately started to claim that if the videotaped evidence was illegal, then any evidence derived from it should be suppressed. In Washington, dozens of ongoing investigations and prosecutions would be jeopardized if this very liberal view of the defendant's right to privacy were upheld. The Justice Department views court ordered video surveillance as a legitimate investigative tool. Indeed, many legal scholars consider video surveillance as less intrusive than audio intercepts produced from wiretaps and bugs. The government filed an appeal to Judge Marshall's decision in April 1990.

Defense attorneys in the Andonian case had not used the legal arguments about the government's lack of statutory authority to conduct video surveillance in their motions to suppress evidence. But several days after Judge Marshall's decision, they filed new motions to suppress the videotaped evidence in the Andonian case to Judge Keller, using the same legal arguments that had been made in the Ropex case. Judge Keller decided quickly on the new motions. On April 11, 1990, he issued a 27-page order in which he ruled that the prosecutors could introduce video surveillance tapes of the defendants' activities inside Andonian Brothers offices. The ruling completely contradicted Judge Marshall.

Judge Keller specifically found that, "There is no foundation for a claim that the court order permitting video surveillance is patently unconstitutional." When he issued the order, Judge Keller told defense attorneys that his order was final and that he was "quite confident" that he would not be reversed on appeal. He also directed that the trial of the Andonian case would commence on April 17, as originally scheduled. Here was an anomaly. Two Federal judges in the same judicial district issued diametrically opposite rulings on an almost identical set of facts.

The Andonian trial started on April 17 with ten defendants. The Ropex trial was postponed pending appeal to the Ninth Circuit Court of Appeals. The delays in the Ninth Circuit Court's ability to decide the issue have turned out to be a blot on the effectiveness of the federal judicial system.

In July 1990, while the Andonian trial was in progress, OCDETF prosecutors in Los Angeles returned a new indictment charging six additional people with money laundering and aiding and abetting the distribution of cocaine arising from the Ropex and Andonian operations. Five of the indictee were jewelers from Los Angeles. The other was Celio Merkin, the

Argentinean who Sergio Hochman identified as one of the original financial backers of the money laundering operation.

The Andonian trial dragged on for months. It would turn out to be the
longest trial in the history of the Los Angeles Federal Courthouse. Testimony was given by almost 100 witnesses. The prosecutors finished their
direct evidence on August 28. Attorneys for all 10 defendants made motions for directed verdicts of acquittal on the basis of insufficient evidence.
Judge Keller denied the motions for nine of the defendants but acquitted
Vasken Anouchian.

Anouchian, who had been employed at Andonian Brothers, had made
many telephone calls transferring funds from Andonian bank accounts to
accounts at banks in New York. Judge Keller found that the government
had failed to prove that Anouchian knew he was participating in a drug
money laundering conspiracy.

The trial continued on with the defense presenting its witnesses and
the prosecution presenting rebuttal testimony. The case finally went to the
jury on November 30, more than six months after it started.

On December 11, after six days of deliberation, the jury acquitted two
of the defendants of all charges. One was an employee of Andonian Brothers. The other was the owner of A&P Jewelers, which was located on the
eighth floor of the same building that housed Andonian Brothers. Evidence
produced during the trial showed that A&P Jewelers had received 26 shipments of packages from New York during June 1988, and that the owner
had turned the packages over to his brother-in-law, Nazareth Andonian.
After the acquittal, attorneys for both men claimed that the government
had not been able to prove that they had any intent to launder money or
traffic in narcotics. They also stated that the government had not proven
guilty knowledge of any money laundering scheme.

On December 18, after 18 days of deliberation, the jury acquitted two
more defendants—two sisters who worked at Andonian Brothers and were
cousins of Nazareth and Vahe Andonian. One was a bookkeeper, the other
a receptionist. Evidence at the trial showed that they both unpacked and
counted currency shipments and then repacked the money in preparation
for deposit into Los Angeles banks. After the not guilty verdicts, attorneys
for the women claimed neither was aware that the money was connected
with any illegal activity.

The jury did not complete its work until January 4, 1991. After 21 days
of deliberations, it found Raul Vivas, Nazareth Andonian, Vahe Andonian,
Ruben Saini, and Juan Carlos Seresi guilty of money laundering charges
and conspiracy. It acquitted the defendants on all charges of aiding and
abetting the distribution of drugs.

The final outcome of the trial was bittersweet for the government. All
of the principal conspirators in the Andonian operation were either found

guilty or had pleaded guilty to money laundering charges, but five of the principal conspirators were acquitted of drug charges, four defendants were acquitted of all charges and Judge Keller had dismissed all charges against a tenth defendant.

The results of the trial were somewhat of an embarrassment for the government in light of the massive publicity that surrounded the arrests and indictments of defendants charged in the case. The government's embarrassment was heightened by an article that in the January 28, 1991 edition of *The Los Angeles Times* titled "Is Government Too Zealous in Pursuing Money Laundering?" The article pointed that the government conducted extensive wiretaps and video surveillances in the case. It also noted that the Andonian phase of the Polar Cap started out with indictments against 17 individuals and one company, but that by the time the case ended, nine of the defendants had been freed. It contained a statement from a defense attorney that the government had "over-indicted the case." The article also stated that there has been no other major federal drug case in Los Angeles in recent years in which such a substantial number of defendants were exonerated.

What happened to the Ropex case? That is a good question. As of early November 1991 it still had not been resolved. The government filed its appeal from Judge Marshall's decision on the issue of videotape surveillance in May 1990. Defense briefs in opposition to the appeal were filed on behalf of Wanis Koyomejian and other defendants in July 1990. Oral arguments before a three-judge panel of the Ninth U.S. Circuit Court of Appeals did not take place until December 1990. Federal prosecutors expected to have a decision by April 1991. Instead, one of the judges on the panel announced his retirement and withdrew from the decision process. The case languished in the Ninth Circuit until October 15, 1991, at which time the appeals court issued a decision reversing Judge Marshall's decision and remanding the case for trial. But the court gave defense attorneys until the end of November to file a motion for a rehearing of the issue.

What a mockery of justice and of our judicial system! It took over one year from the time of arrest for the District Court in Los Angeles to decide that the videotaping of activities at Ropex was unconstitutional, and it took almost another 18 months for the Ninth Circuit to overrule the District Court. Well over two and one-half years have gone by since the defendants were arrested and the appeal process still has not been finally resolved. Justice delayed is justice denied. Justice applies both to the defendants in a case and the prosecution. If the Ropex defendants are not guilty, they deserve to have the onus of criminal charges removed as soon as possible. If they are guilty, the government should have the ability to press for severe punishment as soon as possible.

In the meantime, the principal defendants in the Andonian phase of the case received harsh prison sentences. On August 27, 1991, U.S. District Judge William Keller imposed jail terms on the five principal defendants who were convicted in January 1991. Raul Vivas, Nazareth Andonian, Vahe Andonian, and Juan Carlos Seresi each received sentences of 505 years imprisonment, and Ruben Saini was sentenced to 27 years.

The sentences were a shocker to defense attorneys who had been expecting maximum sentences of 99 years. The sentences also provided a stern warning to drug money launderers.

While the Andonian defendants never made bail and are now serving huge sentences, the Ropex defendants have been free on bail since the spring of 1990.

U.S. Government officials, the media, and Congressional critics frequently disparage the judicial systems in Colombia and Mexico with regard to drug trafficking prosecutions in those countries. Perhaps they should re-examine the U.S. justice system before criticizing others. The Ropex prosecution illustrates some terrible shortcomings in our system. More than two and one-half years after major drug money laundering charges were filed, there have been no trials of defendants who pleaded not guilty in the Ropex case.

There is little doubt that Operation Polar Cap was the largest money laundering operation ever uncovered by the U.S. government. Publicity about the arrests of suspects and the breakup of the operation was massive and put the government's investigation and prosecution in a highly favorable light. Events since the publicity have tended to tarnish the brightness of that light, however.

The government should have been in a position to react to the money laundering problem sooner than it did. A major trial of 10 defendants ended up with five acquittals. The judicial handling of one-half of the Polar Cap case has been mired in a legal quagmire involving a controversial ruling by a judge and an unconscionable delay by the Ninth Circuit Court of Appeals in resolving the ruling. The entire situation raises serious questions about the ability of the federal judicial system to cope with big time drug trafficking and money laundering.

CHAPTER 6

THE BANK OF CREDIT AND COMMERCE INTERNATIONAL (BCCI)

The Bank of Credit and Commerce International, or BCCI, was a rogue elephant, in both the worlds of banking and money laundering. Within some circles, BCCI came to be known as the Bank of Crooks and Criminals International.

The extent of BCCI's proclivity to deal in criminally derived funds became fully apparent during the U.S. Customs sting known as Operation C Chase. It was during that investigation that federal agents discovered just how ready, willing and able BCCI and its key employees were to launder money from cocaine sales.

OPERATION C CHASE

Operation C Chase was launched by Customs in July 1986. C Chase stood for currency chase. Undercover Customs agents, furnished with false identities and business offices, setup shop in a number of cities as money launderers for drug dealers. Arrangements were made with banks to open accounts that could be used by the agents to make large currency deposits, with cooperating bank officials aware of the Customs connection.

Confidential informants in each city introduced the undercover agents to local drug dealers. The agents began to receive currency from the dealers and move it into local banks. Once the currency had been deposited in a bank, the funds would be moved by way of checks or wire transfers according to instructions from the drug dealers. In some cases, the money would be transferred to bank accounts in the same city or in other U.S. cities. In other situations, the funds were moved to foreign bank accounts. Other times, the funds were returned to the dealers in the form of bank or cashier's checks payable to fictitious names. In each situation, the agents withheld a 4% commission for their services.

Successful undercover money laundering businesses were established in New York, Detroit, Chicago, Philadelphia, Los Angeles, Houston, and Tampa. The cornerstone of Operation C Chase was in Tampa, where an intrepid and resourceful undercover agent who went by the name Bob Musella had set himself up as a highly successful businessman.

Musella, whose real name was Robert Mazur, was known to his fellow agents to be a smart, hard-working, and earnest individual. He played the role of a mafia-connected money launderer perfectly, fitting the part in terms of appearance, background, and demeanor. He was in his late thirties and he presented a dapper appearance with a neatly trimmed jet black beard, trim muscular build, dark complexion, and expensive clothing. He had the appearance of a successful accountant and businessman. He had been an IRS agent before joining the Customs Service.

His business empire appeared to control a financial consulting firm, a mortgage business, a brokerage firm, a small charter airline with a Cessna Citation Aircraft, and a chain of costume jewelry stores. The Customs undercover operation provided a service that the drug dealers badly needed—getting large sums of currency into the banking system without drawing attention to themselves and without leaving a paper trail. In some circles, this type of undercover operation has been criticized on the grounds that it facilitates drug trafficking. To a certain extent this criticism is valid. For a period of time, traffickers are being assisted. However, Operation C Chase had some very definite goals. Among them: identifying as many drug traffickers and money launderers as possible and the scope of their operations; seizing cocaine, money, and property; and breaking up trafficking and laundering operations through criminal cases against participants.

All of the goals of Operation C Chase were met and there was an added bonus: a corrupt banking organization and a number of its officers were convicted of money laundering activities.

Operation C Chase was presented by Customs and was accepted as an Organized Crime Drug Enforcement Task Force case (OCDETF) in 1986 in Tampa. The designation paved the way for several IRS agents to work with Customs on the investigation.

An important milestone in Operation C Chase occurred in July 1986 when Gabriel Jaime Mora, a/k/a Jimmy Mora, asked a confidential Customs informant in Miami to open two bank accounts for him. Jimmy Mora was part of a smurfing organization based in Miami and headed by his brother, Gonzalo Mora, Jr., who lived in Medellin, Colombia. The informant told Jimmy Mora that he knew of an organization, based in Tampa, that was capable of laundering large amounts of currency.

In mid-July, the informant introduced Jimmy Mora to the leaders of the Tampa money laundering organization, Customs undercover agents who went by the names of Bob Musella and Emilio Dominguez. The meeting went well, and a deal was struck. The supposed launderers were to open two bank accounts in the Tampa area and the Mora organization was to supply currency to be deposited into these accounts.

Musella and Dominguez were to supply Jimmy Mora with blank, presigned checks that would be used to siphon money out of accounts that would be established in Tampa area banks. The agents told Jimmy Mora they had connections with bankers who would let them deposit large sums of cash and not file Currency Transaction Reports with the government.

During the course of the meeting, Jimmy Mora told the agents he was supposed to have transported 10 kilograms of cocaine to Los Angeles, but that the cocaine was part of a large package of 450 kilograms that had been seized by government agents in Kendall, Florida. Indeed, there had been such a seizure.

In late July1986, the undercover agents opened two accounts in Tampa area banks in the name of Jose Uribe. From August through October 1986, Jimmy Mora and his father made a series of small currency deliveries (amounts ranging between $8,000 and $30,000) to the agents for deposit into the Jose Uribe accounts. Jimmy Mora gave the agents specific instructions from his brother that they were to keep deposits to the accounts under $10,000—this, despite the fact the agents had said they could evade the need for CTRs. Gonzalo Mora, Jr. was paranoid about being identified by the government's CTR forms for large currency deposits.

Presigned checks were delivered to Jimmy Mora. It later turned out that the checks, payable in U.S. dollars, were being converted to Colombian pesos on the Colombian black market by several black market money exchange brokers.

It is worth noting that the currency the agents received from the Moras' prior to October 27, 1986 did not violate laws against money laundering or structuring transactions to evade reporting requirements. A statute establishing the crime of money laundering became law on October 27; the federal antistructuring law went into effect January 27, 1987.

The small currency deliveries made to the undercover agents during the fall of 1986 were an obvious testing process. On December 2, 1986, Gonzalo Mora, Jr. (hereafter referred to as "Mora") came to Tampa to meet with Bob Musella and Emilio Dominguez. He went with them to a suite of offices in New Port Richey, Florida, where Musella described his financial empire and awed Mora with his business acumen. He said that he owned Financial Consulting Inc., a company whose name appeared on the door to the office. He also said that he controlled Dynamic Mortgage Brokers and Tammey Jewels. He described Tammey Jewels as a company that had 50 costume jewelry retail outlets in shopping malls. He also advised that he had an investment in a brokerage house in New York and in a small charter airline named Sunbird Airlines that owned a corporate jet aircraft. Mora took to the agents like a duck to water. Within a short time, he was explaining that he collected large amounts of currency from cocaine sales and that he had to get the U.S. dollars converted to Colombian pesos and back into the hands of major cocaine dealers in Medellin, Colombia. Mora did not realize his meeting with the agents was being recorded on both audio and video tape.

Mora said he was being pressed to handle more money but that he didn't have the people who could get rid of it. He was very much aware of the Bank Secrecy Act, and of the obligation of U.S. banks to file CTRs on currency transactions over $10,000. That was why he had resorted to smurfing.

Musella and Dominguez assured Mora they could handle large amounts of currency without generating CTRs. Musella said he could put some cash through his businesses, and that he knew of some friendly bankers who would not file CTRs. Mora told the agents he was interested in getting an account in a Panamanian bank because he could realize more profit from checks drawn on Panamanian accounts than on checks drawn on U.S. banks. He also liked the security of Panamanian secrecy laws, and he noted that not even the DEA could get information on Panamanian bank accounts.

As the meeting progressed, it became clear that Mora had contacts with Colombian drug dealers and that he needed to move large sums of currency through the banking system. It was also clear that Mora was impressed with the agents. Musella invited Mora to go to New York with him and visit the stock brokerage his Financial Consulting firm had invested in. Mora agreed.

On December 4, 1986, Musella and Mora went to New York on a whirlwind two-day trip. They stayed at the Vista Hotel in lower Manhattan and Musella wined and dined Mora. He brought him to Russo Securities, a brokerage firm in the financial district which he said Financial Consulting had an interest in. The owners went along with the ruse. The trip was a great success. Mora came away convinced Musella's organization could launder large amounts of currency.

On December 9, 1986, Gonzalo Mora met with Bob Musella and Emilio Dominguez in Tampa. Mora was concerned that if he started doing business with Musella's organization he eventually would get cut out of his share of the laundering profits. Musella overcame this problem by suggesting they share equally in the profits of all money laundered and clearly define the responsibilities of each party. It was agreed that Mora would be responsible for recruiting clients and arranging the delivery of all currency to Musella's representatives. Musella's organization was to take possession of currency, get it into banks, and then move the money to Colombia or wherever else Mora wanted it.

Mora liked the arrangement. He assured Musella he would be supplying him with large quantities of currency from a drug dealer and money launderer in Los Angeles.

True to his word, in February 1987, Mora arranged for a series of deliveries totalling over $700,000 in currency to Musella's representatives in Los Angeles. What Mora did not know was that Musella's representatives were also undercover Customs agents. The money received was deposited into a Customs undercover account in a cooperating Los Angeles bank and then wire transferred to an account established in the name of Financial Consulting Inc. at a branch of the Florida National Bank in St. Petersburg. Presigned blank checks were then supplied to Mora in Colombia. He usually made the checks payable to one of several black market currency dealers who converted the dollar-denominated instruments to pesos, which went to Mora's major Colombian drug dealing clients.

BCCI ENTERS THE PICTURE

Customs agents supervising Operation C Chase decided it was time to open a Panamanian bank account. The decision was based on Mora's interest in such an account during his December meeting with the agents.

An international bank was needed for such an account. The Bank of Credit and Commerce International (BCCI) had an office in Tampa and also had offices in Panama, Colombia, the Cayman Islands, and many other countries.

On February 11, 1987, Musella went to BCCI's Tampa office and met with an officer named Richard Argudo. Musella told Argudo he owned two businesses, Financial Consulting and Dynamic Mortgage Brokers, and he explained how he performed financial services for U.S. citizens and clients from Central and South America. He said he wanted to open an account so he could receive payments from his client's accounts in Panama. Argudo explained that an international bank such as BCCI could not accept deposits from U.S. citizens or resident aliens—the bank's business was financing international trade.

Argudo explained that what Musella needed was an escrow account that could only be used to accept funds from foreign clients. He said if Financial Consulting opened an account at BCCI, Tampa, deposits could be made to BCCI Panama on behalf of the Tampa account and within 24 hours the funds would be transferred there. Musella gave Argudo a $10,000 check drawn on the Financial Consulting account at Florida National Bank to open the escrow account. He signed account opening forms and a release permitting BCCI to obtain information from Florida National Bank about Musella and his company. Argudo said he needed minutes of a board meeting and a copy of the corporate resolution.

After the account formalities were over, Argudo asked if there would be a need to move funds in the opposite direction—from the United States to Panama, and Musella indicated he might have such a need. Argudo said BCCI had many clients in Tampa who took advantage of the confidentiality the bank provided in moving funds to Panama. He said these clients made deposits directly to a BCCI affiliate in the Caymans in the past but that he no longer recommended this course of action because the Caymans had entered into a treaty with the IRS which enabled the U.S. government to obtain records of accounts of U.S. citizens in Grand Cayman banks. He said most clients were being directed to have their funds deposited to accounts at BCCI in Panama, and he offered to assist Musella in opening an account in Panama if the need arose.

At this point in time, BCCI was not a suspect or target of Operation C Chase. Customs only wanted to establish a banking procedure whereby they could move funds to Panama. However, Musella thought that Argudo's heavy emphasis on confidentiality and obvious efforts to avoid IRS scrutiny were a bit unusual for an upstanding banker.

It is interesting to note that the procedures Argudo followed in opening the Financial Consulting account represented standard due diligence measures bankers are expected to follow in getting to know a new customer—so-called "Know Your Customer" procedures. Argudo followed up on the information Musella had provided by checking out references and sending officers to visit his business premises.

THE LOS ANGELES CONNECTION

In early April 1987, Gonzalo Mora contacted Bob Musella to say he was coming to the United States and to remind him of his interest in establishing a Panamanian account. Musella agreed to arrange a meeting with his banker. Mora also said he wanted Musella to accompany him to Los Angeles to meet his laundering client there.

On April 8, Musella and Dominguez met with Gonzalo Mora, Jr. and Richard Argudo, the BCCI officer in Tampa, and Argudo reiterated the benefits of Panamanian bank accounts. He recommended that the two maintain accounts in Panama if they wanted to conduct confidential transactions, noting that he had clients who used BCCI accounts in Panama and Miami to handle business that actually occurred between individuals in the United States and South America. He suggested they falsely invoice transactions between themselves, through a Panamanian shell corporation, to avoid taxes. He also suggested Mora and Musella deposit funds at a foreign branch of BCCI and that he would arrange loans of equal amounts at BCCI branches in their respective countries—thus, the funds credited to them would appear to have originated from nontaxable loans.

On April 15, Musella and Dominguez went to Los Angeles where they met with Gonzalo Mora, Jimmy Mora, and a drug dealer/money launderer named Roberto Alcaino, a/k/a the "Jeweler." Alcaino's wife owned a jewelry store in Los Angeles. The meeting went very well. Alcaino talked about importing cocaine into Los Angeles and New York and how he needed to launder large sums of currency from those cities. Musella assured him that his organization could handle quantities of currency anywhere in the United States. It was learned that the currency deliveries to undercover agents in Los Angeles in February had come from Alcaino's organization.

Following the meeting with Alcaino in Los Angeles, there were several currency deliveries to undercover agents in Los Angeles during late April. The average amount of each delivery was about $130,000. The funds were transferred from Los Angeles to the Financial Consulting account in St. Petersburg and moved out of the account via presigned checks sent to Mora in Colombia. During the last week of April, Alcaino and Mora arranged for the delivery of two separate packages of currency to one of Musella's representatives (an undercover agent) in New York; the deliveries amounted to $202,000 and $104,000. The money was moved in a manner similar to the way it was handled in previous transactions.

"PISCES" INTERFERES

By May 1987, it looked as if things were about to pick up for Operation C Chase. There were strong indications of large currency deliveries pending in New York and Los Angeles, and Musella was preparing to open a Panamanian bank account. Then there was an indictment and large number of arrests involving a DEA undercover money laundering sting enterprise known as "Operation Pisces." Publicity surrounding the case put a chill on the entire Musella operation and delayed his Panamanian banking plans.

"Operation Pisces" had been underway for more than three years. DEA agents, posing as money launderers, had washed millions of narco-dollars supplied by dealers in the United States. Most of the drug money had been transferred to accounts at banks in Panama that had been established by representatives of the drug dealers. To make its case, DEA needed to know about the accountholders and where funds from the accounts went. In a situation unheard of until that time, the Panamanian government, with the blessing of General Manuel Noriega agreed to identify the accountholders and provide DEA with records of account transactions.

The decision by Noriega to cooperate was later seen as an effort to appease the U.S. government. Stern voices had been raised within the executive branch and Congress about Noriega's apparent involvement with prominent Colombian cartel members and money laundering activities.

The decision to cooperate enabled DEA to freeze funds in 54 accounts in Panamanian banks. Eighteen of these accounts were located in the Panama City branch of BCCI. When the indictment was made public, Jaime Mora, a/k/a Jimmy Mora, was listed as an unindicted co-conspirator. He decided to return to Colombia.

The "Pisces" indictments and publicity threw a scare into Mora, and he, too, lost interest in establishing a Panamanian bank account.

As a result of all this, Operation C Chase handled very little drug money during the summer of 1987.

During the lull, Bob Musella opened an account at BCCI in Panama. Musella contacted Argudo and was directed to Dane Miller, a new account officer in the Tampa BCCI office. The account was opened in the name of a Panamanian shell corporation, IDC International S.A.

Miller provided several suggestions for protecting the anonymity of Musella's transactions—having BCCI Panama mail IDC statements to BCCI Tampa, in care of him, and establishing accounts in Luxembourg or Liechtenstein for the utmost confidentiality. The suggestions made the agents even more suspicious about BCCI, but the bank still was not added as a target of their investigation.

BCCI BACKGROUND

BCCI was founded in 1972 in Luxembourg by a Pakistani banker named Aga Hassan Abedi. It grew rapidly throughout the world and by the mid-1980s had banking interests in more than 70 countries and assets of approximately $20 billion. The bank was originally financed by Arab money, principally from Sheik Zayed bin Sultan Al-Nahayan, the ruler of Abu Dhabi. There was also an early investment of $2.5 million by the Bank of America, but the bank sold its interest in 1980.

Abedi envisioned BCCI as a champion of the Third World. However, as the bank grew, it developed a reputation for offering first-rate, personal service and special treatment for wealthy customers, third-world or otherwise. BCCI, with lavish offices throughout the world, became known as the kind of bank where wealthy individuals with tax worries and people who made large amounts of money from shady deals could get personal service and secrecy from the prying eyes of enforcement agencies. The bank's controlling offices were set up in countries that exercised little supervision over banks and maximized the advantages of banking secrecy for wealthy investors. The entire institution was controlled by a holding company based in Luxembourg, known as BCCI Holdings S.A. Two principal corporations wholly owned by BCCI Holdings S.A. were BCCI S.A. (based in Luxembourg) and BCCI (Overseas) Limited (based in the Cayman Islands).

By 1987, BCCI S.A. was conducting banking operations through offices in the United Kingdom (with headquarters in London) and through offices in the United States (headquartered in New York). The Florida branches, though, were controlled by BCCI (Overseas) Limited, which also controlled operations in France, the Bahamas, the Caribbean, Central America, and South America.

The operations of BCCI (Overseas) Limited were divided into regions. There was a regional office in Miami that controlled Florida, the Bahamas, Panama, and Colombia.

Rumors started to circulate in 1986 that the solvency of BCCI was in doubt. Other rumors suggested the bank had its hands in shady transactions involving drug money laundering, arms shipments, and bribery. Some observers of the banking scene began referring to the institution as the Bank of Crooks and Criminals International. Actions taken by several senior officials of the bank during the Customs money laundering investigation appear to justify the title. The bank seems to have further earned the name by a series of scandals which led regulators in seven nations to seize control of BCCI operations in their countries during July 1991, citing huge losses and widespread fraud. In fact, by the end of October 1991, a number of criminal investigations were underway with regard to how BCCI obtained control of three banks in the United States and the role that several prominent Americans played in this control.

The Customs undercover money laundering operation, which took place during the late 1980s, provides some amazing insights into the criminal activities of BCCI officials. Indeed, the pattern of shady and illegal conduct in the money laundering case appears to have been so pervasive throughout the organization that it really comes as no surprise that regulators and investigators in a number of countries were able to uncover widespread fraud on the part of BCCI's senior management.

BACK IN BUSINESS

Gonzalo Mora Jr. was eager to begin laundering as soon as things cooled off from the Pisces arrests. In July, he asked Musella to provide him with a letter detailing his various business ventures so that Mora could use the letter to recruit new clients. He wanted to be able to convince prospective customers that Musella was indeed a big time businessman and not an undercover agent. Musella complied, detailing his "financial empire" and providing business references in a July 27, 1987 letter. The letter indicated that Musella either controlled or had a financial interest in Financial Consulting, Inc., Dynamic Mortgage Brokers, Russo Securities, Tammey Jewels, and Sunbird Airlines.

By October 1987, Noriega had reneged on his promise to produce bank records for the DEA in the "Operation Pisces" investigation, which was good news for the Colombian cartel and its money launderers. It was business as usual again with Panamanian bank accounts as a vehicle for moving funds from U.S. drug sales into the hands of Colombian cartel members. Gonzalo Mora Jr. was back in business.

In mid-October, Mora recruited an important client, Javier Ospina, who was reputed to have close ties to the upper echelons of the Medellin cocaine cartel. Ospina said he needed to launder large amounts of currency from cocaine sales in Detroit and Houston.

In late October and continuing into November, Mora arranged with Ospina for three large deliveries of currency to Musella's representatives in Detroit. The total of the three deliveries came to over $2.3 million. In each case, undercover agents deposited the currency into a Detroit bank and wire transferred it to Musella's Financial Consulting account at Florida National Bank in St. Petersburg. Once in Florida, the money was transferred to the IDC International account at BCCI Panama. In one case the transfer was accomplished by a cashier's check which was mailed to BCCI Panama. In the other two situations, the funds were wire transferred from the Financial Consulting account to BCCI Tampa for credit to the account of IDC

International at BCCI Panama. Presigned checks drawn on the IDC account were furnished to Mora in Colombia, who made the checks payable to several big-time black market brokers who, in turn, converted the checks to pesos for Ospina's cocaine distributors.

This entire series of transactions, although conducted by Customs undercover agents, represented a classic flow of funds in a cocaine money laundering operation. It is very difficult for the government to follow a paper trail when funds are moved in this manner.

BCCI BECOMES A TARGET

One of the checks drawn on the IDC account in November 1987, in the amount of $110,300, led to conversations between Bob Musella and an official of BCCI which indicated criminal activity on the part of the bank official.

The check was given by Mora to a black market check dealer, who negotiated it for Colombian pesos. When the check was returned to BCCI for payment, the bank refused to honor it. When Musella learned of this, he phoned BCCI's Panama office and spoke with a bank officer named Syed Aftab Hussain. According to Hussain, the problem was that the numerical amount on the check was $110,300, but the written amount was for $110,000. The two men discussed how the situation could be corrected. Near the end of the conversation, Hussain said his bank was a "full service bank" and he wanted to meet with Musella and discuss how he and the bank could better work with Musella's company. The two men agreed to meet in Miami in early December. Hussain also advised Musella to telephone him prior to future wire transfers and check issuances to avoid any future glitches.

Musella met with Hussain on December 5, 1987. The meeting was remarkable. Hussain provided Musella with all kinds of advice on how to move money with the maximum amount of secrecy. He told the undercover agent to stop using checks to transfer funds, because the paper items breached confidentiality. He cited the Pisces undercover sting operation as an example of how checks were traced to clients in Colombia. He suggested that funds be wire transferred to client's accounts. He said that Musella could send him written instructions on any transactions and that he would keep them confidential. Hussain advised that a numbered Certificate of Deposit (CD) was the most confidential means to transfer funds, and the best way to avoid the web of U.S. enforcement stings, because statements would not be issued and only a few people would know to whom the funds belonged.

Hussain recommended that funds be placed in time deposits in European banks in countries like Luxembourg, Switzerland, London, or Paris. He suggested opening an account for $2 million in Luxembourg which he would arrange to have as the basis for a $2 million loan to Musella from BCCI Panama. He said if Musella had any property in the United States, it could be shown as collateral to provide an excuse by the Panama branch for the issuance of the loan. Hussain told Musella he wanted to introduce him to someone in the Miami office he trusted, and he added that the Miami BCCI officers were top management people who knew when to talk and when not to talk. Musella expressed concern that some of the people he wrote checks to may have been scrutinized in Pisces. He mentioned in particular two names, but Hussain said both were "safe" to the best of his knowledge. The conversation ended with Hussain advising Musella not to speak openly on the telephone and suggesting that they talk in "secret languages."

Musella was amazed by Hussain's openness. All Hussain really knew about Musella was that his business had moved over $2 million in funds through his BCCI account in the space of about two weeks. And yet here he was, at their first meeting, advising Musella on how to avoid pitfalls encountered by the launderers in Pisces who were spotted because they drew checks on their accounts. It was clear from this conversation that Hussain suspected Musella was handling drug money and he wanted to assist him in not getting caught.

The upshot of the entire conversation was that BCCI became a target of the Operation C Chase investigation. All subsequent meetings with BCCI officials were recorded with a body microphone worn by Musella.

On December 8, 1987, undercover agents in Detroit picked up over $1 million in currency from couriers acting on behalf of Mora and Javier Ospina. They deposited the money into a Detroit bank and wire transferred it to the Financial Consulting account at the Florida National Bank in St. Petersburg. On December 8, Musella telephoned Hussain, who was still in Miami, and told him that he was ready to do another deal for a very large amount. They agreed to meet the next day.

The meeting took place at the Miami offices of BCCI. Musella told Hussain he wanted to purchase a CD for over $1 million at the Panama office of BCCI. Hussain told him to wire the funds to his attention at BCCI Panama without any reference to either Musella's name or his numbered account, and he would take care of the details. He said outsiders would never know of the CD and that Musella could provide documents later detailing collateral which the bank would claim was for a loan which would be issued to the IDC account. Internally, the loan would be backed by the funds in the CD, but there would be no records in the CD account indicating a connection to the loan. Hussain assured Musella there was no possibility the transaction would be traced because it wasn't connected to a checking account but was a CD with very little recorded information. If Panamanian authorities did get Musella's account number, he said the bank would deny that the CD existed. Hussain suggested the CD could be further hidden by placing it in Luxembourg, noting that the CD should be purchased in a name different from that which was used on the loan to make it even harder for anyone to trace the transaction. Hussain told Musella that in the future he would speak in code on the telephone, and he requested that Musella use the code name John Hussain when making future telephone calls.

Hussain then produced documents for Musella to sign for the numbered account and CD he was buying, and helped Musella draft a letter instructing BCCI to issue a $1,151,000 loan against the CD in his numbered account. Hussain gave Musella a document showing that his new numbered account was ML 306 and instructions on wiring funds from the United States to BCCI in Panama.

Musella told Hussain one of his client's associates recently had been machine gunned down, and he showed him an article from the December 6, 1987 *St. Petersburg Times* detailing the shooting of Rafael Cardona Salazar, an "enforcer" connected with the Ochoa cocaine organization. Musella said, "The fact of the matter is, that I will discuss only with you but never with anyone else, ever again, that obviously this money comes from some of the largest drug dealers in South America and that is something that needs to be kept between us. But I need to have complete confidence in you as an individual." Hussain replied, "Yes, but I think we need to keep this money in Luxembourg and not Panama."

The two then negotiated a 1.5% fee for BCCI's services in handling the transaction.

On December 11, 1987, Musella commenced the sequence of transactions suggested by Hussain, and checks were subsequently disbursed to several well-known black market check handlers.

Over the next few weeks, Musella and Hussain were on the telephone frequently, working out additional movements of funds. Simultaneously, undercover agents were receiving currency deliveries from Ospina couriers in New York and Detroit, many of whom were identified as known cocaine dealers and/or money launderers. The cash was pooled and wired to the IDC account at BCCI Panama on December 29. The amount transferred came to $1.4 million.

Musella had tried to arrange for a six month CD for the combined deposits, but Hussain told him it couldn't be done because a key BCCI official in Miami was not available at the time. It was later learned that the key official was Amjad Awan.

As their relationship progressed, Hussain kept pressing for funds to be moved through BCCI offices in Europe. It was obvious he wanted the bank to make more money on Musella's transactions. Musella resisted because Customs liked the relative speed with which funds moved to Panama and to the drug cartel; so, too, did the cartel. Musella also resisted Hussain's prodding to wire funds to his "clients" from the BCCI Panama account. Customs liked the paper trail checks left when negotiated by the black market operators.

AWAN AND BILGRAMI ARRIVE ON THE SCENE

Syed Hussain arranged a meeting for January 11, 1988, between himself, Musella, and Amjad Awan, a key official of BCCI whom Hussain trusted. Hussain mentioned there might be a second new individual at the meeting and that this person (a BCCI employee named Akbar Bilgrami) also could be trusted. However, he warned Musella not to mention drugs at the meeting and suggested he indicate his transactions were motivated by tax considerations.

The meeting took place as scheduled and Musella was introduced to Awan and Bilgrami. Musella wore a body microphone and the meetings were recorded. At the time of the meeting, Bilgrami was the Director of the Latin American Division of BCCI (Overseas) Limited, and Awan was Assistant Director of the Latin American Division. Both operated out of BCCI's Miami offices. The meeting was basically a get-acquainted session. Nevertheless, it was enlightening. Comments made by Bilgrami and Awan made it clear that the two were quite interested in helping businessmen evade tax laws. It also became clear that Hussain played a subordinate role to the two officials—he hardly uttered a word after the initial introductions. It was also obvious that Bilgrami and Awan were sizing up Musella.

The two senior bank officials never hesitated in ratifying Hussain's arrangements with Musella for loans issued against CDs where the existence of the CD as collateral would be kept secret. This type of loan deal flies in the face of legal and ethical banking practices in most countries.

After the meeting, Customs supervisors and prosecutors in Tampa decided to go forward with opening an account at a BCCI office in Europe, as recommended by the BCCI officers, to see what doors it might open.

Two days after the meeting, Musella advised Hussain he would open an account at a BCCI European office, with a new $ 1 million deposit, and draw counterbalancing loans from the account. Hussain agreed to prepare the necessary papers. On the morning of January 13, undercover agents in Detroit received over $1.2 million in currency from a courier who worked for Javier Ospina.

On January 20, Musella telephoned Hussain in Panama, and Hussain advised him to use a second company for the deposit. He suggested a Panamanian company, and they agreed on a name, Lamont Maxwell S.A. Arrangements were made for a 90-day CD, to be issued by a BCCI affiliate office in Switzerland, and a loan to the new Panamanian company. Hussain said he would set up a meeting between Musella, Bilgrami, and Awan where all the necessary papers could be signed.

That meeting took place at the BCCI office in Miami on January 25, 1988. Musella told the bank officials that he had over $1 million in his Florida bank which he would place in a 90-day CD at BCCI's Swiss bank (Banque de Commerce and Placement S.A.) in return for a loan of a like amount to a new corporate account which he would open at BCCI Panama. Musella signed all the necessary papers provided by Awan and Bilgrami. He agreed to repay the loan by turning over funds from the matured CD, and he gave Bilgrami power of attorney for Lamont Maxwell, S.A.

During the meeting, Bilgrami received a telephone call from Franz Maissen, an official of Banque de Commerce and Placement S.A. (BCP), during which they discussed the loan. Among other things, he told Maissen to pay a good interest rate on the CD because "this client can be very interesting in the long term." They also agreed that the funds should be routed through First American Bank, New York. The amount of the loan was $1,192,613.

On the following day, January 26, Musella again went to the BCCI office in Miami. Initially he met with Amjad Awan, who told him Luxembourg was a more appropriate location to place CDs because the secrecy there was better than in Switzerland and because BCCI had full control over its Luxembourg operations. He told Musella that BCP in Switzerland was a subsidiary that was only 49% owned by BCCI. (In reality, at the time of the meeting, BCCI owned only 15% to 20% of BCP). During the meeting, Musella signed blank forms for the CDs and the loans. Awan told him that normally it was very difficult to ask somebody to sign things in blank. "We'll do our best to uphold the trust here," Awan said. Musella then said, "Certain things I recognize needn't be said, and when the few times come when something needs to be said, in my opinion they need to be said. I have more at risk than simply the money that's here, and that's some of my Colombian clients have less than an appreciation for the business world. And frankly, between you and I, the gentlemen in the drug business don't generally have an appreciation for anything other than trust." Awan's reaction was to tell Musella to confine all contact at BCCI to himself, Bilgrami, and Hussain. Musella then continued by saying, "I'm very appreciative of the help, to be able to have the loan activity protected as we've described. It's extremely important to me." Awan replied, "Don't worry about that. It's going to be as isolated as possible."

Then, after some additional conversation, Musella again brought up the subject of the source of his funds. He said, "We'll never discuss this again. But the people with whom I'm dealing are the most powerful and largest drug dealers in Colombia, and I don't care to overstate my abilities. I don't care to create any unnecessary concern. We deal on tremendous faith and trust because we've known each other for many, many years. And being able to rely on those two issues of the appearance of the loans coming from the property and the loan activity is to be protected, and secondly, the turnaround time is all that I ask. I want to be very clear and blunt with you." Awan's response was, "I'm not concerned. It's not my business about who your customers are, or whatever. I deal with you." Awan continued by saying, "As long as you and I have a clean, straightforward, legitimate business, we will provide you all security, all sorts of security and anonymity. Further than that, I don't want to know. I'm concerned with you, period."

These statements by Amjad Awan are indicative of the greed and selective blindness that rules some bankers and businessmen. These individuals are more than willing to reap big profits from illegal activity but they don't want to know the details. Awan deliberately stuck his head in the sand; he never wanted to come face-to-face with Musella's clients. As far as he was concerned, he was dealing with Musella. The fact that the funds came from cocaine sales didn't bother him at all. All he wanted was a buffer, and Musella provided that buffer.

On January 26, 1988, Musella directed the wire transfer of over $1.1 million from the Financial Consulting account at Florida National Bank through First American Bank in New York City for credit to a checking account in the name of Lamont Maxwell at BCP, Geneva. The funds were placed in a 90-day time deposit account. A counterbalancing loan for $1,187,595 was granted by BCCI Panama and deposited in the newly-opened checking account of the Lamont Maxwell Corporation S.A. The funds were then transferred to the IDC account at the Panama office, from which checks were disbursed to the usual coterie of black market check handlers who saw to it that the cartel bosses in Colombia ended up with Colombian pesos.

A number of telephone calls were made between Musella and Hussain, Bilgrami, and Awan during the period from January 26 until March 7. Musella also met with Bilgrami and Awan on several occasions during this period. The conversations, for the most part, concerned currency that agents received in Detroit, New York, and two new locations—Chicago and Houston. The currency was initially deposited into local cooperating banks and followed by what was now becoming a standard route—the purchase of CDs, followed by counterbalancing loans, transfers between Panamanian accounts, and checks to black market check handlers. Over $3 million moved through the laundry pipeline during this period. Musella met with Awan and Bilgrami at BCCI Miami on February 1. During this meeting there was an incoming call for Awan. Part of the recorded conversation contained the following quotes from Awan's side of the conversation: "No, that's not the point. The point is that under the circumstances, and I told him this last night, that it will be best if we had the least possible contact, because, who knows who is listening on the telephone. No, what I told him was, you know, if you could just get Montela to call me." After getting off the telephone, Awan said to Musella, "My friend is in deep trouble these days, General Noriega." It would later turn out that Awan acted as a personal banker for General Noriega, dating back to his days as a marketing officer at BCCI Panama in the early 1980s.

On February 2, Musella met with Bilgrami and Awan at BCCI's Miami offices, during which time the bankers cautioned Musella about letting anyone at BCCI Panama know about what was going on in Switzerland or in any other BCCI office. They said they were concerned about investigations that might occur in Panama, and the likelihood that some officer might be subpoenaed. They said they were looking to protect Musella and that the less anyone knew about his business anywhere else, the better it would be for him. They also assured Musella that Hussain was okay and that he knew everything about the loans and the CDs. They said he would remain the contact man in Panama.

THE NORIEGA INDICTMENT

On March 7, 1988, General Manuel Noriega was indicted by a federal grand jury in Miami on drug, money laundering and conspiracy charges. In retaliation, the Panamanian government froze all foreign bank accounts, thereby forcing Operation C Chase to direct more business to BCCI's European banks. At the time of the freeze, there was over $750,000 in the IDC account at BCCI Panama. Two checks had been written on the account, for a combined total of just over $725,000. The checks had not cleared by the time of the freeze.

On March 8, Amjad Awan telephoned Musella and arranged a meeting to discuss the situation. They met at Awan's home, in Coconut Grove, Florida and discussed the effect of the freeze on their business and available alternatives. The idea of moving the funds to the Caymans was discussed and rejected because a recent treaty had opened channels between the United States and the Cayman for the exchange of financial records related to drug cases. As for the Bahamas, Awan expressed concern that

the government might not be able to withstand U.S. pressure for drug-related financial records.

During the course of the meeting, Awan asked Musella where his currency was coming from. He replied that it was coming from U.S. cities
such as Houston, Detroit, and New York, and that he had $1 million in
Houston and Detroit, each, at that point ready to be transferred overseas as
soon as possible. Musella told Awan that he controlled a number of high
volume cash businesses that allowed him to filter funds to his clients. He
noted that with the float in a number of existing bank accounts, he was in
a position to give them almost instant credit. Musella explained that there
was a tremendous back-up of cash because of confusion over the Panama
situation. Awan agreed and suggested the idea of flying the cash directly
out of the United States, either to Uruguay for smuggling to Paraguay and
Brazil, where there was a demand for U.S. dollars, or to Colombia, from
where it could be moved to Bolivia to pay for cocaine labs.

On March 11, Awan and Musella again discussed the Panamanian
freeze and speculated on what might happen if Noriega was thrown out.
Awan felt a new Panamanian government could be beholden to the United
States and might cooperate with U.S. enforcement authorities regarding
Bank Secrecy laws. Awan said he would explore the possibility of getting
the $725,000 from the two checks that had not cleared prior to the freeze.
He also expressed concern that, if Noriega were removed, a new government might look at banking records and BCCI could get caught back-dat-
ing and lose their license.

On March 15, Musella telephoned Awan. He told him he would be
going to Los Angeles in a few days and needed to talk with someone at
the BCCI office there who could arrange for a "loan" based on a CD to
cover an apartment building that was being constructed by a client. (The
client was Roberto Alcaino, the Los Angeles drug dealer.) Awan gave him
the name of a bank officer and told Musella he could speak very freely to
him. Several days later, Musella flew to Los Angeles and met with the
bank officer Awan had referred him to. He was able to have documents
made up that purported to show a $750,000 loan on Alcaino's building.

On March 23, Musella and Emilio Dominguez flew to San Jose, Costa
Rica and met with Mora and Javier Ospina. They discussed the situation in
Panama. Musella said he believed, after several conversations with Awan,
that it would be possible to get the $725,000 in the IDC account released.
They discussed alternatives to doing business in Panama. Ospina said his
bosses were considering Uruguay and Europe. This played directly into
Musella's hand because of previous prodding he had from Awan,
Bilgrami, and Hussain regarding Europe, and recent conversations with
Awan about Uruguay. Musella said he was planning a trip to Europe in
May to finalize plans with his bankers on a new system to move funds

through Luxembourg and other European countries. Ospina told Musella if things went right, he could expect $12 to $20 million a month from Los Angeles, Houston, Detroit, and New York.

During the meeting, Ospina made a call to Colombia and learned that $1.3 million in currency had been delivered to Musella's people (undercover agents) in Houston earlier that day. Ospina said he would have special instructions for at least part of that money before Musella moved it offshore. He also mentioned that the organization he was working for had recently purchased four airplanes.

When Musella returned from Costa Rica, he made a series of telephone calls to Awan. They arranged a trip to New York which would start out with Awan visiting Musella's offices in New Port Richey, Florida on March 28. Musella told Awan he had a girlfriend in Miami named Kathy Erickson and she would accompany them on the trip to New York. What he didn't tell Awan was that "Kathy Erickson" was really an undercover U.S. Customs agent. Musella made arrangements for Erickson and Awan to fly together to Tampa on the jet owned by his charter airline, Sunbird Airlines.

En route to Tampa, Erickson expressed an interest in Awan's background. He told her he had gone to work for BCCI through his connection with the then president of the bank (Aga Hassan Abedi), who had been a family friend. Awan said the president recently had a heart attack and he might not recover sufficiently to return to his job, and that Awan had a better than average chance of becoming the president within the next two to five years. He explained that BCCI had been established, with the support of Saudis, after Pakistan nationalized all banks in that country, sometime around 1973.

When Amjad Awan and Kathy Erickson arrived in Tampa, on March 28, they were met at the airport by Bob Musella who took them to the offices of Financial Consulting, in New Port Richey. He told Awan all about his financial empire, of which Financial Consulting was the cornerstone.

During the March 28 meeting, Awan and Musella discussed their mutual business problems, and the possibility of back-dating wire transfer records so the $725,000 in the IDC account could be released. Awan said it could be done, but that he preferred not to if there was a less risky alternative. He said the bottom line was that if they did it and if it were discovered, BCCI could lose its license. Musella told Awan that the $725,000 was owned by a very powerful client. He conceded the amount was not a big thing, it was the principle of losing anything. He said he had just met with the clients' representatives in Costa Rica and that the client was ready to move up to $20 million a month and would do it through BCCI if the funds could be released. Awan promised to take another look at the problem.

Musella said some of his clients were flying currency directly into Colombia to pay people in Bolivia and Peru who were actually "involved in cooking their stuff." He said this was one of the uses of the funds he moved to Panama for his clients. Musella told Awan that one of his clients, Jorge Ochoa, had sent Noriega a coffin with a note warning that if the Ochoa's lost any of their money in Panama, Noriega would need the coffin.

During the discussions, Awan told Musella that BCCI and five other banks were being scrutinized by a U.S. Senate Subcommittee in connection with the Noriega indictment. Awan said he personally would be investigated because he was the manager of the Panama branch when Steven Kalish, a key government witness against Noriega, said he was doing business with Noriega and had dealings with BCCI. He said he didn't recognize Kalish, but conceded that he might have done business with him. Awan told Musella that BCCI found out about the investigation through friends who were close to the subcommittee's activities.

Amjad Awan also told Musella that BCCI had bought and controlled First American Bank and National Bank of Georgia. He said the banks were bought through private individual names rather than by BCCI itself because U.S. regulators would not have permitted BCCI to purchase and control an American bank. He said former Defense Secretary and renowned Washington attorney Clark Clifford was one of the individuals who worked on behalf of BCCI to gain control of the banks.

This was remarkable information in March 1988. There were only a relatively few people, with an interest in the matter, who suspected that BCCI controlled First American. The Federal Reserve had been reassured in 1981 by BCCI attorneys, including Clark Clifford, that BCCI had no control over the bank.

Subsequent events have shown that BCCI made substantial loans to a number of individuals who invested in First American and gained a controlling interest. The loans never have been repaid and, in fact, were a ruse to enable BCCI to gain control of the bank. Clark Clifford became the chairman of the board of the holding company that owns First American. When the Federal Reserve became aware of the unpaid loans to the private investors, in February 1991, it ordered BCCI to divest itself of whatever stake it had in First American. By October 1991, several U.S. agencies were investigating Clifford's culpability in the relationship between BCCI and First American.

Early publicity about Awan's remarks to Musella, following arrests and indictments in late 1988, were ridiculed by many Washington insiders as grandiose boasting by a minor official who wanted to make himself look like a knowledgeable insider. Subsequent events, however, have proven Awan knew what he was talking about with respect to First American.

On March 29, 1988, Amjad Awan, Bob Musella and Kathy Erickson traveled to New York. While they were en route, Emilio Dominguez received a telephone call from Javier Ospina with instructions on what to do with $300,000 of the $1.3 million undercover agents had picked up from a courier in Houston on March 23. Dominguez was told to wire $300,000 to an account in the name of Rudolf Armbrecht at the First American Bank in Nashville, Tennessee. The money, it later turned out, was used to purchase an airplane for the drug traffickers. The call led to the identity of Armbrecht as an important representative of the drug dealers for whom Operation C Chase was laundering money.

Once in New York, Musella took Awan on a whirlwind tour of Russo Securities and the floor of the New York Stock Exchange. Musella indicated that his firm, Financial Consulting, controlled Russo Securities.

On the morning of March 30, Musella visited Awan at his hotel, and they discussed getting Musella's money out of the account in BCCI Panama. Awan said he was working on back-dating funds transfer records. They also discussed the progress being made by the Los Angeles BCCI office in creating false loan documents for Musella's client. Later that day, Awan telephoned Musella to say he believed he could get Musella's money released but that it would take some time.

THE EUROPEAN ADVENTURE

In early April 1988, Customs officials and federal prosecutors made a decision to keep the investigation going by continuing to receive currency from Mora's clients and transferring the funds to drug traffickers via European accounts. Both BCCI officials and Mora and Ospina were pushing for Europe as a replacement for Panama. Musella also was instructed to keep pressing to get the $725,000 unfrozen from BCCI Panama.

During the first few days of April, Musella had a series of telephone conversations with Mora. He told Mora he and his bankers were ready to begin moving the drug money to Europe, and Mora reacted well to the news. He told Musella that he and Ospina would be meeting with some high level cartel members, and they discussed the possibility of a trip to Europe in May.

On April 8, Musella and Emilio Dominguez met with Mora and Javier Ospina at the Doral Hotel in Miami Beach. Mora said they had met with the "Big Guys," who he described as competitors of Ochoa and Escobar, the two biggest drug lords in Colombia. They discussed a trip to Europe.

Mora and Ospina said their clients, the "Big Guys," would be sending a representative to Europe. They also talked about having all the paperwork ready to open a CD in Europe well before their arrival there. They agreed that the CD would be funded from the next currency pickup in Detroit or Houston.

On April 14, Musella met with Awan. Awan said he had hoped to get Musella's money released prior to their meeting but that there were further delays. They discussed the impact the Panamanian freeze was having on Musella's clients, and Musella indicated he and his clients would probably go to Europe in May. He said they were interested in opening a CD at the BCCI office in Paris. Awan told Musella to be careful about what he said to Syed Hussain and indicated that Hussain talked too much. Near the end of the meeting, Musella said his clients were as professional as Lee Iacocca. Awan laughed. Musella said, "You know, it's just that they have a different kind of business. One sells cars and one sells coke. That's the way it goes." Awan laughed again and agreed.

On April 26, a courier working for Javier Ospina delivered over $1.3 million in currency to a Customs undercover agent in Houston. After being deposited into an undercover account in a local bank, the money was wired to the Financial Consulting account at Florida National Bank. On the same day, Musella telephone Awan. Both men had good news. Awan said the $725,000 in BCCI Panama had been released. Musella said he had a new package of more than $1.2 million and he probably would put it in the Lamont Maxwell account at BCP Geneva. Over the next few days, Musella and Awan had several telephone conversations regarding the placement of the $1.2 million package and the released $725,000. They also discussed the fact that Musella wanted an account opened at BCCI Paris in the name of Lamont Maxwell Corporation. On May 5, Musella wire transferred the $1.2 million from Florida National Bank to the Lamont Maxwell account at BCP Geneva.

On May 10, Musella and Dominguez learned that the name of the representative of the "Big Guys" who would meet them in Europe was Rudolf Armbrecht, the same individual to whom $300,000 had been wire transferred in Nashville several weeks earlier on instructions from Mora. Dominguez received a telephone message from Mora's secretary identifying Armbrecht as the representative.

Plans for the trip to Europe were taking shape. Customs supervisors decided that Musella should be accompanied by a "staff" of three other agents, both for purposes of security and corroboration. One was his girlfriend, Kathy Erickson. Another was Emilio Dominguez. The trip was to include stops at BCCI offices in Geneva, Paris, and London. Musella would be opening new accounts and establishing a money movement system to replace the use of Panama. Musella was to meet with Mora, Ospina, and Armbrecht in Paris sometime around May 22 and would stop in Geneva prior to that.

Before the trip to Europe, Musella met with Amjad Awan and Akbar Bilgrami at the BCCI office in Miami and advised them of his itinerary. They agreed to arrange for him to meet BCCI officials at each location. Awan and Bilgrami expressed concern about what Musella might say to bank officials in Geneva about the nature of his business. They described Franz Maissen, the BCP manager in Geneva, as being too pragmatic and "a little straight down the line." Awan said he had received a call from Geneva seeking information about the nature of Musella's business. Awan suggested Musella not tell the people in Geneva anything at all about the nature of his business. Bilgrami advised Musella to say he had brokerage, real estate, and mortgage companies in the United States and no more. He told him to say the reason he was in Geneva to make transfers directly was because Panama's banking system was closed. Awan said it would be much better to do business in Paris because there would be no questions asked. He said the Swiss asked too many questions. Both bankers told Musella that Paris would be quite happy to do whatever he wanted. They referred him to Nazir Chinoy, the general manager in France, and to Ian Howard, the branch manager in Paris. In London, they referred him to the general manager, Asif Baaksa.

During this meeting, Bilgrami and Awan both asked Musella for some assistance during the waning days of the BCCI fiscal year. They said they were looking for a lot of cash to be sitting in the bank on June 30, the last day of fiscal year. They asked him to try to place large amounts of money in their regional banks before the end of June. They assured him the deposits would just be window dressing and that Musella could withdraw the money on July 1.

Musella said he would try to help the bankers. He explained he was attempting to set up an elaborate system to shelter his clients' money by forming corporations in Gibraltar, Liberia, and Hong Kong, each of which would be owned by a Liechtenstein Trust. He said if the funds were well sheltered he would not have any qualms in putting them in BCCI in Miami. Musella indicated he might be able to place between $2 million and $5 million before the end of June. Awan said they were looking for $25 million.

This solicitation of funds before the end of June 30, 1988 was quite interesting in view of events that came to light in England in 1991. In July 1991, British regulators determined that BCCI had tried to conceal losses of several billions of dollars over the previous 5 years through a pattern of bribery, phony loans, unrecorded deposits, and rapid transfers of funds from one part of the bank to another. A Price Waterhouse audit that led to the seizure of BCCI by British authorities stated that the bank's activities represented "probably one of the most complex deceptions in banking history." It certainly appears that the effort on the part of Awan and Bilgrami to get Musella to place up to $25 million in BCCI before June 30, 1988 was a part of the pattern of deception.

On May 15, 1988, Bob Musella and his "staff" flew to Geneva. Musella held a series of meetings over the course of several days with Franz Maissen and other BCP officials regarding the creation of Swiss corporations in names such as Saintsea, Nicesea, Barkeville, and Fidinam. Musella was careful not to mention anything about the source of his clients' funds.

On May 19, Musella's troupe moved on to Paris. On May 20, the four undercover agents went to a luncheon where they met three officials from BCCI's Paris office—Nazir Chinoy, Ian Howard, and Sibte Hassan. The luncheon meeting had been arranged by Amjad Awan. Afterward, Musella and Emilio Dominguez met privately with Nazir Chinoy at the BCCI office. Chinoy was the area manager in charge of France and Africa. Musella explained that he had South American clients, most of whom had excess capital they needed to place in a manner that provided maximum yield, security, and privacy. Musella went on to tell Chinoy that within the next two days he wanted to transfer $1 million to BCCI Paris for a trusted friend. He said he would leave the money in the account for six months without borrowing against it. Chinoy assured Musella he would find BCCI in Paris very understanding of his client's wishes. He said the bank would protect the identity of the clients and give them as much cover as possible. He said there would be only two people beside himself who would know of Musella's transactions; one of them would be Sibte Hassan, who would be the account officer, the other would be Ian Howard, the Paris branch manager. Chinoy assured Musella he had a great deal of confidence in both officers. He said he knew them well and trusted them.

The conversation, like all those Musella had, was recorded with a body microphone. The following transcript of what was said is most remarkable and illustrates the kind of banking Chinoy and BCCI were prepared to engage in. Musella: "Needless to say, the. . . I think that the professionalism of the people with whom I'm affiliated with is sterling, otherwise we wouldn't be capable of doing what it is we accomplish for as long as we have. Um. . .at the same time, the sensitivity with which the funds must be handled and the confidentiality is of the most extreme method." Chinoy: "Oh yes." Musella: "I don't have to tell you that, you know, drug dealers in Colombia are the types of people that. . ." Chinoy: "Yeah, I've already understood it. That I, I, O.K. I've followed the deal." Musella: "I think if you, eventually if you meet some of my friends, I think if they were in a room with Lee Iacocca, they could easily be mingling with corporate executives, I mean they are that way. Iacocca sells cars and they sell coke and that's the way they deal in their business. Everything is professional, professional, professional. That's why I feel that. . . I'm not trying to desegregate things, but when we speak, we speak alone." Chinoy: "That is how it should be, with every major client, 'cause it's a close personal relationship."

Here was the top official for BCCI operations in all of France and Africa, who had just met Musella for the first time, being told that Musella's clients were Colombian cocaine dealers, and he wasn't dissuaded at all from going forward with anything Musella wanted to do. The only slight discomfort he showed was that he apparently would rather not have heard directly that the money came from drug dealers.

After the meeting, Musella had $1 million wire transferred from a CD account at BCP, Geneva, to a pre-existing account in the name of Rudolf Armbrecht at BCCI Paris, as instructed by Mora. He also opened three new accounts at the Paris office.

On May 22, Mora and Ospina arrived in Paris and met with Musella and Dominguez. They discussed Rudolf Armbrecht. Mora said Armbrecht would be accompanied by another individual who also had placed money for Armbrecht's boss. Armbrecht was described as a German Colombian who had lived in the United States for several years. He spoke Spanish, German and English. He was a pilot who acquired aircraft to be used by his boss to bring cocaine into the United States. According to Mora and Ospina, Armbrecht had the authority to make decisions about how money would be handled in the future. Mora said that Armbrecht would decide whether the $1 million in the BCCI Paris account would remain or be moved somewhere else. He also would accept or reject whatever plans Musella had to substitute money movements through Europe for the Panama arrangement.

On May 23, Armbrecht arrived in Paris, accompanied by a Colombian attorney named Santiago Uribe. Musella and Dominguez met with Armbrecht, Uribe, and Mora that afternoon. Ospina, who had a drinking problem, did not attend the meeting because he was drunk. Armbrecht made it clear that he would call the shots on how money would be handled. He said he had been protecting his boss for a number of years. He identified the boss as "Don Chepe." It was later determined that "Don Chepe" was, in fact, Gerardo Moncada, the same drug boss that Eduardo Martinez laundered money for in the Polar Cap case. Armbrecht stated that his purpose was to establish liquidity and security for Don Chepe's money. He stressed that a system had to be established that would ensure the money could never be traced back. Armbrecht expressed some preference for putting the money in German banks because he was a German citizen and he knew the German government would not freeze it or confiscate it.

Musella described the advantages of doing business at BCCI Paris. He went on to explain how Don Chepe's money could be moved through BCCI's international banking network in a way that could not be traced back. He explained that he had established a number of foreign corporations and bank accounts to facilitate the movement of money. Armbrecht seemed impressed but not convinced. He mentioned that he wanted two pools of funds in Europe—one for money that could be flushed back to Colombia, the other for money that would remain in Europe for the security of the organization.

On May 24, Armbrecht told Musella and Mora he didn't want Ospina involved in any further discussions; he had seen him drunk and didn't trust him. After that discussion, Musella and Mora went with Armbrecht and Uribe to BCCI's Paris office where they met with Nazir Chinoy and Ian Howard. The bankers were very convincing. They spoke of tax advantages in France. They stated that, unlike Swiss banks, no one had ever been able to get information out of French banks. They explained how financially sound the bank was. Armbrecht was convinced. He agreed to leave the $1 million in the BCCI Paris account.

There were separate meetings with Ian Howard and Sibte Hassan on May 25 during which time each official was led to understand the money that would be deposited by Musella's organization came from drug sales. They never flinched or hesitated over the idea of handling drug money. They were ready and willing to go forward with their banking services to accommodate their new clients.

While in Paris, Musella discussed with Nazir Chinoy the request that had been made by Awan and Bilgrami that he place a large amount of money in BCCI before June 30. Chinoy was aware of the request and agreed it would be very helpful.

On May 25, Musella gave instructions which resulted in the transfer of $4 million from the Financial Consulting account at Florida National Bank to a newly-opened three-month time deposit at BCCI Paris. The funds were official U.S. Government budgeted monies. Customs officials had decided to use the money to further the undercover operation.

The main purpose of the European trip was to establish a new system to move the cocaine proceeds, in place of the system that relied so heavily on Panamanian accounts. The manner in which the new system would work was explained to Armbrecht at a meeting in Paris on May 25. He was satisfied with the system and said they would have to test it very shortly. Armbrecht told Musella his people still felt comfortable dealing in Panama, provided that funds went to Banco Occidente from a location other than the United States.

On May 26, 1988, Musella and the other undercover agents left Paris for London, where Musella met with Asif Baaksa, the director of BCCI's corporate unit in London. Musella told Baaksa about his various businesses and about the nature of his clients' business by using the Lee Iacocca analogy that he had used on other BCCI officials. Baaksa was undeterred by the drug connection. He had Musella fill out papers to open a new account in the name of a company called Hardeman Inc. He told Musella about an account that would provide him with utmost confidentiality. He described it as a Manager's Ledger account. Baaksa said that only he and one other individual in the bank would know of the existence of the account. Musella and his fellow agents flew back to the United States on May 29.

On June 2, Musella telephoned Akbar Bilgrami, Director of BCCI's Latin America Regional Office, and arranged for a June 6 meeting at BCCI offices in Miami. He said he would need to open additional accounts. He told Bilgrami he had already placed $4 million in a time deposit in Paris and that he was ready to put another $2 million in an account at BCCI's Miami office.

On June 6, Bilgrami and Musella met as arranged. Until this meeting, the origin of Musella's clients' money had never been discussed in front of Bilgrami. However, at this meeting Musella came right out and recounted the Lee Iacocca analogy. Musella said,"You know, if you were to, and you wouldn't ever, but if you were to meet my clients, you would . . ."

Bilgrami: "No, no, I'm not interested in meeting your clients. I'm only interested in . . ."

Musella: "I don't want you to either. But if you were in a room with Lee Iacocca, they would mix in quite well with him."

Bilgrami: "I'm sure. I'm sure."

Musella: "And he sells cars and they sell cocaine. And that's the end of it, never to be brought up again."

Bilgrami: "I don't . . . (he laughs) I don't want to know this. I don't want to know what they sell."

Musella: "I won't tell you."

Bilgrami: "I'm not interested in what they do, what kind of business in dealing with you. We know your business and we keep all client relations confidential."

Akbar Bilgrami was the director of the Latin America Regional Office of BCCI. His reaction to being told bluntly that Musella's money came from drug dealers was that he really didn't want to know. This attitude permeated the thinking of all BCCI officials Musella and other undercover agents came in contact with.

Musella and Bilgrami next discussed renewing some existing loans and CDs. Musella told him he had opened three accounts in Paris, a fact Bilgrami said he was aware of. Musella said he wanted to open another corporate account in Paris and, in addition, to open one new account in Luxembourg, two in London, one in Geneva, one in Miami, and one in Uruguay. Bilgrami had Musella sign papers to start the process of opening all of the new accounts. The meeting ended with Musella reiterating that he intended to place $2 million in the Miami branch, in addition to the $4 million he had deposited in Paris.

After the Bilgrami meeting, Musella met Rudolf Armbrecht in Miami and flew him aboard his charter jet to Tampa. Armbrecht visited the offices of Financial Consulting in New Port Richey, where he heard the story of Musella's business empire. Musella and Armbrecht flew to New York on the morning of June 7 and visited Russo Securities. All the while, Musella was pushing Armbrecht to start the currency flowing again.

On June 10, on Musella's instructions, $1 million was wired from the Financial Consulting account at Florida National Bank to BCCI Miami, to the attention of A. Bilgrami for deposit to the newly-opened Barkeville Ltd. account. On June 13, a similar transfer of $1 million went from the Financial Consulting account to the Barkeville Ltd. account at BCCI Miami. These two transfers represented the second part of Musella's contribution to the bolstering of BCCI's ledgers for the year-end financial statements. (The first part was the $4 million deposit at BCCI Paris. And like the money deposited in Paris, the $2 million that went into the Barkeville account was also officially budgeted government money.) The money in the Barkeville account went into a 60-day CD that paid 7 9/16% interest.

On June 21, the spigot of drug money once again began to flow through Operation C Chase. Fresh currency from cocaine sales went from Don Chepe's organization to the laundering operation run by Bob Musella. It began with a $500,000 load that was ready to be picked up in New York. Appropriate arrangements were made between Gonzalo Mora and Musella, and $499,016 in currency was delivered to an undercover agent later in the day. The currency was deposited into a Customs undercover account in a New York bank. On June 27, a little over $997,000 in currency was delivered to an undercover account in Houston and was deposited in a local bank.

On June 27, Musella telephoned Amjad Awan and told him he had another $1.5 million that could sit in BCCI until after June 30. On June 28, most of the funds in the Houston and New York accounts were wire transferred to the Financial Consulting account in St. Petersburg.

The next day, Musella met with Awan and Bilgrami at the BCCI office in Miami to discuss how funds would flow through eight bank accounts and four corporations that either had been established or were being established by Musella. It was agreed that an account in the name of Sandart Limited at BCCI Luxembourg would be used as a transit account through which funds would pass to six other BCCI accounts, three in the name of Hardeman Company Limited and three in the name of Berens Limited. The six accounts were to be used as depositories for funds that were collateral for counterbalancing loans. Some of the loan proceeds were to be passed on to a BCCI checking account in the name of Saintsea Shipping Limited which would be used to disburse funds to Musella's clients. Numerous documents were prepared for Musella in connection with the accounts.

Awan and Bilgrami told Musella that they had been busy visiting clients, trying to get them to place funds with BCCI for the next few days to develop "window dressing" for the bank's financial statement which would be prepared for the close of business. These statements and the efforts the bankers made to induce Musella to place millions of dollars in the institution take on added significance in light of revelations in July 1991 that the bank was in the red for over $5 billion and had covered up losses over the years through the rapid movement of funds between countries and branches. The three men agreed to meet the next day to discuss another $1.5 million deposit by Musella and the opening of additional accounts.

The trio met again on June 29 at BCCI's Miami offices. Musella told them he would be sending $1.3 million to the Sandart account in Luxembourg on the next day. He gave instructions to wire some of the money back to the Financial Consulting account and over $900,000 to the Hardeman account in London. The money in the Hardeman account was to be placed in a six-month CD and used as collateral for a loan to Berens Limited in an account at BCCI Nassau. The loan proceeds were then to be transferred back to the Financial Consulting account in St. Petersburg. During this meeting, Musella told the BCCI officials he had seen a *Fortune* magazine in the lobby of the bank and that a picture of one of his clients was on the cover. The issue referred to had a cover story on the drug trade with a photograph of the notorious Colombian cocaine trafficker, Rodriguez Gacha. Both men laughed at what Musella told them, and Bilgrami suggested Musella tell his client about the *Fortune* story.

On June 30, over $1.3 million was wire transferred from the Financial Consulting account at Florida National Bank to the Sandart account in Luxembourg. This money represented most of the cash picked up in New York on June 21 and in Houston on June 27. Later that day, Musella again met with Bilgrami and Awan at BCCI Miami. They told him they would both be leaving the bank by the end of the year to join a small London firm called Capcom Financial Services Limited, and suggested Musella might want to join them in this venture. In any event, they assured him when they left that they would turn over his business to someone who would appreciate the sensitivity of the transactions. They also discussed the possibility of getting currency from the United States to London. Awan said he could dispose of up to $10 million a month in U.S. currency if Musella could get it to London.

The two bankers had another meeting with Musella in Miami on July 1 in which they advised him against transacting future loans in London and Nassau. They said there was too much paperwork and the transactions tended to attract too much attention. They also threw cold water on the previous day's discussion of moving currency to London. Awan felt it was too risky.

On July 6, $457,000 of the money in the Sandart account in Luxembourg was wire transferred to the Financial Consulting account in St. Petersburg. On July 7, $462,000 was wired from the Financial Consulting account to an account at the Banco Exterior de Uruguay in Montevideo, Uruguay. The transfer to the account in Montevideo was based on instructions that Musella received from Rudolf Armbrecht. Also on July 6, over $927,000 was wired from the Sandart account in Luxembourg to the Hardeman account at BCCI London. A counterbalancing loan was granted to Berens Limited in Nassau in the amount of $922,000 and that amount was wired to the Berens account at BCCI Nassau. The $922,000 in the Berens account was wired to the Financial Consulting account in St. Petersburg. Finally, on July 13, the $922,000 was wire transferred to an account at Banco de Occidente in Panama. This final transfer was made on instructions from Rudolf Armbrecht to Musella.

During the two-day period of July 13 and July 14, there were three separate deliveries of currency to the same undercover agent by couriers of the Don Chepe organization in New York City. The three deliveries, combined, totaled over $1.8 million. All of the money was deposited in a Customs undercover account in a local New York bank and was then wire transferred to the Financial Consulting account in St. Petersburg.

On July 14, undercover agents Bob Musella and Kathy Erickson met with Akbar Bilgrami at BCCI's Miami office. Musella said his people had picked up about $2 million in currency and that he had to move it. He also told Bilgrami he expected to receive another $3 million to $5 million in cash over the next few days. As for the $2 million Musella wanted to move, it was agreed that the funds would move from Luxembourg to Nassau, completely bypassing London. They agreed that the money from Luxembourg would go into a CD in the name of Hardeman at BCCI Nassau. There would then be a counterbalancing loan to the Berens Limited account in Nassau.

Events occurred during the currency deliveries in New York on July 13 and 14 which would prevent the $3 to $5 million delivery from taking place. These events would also lead to the termination of the business relationship between Armbrecht and Musella. The events had to do with the fact that after each delivery, the couriers were followed and the couriers became aware of the surveillance. The same undercover agent received all three deliveries. The drug organization in New York reached the conclusion that he was a government agent. The first indication that Musella had about this problem came on July 18 when Gonzalo Mora telephoned undercover agent Emilio Dominguez and told him about the surveillance.

On July 21, Musella transferred over $1.8 million from the Financial Consulting account to the Sandart Limited account at BCCI Luxembourg. Also on July 21, Musella had a telephone conversation with Rudolf Armbrecht in which Armbrecht told him about Don Chepe's people being followed in New York. He said his people were very worried. Armbrecht gave Musella instructions to wire transfer the $1.8 million in the Sandart account to specific accounts at Banco de Occidente in Panama. Musella said he would send his trusted assistant, Emilio Dominguez, to New York for the upcoming deliveries. Dominguez had handled the earliest deliveries from the Don Chepe organization, prior to introducing another agent. Armbrecht said there was so much concern that the next delivery would only be a small one.

On July 25, Emilio Dominguez went to New York and received $500,000 in currency from a woman named Marta. She was one of the couriers who had been followed on July 13. Dominguez asked what the problem had been with the prior delivery. She said that she didn't have a problem with him.

On July 29, a Customs undercover agent in New York picked up almost $2 million in currency from a courier. The pick up was arranged by Gonzalo Mora on behalf of a different Colombian drug organization than Don Chepe's group. This money was deposited into the Financial Consulting account at Florida National Bank. Subsequently, $1.2 million of the money was wired to the Lamont Maxwell account at BCCI Panama. Two $600,000 wire transfers from the Lamont Maxwell account moved the money to accounts in two different Panamanian banks. These accounts were controlled by the drug organization that Mora acted for.

On August 3 and 4, Bob Musella met with Rudolf Armbrecht in Miami. Their discussions did not satisfy the concerns of the Don Chepe organization and no further money was laundered by Musella for Armbrecht.

Musella and Bilgrami spoke by telephone on August 8. Bilgrami proposed a transfer of funds involving the purchase and sale of gold on the same day for no gain. He explained that the gold sales could be used as a cover to explain the movement of funds. He talked about making the gold transactions through Capcom Financial, the firm he was to join in a few months.

By August 10, the status of Operation C Chase looked something like this. The Don Chepe organization, with Rudolf Armbrecht as its spokesman, was spooked by law enforcement surveillance activity in New York and would no longer make currency deliveries to Bob Musella's representatives. Gonzalo Mora promised to work hard to get more currency from existing customers and to develop new customers. He lined up a $1 million delivery in New York shortly after Armbrecht shut off Musella. Amjad Awan and Akbar Bilgrami had announced they were going to leave BCCI. They were trying to convince Musella to move his funds through the firm they were going to join, Capcom Financial. A Senate Subcommittee was holding hearings on General Noriega's connection to drugs and money laundering and was looking to call Amjad Awan as a witness. Solid money laundering cases had been developed against a number of BCCI officials. Operation C Chase was in a position to file charges against another 60 or more individuals in six cities for drug and money laundering violations. Prosecutors and Customs officials agreed that it was getting close to the time to end the Operation by making arrests. They agreed that an effort would be made to develop a case against Capcom Financial.

On August 11, Gonzalo Mora arranged for the delivery of almost $1 million in currency to an undercover agent in New York. (The actual amount was $999,800.) After being deposited in a New York bank, the money was wired to the Financial Consulting account in Florida. Subsequently, $930,000 was wire transferred to the Sandart account in Luxembourg and then wired to the Barkeville account at BCCI Paris. Finally, $910,000 of the money was wired to Mora's client's account at the BCCI office in Colon, Panama.

On August 16, Bob Musella and Kathy Erickson met with Akbar Bilgrami. Bilgrami again discussed the prospect of moving Musella's funds through Capcom Financial by way of the simultaneous purchase and sale of gold. Bilgrami said the cost of using Capcom would be cheaper for Musella than BCCI and would involve much less red tape in the form of account records, loan documents, and corporate papers. He said that Capcom could act as a buffer between Musella's organization and the banks. Musella said he was interested and indicated that he would take a trip to London in September to meet with the head of Capcom Financial. During their meeting, Bilgrami cautioned Musella about his Panamanian accounts; he observed that the United States might eventually be able to obtain Panamanian banking records.

Musella met with Awan and Bilgrami on August 17, and they told him about a Senate Subcommittee investigation and the likelihood of Awan being called as a witness because he had past financial ties to General

Noriega. They also advised him that the Congressional panel had requested records of Panamanian accounts and of loans being generated from BCCI's Panama offices. They advised Musella that the request for records would not result in his transactions being disclosed. Bilgrami said BCCI would not furnish the Subcommittee with any records from Panama because it would violate Panamanian law. Nevertheless, the bankers suggested Musella prepay the interest due on his Panamanian loans, free up CDs in Switzerland, and take care of Panamanian accounts with other banks. In effect, they were suggesting Musella wipe out any indebtedness to BCCI Panama, to be on the safe side. Awan told Musella he would be going to Washington that night to meet with lawyers to prepare a defense for the upcoming hearings.

Musella again met with Bilgrami on August 22, and they further discussed moving funds through Capcom Financial. Musella indicated he would definitely do so.

On August 23, one of Mora's drug contacts in Houston delivered over $400,000 to an undercover agent. The money was moved to the Financial Consulting account at Florida National Bank, and after several wire transfers, the funds ended up in the Saintsea Shipping account at BCCI Nassau. The money went to Mora's clients via checks drawn on the Saintsea account at BCCI Panama.

Bob Musella and his undercover girlfriend, Kathy Erickson, went to Nassau, Bahamas on August 25. They had three separate meetings with Saad Shafi, the manager of the BCCI branch there. The meetings had been pre-arranged by Akbar Bilgrami. By the time of the visit, Musella had established accounts at the Bahamas branch in the names of three different corporate entities. The nature of remarks made by both parties during the meetings threw additional light on the type of ethical culture that existed at BCCI.

Shafi said the Nassau branch had $180 million in deposits, all but $2 million of which came from offshore sources. He said the Nassau branch had only granted about $40 million in loans. He told Musella that Bahamian government officials had been very supportive of BCCI in not relinquishing records to U.S. authorities. Shafi stated that Amjad Awan and Akbar Bilgrami were responsible for the bulk of BCCI's South American clients. He added that Awan was a financial advisor to Noriega. Musella said he needed secrecy for his client's funds. Shafi said he would handle matters for Musella with the maximum of security and the utmost confidentiality. He said he could insure confidentiality in Nassau because he had the support of government authorities.

Musella told Shafi he bought and sold currency for a percentage. He explained that he received cash in the United States from clients who were both Colombians and Americans. He said he needed to disguise the money to make it look as though it came from legitimate businesses, so he filtered it through many cash generating businesses and subsequently had it transferred to his investment company. He said he then needed a vehicle to transfer funds out of the United States and transform it to appear, upon return to his clients, as a loan from a foreign source. Musella then went into his Lee Iacocca analogy for describing his clients. Shafi's response was to immediately assure Musella that his branch could handle any amount of cash. He also said he could accept unlimited amounts of funds for CD purchases and issue counterbalancing loans. He said he could insure that the paperwork which might link CDs with loans would not be given to anyone outside the bank.

Once again, a BCCI official had no qualms about taking drug money or about covering up the security for loans. The culture of BCCI was, give us your money and we'll guarantee secrecy and confidentiality. No one will know there is a link between a CD and a loan.

When Bob Musella returned to Florida from Nassau, he was involved in a series of telephone calls and meetings with Akbar Bilgrami. During one call on August 29, Bilgrami said that, as a result of subpoenas served on the bank from the Senate Subcommittee, there were internal auditors looking over activities. He said they had discovered some incomplete documentation regarding some of Musella's new companies, and he suggested that transactions be suspended until all documentation was completed.

On September 2, Bilgrami and Musella met at the Miami BCCI office to complete documentation on some of the companies. They discussed the fact that Musella would go to London on or about September 20 to meet with S.R. Ali Akbar, the director of Capcom Financial Services Limited. Bilgrami told Musella that he and Awan had told Akbar about the sensitivity of Musella's funds. He advised Musella not to mention to Akbar that his clients were drug dealers and that his money came from cocaine sales. He suggested that he tell Akbar he would be conducting transactions for "tax purposes." Musella and Bilgrami filled out Capcom Financial Services Inc. account forms in the name of Sandart Limited, and Musella signed the forms. Bilgrami advised Musella to close out his BCCI accounts in Panama because of increased pressure the U.S. Government was exerting on international banks, such as BCCI, with offices in the United States. He predicted the banks would eventually have to disclose records to Senate investigators.

Bob Musella had his last face-to-face meeting with Amjad Awan on September 9, 1988. Awan said BCCI had received three subpoenas from the Senate Subcommittee. One was for records of all transactions conducted on behalf of Panamanian corporations. Awan said the bank could not provide that information because the government of Panama would not allow the release of those records. He said he would try to enlist a friend in the BCCI Panama office to remove all but the most essential records of Musella's account activity. He recommended Musella close out all of his Panamanian accounts.

Awan told Musella he had been subpoenaed to appear before the Subcommittee as had been Mr. Shafi, the general manager of the Latin American Division of BCCI (and the father of Saad Shafi, the BCCI country manager in Nassau, Bahamas). Awan said he believed he had been subpoenaed because of his former association with General Noriega. He told Musella the bank's attorney, Robert Altman, had advised that Awan should be transferred to Paris to slow down the Senate investigation. Awan said he could hurt the bank badly if he were to cooperate fully, which he said he would not do. He said he did not want to go to Paris because he would be looking over his shoulder forever. He said he had worked out a solution. He was going to submit his resignation. The following Sunday he would fly to Washington to meet with a heavyweight lawyer he had retained and meet the Subcommittee Counsel on Monday. Awan said he felt he had developed a good rapport with the subcommittee lawyer. Awan told Musella he believed he could extricate himself from the whole situation quite cleanly without really damaging the bank.

The Senate Subcommittee that subpoenaed records of BCCI and Amjad Awan was the Foreign Relations Subcommittee on Terrorism, Narcotics and International Operations, which was chaired by Senator John F. Kerry of Massachusetts. This was the same Congressional panel that went off the deep end and was embarrassed by Ramon Milian Rodriguez during earlier hearings in 1987 and 1988.

The Subcommittee Counsel, Jack Blum, had been making numerous inquiries regarding General Manuel Noriega's involvement in drugs and money laundering. He learned that Noriega had conducted business with BCCI in Panama and in other countries and that Amjad Awan, a BCCI official, had been Noriega's personal banker when Awan worked in BCCI's Panama branch. In the course of gathering information about Awan, Blum met with Customs and Justice officials in Florida. He learned there was a highly sensitive Customs undercover operation that involved Awan. He was told that a subpoena to Awan could possibly damage the undercover operation. Blum told the government officials he would not subpoena Amjad Awan until the Customs case was completed.

But Senator Kerry and Jack Blum had bigger fish to fry. There was an election coming up in November. Vice President Bush was ahead in the polls. It was more important to try to embarrass the existing administration and candidate George Bush by trying to show that it mishandled General Manuel Noriega than it was to protect a Customs drug money laundering and drug case. So, Amjad Awan was subpoenaed.

The subpoena had a chilling effect on the C Chase investigation. After Bob Musella's meeting with Awan on September 9, Customs supervisors and prosecutors in Tampa met to plan a strategy. They decided the Awan subpoena would have to bring the case to an untimely end. They had wanted to attempt to move funds through Capcom Financial Services in London and to see what the involvement of its subsidiary, Capcom Futures, in Chicago, would be. But they couldn't take the chance that testimony by Awan or some leak by Senate investigators might compromise Bob Musella and other undercover agents involved in the investigation. Besides, it was clear that Armbrecht and the "Don Chepe" organization were suspicious of Musella and his associates. So they made plans to wrap up the case. It was decided to make arrests in the first week of October.

An ingenious plan was developed. It grew out of two factors: that arrests would have to be made all over the United States and the world, and that Musella and Kathy Erickson had intimated that they were romantically involved (and in reality, in their off-duty lives, they were). With these factors in mind, the investigators decided to announce the wedding of Musella and Erickson and invite many of the people who would be charged in the case. Invitations were printed and mailed out in mid-September. The wedding was to be held at 10:00 a.m. on Sunday, October 9, 1988, at the Innisbrook Resort and Golf Club, Tarpon Springs, Florida. Both agents began to make telephone calls to prospective defendants to advise them of the wedding plans and to tell them that formal invitations would be forthcoming.

In the meantime, there were still investigative matters to be attended to. It was decided Bob Musella should proceed with plans to visit London and Paris to meet with S.R. Ali Akbar of Capcom Financial Services and to have additional meetings with Nazir Chinoy and Ian Howard at BCCI in Paris. Musella continued to converse with Akbar Bilgrami. There was a telephone conversation on September 12 in which Musella told Bilgrami that, after meeting with Awan on the 9th, he now understood why Bilgrami advised him to close out his Panamanian bank accounts. Bilgrami said it would be best to lay low for the time being. He said he would let Musella know when everything was all clear. On the next day, Bilgrami telephoned Musella and told him there were no documents remaining on the Lamont Maxwell account.

BACK TO EUROPE

On September 20, Bob Musella flew to London. The following day he met with S.R. Ali Akbar at the offices of Capcom Financial Services Limited in

London. During the meeting, Musella explained he would be receiving millions of dollars in currency in the United States from Colombian clients. Despite the prior admonition by Bilgrami not to tell the nature of his client's business, Musella went on to tell Akbar that his clients sold cocaine in the United States. Akbar had two reactions—he told Musella what he and his clients did was their own business, and then he proceeded with the paperwork for Musella to open two corporate accounts at Capcom. One of the accounts was for Berens Limited and the other was in the name of Hardeman Company Limited. What Musella did not realize at the time of this meeting was that Akbar was the former treasury officer of BCCI in London and had been involved in trading activity that resulted in hundreds of millions of dollars in losses to the bank.

Beginning on September 23, Musella spent several days in Paris. He met with Nazir Chinoy, Ian Howard, and Sibte Hassan on several occasions. In the first meeting, on September 23, all three bankers were present. Musella advised them he expected to move large amounts of money through his Paris accounts during the next several months. Chinoy said Musella's organization had the complete support of the upper echelons of BCCI. Musella executed a number of documents for his accounts at the Paris branch. Sibte Hassan showed Musella records indicating that Rudolf Armbrecht had removed Musella's name as a signatory on the Nicesea Shipping Limited account back on July 22. Musella had agreed to this removal with Armbrecht after the Don Chepe organization became suspicious of a government investigation. Hassan showed him two replacement names on the account. Musella recognized the names as those of launderers for the Don Chepe organization—individuals to whom checks were issued from Musella's Panamanian accounts.

On September 25, Musella met alone with Nazir Chinoy. Chinoy said he intended to call the president of BCCI to explain to him the volume of business that Musella had promised to bring in before the end of the year. He said he would tell the president about this so he could get excused from a board meeting in London on October 8, that would enable him to attend Musella's wedding in Florida on October 9.

Musella returned to Tampa on September 26. Things were astir at Operation C Chase. Agents and prosecutors were working feverishly to prepare arrest warrants and affidavits for search warrants. Plans were being made for the Musella/Erickson "wedding." Invitees who indicated they would attend the wedding were being put up in rooms at the Innisbrook Resort and Golf Club. Plans were being made for a "wild" bachelor party at a restaurant located on the top floor of an office building in downtown Tampa. The fact that the office building was located across the street from the U.S. Courthouse provides some inkling of what was in store for the invited guests.

Bob Musella had two more meetings with Akbar Bilgrami before the events of the night of October 8, 1988. One was on September 30, at which time they discussed the accounts that had been opened at Capcom. Bilgrami said S.R. Ali Akbar was upset by the fact that Musella had discussed the nature of his client's business so bluntly during their meeting in London. The other meeting was on October 3 and involved papers that had to be completed before Musella could begin sending money on a regular basis to Capcom.

On September 30, Amjad Awan testified before a closed hearing of the Senate Subcommittee on Terrorism, Narcotics and International Operations. Chief Counsel Jack Blum presided. The hearing was classified at the Committee Sensitive level, which theoretically meant that no information about the testimony was to be made public until authorized by a vote of the subcommittee. Awan testified about the banking services that he and BCCI provided to General Noriega. He testified that Noriega had opened a Secret Service intelligence account at BCCI with several hundred thousand dollars in cash and used the account to pay off politicians in cash and to pay for his own personal expenses on foreign trips. On several occasions during the hearing, Awan was asked if he had ever laundered drug money, and he replied no.

THE END OF THE LINE

Eighteen key players in the money laundering conspiracy were invited to the Musella/Erickson "wedding." Eleven checked into the Innisbrook Resort and Golf Club in Tarpon Springs on the afternoon of October 8. They mingled with other guests who were Customs agents. Five of the nine BCCI officials who were invited appeared: Ian Howard and Sibte Hassan from Paris (Nazir Chinoy could not get permission to come), Syed Hussain from Panama, and Amjad Awan and Akbar Bilgrami from Miami. Gonzalo Mora, Jr. flew in from Colombia. Bob Musella made a brief cameo appearance. He thanked the guests for coming and said he would see them at the bachelor party that evening. He then left, saying he had last minute business to attend to.

The guests were told the bachelor party would be the experience of a lifetime. It was to be held at MacBeth's Restaurant in downtown Tampa. Limos would pick everyone up at 7:00 p.m. On schedule, a number of stretch limousines appeared at Innisbrook just before 7:00 p.m. Guests were loaded in and driven to downtown Tampa. They were escorted to MacBeth's Restaurant, which was located on the top floor of a high rise building. It is not known if some of the key invitees noticed the U.S. Courthouse across the street from MacBeth's as they arrived. If they did not, they certainly became aware of it on their departure. Once the group arrived at the parking lot in the building that housed MacBeth's, they were greeted by a large contingent of law enforcement officers who placed them all under arrest.

More than 40 additional arrests were made over the weekend in Detroit, Chicago, Houston, Los Angeles, and New York. Those arrested were cocaine dealers and their money launderers, and couriers who had been making currency deliveries to Customs undercover agents for the previous two years. S.R. Ali Akbar (Capcom) and Asif Baaksa (BCCI) were arrested in London. S.R. Ali Akbar was convicted of a money laundering charge under British law and served a year in prison during most of 1989.

Dozens of search warrants were executed in connection with the arrests. On Monday morning, October 10, scores of agents invaded the offices of BCCI in Tampa, Miami and Boca Raton. Armed with search warrants, they walked out with boxes of records, particularly from the Latin American Caribbean Regional Offices in Miami. Search warrants were also executed at the residences and offices of the drug dealers, money launderers, and couriers around the country who had been supplying undercover agents with currency. In many instances, these searches produced vital evidence—cocaine and/or caches of drug proceeds.

A prime example occurred in New York. The leader of the money handling operation for the "Don Chepe" cocaine distribution organization in New York was Pedro Charria. Charria and his couriers had made a number of currency deliveries to undercover agent Nelson Chen during 1987 and 1988. Charria lived in Dix Hills in the Queens borough of New York City. When it was decided to close down Operation C Chase, a separate indictment was obtained in Federal Court in the Southern District of New York charging Charria and 15 subordinates with counts of money laundering and drug conspiracy. After Charria was arrested a search of his residence yielded voluminous records of currency transactions. The records included money ledgers showing the receipt and distribution of over $35 million in currency during the six-month period ending October 6, 1990. In addition to $12.3 million that had been delivered to the Customs undercover agent during this period, there were entries for accounts labeled, "Mina 20," "Mina 11," "Mina 30," and "Paolo Mina," thereby tying the couriers in with the Polar Cap laundering operation.

The arrests and seizures in cities other than Tampa pointed up the overall value of the C Chase operation. Not only were a crooked bank and a number of key employees facing criminal charges, but drug dealing and money laundering organizations in a number of cities were put out of business and a link was established between targets of C Chase and the large money laundering organization that was being investigated in Operation Polar Cap.

On Tuesday, October 11, 1988, federal prosecutors unsealed three separate indictments in Tampa that, together with indictments in five other cities, charged 85 defendants with a variety of counts, including money laundering, cocaine importation, cocaine possession, and conspiracy. Three separate corporate entities of BCCI were among the 85 defendants. There was massive publicity connected with the case. It marked the first time that a bank had been charged with money laundering offenses. Previous cases had involved officials of banks but none had actually charged the banks.

When the indictments became public, the defendants were in for a shock; they discovered that Bob Musella, the owner of the Financial Consulting business empire, and his "girlfriend" were, in reality, Special Agents of the U.S. Customs Service, and that their real names were Robert Mazur and Kathleen Ertz.

What happened in the period of a little more than two years after the arrests and indictments has been described by one federal investigator as a "legal feeding frenzy" as attorneys and law firms ran up massive bills representing BCCI and the officers of the bank who faced charges of criminal misconduct. Investigations were conducted, witnesses interviewed, motions filed, and hearings were held. In one lengthy motion prepared by two law firms, the contention was made that the indictment against the bank and its employees should be dismissed because of government misconduct. The prosecutors replied that the government's behavior was legal and proper in all respects. After a hearing, the trial judge dismissed the defense motion and ruled that the undercover measures were appropriate.

It has been estimated that legal fees to eight different law firms who represented the bank and its indicted employees amounted to between $32 million and $35 million.

In December 1989, the trial judge denied all defense motions and ordered BCCI, five of its officers, and Rudolf Armbrecht to proceed to trial. By this time, Gonzalo Mora, Jr. had already entered a guilty plea. At the last minute, just before the trial was to begin in January 1990, two of the three BCCI corporate entities that had been indicted entered into a plea bargain, agreeing to plead guilty to a number of charges and to forfeit $14 million. BCC International S.A. agreed to plead guilty to one conspiracy count and two money laundering counts. BCCI (Overseas) Limited pled to one conspiracy count and 27 money laundering counts. Charges against the holding company in Luxembourg, BCCI Holdings, were dismissed.

The guilty pleas were accepted by U.S. District Court Judge W. Terrell Hodges. He imposed the $14 million penalty (which had grown to $15.3

million with interest) and placed the two bank units on probation for five years each. The sentence was the largest single monetary penalty ever imposed on a bank in the United States for money laundering or laundering-related charges. By the time of the sentence, BCCI had closed its offices in Tampa and Boca Raton. Immediately after the sentence, the Florida Comptroller, the state's chief bank regulator, revoked BCCI's license to do business in Florida. BCCI appealed and won a reversal of the license revocation. A Florida appellate court ruled that BCCI was entitled to a hearing. However, rather than face a hearing that would subject its activities to intense scrutiny, BCCI shut down its Miami office and indicated that it would not do business in Florida again.

In January 1990, the five BCCI bankers who were arrested at Bob Musella's "bachelor party" went on trial along with Rudolf Armbrecht in U.S. District Court in Tampa. The trial lasted an exhausting six months. The prosecutors were Assistant United States Attorneys Mark Jackowski and Michael Rubinstein. They did an outstanding job of presenting the government's case, cross-examining defense witnesses, and presenting final arguments. Customs Special Agent Robert Mazur (Musella) and other Customs agents capped off their outstanding undercover performances by presenting themselves as excellent witnesses. Their testimony was backed up by hundreds of tapes of recorded conversations they had with the defendants in the United States and in Europe. Time and again the jury heard tapes of Mazur telling various defendants his client's money came from drug sales. They heard the Lee Iacocca story run at each of the banking defendants. They either heard the bankers complain about not wanting to know where the money came from or just proceeding with transactions after a brief acknowledgement of what had been said. They never heard any defendant say, "Stop. I won't handle drug money." The case relied heavily upon testimony from Customs agents and hundreds of tapes of recorded conversations.

The quality and quantity of the government's case was too much for the defense to overcome. The jury found all of the defendants guilty of all counts. When the guilty verdicts were returned on July 15, 1990, it was seen as a resounding victory for the government.

On November 30, 1990, U.S. District Judge W. Terrell Hodges sentenced all six defendants to jail terms. Amjad Awan was sentenced to 12 years, Rudolf Armbrecht got 12 years and seven months, Akbar Bilgrami received 12 years, Syed Hussain was sentenced to seven years and three months, Ian Howard got four years and nine months, and Sibte Hassan received a sentence of three years and one month. Nazir Chinoy was extradited from France to the United States during the summer of 1991. He is awaiting trial on the original money laundering indictment.

ADDITIONAL PROBLEMS

The conviction of BCCI banking units and employees in Operation C Chase was the forerunner of much more serious problems for the world-wide banking organization. Operation C Chase was the tip of the iceburg.

On July 5, 1991, the central banks of seven countries took coordination action to immediately shut down BCCI operations within their borders. The action was taken after the Bank of England reviewed a confidential audit report prepared by Price Waterhouse, the international accounting firm. The report revealed that BCCI had suffered massive losses, approaching the range of $4 to $5 billion and had been covering up the losses since as early as 1984 by a system of false loans and fraudulent accounting practices.

The losses came from trading in currency futures, unpaid loans, and money spent on the illegal acquisition of several banks in the United States. The cost of financing the cover-up of the losses was staggering and has been estimated as being about $2 billion.

BCCI set up a central treasury operation in its London office in 1982 to take advantage of the pools of currency accumulated in its 70-nation banking network. The treasury operation bought and sold currencies and traded in currency futures. It was headed by S.R. Ali Akbar, under whose capable stewardship the operation lost over $800 million by 1985. Akbar was fired and went on to run Capcom Financial Services, Ltd. until his involvement in C Chase.

BCCI carried unpaid loans made to a number of internationally known Arab businessmen of well over $1 billion.

BCCI's problems in the United States primarily involved improper and illegal control of several banks and money laundering. As it turns out, BCCI gained control of First American Bancshares, a holding company that owns First American Bank of Washington, D.C., in 1981. The control was obtained improperly by using nominees to purchase shares in the holding company. The nominees were 14 Arab businessmen who received loans from BCCI to purchase the shares. Most of the loans were never repaid and the purchasers pledged their shares to BCCI. The Federal Reserve Bank approved the First American Bancshares takeover in 1981 based on representations made by Clark Clifford, the famous adviser to presidents, and his law partner and protege, Robert Altman. Both were attorneys for the investors and BCCI. The representations were to the effect that the Arab businessmen who purchased the stock were acting independently and that they were not serving as fronts for any other entity. Clifford and Altman further assured the Federal Reserve that BCCI did not own any of the shares and would not exercise any control of the holding company.

The Federal Reserve finally approved the takeover when Clifford and Altman stated that they would run First American Bancshares to assure that there would be no control by BCCI. Clifford became the chairman and Altman the president.

In 1989, the Federal Reserve began an investigation of BCCI's possible hidden ownership of First American Bancshares and of the National Bank of Georgia, which had been acquired by First American in 1987. By late 1990, the investigation determined that BCCI controlled at least 25 percent of the stock and the Federal Reserve ordered BCCI to divest itself of whatever financial interest it had in First American Bancshares.

In July 1990, the Federal Reserve imposed a civil penalty of $200 million against BCCI for having engaged in a pattern of deceit in obtaining ownership interests in First American Bancshares, the National Bank of Georgia, and two other U.S. banks, Independence Bank of Encino (California) and Centrust Savings (a failed savings and loan institution in Miami).

On July 29, 1991, the New York County (Manhattan) District Attorney, Robert Morgenthau, announced a 12-count indictment against BCCI for what he described as the "largest bank fraud in world financial history." The indictment included three counts of grand larceny and eight counts of money laundering. In a press conference, Morgenthau stated, "The defendants created the appearance of respectability by persuading world leaders to appear with them." He cited Jimmy Carter, Andrew Young, U.N. Secretary Javier Perez de Cuellar, and former British Prime Minister James Callaghan as individuals who fell into this category.

On August 23, 1991, a federal grand jury in Tampa returned an indictment charging six former officials of BCCI and Gerardo Moncada, the Colombian cocaine trafficker, with racketeering and money laundering violations stemming from the C Chase investigation. S.R. Ali Akbar was one of the former BCCI officials charged along with his firm, Capcom Financial Services, Ltd. It is believed that the indictment was based on new information provided by Amjad Awan and Nazir Chinoy, who are now reported to be cooperating with the government. Chinoy, the former BCCI official in charge of France and Africa, is in custody in the United States awaiting the disposition of charges against him in the original C Chase indictment.

On November 14, 1991, a federal grand jury in Washington, D.C. indicted the two highest officials in BCCI and a major shareholder of the bank on fraud and racketeering charges in connection with efforts to gain control of the Independence Bank of Encino, California and a fraudulent stock scheme involving the Centrust Savings Bank in Miami. Charged in the indictment were Agha Hasan Abedi, BCCI's founder and former president, Swaleh Naqvi, the acting president, and the internationally-known businessman, Gaith Pharaon, who was a major shareholder in the bank.

This same grand jury in Washington is looking into the possibility of further criminal charges in connection with the control which BCCI obtained over First American Bancshares and the National Bank of Georgia. The involvement of Clark Clifford and Robert Altman in the BCCI control of these banks is being examined by the grand jury.

For their part, Clifford and Altman have maintained in testimony before several Congressional committees that they were innocent dupes who did not know anything about loans from BCCI to the investors who bought the controlling shares in First American Bancshares. They maintain that BCCI never exercised any control while they served as the principal officers of the holding company.

It is ironic that Clark Clifford once referred to Ronald Reagan as an amiable dunce. It is now clear that Clifford, the adviser to Presidents, the ultimate insider, the man who could see behind every intrigue, would prefer to be seen as an amiable dunce in the First American Bancshares situation than to be identified in a criminal scheme to deceive the Federal Reserve Bank.

Clifford and Altman have not been helped by revelations that they borrowed $18 million from BCCI in 1987 to buy stock in First American Bancshares. In 1989, they sold 60% of the stock they owned and realized a pre-tax profit of more than $9 million. They sold the stock to one of the original nominee investors who may now be deceased.

SOME OBSERVATIONS

The events of 1991 with regard to the seven-nation shutdown of BCCI operations, the New York indictment, and the $200 million fine by the Federal Reserve have led to a "feeding frenzy" by the world's media. Some of the reporting has been excellent and has actually pushed government officials to take action on hidden ownership issues. A considerable amount of the reporting has been flat-out inaccurate, laced with innuendo and unsupportable allegations and influenced by political bias.

Perhaps the worst of the articles written was the *Time* cover story piece of July 29, 1991 entitled, "The World's Sleaziest Bank." A major premise of the article is that the U.S. Government is trying to cover up its role with BCCI and that the White House has become entangled. An unnamed "U.S. Intelligence Officer" is quoted as attributing the government's lack of action against BCCI as being related to "the blind eye that the U.S. turned to the heroin trafficking in Pakistan." How any responsible journalist could espouse such a premise in a lengthy article without once mentioning that it was the U.S. Government in the form of the U.S. Customs Service and the U.S. Justice Department that successfully prosecuted and convicted BCCI and a number of its officials on money laundering charges in 1990, is incomprehensible. The entire article is laced with James Bond-type scenarios of terrorist networks and arms and drug conspiracies all engineered by some all-powerful, all-seeing force named BCCI. The article was a disgrace to honest journalism and was the stuff of the supermarket tabloids.

The Justice Department has come in for considerable congressional and media criticism for not taking action against BCCI. Most of the critics fail to mention that Justice prosecuted BCCI in Operation C Chase and that the Justice action in that case is the only recorded criminal conviction of the bank in the world. In all fairness, Justice appears to have been slow to react to the hidden ownership issue with regard to First American Bancshares. They seem to have left this issue to the Federal Reserve as a civil matter. On the other hand, it appears that Justice is now vigorously pursuing several criminal allegations concerning BCCI control of First American Bancshares and the people connected to it.

Some media stories, in discussing Operation C Chase, have referred to sources who claim that the U.S. Government stepped in and stopped the investigation before it went further and embarrassed the United States. This is nonsense. The Customs undercover operation had gone about as far as it could with BCCI. The investigators would have liked to go further with Capcom Financial Services, but precipitous action by the Kerry Subcommittee and several other factors led to the shutdown of the investigation sooner than was desired.

Much has been made by the media of possible involvement by the CIA with BCCI and the use by the CIA of BCCI's banking facilities. The thrust of some of these stories is that there is somehow something inherently wrong and/or sinister with the CIA using BCCI or any other bank's services to move funds. This is not the case. It is clear that the CIA and the intelligence agencies of numerous other countries used BCCI accounts and funds transfer facilities to move monies in covert operations. The facilities of many banks are similarly used. It was quite logical to use an international bank such as BCCI that had offices in 70 countries.

As a matter of fact, in Operation C Chase, Customs undercover agents started out by using BCCI facilities to open an account in Panama as part of a covert operation. BCCI was not a target at the time. Customs found it convenient to use a bank that happened to have offices in both Tampa and Panama. If BCCI officials had not involved themselves in criminal misconduct, Customs would have been sitting in the same boat as the CIA today. Would anyone seriously suggest that it would have been improper for the Customs undercover agents to have moved money in undercover accounts at BCCI to develop criminal cases against cocaine dealers and money launderers? As a practical matter, the CIA and the intelligence services routinely use the banking facilities of international banks to surreptitiously move funds. There is nothing wrong with this. By October 1991, nothing concrete had been developed to indicate that the CIA had any improper relationship with BCCI. Contrary to any impropriety, it appears that the CIA, as early as 1984, recognized the sleazy nature of BCCI and furnished a number of reports about the bank's improper conduct to other U.S. Government agencies.

Media accounts have highlighted the fact that Abu Nidal and other terrorist organizations used BCCI banking facilities to shelter and transfer funds. The truth is that several intelligence agencies from concerned countries were on to the Abu Nidal accounts at BCCI and were able to monitor the activities in these accounts. MI5, Britain's version of the CIA, received information from an employee of BCCI about the existence of the Abu Nidal accounts. Several print media stories identified the employee by name and at least one television network named him and showed footage of him leaving the bank in London. Can there be anything more irresponsible than letting the Abu Nidal terrorists know the identity of the individual who fingered them?

In conclusion, there is no doubt that there was a corporate culture at BCCI of secrecy, fraud, deception, and looking the other way at money coming from criminal enterprises. The culture extended to the highest levels of the bank and had probably started in the early 1980s. Nine bank officials were advised by Customs undercover agents in Operation C Chase that money being put into the bank came from cocaine sales. All nine officials continued to take the money without blinking an eye. The only protest heard was that some of the officers didn't really want to know where the money was coming from. The nine officers and two other BCCI employees who were first approached to open accounts were willing to assist the undercover agents with secretive and deceptive transactions that would assist in evading taxes and provide secrecy and confidentiality from government investigators. It is not surprising that this culture extended to the very highest officials of the bank who were trying to cover up losses by a variety of deceptive practices. Recall the efforts by Amjad Awan and Akbar Bilgrami to get "Bob Musella" to load as much money as possible in the bank before the June 30, 1988 end of the fiscal year to make things look good. It is easy to imagine that hundreds of bank officials were doing the same thing with wealthy clients around the world. Such activity would tend to cover up losses and make the bank's balance sheet look good.

The culture of extreme confidentiality and deceptive practices made BCCI a natural for drug dealers, arms merchants, terrorists, swindlers, tax evaders, dictators, and intelligence agencies, all of whom wanted strict confidentiality and the ability to move their funds from country to country. The point is that BCCI willingly allowed itself to be used by these people to get money in the front door. A strong part of the reason the bank wanted this kind of money was that it was attempting to cover up massive loan and trading losses. It is not the case that BCCI was masterminding spy operations, terrorist activities, drug conspiracies, illegal arms sales, or tax evasion conspiracies. It was the case that BCCI provided a convenient and friendly place for individuals involved in a wide range of illegal activities. In some cases, the bank knew what was behind the money and in other cases it didn't. The bank needed the funds to make up for losses. In all cases, BCCI really didn't care where the money came from. Money laundering of drug proceeds becomes a relatively easy thing to do when a banking institution, such as BCCI, and a number of its key officials cooperate fully in the laundering activity.

CHAPTER 7

THE WAR ON DRUGS

This chapter deals with two declarations of war against drugs, one by the Reagan Administration in 1981 and the second by the Bush Administration in 1989. It reviews some of the actions taken as a result of these declarations and the impact of these actions. It contains some concrete suggestions on how the drug wars can be fought more effectively.

An observer may question why there is a chapter about the "War on Drugs" in a book about money laundering and money launderers. The answer is that illegal drug dealing and money laundering are inseparable. In the words of the old popular tune, "You can't have one without the other." Not all money laundering involves cash from drugs sales. However, almost all drug sales require some form of money laundering. During the decade of the 1980s and continuing into the 1990s, billions of dollars in currency from illegal drug trafficking have been laundered. Experience has proven that all major drug trafficking organizations have a support structure that launders the money from drug sales. No single type of criminal activity generates as much currency that must be laundered as the illicit drug trade.

239

This chapter does not attempt to present a comprehensive historical review of government efforts to suppress narcotics use. While most of the chapter deals with enforcement efforts to curtail drug use and trafficking, there are also comments on nonenforcement activities and programs.

THE CARTER YEARS

To better appreciate the efforts of the Reagan Administration's efforts against drugs, it is important to understand what the Carter Administration did and did not do in its four years in office from 1977 to 1981. The Carter Administration's enforcement efforts were best summarized by Congressman William Hughes of New Jersey, the chairman of the House Subcommittee on Crime, in 1982. "The enforcement efforts of the Carter Administration against drugs were pitiful," he said.

During the four years of Carter's reign, enforcement budgets were cut. The Customs Service, guardian of the federal borders, was taken out of the drug enforcement loop. A Customs Commissioner was appointed who established, as the highest priority of the agency, the interdiction of merchandise upon which no tariff or too little tariff had been paid.

Even worse than the lack of enforcement effort was the message the White House sent to the public about drug use—that cocaine was acutely pleasurable and nonaddictive, and that moderate use of cocaine and marijuana was acceptable social behavior.

To understand the message from the Carter White House more clearly, the following excerpt is quoted from an article entitled, "The Great Cocaine Myth," written by Dr. Peter Bourne, the President's Drug Policy Advisor. The article appeared in the *Drugs and Drug Abuse Education Newsletter* issue of August 1974. "At least as strong a case could probably be made of legalizing [cocaine] as for legalizing marijuana," Dr. Bourne wrote. "Short acting—about 15 minutes—not physically addicting, and acutely pleasurable, cocaine has found increasing favor at all socioeconomic levels in the last year. Although it is capable of producing psychosis with heavy, repeated use, and chronic inhalers can suffer eventual erosion of the nasal membrane and cartilage, the number of people seeking treatment as a result of cocaine use is for all practical purposes zero.... One must ask what possible justification there can be for the obsession which DEA officials have with it, and what criteria they use to determine the priority they give the interdiction of a drug if it is not the degree of harm which it causes the user."

The message given is absolutely incredible in light of the experience with cocaine in the United States in the late 1970s and throughout the 1980s. One must wonder how many lives were ruined because people believed this message—that cocaine was not addictive and was acutely pleasurable.

THE REAGAN WAR ON DRUGS

Shortly after assuming office in 1981, President Reagan declared war against drugs. It was a period when heroin addiction was increasing and marijuana usage was rampant. It also marked the beginning of the U.S. cocaine explosion.

While cocaine was a serious problem in 1981, the full extent of its prevalence and the devastating impact it would have on the country were not fully realized at the time.

The Reagan Administration strategy for winning the war on drugs incorporated a number of enforcement initiatives and a major demand reduction initiative. Despite some significant improvements and some victories, however, the war was not won and the battle continues.

Although the war was not won, more was done to fight the problem during the Reagan years than had ever been undertaken in the past, and the tide of battle was turned. Most of the Reagan initiatives went unrecognized or were criticized by Congress and by the media. While much of the criticism was unfair, the bottom line was that the Reagan Administration did not win the war against drugs because it did not put enough into the effort.

Some of the earliest Reagan Administration efforts against drugs occurred in the Treasury Department. None of these efforts involved additional funding, but instead a reordering of priorities at IRS and the Customs Service.

Customs was instructed to make drug interdiction a high priority, and it did so. William Von Raab was appointed Commissioner of Customs in September 1981. Almost overnight he was able to get through to over 13,000 Customs employees that drug interdiction was a top priority. An organization that had been told by the previous administration to stay away from drug enforcement turned around and began making seizures of drugs being smuggled into the country. Indeed, drug seizures soared almost immediately.

The IRS, Criminal Investigation Division (CID), was instructed to vigorously pursue tax cases against high level drug dealers and to devote more resources to investigating money laundering activities which violated the Bank Secrecy Act. An aggressive and highly-competent manager named Dick Wassanaar was appointed Assistant Commissioner for Criminal Enforcement at IRS. He quickly changed CID priorities and more agents were committed to BSA cases and to investigating high level drug dealers for tax evasion.

IRS participation and involvement against major drug traffickers is important. In many cases, it is difficult to develop drug cases against high level dealers. However, their lifestyles, with expensive homes and fancy cars, etc., make them ripe targets for tax evasion cases. It is an understatement to say that drug dealers usually do not file tax returns that accurately reflect the source and amount of their income.

Treasury also placed a high priority on enforcement activity against money launderers. Operation Greenback, the multiagency financial task force in Miami, was beefed up with more Customs and IRS agents and additional prosecutors. A number of mini-Greenback financial task forces were created in other cities, comprised, for the most part, of IRS and Customs agents with support from local U.S. Attorney's offices. By mid-1982, there were financial task forces operating in 26 cities.

The Treasury Department effort in the war on drugs was both significant and substantial. In 1981, it resulted in the reassignment of hundreds of enforcement personnel to activities related to drug enforcement. The priorities of entire organizations such as IRS and Customs were changed from little involvement in the war against drugs to a high priority significant role. There were many critics of the Reagan Administration's drug war in the media and in the Congress. The critics carped on what was perceived to be the Administration's unwillingness to spend additional funds for resources. While there was some basis for valid criticism in this area, hardly anyone recognized the substantial reallocation of resources and priorities that took place in the IRS and the Customs Service.

ROLE OF THE JUSTICE DEPARTMENT

In the Reagan Justice Department, the decks were also cleared for battle. U.S. Attorneys, the chief prosecutors in federal judicial districts, were being appointed. For the most part they were young, aggressive, pro-law enforcement types who were more concerned with the rights of victims than the rights of defendants. Federal judges were appointed with conservative views of the criminal justice system and a belief that defendants convicted of serious crimes should serve long jail terms.

The Reagan appointees of prosecutors and judges were in sharp contrast to the Carter appointees who tended to have liberal views of the criminal justice system that emphasized the rights of criminal defendants. These attitudes resulted in nonaggressive prosecution policies and light jail sentences.

Obviously, not all of the Carter appointees were bad and not all of the Reagan appointees were good. Generally, however, the Reagan prosecutors and judges were much more aggressive in prosecuting and sentencing major drug traffickers than their predecessors had been.

The difference in philosophies and aggressiveness of prosecutors was important in the war on drugs. Nowhere was this more evident than in the Southern Judicial District of Florida which encompassed Miami and all of South Florida—an area that had become known as the cocaine capital of the United States. During the four years of the Carter Administration there had been two appointments to the U.S. Attorney's position. Both individuals were weak, indecisive, and lacked aggressiveness. They declined to prosecute a number of major cases for a variety of inconsequential reasons. All of the federal enforcement agencies were up in arms. Strong cases against important offenders were not pursued. Major cocaine dealers were walking the streets and thumbing their noses at federal investigators.

In one of the best moves it made in the war on drugs, the Reagan Justice Department appointed Stanley Marcus as U.S. Attorney for the Southern District of Florida. Marcus was bright, aggressive, and knowledgeable. He had been a prosecutor for a number of years and had a good record of successful prosecutions of major cases. At the time of his appointment in 1981, he was serving as the head of the Justice Department's Organized Crime Strike Force in Detroit.

Almost overnight Marcus turned things around in the prosecution arena. He beefed up his staff with aggressive, competent lawyers from all over the country. A new aggressive prosecution policy was instituted, and cases which previously had been considered impossible to prosecute were taken to trial and won. Defense attorneys who had been having a field day suddenly saw Assistant U.S. Attorneys going to the wall on every issue and winning most of them. Federal agents developed a new respect for and confidence in the U.S. Attorney's office. In a matter of less than 90 days the U.S. Attorney's office went from a weak, ineffective, bumbling organization to a decisive, aggressive, and successful prosecutorial team. It was a classic example of how a dynamic leader can affect an organization. It was the best example of the difference in appointments between the Carter and Reagan Justice Departments.

In August 1981, the Justice Department made a major resource reallocation in the enforcement effort against drugs. The FBI was given concurrent jurisdiction over all federal drug statutes that previously had been the sole province of the DEA. There were many critics of this move, but the inescapable fact is that hundreds of federal agents were instantly added to investigation of major drug trafficking organizations. In the decade since that reassignment of jurisdiction, the FBI has made dozens of major cases against big time drug trafficking organizations and arrested and convicted hundreds of dealers. Most of the cases would not have made had it not been for the FBI's involvement.

BUDGET DEFICIENCIES

While many positive measures were taken during the first year of the Reagan Administration's war against drugs, the entire effort was tarnished by a budget controversy. Reagan was swept into power with a pledge to cut government spending. His first budget proposal called for 12% government-wide spending cuts, except for the Defense Department. Incredibly, despite the President's declaration of war against drugs, the spending cuts severely restrained resources at the Justice and Treasury agencies involved in the war. The FBI, DEA, IRS, and the Customs Service were all scheduled for cuts.

The fallout was both swift and lasting. The Democrats in Congress, many of whom were mum during the Carter years of inaction, became very vocal. They ridiculed the Administration's commitment to fighting the war on drugs at the same time it was proposing to reduce the number of enforcement agents dedicated to the fight. The media picked up on the budget cut issue, too, depicting the drug war as all smoke and mirrors and no substance.

No matter what it did, the Reagan Administration was not able to overcome the theme. Indeed, the perception still exists that Reagan was not serious about fighting the drug problem.

The budget issue was unfortunate. It was an unnecessary political embarrassment. On the one hand was the President, who was firmly committed to fighting drugs. On the other hand were bean counters at the Office of Management and Budget (OMB), then headed by David Stockman, who insisted that budget cutting be done across-the-board for all agencies. Stockman and his staff never appreciated the political aspects of the drug war issue.

At the Justice Department, the Attorney General, William French Smith, fought against the OMB-proposed budget cuts. He won internal fights within the administration. Proposed cuts of DEA and FBI agents were withdrawn.

Over at Treasury, it was a different story. Neither Treasury Secretary Donald Regan, nor his deputy, Timothy McNamara, had any real understanding of enforcement issues and no feeling for the politics of the drug issue. Their commitment to budget cuts was unshakable. In their view, Treasury enforcement bureaus, including those fighting the war on drugs, had to accept across-the-board cuts along with all other Treasury agencies.

Never mind that the President was committed to an era of law and order. Never mind that the President had declared war on drugs. Regan and Mc-Namara went along with the OMB budget cuts. President Reagan's first budget went to Congress with recommendations to cut spending at the Customs Service and IRS.

Once before Congress, the Customs budget was restored and even enhanced. The Democrats had a field day. In hearing after hearing, they lambasted the Administration's drug efforts and made the point that Congressional Democrats were more concerned about fighting drugs than was the Republican Administration. The Customs budget became an annual embarrassment from a drug enforcement perspective during the Reagan years. The Administration repeatedly tried to reduce expenditures only to have them restored and enhanced by Congress. The budget debates were particularly embarrassing when it came to items like aircraft, radar, and boats that Customs needed to interdict drug smugglers. The Democrats in Congress were basking in their glory as champions of the enforcement process.

THE SOUTH FLORIDA TASK FORCE

Miami in 1981 was a city with an enormous crime problem brought on by drug trafficking. What plagued Miami was more than the ordinary crime problems associated with drug dealing and drug use. The city had become the central point in the United States where Colombian cocaine and marijuana dealers did their business. They made deals with buyers and received payments for drugs in Miami and, in many instances, also made deliveries there. It was also at this time that the Colombian and Cuban dealers began slugging it out for control of the illegal drug trade.

There were unspeakable crimes of violence as different organizations sought to intimidate their rivals or to retaliate for actions taken against them. Shootouts were commonplace, often occurring in broad daylight, and innocent bystanders were often killed and wounded. Drug dealers were buying expensive homes, yachts, airplanes, and fancy cars with cash. Real estate prices were being inflated by an influx of apparently wealthy Colombians who did not argue about price.

The existing criminal justice system was incapable of coping with the problem. Miami, and all of South Florida, had been taken over by drug dealers.

Against this backdrop, the Reagan Administration started to receive political pressure from business and citizen groups to take action. The pressure was particularly strong from Cuban American business groups that had supported the 1980 Reagan campaign. The Administration decided to act. Vice President George Bush was told to examine the situation and to propose a course of action that could have some immediate impact. The Vice President could have ducked this assignment, but he did not. Despite advice that drug battles can't be won, and the potential for political embarrassment, George Bush plunged into the fray and came up with the South Florida Task Force.

The South Florida Task Force was announced by Bush at the end of January 1982, and it commenced operations on February 15, 1982. The task force involved bolstering existing federal enforcement resources in South Florida by assigning large numbers of temporary personnel in a coordinated effort to bring maximum pressure against major drug trafficking organizations. It was a multipronged effort; federal judges, Assistant U.S. Attorneys, Deputy U.S. Marshals, and probation officers moved in to handle an anticipated increase in criminal prosecutions. Admiral Daniel Murphy, the Vice President's Chief of Staff, was assigned to oversee the program.

Charles Rinkevich, an outstanding administrator with years of experience with local law enforcement and the Law Enforcement Assistance Administration (LEAA), was designated on-site coordinator of the task force in Miami. He did an excellent job of placating the local business groups, keeping the media happy, and prodding the various enforcement agencies without bruising egos or getting entangled in free-for-alls.

Agents of the Bureau of Alcohol, Tobacco and Firearms (BATF) were sent in to supplement the existing staff and to work on cases involving the use of illegal firearms by drug trafficking organizations. BATF agents made a remarkable contribution to the overall effort. Fifty-six temporary duty agents made 109 arrests of firearms traffickers with connections to drug organizations and seized 2,094 firearms between February 15, 1982 and December 31, 1982. Additionally they participated in a number of drug arrests and were involved in many drug seizures. There was never any question in the minds of these agents that there was a real war on drugs going on in South Florida and that they were in the front lines of that war. Two outstanding BATF agents were killed and a third badly wounded in two separate shootouts involving undercover operations against suspects dealing in firearms and cocaine. The killing of BATF agents Ariel Rios and Eddie Benitez on the South Florida Task Force was one of the most unheralded and least reported events of the war on drugs.

The U.S. Customs Service made the greatest resource commitment of temporary manpower to the task force. A total of 153 Customs personnel were sent on temporary duty assignments to South Florida. Some Customs personnel augmented the permanent air and sea interdiction capabilities of the agency. Others formed the cadre of the administrative staff of the

South Florida Task Force Coordinator in Miami. Some 124 Customs agents and patrol officers were assigned to work with DEA agents, developing drug smuggling conspiracy cases and conducting follow-up investigations on smuggling arrests.

An important aspect of the combined Customs/DEA investigative effort was that personnel from each agency assigned to the task force received a cross-designation to investigate cases under the jurisdiction of the other agency. Customs agents were authorized to work on drug statutes and DEA were given authority to work on Customs smuggling statutes. The cross designation was spelled out in strict guidelines. The issue of Customs being able to work on drug cases had been, and continues to be, a major turf issue between the two agencies.

DEA agreed to the cross-designation only on the condition that a DEA supervisor be in charge of each investigative team. A Customs supervisor was designated as the number two person on each team.

DEA dispatched 55 personnel on temporary assignment to augment a permanent cadre of 130 it had in South Florida. DEA's heart was never in the South Florida Task Force effort. DEA Administrator Francis M. "Bud" Mullen saw the task force as an incursion on DEA's lead agency role in the anti-drug effort. He and his agents didn't want to be coordinated or participate in joint operations. They made a show of cooperation on paper, but in reality they often ignored calls for help. The best indication of DEA's attitude is summed up in a passage in Elaine Shannon's book, *Desperados*. The passage is quoted as follows: "Mullen's aides met Murphy's demands by assigning agents on paper to the task force. 'It was all smoke and mirrors,' a top DEA official later said. 'Admiral Murphy would call over and say, how many people do you have there today working on the task force?' We'd say, 'How many do you want.' We'd call Pete (Gruden, the head of the DEA Miami office) and say, 'Pete, the Admiral wants more people.' He'd say, 'Okay, tell him I've assigned a hundred people.'" The Admiral Murphy referred to was the Vice President's Chief of Staff.

Despite attitudes at the top in DEA, there actually was a Joint Task Group comprised of almost 200 DEA and Customs agents that worked harmoniously and successfully during 1982 and early 1983. In fact, Pete Gruden, the DEA chief in Miami, submitted a report in early 1983 in which he praised the performance of the DEA and Customs agents who served on the task group and their ability to work together.

The FBI did not participate in the South Florida Task Force, except on a few specific investigations. No temporary duty FBI personnel were assigned to Florida for task force assignments. An FBI agent from the Miami office was assigned in a liaison capacity. The FBI at that time was unwilling to participate in a joint operation despite a request from the Vice Presi-

dent to do so, and the Justice Department did not order the FBI to participate.

The South Florida Task Force set up a drug interdiction coordination
operation, known as the Interdiction Operations Information Center
(IOIC). IOIC coordinated interdiction efforts of the Coast Guard and the
Customs Service and brought in assistance from the Navy and Air Force.
The task force operation marked the first time military assets were used to
gather information about suspicious aircraft and ships that might be smuggling drugs.

There were and are varying views about whether or not the South
Florida Task Force was a successful operation. Critics maintained it was a
political grandstand play that didn't accomplish anything. Critics complained that the Administration did not seek additional funding for the
operation, but rather drew down on existing budgets and resources of the
involved agencies. DEA officials complained that the operation involved
the politicalization of the law enforcement system to enhance the images of
the President and Vice President.

Democratic politicians were critical that the South Florida Task Force
drew resources from other areas of the country, leaving these areas more
vulnerable to the drug menace. They also complained that the task force
failed to solve the drug problem; it merely shifted the delivery points from
South Florida to California and other coastal and border states. This latter
criticism, although valid, also amounted to a recognition of the success of
the operation, in that the drug smugglers had been forced to relocate some
of their operations.

On balance, the operation was successful. It certainly was political, but
in the very best sense of the term. The South Florida Task Force represented a recognition by political leaders that there was a serious problem
maintaining law and order in South Florida and that the entrenched federal law enforcement bureaucracy was unwilling or unable to prioritize
resources to cope with the problem.

The Miami drug situation and associated crime problems had been
getting worse for several years. However, very few of the federal enforcement bureaus had moved in sufficient personnel to deal with the problem.
The task force provided leadership and action to pour in resources in pursuit of the problem.

The task force ushered in successes on many fronts. There were more
arrests and drug seizures, with more than 1,000 people apprehended for
drug-related violations who might not otherwise have been arrested. The
number of violent crimes in South Florida dropped significantly, due in
part to the crack-down on illegal firearms. Federal law enforcement agencies all increased the number of permanent personnel assigned to Florida,
as did the U.S. Attorney's office, the U.S. Probation Office, and the Coast

Guard. And drug smugglers were constantly forced to find new entry points. If nothing else, the South Florida Task Force proved that concerted, decisive action can affect drug trafficking operations in a limited geographic area.

Politics and turf battles have been the bane of successful drug enforcement efforts for years. Mixed together, they can become devastating.

A case in point. Mention was previously made that BATF agents Ariel Rios and Eddie Benitez were killed in two separate undercover operations while assigned to the South Florida Task Force. Congressman Charles B. Rangel (D-N.Y.) was Chairman of the House Select Subcommittee on Narcotics Abuse and Control. He had been openly critical of the Reagan Administration's efforts to combat drugs, and he was a staunch ally of DEA in the turf battles that were constantly being played out on the sidelines of the "War on Drugs." On July 26, 1983, less than three weeks after BATF agent Eddie Benitez was shot and killed in Miami, Rangel wrote a particularly vicious and demeaning letter to Assistant Treasury Secretary John M. Walker, Jr., who oversaw Treasury's enforcement agencies, including BATF. The letter combined the worst elements of political criticism and turf fighting. It totally ignored the heroism of Benitez and Ariel Rios, the other BATF agent who had been killed in the Miami operation.

The thrust of the Rangel letter was threefold. First, he indicatd that the Vice President's South Florida Task Force was poorly coordinated and controlled, and secondly, that the BATF agents lacked proper training for their assignment. Thirdly, he indicated that all investigative activities in the task force should be "performed under the leadership of our nation's lead drug enforcement agency—the Drug Enforcement Administration."

Rangel's letter was a demoralizing "kick in the ass" to BATF agents who were mourning the deaths of Benitez and Rios and who were hoping for the full recovery of Alex D'Atri, who was still being treated for multiple gunshot wounds sustained in the shootout in which Rios died.

Walker's reply was a masterpiece of understatement which said, nicely, that Rangel did not know what he was talking about and had been badly misinformed about the two incidents. The letter went on to detail the full coordination that had been worked out with DEA in both investigations; the fact that a DEA agent was a member of the surveillance team during the Rios shooting; the fact that both investigations involved illegal firearms as well as narcotics; the background of agents Rios, D'Atri, and Benitez, including the fact that they were all experienced in undercover operations; and the kind of training and type of work BATF agents perform. An attachment to Walker's letter contained a detailed chronology of the investigations conducted in both shooting incidents. The chronology of the Ariel Rios case is laid out here because it so graphically illustrates the violent life of BATF agents assigned to the Miami task force.

THE ARIEL RIOS SHOOTING

The attachment to Walker's letter follows in its entirety:

On October 25, 1982 ATF agents received information from an informant that a suspect named Ismael Copa had contacts for automatic weapons and silencers. On November 4, 1982, ATF undercover agents Ariel Rios and Joe Tirado met Copa in Homestead, Florida and discussed a weapons purchase. Later on the same day Copa introduced the agents to Jose Dearmas. On the following day, November 5, 1982, the undercover agents purchased a RPB M-10 converted to fire fully automatic with an attached silencer from Dearmas and another suspect. At the time they also purchased a stolen handgun and a paratrooper M-1 carbine. Dearmas and the other suspect indicated that they had access to large quantities of weapons and silencers.

On November 4, 1982, suspect Copa introduced undercover agents Rios and Tirado to an individual named Ramon Raymond. Raymond offered to sell the agents automatic weapons and cocaine. On November 18, 1982 agents Rios and Tirado met with Raymond in Homestead, Florida. Raymond introduced them to Rolando Rios. Rios offered to sell them cocaine and firearms, including machine guns and silencers. Rolando Rios furnished the agents with a one gram sample of cocaine on November 18, 1982.

Shortly after the meeting on November 18, 1982 the ATF undercover agents delivered the cocaine sample to the South Florida Joint Task Group. In case you are not aware, this Task Group was composed of DEA and Customs agents. It was organized to follow-up on drug smuggling arrests and to develop information on drug smuggling activities. The Task Group was under the leadership of DEA. The cocaine sample was delivered to the Task Group and the Task Group was fully advised of the identities of the suspects and other circumstances surrounding the transactions so that proper coordination could be effected.

On November 29, 1982 agents Rios and Tirado again met with Ramon Raymond in Homestead, Florida. They discussed the purchase of automatic weapons and silencers and agreed to meet on the following day. On November 30, 1982, Rios and Tirado met with Ismael Copa and Ramon Raymond in Homestead, Florida and discussed the delivery of automatic weapons and two kilos of cocaine on the afternoon of December 1, 1982. On the same day in a separate transaction undercover agents met Jose Dearmas and discussed the purchase of automatic weapons and silencers which were to be delivered on the afternoon of December 1.

Shortly after 5:00 p.m. on December 1, 1982 agents Rios and Tirado met with Jose Dearmas and Miguel Vazquez. Dearmas and Vazquez left the meeting site and returned a short time later with two RPB SM-11A1's and one Ruger pistol, all with attached silencers. Dearmas and Vazquez were arrested and a .12 gauge shotgun with a folding stock was taken from them. The suspects had been followed when they left the meeting site and a search was conducted of the location where they had obtained the weapons. The search resulted in the seizure of 13 firearms, including four pistols, one rifle, one KG-9 pistol, 7 RPB SM-11A1's pistols. Also seized were 20 silencer kits, a stolen U.S. Customs badge and credentials, two fictitious police badges and credentials, a box of lockpicks, hundreds of stolen credit cards and numerous other stolen items including watches and jewelry. Also seized were scramblers for monitoring police radio frequencies and a large quantity of ammunition.

After the arrests and seizures ATF undercover agents Rios and Tirado joined by two other undercover agents, Eddie Benitez and Alex D'Atri, went to another location in Homestead where they met Ramon Raymond and Rolando Rios. They discussed the purchase of cocaine, machine guns and silencers. Raymond and Rios said that they were waiting for a delivery from Miami. While they were waiting the undercover agents were introduced by Ramon Raymond and Rios to Eduardo Portal. Portal made a telephone call and then advised the agents that he could provide kilo-quantities of cocaine on the following day. He furnished the agents with a telephone number and then departed.

While continuing to wait for Raymond's delivery the agents were also introduced to Eduardo Machin. Machin told agents Rios and Benitez that he could contact someone who could deal cocaine immediately but that it would have to be at least five kilos. The agents indicated that the money was available. Machin made a telephone call and arrangements were then made for a delivery of five kilos of cocaine in a shopping center in the Kendall area of Dade County. The four ATF agents and the surveillance team then went to the shopping center. You should note that the surveillance team included Customs agents from the South Florida Joint Task Group. The undercover agents met with Machin and Hernando Sierra in the shopping center. Sierra showed agent Rios a quantity of cocaine. Rios gave a signal and arrests of Sierra and Machin were effected. In the course of the arrests Machin went for his firearm and attempted to shoot agent Tirado. A violent struggle ensued and Machin was subdued. Seized at the time of the arrest were four kilos of cocaine, $82,000 in cash and a firearm. It has subsequently been determined that Machin and Sierra were involved in large-scale cocaine trafficking activities.

On December 2, 1982, Eduardo Portal was telephoned by ATF undercover agent Ariel Rios. He was told that cocaine was available and a meeting was arranged. Agents Rios and D'Atri met Portal and an accomplice named Victoriano Concepcion at a restaurant parking lot in Miami. The agents then went with the suspects to the Hurricane Motel where they met Augustin Alvarez, Oscar Hernandez, Jose Lopez and Mario Simon. They were told to return to the motel in an hour at which time three kilos of cocaine would be delivered at separate intervals. The undercover agents left the motel and met covertly with the surveillance team. At that point the surveillance team was increased from nine agents to 15 agents because of the number of suspects. Eleven of the surveillance team agents were from ATF, the other four agents were from the Florida Joint Task Group. . . . The Florida Joint Task Group was headed by DEA. The four Task Force Group agents on the surveillance team consisted of three Customs agents and one DEA agent. The flashroll [buy money] to be used by the undercover agents was obtained from DEA.

Undercover agents Rios and D'Atri returned to the motel at approximately 4:00 p.m. They left almost immediately after being advised that the cocaine had not yet arrived. Several suspects were seen entering and leaving the motel. The undercover agents returned a short time later and entered the motel office. Suspect Mario Simon then left the motel and removed a blue and white bag from a car. He then returned to the motel office. Agent Rios then left the motel and went to his vehicle at which time he gave a prearranged signal for arrests to be made. Rios went back into the motel office and surveillance agents moved in for the arrest. At the time that the surveillance agents arrived at the motel door a number of gun shots were heard. Before entry could be effected by the surveillance agents Ariel Rios was shot and killed and Alex D'Atri was seriously wounded. One of the suspects was also shot. The other suspects were arrested. Following the arrests a kilo of cocaine was recovered together with $48,000 in U.S. Government

funds, *which had been provided by DEA.* Four firearms which belonged to the suspects were also seized.

This chronology not only depicts, graphically, the dangerous, hectic
and hair-raising type of investigative work the BATF agents and the agents
on the Joint Task Group performed, but also shows the type of vicious
criminals the South Florida Task Force pursued. It certainly demonstrates a
measure of the success of the task force efforts.

THE NATIONAL NARCOTICS BORDER
INTERDICTION SYSTEM (NNBIS)

It became clear during the South Florida Task Force that there was a need
to coordinate drug smuggling enforcement activities. Illegal narcotics such
as heroin, cocaine, and marijuana (with the exception of domestically
grown marijuana) all enter the United States from foreign countries.

The primary agencies with a border interdiction jurisdiction are the
U.S. Coast Guard, a agency of the Department of Transportation, and the
U.S. Customs Service, a Treasury Department agency. Other agencies that
play important supportive roles in drug interdiction are the Immigration
and Naturalization Service (INS), DEA, the FBI, and the military, particularly the Navy and the Air Force.

The Interdiction Operations Information Center (IOIC) in the South
Florida Task Force proved coordination of interdiction efforts was necessary and that it could improve performance.

The need for coordinating interdiction activities and enhancing drug
smuggling intelligence was apparent from the start of the war on drugs.
The big question was who would undertake it and how would it be done?
Once again, George Bush accepted the task. Bush had expected political
and media criticism for his actions. But what he didn't expect was the criticism that came from within the federal law enforcement community,
namely from DEA Administrator Bud Mullen.

On March 23, 1983, President Reagan announced the National Narcotics Border Interdiction System (NNBIS), (pronounced as EN BIS). Bush was
placed in charge of the program.

The role of NNBIS was to coordinate drug smuggling interdiction activities through the establishment of six regional centers. Key elements of
the program included obtaining better intelligence on drug smuggling ac-

tivities and leveraging military assets to improve intelligence and to assist in physical interdiction efforts. Each regional center was headed by a Coast Guard officer or a Customs official. The center in Florida was opened in March, concurrent with the President's announcement. Five other regional centers were opened in June in New Orleans, El Paso (Texas), Long Beach (California), Chicago and New York. Each center had representatives from Customs, the Coast Guard, DEA, FBI, INS, CIA, and the military.

NNBIS was coordinated by the Vice President's Chief of Staff, Admiral Dan Murphy. Murphy had been the Commander of the Sixth Fleet and the Deputy Director of the CIA before going with the Vice President.

Overall, NNBIS accomplished its primary objectives. It improved the quality of intelligence that was collected and furnished to the interdiction agencies. There were significant seizures in the Miami, New Orleans, and Los Angeles districts. Accomplishments, however, were continually overshadowed by media and Congressional criticism and, worst of all, by criticism from Mullen at DEA.

Mullen had been an Associate Director in the FBI prior to his appointment as DEA Administrator. He came up through the ranks of the FBI in the days of J. Edgar Hoover and was known in the bureau as a turf fighter. He brought his turf fighting attitude with him to DEA. It didn't matter that DEA didn't have the resources to even begin to cope with the exploding drug problem. His position was that turf was turf and it had to be protected at all costs.

During the South Florida Task Force operation, Mullen had numerous run-ins with Admiral Murphy, mostly over credit for cases and the usurpation of DEA's lead agency role. When NNBIS came along, Mullen and Murphy clashed even more frequently. At the very first NNBIS planning meeting, Mullen made it clear that he did not believe NNBIS was necessary.

The fact was that Mullen did not really believe interdiction activities were worth the effort or the cost. In his view, the seizure of intercepted drugs and the arrest of pilots, boat crews, and couriers did not get at the drug kingpins or their assets. Of course, this view ignored the fact that pilots and boat captains often know a great deal about the organizations they work for and that sometimes they cooperate when arrested. Mullen also believed the purchase of expensive aircraft and radar equipment reduced the amount of funds for badly-needed DEA agents.

Mullen saw NNBIS as political empire-building on the part of Murphy and the Vice President. He resented the fact that law enforcement activities were being coordinated by the White House.

Mullen complained to Attorney General William French Smith about NNBIS activities. Smith told him to document his complaints in a report, and Mullen submitted a report to Smith in February 1984. The report constituted a savage and inflammatory attack on NNBIS, complete with inaccurate statements and gross exaggerations. By May of 1984, no action had been taken on Mullen's report. It was then "leaked" to Joel Brinkley in the *New York Times*. Brinkley wrote about the report in a May 13, 1984, story headlined: "Director of Federal Drug Agency Calls Reagan Drug Program 'Liability.'" Among the statements quoted from Mullen's report were the following:

> False credit claimed by NNBIS spokesmen demoralizes the personnel working for a number of federal agencies whose bona fide accomplishments either go unrecognized or are related to unwise overemphasis on NNBIS and the South Florida Task Force interdiction programs.

> NNBIS has made no material contribution to the administration's interdiction efforts—nor should it. Yet the credits claimed by NNBIS create the impression that NNBIS is operating in virtually all aspects of drug law enforcement. Such impressions, reinforced by unbridled activities of NNBIS regional coordinators as well as Admiral Murphy, are confusing foreign, state and local law enforcement officials.

It was clear that Bud Mullen was not a team player. It was also clear that he did not understand that he was an executive branch manager working for the President. What he did was clearly an act of insubordination.

Mullen's tirade represented the worst of the turf wars that have plagued the antidrug efforts in the United States for more than 30 years. Almost as much effort has been spent by high level administrators and managers in protecting turf and defending their agencies against attacks from other agencies as has been devoted to leading those agencies in the battle against drug kingpins. Bud Mullen should have been summarily fired. He was not. If the head of one of the Armed Forces had done what Mullen did, he would have been instantly removed. Perhaps the current Administration can learn something from the military in executing its war on drugs. There is a lesson to be learned about discipline and marching to the tune of the Commander in Chief, and there are lessons to be learned about joint command operations under the direction of a selected commander.

The reaction to the *New York Times* article and a wave of other negative publicity which followed was mild from the Vice President's office. George Bush and Dan Murphy knew that there would be no benefit to the Vice President by trading barbs with someone as "off the wall" as Mullen. Publicly, Murphy acknowledged that there had been some poor staff work by some of his people and let it go at that. Inwardly, Murphy was ripping mad. He believed Mullen's accusations were false and reflected the DEA leader's bias against any form of interdiction activity. He also felt that Vice President Bush deserved credit for attempting to coordinate the activities of agencies that, left to their own devices, fought more with themselves than with the real enemy.

Mullen's highly negative and much publicized report to the Attorney General hurt NNBIS and the South Florida Task Force in particular, and the entire Reagan Administration antidrug effort. Congressional Democrats and the media never looked behind the Mullen accusations. They accepted them as coming from a law enforcement professional instead of from an intemperate turf fighter who was negative about anything he couldn't control. Hardly any of the good work of the NNBIS program ever received any recognition other than ridicule.

ORGANIZED CRIME DRUG ENFORCEMENT TASK FORCES

The most successful initiative developed in the Reagan Administration's "War on Drugs" was the creation of the Organized Crime Drug Enforcement Task Force program (OCDETF).

The OCDETF program was the creation of Rudy Giulliani. In 1982, Giulliani was the Associate Attorney General. He occupied the number three position in the Justice Department. He was a vigorous and aggressive former federal prosecutor from New York, who recognized the need to mount a comprehensive drive against drug trafficking organizations. Giulliani knew no single agency could cope with the drug problem. He had seen the results of some successful interagency coordination efforts in the South Florida Task Force and in the Operation Greenback financial task force in Miami.

Rudy Giulliani came up with a plan to create 12 multiagency task forces in various areas of the country, utilizing the resources of federal, state, and local enforcement agencies to deal with the drug trafficking problem. The concept was in some ways based on the Justice Department's organized crime strike force program which had been in existence since the early 1960s. It was also based on Operation Greenback, but was much broader with more enforcement agencies participating. Giulliani sold the Attorney General on the plan and it was put into effect with much fanfare.

President Reagan announced the formation of the OCDETF program on October 14, 1982. In December of that year, Congress authorized funds for the program which would provide 1,000 additional personnel for the federal enforcement agencies and 200 additional federal prosecutors.

Within 30 days of the Presidential announcement, guidelines for the program were drawn up, and operating principles and an organizational structure were outlined. The original participating agencies were BATF, DEA, FBI, IRS, the Customs Service, the U.S. Marshal's Service, the Coast Guard, and the various U.S. Attorneys' offices. (INS would join the program later.) Senior officials of all the agencies formed what was initially known as the OCDETF Working Group, and later became known as the Executive Review Board (ERB). Just below the ERB, organizationally, was a Washington Agency Representatives Group (WAR Group) consisting of program managers and operating officers from the various agencies. A small administrative staff, housed in the Department of Justice, provided support for the task forces.

In the field, each of the 12 original regions was structured to include a number of federal judicial districts, with a major "core city" designated as regional headquarters. (A thirteenth region, Florida and the Caribbean Basin, was added to the program in 1984.) The U.S. Attorney in each core city was accountable to the Associate Attorney General (Rudy Giuliani) and was responsible for establishing a Task Force Advisory Committee (a coordinating group) and for selecting an Assistant U.S. Attorney (AUSA) Task Force Coordinator. Additionally, each federal enforcement agency was required to name a full-time Agency Task Force Coordinator.

The OCDETF program was, by any measure, a success during the Reagan years and it continues to be successful in the Bush Administration. There were a number of successful prosecutions of major drug and money laundering organizations, among them: the Pizza Connection, Polar Cap, and Operation C Chase. By the end of 1987, the program had initiated 1,901 investigations, resulting in 3,943 indictments and the conviction of more than 8,400 individuals. Of those convicted, over 6,700 were considered to be top and mid-level organization leaders and major drug suppliers. In most of the successful investigations, there was good interagency cooperation and information sharing which might not otherwise have occurred.

The task force program demonstrated that multiagency operations can be carried out successfully under good leadership. The OCDETF program had its flaws. Some of the core city regional task forces were not as successful as others. Generally, the OCDETFs, with a strong U.S. Attorney at the top and a strong AUSA task force coordinator, were more successful than those with weak leadership. A measure of the success of the OCDETF program is that it is still in existence and has become the cornerstone of the Bush Administration's investigative strategy in its "War on Drugs."

THE DRUG WAR UNDER ED MEESE

Ed Meese became President Reagan's Attorney General in 1985. He went through bitter and acrimonious hearings in gaining Senate confirmation, and his tenure as Attorney General was marred by continual attacks from the media and Congress.

Many of the attacks stemmed from alleged improprieties during his tenure as a Presidential advisor—allegations of which he was eventually cleared. He was also criticized for his conservative views on defendants' rights and his efforts to chip away at the Supreme Court's decades old Miranda decision. Overlooked in the attacks and charges, however, was the excellent job Meese did in coordinating the Reagan Administration's War on Drugs during the three years he was the Attorney General.

Congressional Democrats, led by Senator Joseph Biden of Delaware, had been pushing the Administration to name a "Drug Czar" since 1981. Senator Biden, in fact, had introduced legislation that would have created an administrative structure and specific duties and responsibilities for a Drug Czar. The theory was that a Czar was needed to coordinate all of the activities of the many agencies and cabinet departments involved in anti-drug activity, and also to formulate and carry out a national strategy against drugs.

The Reagan Administration did not like the Drug Czar proposal. It was seen as a gimmick that would add another bureaucratic layer to an already confused multiagency mission. In 1985, a deal was struck between the Administration and key Congressional leaders. Congress would not pass the Drug Czar bill if the Administration would create a National Drug Policy Board that would be actively directed by the Attorney General. The Drug Policy Board was to formulate a national strategy and coordinate the activities of the agencies and bureaus involved in carrying out that strategy.

Meese established a workable National Drug Policy Board. He set up a number of committees to coordinate action in specific areas and to develop strategic plans for these areas. He wanted to come up with a good strategic plan for the entire drug effort, which was something that was admittedly lacking during the first four years of the Reagan Administration.

Under the hands-on leadership and direction of Meese, the Drug Policy Board formulated a strategy that covered all areas of drug enforcement and efforts to reduce the demand for drugs. Demand reduction initiatives in the areas of education, prevention, and treatment were integral to the strategy. These areas had been largely overlooked and grossly under-funded during Reagan's first term.

On the enforcement side, committees were formed to coordinate and plan strategies on prosecutions, intelligence, investigations, interdiction, and international matters. The Customs Commissioner, Willie Von Raab, was the Chairman of the Interdiction Committee. That committee eventually supplanted NNBIS in the coordination of all interdiction activity.

Meese was able to bring the drug problem—and efforts to combat it—to a level of focus within the Administration that far exceeded anything that had been done in the past. He convinced the President to hold monthly Cabinet meetings devoted exclusively to the drug problem. There were more than 30 of these meetings during Meese's tenure as the Attorney General, and they were attended by the President and Vice President. Problems were identified and discussed during the meetings, solutions were proposed, hitherto unrecognized assets were identified and more energy, ideas, and resources were brought to bear on the problem. As each committee completed its strategic plan, and after review and approval by the Drug Policy Board, the committee chairman made a presentation on the plan at a Cabinet meeting.

Meese was also able to instill a greater sense of cooperation among enforcement agencies than had been seen in the past. Meese had a tremendous knowledge of and interest in law enforcement problems. He possessed a high level of energy and drive and stayed in close touch with agency heads and their problems. By dint of drive, determination, and leadership, Ed Meese was able to improve cooperative efforts. It was almost as if agency heads and senior staff people were embarrassed to engage in turf battles that might come to his attention.

In the final analysis, Ed Meese received little credit or recognition for his efforts in the Reagan Administration's War on Drugs. His accomplishments were substantial. As the Attorney General, he formulated an Administration strategy to confront the drug problem; he obtained additional resources for the entire antidrug effort; he created a mechanism (the Drug Policy Board) to coordinate all antidrug efforts under one roof; and he placed an emphasis on demand reduction that had been sorely lacking in earlier years. His accomplishments, however, were overshadowed by the cacophony of media hype, reinforced by Congressional criticism that the Reagan Administration's Drug War was all smoke and mirrors, that it was not serious and that it was not adequately funded. Add to this the personal attacks on Meese regarding improprieties alleged in the Wedtech scandal over defense contracts and other matters, and it's clear that he was haunted by a negative image that was undeserved.

"JUST SAY NO"

When Ronald Reagan became President in 1981, he indicated education and prevention should be the prime methods of overcoming drug use. Yet, his Administration did very little in the way of funding prevention and education efforts until 1986 when Ed Meese elevated demand reduction efforts to a significant role in the national drug strategy and obtained funding for a number of projects in this area.

There were valid criticisms of the failure to fund education and rehabilitation programs prior to 1986. However, while funding was not there, a very important approach emerged from the White House that had a profound and important effect on the decision-making processes of thousands of young people during the decade of the 1980s.

The "Just Say No" program inaugurated by Nancy Reagan in 1981 became the Administration's main drug education initiative, and it was effective. The program sent a loud and clear message from the very highest level, the White House. The message was that drugs are harmful, they ruin lives, they destroy people physically, mentally, emotionally, and spiritually. Nancy Reagan appeared at high schools all over the country heralding the message that illegal drug use would not be tolerated. "Just Say No" became a household phrase.

The First Lady urged a number of programs to reduce drug use, including the development of community drug education programs, the suspension of drug users and pushers by schools, and a variety of volunteer drug education programs. The drug intolerance message from the Reagan White House was in sharp contrast to the permissive message of the Carter years.

Although it is difficult to measure the success of antidrug efforts, the "Just Say No" program was a successful tool in dissuading young people from abusing drugs, particularly given the fact that it required no tax dollars. One measure of its success comes from the National Household Survey on Drug Abuse, conducted by the National Institute on Drug Abuse (NIDA). In 1985 the survey identified an estimated 23 million drug users in America. Three years later, in 1988, the number of current users had fallen to 14.5 million. If these figures are accurate, and there are those who challenge them, there was a remarkable turn-around. Certainly there was an indication of a considerable reduction in drug use.

THE INTERDICTION WARS

In 1981, when the War on Drugs was declared, the nation was seriously lacking in interdiction tools. The military's radar detection system was not equipped to detect low and slow-flying aircraft along the southern borders from Florida to California. In the Miami area, Customs and the Coast Guard had just one radar system between them to identify aircraft coming in from the south in only a very narrow band of airspace at an altitude below 10,000 feet. Otherwise, there was nothing but military radar to pick up aircraft flying above 10,000 feet. There was no system designed to monitor low and slow-flying aircraft of the type used by smugglers to bring in cocaine and marijuana from Colombia or from trans-shipment points such as the Bahamas.

Customs and the Coast Guard also had only a few aircraft for interdiction missions. Customs had two Cobra helicopters which had been obtained from the military. The theory was that a Customs fixed-wing aircraft would identify and track a suspected drug smuggling airplane as it came in over water to the Florida mainland and then call up one of the Cobra helicopters to follow the aircraft down onto a landing strip to conduct a search of the aircraft and to make arrests and seizures, if necessary.

The problem was that the Cobra was only a two-seater and, in most situations, only one Customs officer could quickly alight from the helicopter to conduct a search. Smuggling aircraft frequently landed at remote airstrips and were met by armed members of a drug organization who had vehicles to transport the drugs. The odds were against Customs. It was one or two lightly armed Customs officers versus six to ten heavily armed drug smugglers. And neither Customs nor the Coast Guard had high-speed boats to counteract the cigarette boats used by the smugglers to pick up drug packages air-dropped into the sea.

It was obvious that the Customs Service needed an infusion of aircraft and boats to keep from being completely outpaced by the Colombian smuggling organizations.

The first thing to come along was the Blackhawk helicopter. It was bigger and much faster than the Cobra. It could put six heavily-armed officers on the ground. It could be reconfigured by adding a gasoline tank to increase its range. It was very expensive for an agency the size of Customs to afford . . . unless . . . the Defense Department would fund it.

The next thing to be proposed was an aerostat balloon. The balloon would be tethered to a fixed platform and carry a radar unit aloft that would keep a look-out for low, slow-flying aircraft. If enough of these were strategically placed along the Florida coastline and perhaps on an island in the Bahamas, an effective radar picketline could be established to spot incoming smuggler aircraft. Like Blackhawk helicopters, aerostat balloons would be very expensive for an agency the size of Customs to afford . . . unless . . . the Defense Department would fund them.

Still another proposal involved the use of the E2C radar aircraft, the type used by the military to keep tabs on aircraft and ground movements in combat situations. Once in the air, this type of plane could provide aircraft surveillance over a very wide area. The E2C was even more expensive than the Blackhawk helicopter or the aerostat balloon, and definitely couldn't be supported by Customs' budget.

As a result of these proposals, interdiction wars developed within the Administration and between the Administration and Congress.

Some, like DEA Administrator Mullen, and his successor Jack Lawn, considered interdiction efforts a waste of time and money, and akin to looking for a needle in a haystack. The money was better spent assigning more agents to source countries, they argued.

The Customs Service and Coast Guard took the view that it was better to stop drug shipments before they entered the country. Once drugs were smuggled into the country, time-consuming and labor-intensive investigations didn't always succeed in identifying distribution networks, they reasoned. Customs wanted to be able to acquire aircraft and radar devices.

Not everyone within the Treasury Department agreed with the Customs view, however. Some departmental officials wanted to slash budget expenditures across the board; they recoiled at the thought of costly new expenditures for new interdiction resources. There was also a small battle on the side between Customs and the Coast Guard over which agency would play the lead role in air and marine interdiction campaign.

The military took the position, in the early 1980s, that it did not want an active role in air and marine drug interdiction efforts. Military officials were ready to and did assist civilian agencies in this mission, but there was a genuine concern that a greater involvement would detract from their combat readiness. The Defense Department was willing to provide some aircraft and radar, provided it received funding within the Administration and from Congress.

Congress played a major role in the interdiction wars. The Congressional view, and ultimately that of the Administration, was that a multipronged law enforcement approach was needed. Investigative and interdiction efforts were seen as equally important, with each complementing the other. This view was rooted in the position that the United States could not allow Colombian drug organizations to brazenly fly cocaine and marijuana onto U.S. landing strips without fear of being caught. There was also a strong conviction that U.S. maritime borders could not be left unprotected. Congressman Glenn English of Oklahoma and Senator Dennis DeConcini of Arizona were the principal architects of efforts to improve air and sea interdiction capabilities. The two, both Democrats, frequently clashed with Administration representatives, particularly from the Treasury Department, over appropriate funding levels for interdiction efforts.

During the South Florida Task Force operation, the Customs Service was supplied with a Blackhawk helicopter from the military. It was operated by Customs personnel. It proved its worth on several occasions when smuggling aircraft were intercepted and followed to landing strips. Armed Customs officers from the Blackhawk were able to exit the helicopter to make arrests and drug seizures. Military aircraft also were used to assist Customs and the Coast Guard in South Florida. Despite modest successes, there was a recognition that air interdiction resources were simply inadequate against organizations using private aircraft to smuggle narcotics.

There were gradual additions to the Customs air and maritime interdiction assets during 1983 and 1984. Several Blackhawk helicopters were acquired and two aerostat balloons with radar platforms were put into service in Florida. A few high-speed chase boats were bought to try to cope with the smugglers' cigarette boats. The helicopters and radar platforms were obtained from the Defense Department. There were budget battles every inch of the way. Treasury repeatedly went before the House and Senate Appropriations Committees expressing support for interdiction programs but seeking to get the Defense Department to fund aircraft and radar items. The Democrats in Congress had a field day. They used the lack of Treasury funding as an indication that the Administration was not serious about the drug effort, and they generated a great deal of media coverage about the President's lack of commitment.

One of the worst examples of the interdiction wars and the Customs budget mess came in Administration proposals in 1984 for the Customs budget for fiscal 1985. The Treasury Department stated it supported a $32 million Customs air interdiction program, but only requested funding in the amount of $17 million. Treasury said it hoped to get $11 million from the Department of Defense for the operation and maintenance of military aircraft that had been given to Customs. Treasury said it would attempt to find $4 million for a third aerostat balloon from other areas within the departmental budget request. When advised that the Defense Department would not come up with the $11 million, Treasury told the Congress it would also try to find that amount from other sources within the department's overall budget. The Appropriations Committees appropriated the full $32 million for Customs.

In 1986, Senator DeConcini and Congressman English sponsored legislation that provided almost $300 million for Customs and Defense Department budgets for military surveillance aircraft, radar balloons, and Blackhawk helicopters. That measure was incorporated into the Anti-Drug Abuse Act of 1986. Initially, the Reagan Administration opposed the legislation on the grounds that it was too expensive. But when it became evident the bill would pass by a landslide vote, the decision was made to support the air interdiction funding.

Air and marine interdiction capabilities were significantly enhanced during the Reagan years. Some of the credit for this belongs to Congressman English and Senator DeConcini and a number of other legislators on the Treasury Appropriations Committees of both Houses. Some of the credit also should go to a variety of officials in the Coast Guard, Customs Service, Treasury Department, and Defense Department who fought within the Administration for a credible air and sea interdiction program, despite high level opposition at OMB and Treasury.

It is important to understand that successful interdiction efforts are not measured in terms of being able to shut U.S. borders down to all drug smuggling activity. This would be a physical and practical impossibility given the vast extent of air space and land and sea borders that surround the country. Success is measured rather by seizures of drugs and by how much more difficult and costly it becomes for smugglers to operate.

Drug smuggling is not restricted to private aircraft or to cigarette boats and fishing vessels. Drugs are also smuggled in ship cargoes, on commercial air freight shipments, in suitcases, and on the person of commercial airline passengers, and in cars and trucks driving across land borders. Traffickers frequently change their tactics when enforcement efforts start to be effective against certain types of smuggling activity. By the end of the Reagan Administration, it was certainly more difficult to smuggle cocaine and marijuana into the country by air and by sea.

THE REAGAN ADMINISTRATION: A SUMMATION

In summary, much was accomplished during the Reagan Administration's "War on Drugs." Enforcement efforts were increased significantly. The "Just Say No" program carried on by Nancy Reagan was an effective weapon in reducing the demand for drugs. A national strategy was developed to coordinate supply reduction and demand reduction efforts.

There was a great deal of criticism from the media and from Congressional Democrats. There was hardly any recognition of many positive accomplishments. Some of the criticism was appropriate; much of it was undeserved. Certainly, funding for drug rehabilitation and education programs was woefully inadequate. Attempts to weasel out of some interdiction budget responsibilities were fair game for attack. The Reagan Administration did not win the "War on Drugs." It won many battles, but the war raged on into the Bush Administration. It probably changed the tide of battle in favor of the good guys. The ultimate outcome of the war at the end of 1988, though, was still in doubt. It is fair to say that the Reagan Administration underestimated the magnitude and seriousness of the drug problem and failed to make sufficient budget and resource commitments to do an even better job.

THE BUSH ADMINISTRATION

Like his predecessor, George Bush declared a "War on Drugs" shortly after he was inaugurated. By this time, legislation had been enacted requiring the President to nominate a "Drug Czar" and to provide appropriate staffing. Ed Meese had resigned as Attorney General in March 1988. His successor, Richard Thornburgh, was not confirmed until the fall of 1988. In the interim, there was no "hands on" guidance and coordination of the drug effort as had been provided by Meese.

By the time Thornburgh was confirmed, the "Drug Czar" bill had been enacted and preparations were being made to nominate someone for the job. The hiatus in the coordination and leadership of the antidrug program continued.

William J. Bennett, the outspoken and somewhat controversial former Secretary of the Department of Education, was named by President Bush as the first "Drug Czar." Bennett's actual title was Director of the Office of National Drug Control Policy.

The legislation creating the Office of National Drug Control Policy (ONDCP), the Anti-Drug Abuse Act of 1988, contained a number of mandates, including the development of a strategy document to be updated annually, studies of potential Executive Branch organizational changes to improve policy development and implementation, and research and development of enforcement technologies.

Bennett and his new organization set about their tasks with some dispatch. By September 1989, President Bush unveiled the first National Drug Control Strategy document of his Administration. The principal goal was to reduce the level of illegal drug use in America. The strategy involved creating coordinating mechanisms in the two broad areas of supply reduction and demand reduction. The first strategy position benefitted greatly by the one developed by Ed Meese in 1987.

The entire drug war situation faced by the Bush Administration was easier to cope with than the problems faced by the Reagan Administration in 1981. The drug problem was just as severe, but the tools available to cope with the problem were vastly improved. On the enforcement side, budgets, equipment, and personnel had been increased significantly. The OCDETF program had a five-year track record, and military-assisted interdiction programs were making life more difficult for drug smugglers. A number of major drug trafficking organizations, including some big-time Colombian cocaine rings, had been put out of business. The problem, of course, was that each time a big organization went down, another one moved in to pick up the slack.

On the demand reduction side, a number of programs were being funded and more services were being provided for rehabilitation and education. Over $1 billion was in the fiscal 1989 budget for demand reduction programs. The federal government was much better equipped to deal with the drug problems of 1989 than it was those of 1981.

Bennett set about his task as "Drug Czar" with considerable fervor. He made speeches, appeared on television, and maintained a generally high profile. His thrust was to deal with the drug problem in a political and philosophical context. He spoke eloquently about the responsibility of the individual in choosing to use drugs. He spoke about the role of government in the drug war and correctly pointed out that many of the state and local governments clamoring for federal assistance in the drug fight had not devoted sufficient resources to fund their own local narcotic enforcement efforts.

Bennett was a brilliant man who spoke eloquently and who was up to any give and take session with a television interviewer or any critic of the Administration's antidrug efforts. He spoke of concepts such as drug-free schools and drug-free workplaces. He elevated the nation's awareness to the magnitude and seriousness of the drug problem. He pressed an international drug strategy that attempted to foster a broad, cooperative effort to reduce the foreign supply of drugs while working with other countries to dismantle their own illicit drug operations, reduce the demand for drugs, and combat the worldwide drug trade.

Despite his accomplishments and his obvious brilliance, Bennett did not have the capacity to have a real impact on the numerous agencies involved in the drug war, either in the enforcement area or in the demand reduction area. He was intellectual and cerebral. He articulated drug strategy and contributed a great deal of information to the public about drug problems and drug cultures. However, he was unable to provide leadership to the agencies within the federal structure, nor was he able to motivate these agencies to enthusiastically support the strategy.

Federal agencies had little input into Bennett's operation. He lacked the ability Ed Meese had to provide hands-on leadership to the drug-fighting agencies. Conversely, Meese had not been able to articulate strategy and policy with the same effectiveness as Bennett.

DEMAND REDUCTION

Under Bennett, National Drug Control Strategy documents were issued by the Bush Administration in January 1990 and 1991. These documents reflected increasing awareness of the need for demand reduction.

More funding was proposed each year for drug treatment and education. The strategy in the treatment area was to get more drug users to stop using drugs through treatment and to make the treatment more effective.

The strategy in the education area was to reduce the overall level of drug use by preventing it before it started. The prevention strategy included instilling in children the values and attitudes that contribute to a drug-free life; informing families and communities of the harmful effects of drugs; developing formal antidrug educational programs and policies in schools; organizing communities to take responsibility for solving local drug problems; and creating employee assistance programs and personnel policies in businesses to help remove drugs from the workplace. The strategy recognized that prevention efforts, to be truly effective, must engage the entire community—not just the family, the schools, the churches, social service organizations, or the workplace separately, but all together simultaneously.

By fiscal 1991, federal spending for drug treatment and education prevention programs was just over $2.5 billion. Of this amount, $1.5 billion was allocated for a variety of treatment programs. The treatment funds go to block grants to states, to veterans programs, to treatment services for pregnant women and drug-affected babies, and to enhanced treatment research. State and local communities are estimated to spend slightly more on treatment programs than the federal government. Federal spending on treatment and education had been $1.5 billion in 1989.

SUPPLY REDUCTION

The strategy of the ONDCP during the first three years of the Bush Administration in the supply reduction area was focused on the criminal justice system, international initiatives, and interdiction efforts. The thrust of attempts to improve the criminal justice system was to increase the number of DEA and FBI agents and support personnel and to provide additional resources for the Organized Crime Drug Enforcement Task Forces. The OCDETF program was carried over into the Bush Administration and has become the cornerstone of coordinated investigative efforts to dismantle major drug trafficking organizations. Other criminal justice system initiatives include increased assistance to state and local law enforcement (over $500 million in 1991), expanded resources for money laundering investigations, and increased capacity in the U.S. courts and in the federal prison system.

International initiatives focused on cooperation with and assistance for drug source and transit countries (such as Colombia, Peru, Bolivia, Mexico, Ecuador, Venezuela, Paraguay, Argentina, and Chile). Economic, military, and law enforcement assistance was provided to Colombia, Peru, and Bolivia. Cooperative efforts in law enforcement programs are underway with the other countries. An international strategy has been developed to focus on opium and heroin. There are broadened domestic and foreign efforts to counter international drug money laundering activities. There have been expanded efforts to reduce the illegal manufacture and shipment of chemicals essential to illicit drug production.

Interdiction strategy focused on intercepting drug smugglers and their shipments so that trafficking operations could be consistently disrupted. Approximately $2.5 billion in funding was provided for interdiction in fiscal year 1991. Interdiction efforts have been highlighted by an enhanced and expanded role for the Department of Defense in the detection and monitoring of drug trafficking. There have been improvements in the coordination of air, land, and maritime interdiction efforts by the various involved agencies. There has been an increased focus on the southwest border as a primary smuggling area for drugs. Additional Customs and INS personnel have been added to the antismuggling program. Enhanced drug detection technology is being developed to increase cargo and baggage inspection at ports of entry.

THE OCDETF PROGRAM

As the cornerstone of the Bush Administration's coordinated effort to attack major drug trafficking organizations, the OCDETF program tends to highlight the best and the worst of federal drug law enforcement efforts over the last 40 years. The major problems have always been turf battles between agencies, a lack of interagency cooperation, and a lack of coordination of activities directed against major targets. The OCDETF program was designed to overcome these obstacles by having agencies work together under a joint command structure.

Make no mistake about it, there have been and continue to be excellent cases developed under the framework of OCDETF programs. There have also been significant problems involving coordination and a lack of cooperation. The OCDETF program has conducted annual management studies of its operations, as far back as 1983. The studies, conducted by outside contractors, have been designed to evaluate the effectiveness of the program. A study submitted in November 1989 contained some interesting comments on the strengths and weaknesses of the program in terms of coordination and cooperation. The study scored the top five performing task forces and the bottom five, and commented on differences in the operating characteristics between the top and bottom performers.

The study found that in the top five performing task forces, the coordinators were co-located in common office space and exclusively performed

OCDETF duties to a much greater degree than in the five lowest ranking districts. The result was that there was greater interaction between coordinators and their staffs and conflicts over case selection and case management were resolved at much lower levels in the top five performing groups.

The OCDETF management study also identified problems with the way agencies treated cases. Problems included withholding cases (not submitting high quality cases for OCDEFT consideration), holding back cases (submitting them for consideration only in the later stages of development) and refusing to participate in cases. All three of these practices occurred more frequently in the five core cities with the lowest performance scores, and occurred with much less frequency in the five core cities with the highest scores.

The 1989 study found that disputes over Title 21 (Drug Statutes) and cross designation of non-Title 21 agency personnel were almost unresolvable issues. Title 21 is the portion of the Federal Criminal Code that details all drug offenses. DEA had exclusive jurisdiction over the investigation of these offenses, but the FBI was designated by the Attorney General to share investigative jurisdiction over Title 21 offenses when it was brought into the drug war in 1981. The problem was that DEA and the FBI were unwilling to cross-designate their jurisdictional authority to agents from other bureaus to work on drug cases under the task force umbrella.

The top five core city districts had not allowed questions of Title 21 jurisdiction to impede the development of cases as had the bottom five districts, even though all the task forces worked with the same policy directives and with the same combination of investigative agencies. Most of the rationale for refusing to cross-designate seemed to turn on a lack of training and experience by agents from other enforcement bureaus. Little evidence existed that supported the claim.

Despite these problems and others noted in the report, the study group found the OCDETF program to be highly effective. Among its accomplishments:

- Initiation of 2,532 investigations, resulting in 4,917 indictments and criminal informations against 16,859 defendants.

- Charges against 8,208 top and mid-level leaders and major drug suppliers.

- The seizure of cash and property assets totaling $916 million.

- Over 10,000 individual defendants were found, or pled, guilty to at least one charge, and more than 80% were sent to prison, many for life.

The overall opinion expressed in the 1989 study was that the OCDEFT program was a success.

There is no denying this assessment. The problem areas of "turf" and "coordination" have plagued drug enforcement efforts for over 40 years. There are indications that significant improvements have been made in many of the problem areas cited in the 1989 report. Coordination now appears to be better, although turf battles continue.

CURRENT STATUS OF THE DRUG WAR

What is the status of the drug war as we come to the end of the third year of the Bush Administration? It depends on who you talk to.

Administration sources maintain the tide of battle has turned. They point to a strategy designed to go after every aspect of the drug problem. They talk about over $10 billion in funding for the drug war in fiscal 1991 and the fact that more resources than ever before have been brought to bear against the problem. They point to huge drug seizures, large cash seizures, hundreds of millions of dollars in seized assets, and major drug trafficking and money laundering cases being made, all with some frequency and regularity. Administration sources also note that all of the big shots who controlled the Colombian cocaine cartel are either dead or in jail. The likes of the Ochoas, Carlos Lehder, Pablo Escobar, and Gonzalo Rodriguez Gacha are among those taken out of action.

There are indications from a number of sources and surveys that drug use is declining, particularly among young people. The National Household Survey on Drug Abuse conducted in 1990 revealed that the number of current users had declined to 12.9 million, an 11% decrease from the 1990 figure of 14.5 million. The 1991 survey revealed even further declines in the number of users. The Administration believes that the war will be a long one, but that it is being won and success is attainable.

If you listen to Congressional Democrats, particularly those from inner city districts, the drug war is not being won. They believe the drug problem in the inner cities is worse than ever, with no sign of improvement in sight. They acknowledge successes against specific organizations, but indicate that the flow of drugs into the country is as strong as ever. They point to some of the large drug seizures heralded by the Administration as evidence that drugs keep pouring in. Some are willing to concede that there might be a stand-off in the battle against cocaine, but they state heroin use and addiction is on the rise in big cities.

Who is right? Is this just a political argument with one or both sides exaggerating for political gain? It appears both views have considerable merit. But there is also some exaggeration for political advantage.

There certainly are indications on a national level that drug use is declining. Years of educational effort about the health dangers associated with drugs appear to be paying off. In small and medium-sized towns and cities all across the country, the dangers of drug use are apparently turning away previous and potential users. On the enforcement side, there have been major successes which have dismantled some big-time trafficking organizations.

On the other side of the coin, drugs continue to flow into the United States in substantial quantities. Large seizures that are being made indicate more effective interdiction and investigative efforts. These efforts have put some major organizations out of business and forced smugglers to alter their tactics and routes. There appears to be an abundance of up and coming entrepreneurs to replace the drug bosses who have been jailed. There is no shortage of supply of any kind of drug, and prices are falling. This may be related to decreased use or it may be connected with increased production and smuggling activity.

Despite apparent improvement in the rest of the country, the inner city drug problem is out of control. Inner city kids become drug users at astoundingly young ages. Whole families become addicted to crack cocaine. Role models for inner city Black and Hispanic kids are the drug dealer with gold chains, new cars, and a thick wad of bills stuffed in their pockets. Some of the dealers are in their mid-teens.

There is a wave of crime and violence associated with inner city drug use as users rob and steal to get drug money, drug dealing organizations fight over territory, and street gangs fight with each other for pieces of the drug action. Money launderers hire young people as "smurfs" to buy money orders from convenience stores, check cashers, and post offices with currency from drug sales. In Philadelphia in 1989, 80% of all people arrested tested positive for drug use.

Drug treatment is available in many inner city areas, but in many cases there are long waiting periods and the people seeking help need it immediately. The picture of the inner city drug epidemic is not a pretty one, but it is reality.

Part of the problem with drug use in major cities has to do with a near total breakdown of the criminal justice system. The problem is bad everywhere, but it is worse in large cities. Vast numbers of crimes go unreported. In some areas of New York City, it is estimated that only about one third of crimes committed are actually reported. Thousands of assaults, burglaries, rapes, and shootings are not reported. Nationally, there are millions of dollars of losses from stolen and forged checks and from stolen and fraudulently used credit cards that either are not reported or, if reported, are not investigated. A considerable amount of the drug economy is supported by these types of crimes.

Some examples highlight the problem. In September 1991, a cooperative citizen became aware of the identity and location of an individual with an attache case full of stolen credit cards and passbooks for bank accounts that were opened fraudulently. He contacted two federal enforcement agencies and two detective squads, but could not get anyone to respond. A $28,000 embezzlement case went unreported in New Jersey because neither the local police nor any federal enforcement agency was interested in pursuing the matter. These are but two of thousands of situations that occur regularly.

In many inner city areas, the streets are controlled by thugs. Drug dealers reign supreme. Criminals roam the streets freely. In their encounters with the criminal justice system, they frequently come off with suspended sentences, probation, or reduced pleas to misdemeanor offenses. They are freed on bail pending appeals and frequently receive very light sentences. While it may not be the intent of the criminal justice system, the reality is that these criminals have more rights than the law abiding citizens who are their victims. The police are practically powerless in enforcing laws and maintaining public safety. This is the milieu in which drug trafficking and drug use flourishes in our inner cities.

It is possible, even probable, that the corner has been turned in the Bush Administration's War on Drugs. Many battles have been won and the tide appears to be turning in favor of the government. However, demand for drugs is still strong. The profit potential is so great from drug trafficking that people will always be found to step in and take the place of those who are jailed or killed.

The fact is that the federal government has never been better positioned to fight the War on Drugs. Never before has there been so much funding and so many resources committed to the antidrug effort. The Congress and the Administration have finally agreed on overall funding and resource levels. Many new resources and assets have been put into place. It is time to see if the overall strategy and the tactical use of the assets provided will lead to a victory in this war.

In the past, we fought the drug war the same way we fought in Korea and Vietnam, without a full, all-out commitment to win. Intentions were not always matched with the planning or resources needed to do the job. The Bush Administration and Congress appear to have the moral commitment to win the war and have committed substantial resources. Whether or not these resources are enough to win the war remains to be seen. Even with a greater commitment than has ever been made, it still appears that we may be coming up short on funding the drug war when one considers the inner city drug problem. We still appear to be short of the all-out commitment the nation made in Desert Storm.

WHAT NEEDS TO BE DONE

There are many reasons given for the explosion of drug use in the United States over the past 15 years. Social scientists ascribe it to poverty, illiteracy, joblessness, despair, poor housing, a breakdown of the family unit, an absence of moral values, peer pressure, and a variety of other reasons. Many people become involved with drugs without any of these causes apparent. It is clear, however, that drug use is much more prevalent in economically depressed inner cities than in any other areas of the nation.

Most of the causes given for drug use are hallmarks of the inner city. Poverty, despair, joblessness, substandard housing, broken families, crime, and violence dominate inner city life. Public education is at its worst in the inner city. Dropout rates and illiteracy are higher there than in any other geographic unit of our society. There is an apparent correlation between the social ills of the inner city and drug use. To the extent that these ills can be cured or improved, one would hope and expect that drug use would recede.

There is no pretense that recommendations in this book provide an overall solution to the drug problem. Great minds have examined this complex problem without arriving at completely effective solutions. Presented here are some suggestions and recommendations that could help reduce the severity of the problem and/or increase the effectiveness of the War on Drugs.

Overall Strategy

The drug problem should be attacked in a manner akin to a full court press. In basketball, the full court press strategy requires going after the other team even before they take the ball out of bounds. It means pressing them all over the court and trying to steal the ball and/or disrupt their offensive strategy. The objective is to demoralize and confuse the opposing team, to force them to make turnovers and take them out of their offense.

Translated into the war against drugs, the full court press would require a vigorous attack without let-up on every aspect of the drug problem, from the root social causes, if they are truly identifiable, to reducing the demand for and the supply of drugs. Law enforcement activity by itself will never solve the drug problem. Likewise, drug education and treatment programs alone cannot solve the problem. Programs that provide adequate housing, better education, more jobs, and more stability to family units will not, by themselves, cure the drug problem. Rather, a combination of all three avenues must be pursued in order to win the war on drugs.

The National Drug Control Strategies developed by the Bush Administration in 1989, 1990, and 1991 seem to identify and address the areas of supply and demand reduction. There are some questions, however, about the strength and magnitude of the attacks in these areas. The drug strategies of the Bush Administration do not address problems such as housing, joblessness, and the need for better educational systems and they probably should not. These problems, even though they are problems related to drug use, should be addressed in a broader context than just drug use.

Demand Reduction

Federal government funding for drug treatment amounted to just over $1.5 billion in fiscal 1991. Drug treatment programs appear to be severely under-funded. There are not enough programs and facilities in many large cities where the need is far more urgent than anywhere else.

There are two phases to treatment and rehabilitation. The first involves a detoxification program of about five to 14 days where the addict is denied drugs. The addict remains at a detox center until blood tests show he or she is no longer physically controlled by a narcotic substance. The second phase involves a long-term treatment and rehabilitation program. The most successful programs rely on residential and out-patient counseling for periods from 18 months to two years, depending upon the severity of the addiction. There are some treatment programs that last for 30 to 60 days. The longer-term programs have much higher success rates.

The most important time for an addict to enter a treatment program is immediately after detoxification. Most large cities have sufficient detoxification centers, but do not have sufficient treatment facilities. Waiting periods of 30 days to six months are common. In New York City, for example, there is a six-month waiting period for an addict to be admitted to the better long-term treatment programs. There are two large sections in New York City, the Williamsburg and Bushwick sections of Brooklyn, that are overwhelmed by drug use and neither section has a residential drug treatment program. This situation is not uncommon in large cities. Frequently, the addict who does not receive treatment after detoxification goes back to drug using, becomes involved in criminal activity, and or ends up in jail and the cycle repeats itself.

Demand reduction is so important that all phases of it must be adequately funded. If we are to wean people away from drug use, there must be enough treatment facilities to attempt to rehabilitate addicts. This means a substantial increase in spending, but budget constraints and the need to spend wisely cannot be ignored.

An interesting situation was uncovered in New York City while conducting research for this book. It involves millions of federal and city dollars being wasted in trying to provide shelter for the homeless, a sociological problem sometimes related to drug use. Under current rent control law in New York City, a landlord can raise rents up to certain limits. The limits far exceed what a family on welfare receives for a housing allowance. For example, a family of six is allowed $330 per month for housing under welfare rules. In most sections of Brooklyn, the minimum rent for a four-room apartment to house a six-person family is $650 per month. Landlords can and do evict families who cannot afford regulated rents. Thousands of families who have been evicted receive emergency housing at so-called "welfare hotels." A six-person family would be entitled to four rooms at one of these hotels, for which the city pays $1900 per month with money from federal funds designated for the homeless. Living conditions at the hotels are much worse than in almost any apartment, particularly with regard to drug use and criminal activity. If the family received an increase in the allowance to cover the $650 rent, they could stay in the apartment, which provides at least a somewhat more stable environment than a welfare hotel at less than half the cost. The millions of dollars being wasted could provide funds for some of the badly needed drug treatment programs.

The money being wasted on shelter programs highlights the need for prudent spending on programs that have a good track record. Management controls and audit procedures should be established to ensure that fraud, waste, and abuse do not overrun the programs.

Education is a vital part of demand reduction and a relatively inexpensive one. There are several community programs aimed at prevention of drug involvement by young people. Again, the most successful programs need to involve a full court press by families, community organizations, schools, churches, and the media. The effectiveness of these educational efforts will have to be judged in the future, but several appear to be working to some degree.

Supply Reduction

The National Drug Control Strategy addresses supply reduction by law enforcement programs. Some people have suggested that the money spent on drug enforcement activity should be used for demand reduction programs. It is preposterous to think what our nation would be like if we did not take action against the leaders and members of criminal enterprises who are responsible for the sale of between $80 billion and $120 billion of illegal narcotics annually. The very illegality of trafficking, the debilitating results of drug use on the health of large numbers of people, the vast amounts of untaxed wealth accumulated by traffickers, and the corrupting influence that the drug business has on politicians, enforcement officers, and people in financial institutions all mandate the need for aggressive and effective law enforcement action. While funding for demand reduction should be increased, there is also a need for more funding and better utilization of resources in some law enforcement areas.

IRS

One of the principal shortcomings in both the Reagan and Bush Administrations' prosecution of the war on drugs has been the failure to adequately staff the IRS Criminal Investigations Division (CID). Congress must share the blame for this failure. In addition, the internal organizational structure of IRS limits the effectiveness of the Criminal Investigations Division, and there has been a reluctance on the part of IRS managers to commit resources to drug traffickers and high level criminals, as opposed to tax evaders.

IRS should be a major player in the war on drugs. Its jurisdiction over violations of the tax statutes and violations of the Bank Secrecy Act, together with the financial investigative expertise of its agents places the CID in a vital position to investigate and prosecute drug money laundering activity. CID accumulates vast amounts of suspicious transaction information from financial institutions. IRS has the responsibility to enforce the reporting requirements of the statute which mandates that businesses file an IRS form for currency and monetary instrument transactions over $10,000. Drug dealers do not pay taxes on their profits. Drug traffickers and their money launderers regularly violate the Bank Secrecy Act and money laundering statutes. IRS's responsibilities should place them in a major role in pursuing money laundering activity.

The importance of IRS agents in drug and money laundering investigations has long been recognized. Prosecutors in the Justice Department and in the U.S. Attorneys' offices have been clamoring for IRS agent support in drug and money laundering cases for years. IRS agents play a vital role in OCDETF cases in all of the 13 task force regions. IRS agents made a tremendous contribution to Operation Greenback, the financial investigative task force that operated so successfully in Florida during the early and mid-1980s.

During the Nixon Administration there was a significant heroin problem in a number of major cities and a corresponding push to put heroin trafficking organizations out of business. One of the initiatives developed was an IRS program named the Narcotics Trafficker's Project (NTP). In this program, some 200 IRS agents were assigned to work with the Bureau of Narcotics and Dangerous Drugs, the predecessor agency to DEA, to target major heroin dealers for tax evasion violations. The project was very successful. A number of joint drug and tax cases were made against major heroin traffickers. In some cases, tax cases were successfully prosecuted where not enough evidence could be collected to make a drug case.

The combination of drug, money laundering, and tax investigations appears to be an obvious natural progression.

Despite the importance of IRS in drug investigations and prosecutions, understaffing and underfunding of CID is a major problem. The number of IRS CID agents has not changed significantly in the past 13 years, ranging from 2,850 to 3,000. Between 1989 and 1990, the number actually decreased from 2,996 to 2,846. About half the agent force is involved in special enforcement programs related to drug dealers and money launderers. These programs lost agent support at a time when all other enforcement agencies were substantially increasing personnel to work on drug-related matters. Indeed, the IRS personnel loss came at a time when the following conditions prevailed:

- Treasury was encouraging banks and other financial institutions to report to the IRS suspicious transactions that might involve money laundering or Bank Secrecy Act violations. IRS was being overwhelmed with suspicious transaction information—over 30,000 reports since January 1990—and could not adequately respond.

- Congress severely criticized Treasury and IRS for not adequately enforcing or investigating criminal noncompliance with the requirement of businesses and trades to report to the IRS currency and monetary instrument transactions over $10,000. The staffing situation in CID was woefully inadequate to handle the volume of offenses.

- OCDETF investigative activity was increasing with additional prosecutors and investigators from other agencies. IRS was forced to reduce its personnel commitment to most of the task forces in 1991.

Another problem for CID is that the organizational structure of IRS appears to be designed to guarantee ineffectiveness on the part of CID. CID agents in the field ultimately report to nonenforcement managers. The assistant commissioner for CID has only dotted line authority over his agents and has limited ability to move them from one location to another. CID field personnel report to district directors of IRS and eventually to regional commissioners in seven regions. These district directors and regional commissioners are tax specialists and administrators with little or no law enforcement backgrounds. On some occasions, they have blocked proposed undercover operations by CID agents because they did not understand the law enforcement benefit of the investigation even though the proposal had been approved by the local U.S. Attorney.

Another problem has been a reluctance on the part of IRS managers to commit resources to drug traffickers and high level criminals. A succession of IRS commissioners and top managers over a period of years have construed the primary IRS function in criminal enforcement field to be the pursuit of ordinary tax cheats who make money lawfully. The theory is that the entire taxing system works basically on voluntary compliance. To the extent taxpayers believe their returns will be checked, sometimes audited, and that they will be prosecuted if they cheat, the level of voluntary compliance is high. The IRS top management position has been that a concentration of resources on drug traffickers and high profile criminals reduces the agency's ability to develop cases against the ordinary tax cheat.

The top managers who hold these views have invariably been individuals without any criminal enforcement background and without any appreciation for the importance of CID agents to pursue money laundering and drug trafficking investigations. They tend to see drug-related investigations as messy and loaded with problems. As managers, they don't like problems. Most IRS commissioners have been very successful accountants and/or attorneys associated with major law firms and accounting firms as senior partners. Most senior managers in IRS have come up through the ranks as accountants who have been involved in the administrative and civil areas of tax administration. The commissioners and managers like clean, neat and well-organized tax cheat prosecutions. Most have found the undercover operations, wiretaps, and surveillances connected with drug money laundering cases to be dirty, messy, somewhat disorganized, dangerous, and loaded with problems. They don't like this activity and invariably point to how it detracts from the IRS enforcement mission to deter tax cheating by the vast majority of taxpayers who earn money from legitimate sources.

In addition to the structure of the organization and the attitude of IRS top management, there is a historical reason for problems. There were a number of abuses of IRS confidential tax return records during the Nixon Administration. There was the famous "enemies list" where some of Nixon's enemies were targeted for tax investigations. There were alleged improprieties involving CID agents. The result was that Congress, with the concurrence of the Ford Administration, put IRS, and particularly the CID, in a box. Tax return information was made so sacrosanct that it was difficult to obtain even for criminal prosecutions. Oversight of IRS activity by the Executive Branch was greatly reduced, while Congressional oversight was increased. CID appropriations have been reduced or held in check by Congressional action. This set of circumstances has restricted CID from obtaining resource allocations proportionate to other agencies involved in the drug war.

To underscore the intensity of efforts to reduce the IRS role in the drug war, an American Bar Association subcommittee released a report in August 1991 that accused IRS of spending too much time chasing drug dealers, mobsters, and other high profile crooks for tax fraud. The report urged the IRS to focus more on lower profile, ordinary tax evasion cases. Eight former IRS commissioners wrote IRS agreeing with the ABA report and warning that a tilt away from general enforcement will "create the impression among great numbers of taxpayers who earn legitimate income that it is safe to cheat."

Several steps must be taken to make IRS a more significant and effective player in the War on Drugs. These include:

- Significant increases in funding for agent personnel and CID support staff. IRS CID is scheduled to get 325 new agents in 1992. About 118 of these agents will go into OCDETF programs. This is a drop in the bucket in terms of total need. Resources applied to the drug effort should be at least doubled. Personnel increases are also needed in the general enforcement area to work on more routine tax evasion cases.

- Suggestions that IRS should not be involved in tax fraud and Bank Secrecy Act investigations against drug traffickers and major criminals should be put to bed with strong policy statements from Treasury and Justice and from the "Drug Czar."

- Line authority over CID agents should be removed from district directors and regional commissioners, as is the case today, and given to the Assistant Commissioner for Criminal Enforcement.

- Consideration should be given to moving CID out of IRS. It may be more effective as a separate agency in the Treasury Department.

Joint Command Structures and Co-located Task Forces

Federal drug enforcement efforts have, for a period of years, been characterized by a lack of coordination, turf battles, fragmented efforts, and failed programs. Numerous attempts have been made to improve coordination and cooperation. Overall, a national drug policy strategy has evolved from the Justice Department in the Reagan Administration and from the Drug Czars in the Bush Administration. Enforcement strategy focuses on the criminal justice system, international initiatives, interdiction, and intelligence. In the criminal justice area, it has become clear that the most effective major investigative efforts come from joint task force operations.

The OCDETF program is the major cooperative investigative program at the federal level. The program has demonstrated a considerable amount of success since its inception in 1982. Studies of the program have determined that the most successful task forces have had their Assistant U.S.

Attorneys and agency coordinators co-located. Coordination appears to work reasonably well when there is a target within the geographic confines of a task force. However, when more than one task force is involved, coordination becomes more of a problem.

In Operation Polar Cap, an ad hoc coordination mechanism was set up in Washington with the head of the Narcotics Section of the Justice Department chairing a committee of senior officials from the involved investigative agencies. Coordination and direction worked reasonably well, but it did not prevent DEA agents in New York from making a precipitous seizure of $4.8 million in currency, which led to a somewhat untimely termination of the investigation.

There appears to be a need for some kind of a joint command structure to direct and coordinate multiple task force operations against major targets. Cases such as Polar Cap need full-time operational control and direction. An ad hoc committee, whose participants have a myriad of other duties and responsibilities, cannot devote the time and effort needed for effective control. A study should be made of the Department of Defense joint command structures to determine if there is a model that might apply to the drug enforcement arena. Potential joint command structures may apply to a particular target trafficking organization, a major problem in a specific geographic area, or to a multidistrict OCDETF case.

There are strong indications that the most successful multiagency task force operations have involved agents from different agencies co-located in the same working space. There have been a number of successful models of these types of operations in drug and money laundering investigations. Operation Greenback in Miami and the South Florida Task Force are good examples.

There is a fairly new and successful drug-related money laundering task force currently operating in South Florida. It operates under the umbrella of OCDETF, however, special funding is provided to agencies who co-locate agents in the same office space. The special funding comes from a provision in the "Drug Czar" legislation which enabled ONDCP to designate certain "high intensity drug trafficking areas" (HIDTA) which would receive special funds through a variety of programs involving federal, state, and local cooperative efforts. HIDTA areas have been designated in Miami, Houston, Los Angeles, New York City, and the southwest border. The early results of the Miami HIDTA-funded task force have been so good and cooperation has been at such a high level that consideration should be given to replicating this model in other locations, probably within the framework of the OCDETF program. It is interesting to note that the coordinator of the Miami HIDTA-funded task force operation is a highly respected state law enforcement officer.

DEA State Local Task Forces

One of the best examples of co-located joint agency operations is the DEA State and Local Task Force program that has been in effect for a number of years. This is an excellent program that has been targeting high level violators in local drug markets. It is particularly important to target this level of violator as significant resources are poured into efforts to dismantle entire international drug trafficking organizations. There are two prime factors that make high level local violators important targets. One is that it helps to knock out the lower level infrastructures of the larger drug organizations. The other is that cases against important local violators sometimes lead to successful efforts against higher level traffickers. Indeed, many OCDETF cases are initiated as the result of DEA State and Local Task Force investigations. This effective program had $50 million in funding in 1991. Substantial increases in resources would appear to be in order to target the high level local drug dealers.

Outbound Currency

There are many indicators that large amounts of U.S. currency are being smuggled directly out of the country to a number of overseas locations. Several cases mentioned in this book involved outbound currency smuggling. The "Pizza Connection" launderers smuggled U.S. dollars to Switzerland, the Caymans, and the Bahamas. Ramon Milan Rodriguez transported over $100 million in U.S. dollars to Panama in his private jet. In the BCCI case, a Customs undercover agent had discussions with a BCCI official about moving millions of U.S. dollars to Colombia and to London.

During Congressional testimony in 1989, Federal Reserve Chairman Alan Greenspan estimated that half of all U.S. currency is located outside the United States. In early 1990, there was approximately $180 billion worth of U.S. currency that could not be accounted for in the United States. It appears that almost all of it had moved to foreign countries. Most experts attribute the outflow of dollars to drug trafficking and other illegal activities.

The demand for U.S. dollars in foreign countries is insatiable. It has always been very high in South American countries, particularly in Argentina and Brazil. Argentina has two working currencies, the dollar and the Austral. The dollar is in much greater demand because the Austral has been frequently devalued since it became the official currency in 1985. At the present time, there is a tremendous demand for dollars in the Eastern Bloc countries and in Russia. There is a flourishing black market in dollars all over Europe and in the Mid-East. The dollar has become the world's principal means of black market currency exchange. It is accepted in every country.

The demand for dollars overseas has made it very attractive for drug money launderers to move more and more dollars directly out of the country. There is a premium paid for United States currency in most areas of the world. If the drug dealers or their money launderers can get dollars out of the United States, they will have avoided the necessity to launder the money through domestic financial institutions and there will be no paper trails left behind. This is convenient because government regulatory and enforcement efforts are putting pressure on domestic financial institutions to report all suspicious transactions.

There is every indication that dollars are hemorrhaging out of the United States. They are departing across our land borders with Mexico and Canada. They leave on checked baggage and on the bodies of travelers on flights from the United States to foreign countries. Dollars are also shipped as air freight and cargo on ocean going vessels. The U.S. Customs Service has had outbound currency enforcement programs in place for a number of years. The problem is that Customs does not have sufficient personnel to be effective against outbound currency smuggling. The Customs Service is well aware of its personnel limitations. It entered into an agreement with the National Guard some years ago for personnel to augment its efforts to detect drug smuggling. Most Customs enforcement efforts are directed to inbound passengers, cargo on planes, and to land vehicles at land borders. Outbound enforcement efforts have mostly concentrated on flights from certain airports, such as J.F.K. in New York and Miami International to specific destinations such as Colombia and Panama. Just about every time Customs has had a special enforcement operation aimed at these flights, there have been significant currency seizures.

In 1990, Customs personnel seized over $50 million in currency as it was being smuggled out of the country without a Customs Currency and Monetary Instrument Report (CMIR) having been filed. There was a cargo seizure of $6.4 million at J.F.K. Airport in New York. The currency was packed into 25 canisters of bull semen that was being shipped to Colombia on Avianca Airlines. There was a $1.2 million seizure from two sport-utility vehicles on the Mexican border at Douglas, Arizona. A unique seizure of $1.1 million occurred at Los Angeles International Airport. The currency, all in $100 bills, was strapped to the body of a man who was flying to Russia. Customs has done a good job with limited resources, but it is clear that massive amounts of dollars are exiting the country and more needs to be done. The amount of currency being smuggled out is a factor of guesswork, but educated estimates range from a low of $10 billion to $20 billion or more annually.

Outbound currency enforcement should be an important part of the full court press needed to attack the international drug trafficking organizations at every level of their operations. Resources in the form of additional personnel and technical equipment should be provided to the Customs Service to concentrate special enforcement operations against cargo shipments, private aircraft flights, land border vehicle traffic, and commercial passenger traffic headed to likely destination countries for outbound currency shipments. Customs presently utilizes some National Guard personnel to assist in outbound searches. Much more assistance is needed. The task is a massive one and it is impossible to even begin to check everything going out. However, aggressive and intelligent enforcement efforts bolstered by profiles of smuggling procedures and additional resources can lead to seizures and deterrence and force smugglers to adopt different methods.

Leadership

Although most federal law enforcement agencies do a fairly good job of developing middle management types to run field offices and to fill headquarters staff positions, they have generally not produced outstanding leaders to effectively head their agencies and command respect on a national level as articulate and knowledgeable spokespersons for federal enforcement. Career enforcement agents have ascended to top positions in some of the Treasury enforcement bureaus and many have done a good job in running their own organizations. None have become nationally recognized law enforcement spokesmen. In the FBI and DEA, the trend has been to appoint leaders from outside those agencies—federal judges, prosecutors, and attorneys. A few have become articulate spokespersons for law enforcement, but many of them never came to understand how the agencies they headed operated or how those agencies co-existed with the world beyond their own organizations.

One of the problems encountered in the "War on Drugs" is that there has not been first class leadership at the top of the various federal law enforcement agencies that work on drug related issues. This is particularly true in DEA. It is the only federal agency whose sole mission is drug enforcement. It has suffered from poor leadership at the top for over 20 years. Since 1968, all of the administrators of DEA have come from outside the agency. With the exception of Jack Lawn, a professional law enforcement officer who came from the FBI, they have been a lackluster group. Rob Bonner, the present administrator of DEA, is no exception. He is not providing dynamic leadership to the organization. DEA needs quick decisions and risk taking to be effective. However, conservative approaches and slow decisions emanate from his office. DEA needs leadership from a career official who understands problems that agents face in the street and overseas and who understands the international drug trafficking and enforcement arena.

There is a need for a leadership training program for senior federal law enforcement officials similar to the War Colleges and the Armed Forces Staff College that the military services conduct. Because of the size of their organizations, no single enforcement agency can afford to run its own "War College"-type senior leadership program. Consideration should be given to the establishment of a Federal Enforcement Senior Executive Leadership Course that would be geared to the development of qualities in senior officials who might be in line to become heads of their agencies or to fill senior staff roles. The executives chosen for this program should have already demonstrated strong leadership qualities in their prior careers. The object would be to make them more effective by broadening their knowledge and skills in areas outside of law enforcement.

Above all, those selected should have demonstrated skills as street agents and as leaders capable of directing successful major enforcement operations. They should not come from the ranks of administrative paper pushers who have spent most of their careers in headquarter staff positions. Such a course of training should be of sufficient length to deal with problems such as media relations, departmental relations, Congressional relations, national security problems, interface with the military, state and local enforcement problems, international enforcement, budgetary considerations, the role of OMB, political problems involving law enforcement, environmental issues, and personnel problems. There should be time to war game on both law enforcement situations and other unique problems that might be encountered by law enforcement agencies. The goal of this kind of a program would be to develop better senior executives in all of the enforcement agencies, the kind of individuals who would have the ability to lead their own agencies effectively, interact with other law enforcement agencies, and articulate their mission to those outside law enforcement.

WHAT WE SHOULD NOT DO

One thing we shouldn't do is legalize drug use. That suggestion is made from time to time. Some who make this proposal are wearying of the drug effort. Others argue that legalization would take the profit out of illegal drug use and do away with the cartels that run trafficking operations. Still others propose that legalization would bring users into government centers where drugs would be administered in supervised programs that would be combined with treatment which might lead to recovery.

These suggestions ignore the fact that heroin and cocaine are addictive and have severe physical, mental, and emotional consequences. Both drugs have the capability of producing psychosis. Chronic inhalers of cocaine suffer eventual erosion of the nasal membrane and cartilage. Marijuana, while not addictive, is habit-forming and research has shown that habitual use has severe long-term health consequences. The addictive and habit-forming qualities of drugs will always lead users to seek more drugs from the illegal market than they can obtain legally. Thus, the dream of the dissolution of the illegal market will not be fulfilled. Knowing the severe consequences of drug use, it is difficult to see how any self-respecting nation or society can advocate legalization as a solution to the drug problem. Legalization has been tried in several countries, without success.

Another thing that should not be done is to eliminate DEA by folding it into the FBI. This idea was being seriously considered by the Justice Department in the fall of 1991. A similar proposal had been considered and rejected by the Reagan Administration in 1981.

Folding DEA into the FBI would be a serious setback to drug enforcement effectiveness. DEA is the only enforcement agency whose mission is solely directed at drug enforcement. It is important to retain an independent agency with this single mission focus when dealing with an enforcement problem of the magnitude posed by illegal drug use.

While DEA has suffered from poor leadership at the top, it has talented and experienced enforcement personnel who have unique skills in street investigations and undercover operations and in overseas liaison with foreign police and security forces in anti-drug efforts. DEA has become characterized as a fast-moving, risk-taking organization that has been effective against a number of major trafficking organizations. In the totality of the drug enforcement effort it became overwhelmed by the magnitude of the problem. Since the early 1980s, DEA has been augmented by numerous other enforcement agencies in a variety of joint task force operations that have increased the effectiveness of the overall drug enforcement effort.

The FBI, contrasted with DEA, is identified as a slow-moving, plodding, bureaucratic giant that has a wide variety of criminal enforcement responsibilities. Many knowledgeable individuals in the ranks of enforcement and prosecutorial agencies seriously question the overall effectiveness of the FBI in its criminal investigative mission. The FBI was given investigative jurisdiction in the drug enforcement area in 1981. There is no question that the additional resources from the FBI resulted in a number of convictions against major drug traffickers that would not otherwise have happened. There are serious questions about how effectively FBI resources have been utilized in the drug enforcement effort.

Turf battles that seemed to have subsided to some degree in the drug enforcement area in the late 1980s reappeared in 1990 and 1991. The FBI appears to be the primary offender in turf fights with DEA, Customs, and BATF. Turf wars are also being waged by the FBI against other enforcement agencies in other areas of criminal enforcement. It appears that the current FBI Director, Judge Williams Sessions, has regressed to a J. Edgar Hoover mentality in attempting to exert dominance over all areas of federal criminal enforcement activity.

Assimilating DEA into the FBI would be a step backward in effective drug enforcement.

AN OVERALL ASSESSMENT

The Bush Administration, in its last two strategy documents published in January 1990 and February 1991, has identified the principal goal of the national strategy as the *reduction* of illegal drug use in America. This suggests that we recognize the drug situation as a long-term criminal and sociological problem that will not go away, much as we now address burglary and assault. In this scenario, we would continue to fight against drugs with current budget levels and personnel resources in order to diminish the problem and keep it somewhat under control. Perhaps the goal of reduction of illegal drug use is a more attainable goal than that of winning an all-out victory in the "War on Drugs." Either scenario requires commitment, leadership, and resources devoted to effective, well-managed programs.

Two administrations have come a long way in the "War on Drugs" since the bleak days of 1980. Substantial resources and good strategies are now in place in efforts to attack and cope with the drug problem. It is probable that the corner has been turned and that we might be winning the war. There are some indications that drug use is starting to decline on a national level.

Despite the positive indicators, there continue to be serious concerns. Leadership has always been a very significant factor in winning a war. Victories are reached when there is an all-out commitment of resources and people. Does the leadership, drive, and commitment now exist to continue fighting the war? Does the drug war have competent leadership? Have we committed sufficient resources? The jury is still out on the effectiveness of the "Drug Czar" legislation which mandated the Drug Czar and the OCNDP mechanism that has been set up to administer the anti-drug effort. The Drug Czar legislation has spawned a new bureaucratic layer of supervision and oversight over all the federal drug efforts. The OCNDP now has a large staff and a 1991 budget estimated at $100 million. There have been some positive accomplishments. The strategies developed appear to be cohesive and all-encompassing. There is improved coordination between the various agencies and programs involved in demand reduction and supply reduction. Prior helter-skelter approaches appear to have been replaced with well-thought-out and organized programs and strategies.

There is not, however, the lightning rod dynamic leadership that is needed to energize the various federal bureaus and agencies engaged in the fight. Bill Bennett, the first drug czar, was an effective spokesman for the antidrug effort, but he did not provide leadership to the agencies. The new drug czar is Bob Martinez, the former governor of Florida. He has only been in office for a few months, and this may be unfair, but there are early indications that he is not up to the task of being an effective spokesman for federal efforts or a strong leader who can motivate the agencies involved.

In 1991, $2.7 billion was earmarked for demand reduction. Is this enough when thousands of drug users are not able to obtain timely treatment and our inner cities are being overwhelmed by drugs and associated problems? Conservatively, it appears that the federal government should be spending somewhere between $8 billion to $10 billion on demand reduction problems.

Over $7 billion was designated for supply reduction in 1991. Is this enough when it is clear that drugs keep pouring into the United States? There is a need for more enforcement personnel, particularly in Customs and IRS, for more prosecutors, judges, and prisons. Special programs such as OCDETF, HIDTA, the DEA state and local task forces, and Customs outbound currency enforcement programs need more resources than currently provided.

The argument can well be made that we are in a budget crisis and that we cannot afford additional billions for the "War on Drugs." A more important question to be raised is, "Can we afford not to?" A strong argument can be made that widespread drug use undermines the very fabric of our society, encourages criminal activity, and destroys a segment of our younger generation.

CHAPTER 8

LESSONS FOR FINANCIAL INSTITUTIONS

The "War on Drugs" continues at a hectic pace. While government efforts are unprecedented, the drug cartels have not backed off. Drugs continue to flow into the United States, generating enormous profits. As soon as one trafficking organization gets knocked off, another one steps forward to take its place. While there are indications of a slackening in the demand for drugs, the market remains strong. Estimates are that Americans spend over $100 billion a year on illegal drugs. Almost all of the drug purchases are made with currency. As much as 80% to 85% of all the currency used to purchase drugs finds its way into U.S. financial institutions, one way or another. The other 15% to 20% is smuggled directly out of the country.

Many banks and other financial institutions have been and continue to be used by drug dealers and their money launderers. Some, have been lax in complying with the requirements of federal laws and regulations. In almost every known case where a financial institution has been used or has gotten into trouble with regulators, the institution either knew or should have known better. Most money laundering activity results in unusual and unique transactions occurring at financial institutions.

BANK OF BOSTON

A good example is the Bank of Boston case which gained widespread notoriety in early 1985. Part of the bank's problem had to do with 1980 changes in Treasury reporting rules that required all banks to file Currency Transaction Reports on currency transactions involving foreign banks, even if the foreign bank was a wholly-owned subsidiary of the domestic bank. Bank of Boston didn't pick up on the change and continued to conduct currency transactions with foreign banks, including its own subsidiaries, without filing CTRs. This practice continued until 1984.

Another problem encountered by Bank of Boston was that one of its branches had been doing business with a notorious organized crime figure for years. The individual owned a realty business, and the branch exempted the business from the currency reporting requirements even though it did not qualify for an exemption under Treasury regulations. For years, the mobster and his brothers would bring shopping bags full of cash into the bank and make deposits or buy cashier's checks. No CTRs were filed by the bank because the business account had been exempted.

A Treasury Department investigation uncovered the failure to file reports on transactions with international banks and an IRS investigation uncovered the situation with the organized crime figure. The investigations led to criminal charges against Bank of Boston. The bank pled guilty and was fined $500,000.

Bank of Boston was engulfed in a tremendous amount of negative publicity from the criminal conviction. In both situations, the bank and its employees professed misunderstanding of the law and Treasury regulations. But, frankly, there was no excuse. The bank certainly should have known and understood the reporting requirements.

What happened at Bank of Boston was a compliance failure of major proportions. In addition, the situation with the organized crime figure represented a major failure of the "Know Your Customer" policy banks are expected to embrace. Bank of Boston employees knew of the customer's reputation as a mobster. They certainly should have been suspicious of repetitive large currency transactions coming from a nonretail business. The continuation of business with the mobster represented a "see no evil, hear no evil" attitude.

LEARNING FROM MISTAKES

Some institutions have learned from their mistakes. Chemical Bank in New York was burned in 1977 when a branch manager agreed to accept payoffs from drug dealers for not filing CTRs on large currency deposits. The branch failed to file CTRs for over 500 transactions totaling roughly $8.5 million. The manager enlisted other employees in the scheme, who believed they were helping the manager's cousin dispose of gambling proceeds. The manager received a jail sentence. Chemical pled guilty to 200 misdemeanor violations and was fined $200,000.

Two years later, Chemical, having been once burned, refused to accept a suspicious currency transaction and was victorious in a civil suit that resulted from the refusal. The situation arose out of a lease agreement, entered into in 1979, between a leasing subsidiary of Chemical and an aircraft company in North Carolina. The aircraft firm leased a large aircraft from the Chemical subsidiary. The plane was then subleased to Tampa Airlines, a Colombian cargo carrier, for $400,000, which was to be paid by Tampa Airlines to a small bank that Chemical owned in Miami. On October 26, 1979, a Tampa Airlines official showed up at the Miami bank with two suitcases and a man who appeared to be a bodyguard. The suitcases contained $400,000 in currency, in bundles of old $5, $10 and $20 bills tied together with rubber bands. The bank manager initially accepted the money, but after conferring with New York, returned the cash to Tampa Airlines, whereupon Chemical's leasing company canceled the lease arrangement.

Several years later, Chemical was sued in New York by the North Carolina aircraft firm for breach of contract and alleged damages, in the amount of $10 million. It was determined that Tampa Airlines aircraft frequently carried cocaine, some of which was seized by Customs. The lawsuit was not resolved until 1990, when a New York State Supreme Court Judge granted a summary judgment to Chemical and dismissed the case. The judge ruled that, based on the manner in which Tampa Airlines delivered the $400,000, Chemical was justified in concluding that Tampa was involved in money laundering and the aircraft would ultimately be used to transport drugs. The judge's decision stated that a party to an illegal contract cannot seek the court's assistance in carrying out an illegal objective. The court noted that the plaintiff failed to come forward with any reasonable explanation for the apparently improper cash transaction.

The decision in this case may have far-reaching implications for financial institutions. Even though the decision was made by a state court in New York, it gives an indication that courts will recognize obvious money laundering transactions as a basis for refusing to honor contractual obligations. It should provide financial institutions with a certain comfort level in deciding to decline transactions where payments apparently come from illegal activity, even where there is a contractual relationship.

BROKER DEALER PROBLEMS

Some of the money laundering transactions in the Pizza Connection case were highly unusual and the financial institutions involved certainly should have known better than to proceed with them. Merrill Lynch officials in New York should have known better than to accept three currency deposits in the total amount of $3 million in March 1982 from Franco Della Torre. Even after a security officer of the firm wrote an internal memo pointing out that the transactions were suspicious, officials accepted two more large currency transactions of almost $3 million from Della Torre. The account was finally closed out after $4.9 million in small bills had been received in five transactions over a one-month period. Merrill Lynch filed CTRs, but took no official action to notify any government agency that it considered the transactions suspicious and unusual.

If Merrill Lynch was lax, then officials at E.F. Hutton were almost criminally negligent in accepting 22 currency deposits totalling $15.6 million from Della Torre during the summer of 1982. Hutton continued to accept currency from Della Torre even though a bank officer warned a Hutton official that the money might be coming from illegal activity. Hutton filed CTRs for all the transactions, but took no action to officially notify any government agency about the suspicious nature of the transactions. Even worse, Hutton tipped off Della Torre's company in Switzerland that a subpoena had been issued for the records of the account where the currency had been placed and that the FBI was asking questions about Della Torre.

Deservedly, E.F. Hutton received a great deal of negative publicity over its handling of Della Torre. In 1985, Hutton received another spate of bad publicity when its Providence, Rhode Island office pleaded guilty to failing to file CTRs for currency transactions received from drug dealers. This occurred almost simultaneously with revelations about a check kiting scheme that enabled Hutton to rake in money at the expense of its clients.

The three incidents combined to shake public confidence in the brokerage. Investors moved to other firms and Hutton's lending banks declined further extensions of credit. Hutton was forced to sell out to Shearson Lehman or go bankrupt.

Contrast E.F. Hutton's dealings with Della Torre with the actions of Donaldson Lufkin Jenrette, in dealing with Isaac Kattan. Shortly after Kattan opened an account at Donaldson's Miami office, in January 1981, couriers began making huge currency deposits to the account. The Donaldson manager contacted the Miami Police Department, the Customs Service, and the FBI because he suspected that the money was coming from drug sales. When arrests did not quickly materialize, the account was closed out, because the manager did not want the firm's good name tarnished by helping to launder what was obviously drug money. The information provided by the Donaldson firm ultimately led to Kattan's arrest nearly two months later, and the brokerage house received good publicity for its actions.

The E.F. Hutton case offers some great lessons for financial institutions. One of those lessons is to refuse to conduct suspicious transactions if it possible and practical to do so. The second is to report suspicious transactions to an appropriate federal enforcement agency, consistent with the Right to Financial Privacy Act. A third lesson is the devastating effect negative publicity can have on an institution that allows itself to be used by drug money launderers.

There is a special lesson for broker-dealers: don't accept currency from customers. Most major brokerage houses have in place policies against accepting currency payments from customers. Some individual brokers, however, have circumvented the policies by accepting the cash themselves and laundering it through structured transactions to purchase monetary instruments that are then used to pay for investments. Brokerage houses should take a hard look at repetitive payments to accounts made by monetary instruments such as cashier's checks, bank checks, and money orders.

OUTRIGHT CRIMINAL ACTIVITY

Many financial institutions have been victimized by outright criminal activity on the part of employees. In some instances, financial institutions themselves have embarked on patterns of criminal involvement with launderers. There were numerous examples of both types of activity in Miami during the late 1970s and early 1980s, as launderers, laden with currency from cocaine sales, approached banks with outright bribes and offers of "fees" for processing their cash.

Popular Bank and Northside Bank, the two institutions controlled by Andres Rodriquez, were prime examples of institutional involvement in money laundering Rodriquez and his top officers entered into agreements with the likes of Isaac Kattan to receive large cash deposits without filing CTRs, in return for processing fees. The agreements only began to unravel when Rodriguez started cheating the launderers by shorting their deposits.

Great American Bank was an example of criminal activity by key employees of a bank that apparently fell short of institutional involvement. Three key officers of the bank arranged with Isaac Kattan and another money laundering organization to accept large cash deposits without filing CTRs and to issue cashier's checks in fictitious names for a fee.

The actions of three key officers of Landmark First National Bank of Fort Lauderdale in accepting $55 million in currency deposits from representatives of Hernan Botero was another example of criminal activity by employees. The three agreed to accept large currency deposits into a number of accounts. They prepared CTRs, but never filed the originals with the IRS. They received a fee of 0.75% on all transactions for their efforts.

The Capital Bank situation in Miami was a slightly different matter. There was institutional involvement in that the owner of the bank and top officials agreed to accept, for a fee, large volumes of currency ($242 million during eight months in 1981) from a business account maintained by Beno Ghitis. The bank initially filed CTRs for the transactions and then switched and began to file CMIRs because Ghitis had told them the money was being shipped to Miami by Colombian money exchange houses. The bank avoided prosecution because the U.S. Attorney in Miami decided a conviction could not be obtained on a Bank Secrecy Act violation. The criminal offense of money laundering was not established until 1986. Had money laundering statutes existed in 1981, the government may have been able to convict Capital Bank of those offenses.

A judge in a civil action involving a $10 million penalty and seizure of currency from Ghitis' company had no difficulty concluding that the currency came from drug sales.

A financial institution can never guarantee that its employees will not become involved with money laundering or any other financial crime connected with the institution. As a result of lessons learned in Miami in the early 1980s, when a number of banks became involved in Bank Secrecy Act violations, most financial institutions have established internal controls and compliance procedures that seek to avoid and deter malfeasance by employees. Some of these measures include:

- One or two levels of review before CTRs are filed;

- Centralized filing from an institution's headquarters rather than from branches;

- Daily checks of currency activity against CTRs filed;

- Training for all employees on BSA requirements, on money laundering awareness and the recognition of suspicious transactions;

- Internal audits to check on the effectiveness of BSA compliance and the level of money laundering awareness;

- The designation of an officer and an adequate staff to oversee BSA compliance and problems related to possible money laundering activity.

Financial institutions must understand that information known to their employees, acting within the scope of their employment, can be attributed to the institution. This holding was articulated in a judicial opinion and is known as the doctrine of "collective knowledge." The opinion was rendered by the First Circuit Court of Appeals in a decision in *United States* v. *Bank of New England, N.A., 821 F.2d 844, 855 (1st Cir.), cert. denied, 108 S. Ct. 328 (1987).* In that case, the Circuit Court of Appeals upheld the District Court's use of jury instructions that permitted the jury to attribute to the bank the total knowledge of the bank's employees acting within the scope of their employment. The court reasoned that "the knowledge obtained by corporate employees acting within the scope of their employment is imputed to the corporation."

The Court of Appeals upheld a separate portion of the jury instructions that permitted an inference of specific intent from evidence of the bank's "flagrant organizational indifference" to its obligations under the Bank Secrecy Act.

While the doctrines of "collective knowledge" and "flagrant organizational indifference" were set forth in a case where bank employees failed to file CTRs, they could also be applied to the a situation where a financial institution's employees become aware of unusual or suspicious transactions that may indicate money laundering. For example, a bank's employees might become aware of large and unusual currency deposits by a customer that seem indicative of money laundering activity. Even though CTRs had been filed, the bank could have a problem with a money laundering violation if another employee knew that the currency came from drug sales and assisted in the transactions. The employee could be charged with money laundering and, under the doctrines of "collective knowledge" and "flagrant organizational indifference," the bank could face exposure to a criminal charge.

The doctrines of "collective knowledge" and "flagrant organizational indifference," along with the money laundering statutes are reasons why financial institutions must train employees to recognize unusual transactions that might be related to money laundering and to establish internal reporting mechanisms so that all unusual or suspicious activity can be reported to a central location for appropriate action.

RECOGNIZING THE SMURFS

Most people working in financial institutions can recognize suspicious transactions connected with money laundering. Some are easier to recognize than others. Smurfing has always been an easy money laundering activity for employees in financial institutions to identify.

Smurfing involves the use of couriers (referred to as smurfs) to purchase monetary instruments with currency in amounts under $10,000. The monetary instruments are later deposited in bank accounts and, in most instances, the funds are eventually wire transferred to accounts in foreign countries that have strict bank secrecy laws.

During the "Papa Smurf" investigation, numerous tips were received by law enforcement agencies from banks about suspicious transactions involving the purchase of cashier's checks, bank checks, and money orders in amounts under $10,000. It was clear to bank tellers that the smurfs were trying to evade the reporting requirements of the Bank Secrecy Act. The money launderers did not want to conduct currency transactions over $10,000 that would be reported to the IRS on CTR forms.

The tips came from banks in Phoenix, Denver, Cape Coral, Florida, Macon and Columbus, Georgia, and Birmingham, Alabama. Aside from direct tips, there were instances where agents investigating the case went to banks to inquire about cashier's checks and money orders that had been purchased previously, and found that tellers were able to recall the incidents and identify the purchasers because of the suspicious nature of the transactions. In some situations, tellers even had turned on the bank surveillance camera and photographed purchasers.

In 1986, the structuring of transactions to evade the BSA reporting requirements was made a criminal offense. It then became easier to prosecute smurfing and other types of structuring cases. In 1989, Treasury clearly defined, by regulation, what structuring meant. In the *Federal Register* notice that announced the definition, Treasury referred to a Federal Circuit Court of Appeals decision that established the doctrine of "willful blindness." In that decision, set forth in *United States* v. *Jewell, 532 F.2d 697(9th Cir.), cert. denied, 426 U.S.951(1976),* the court stated, "if a person has his suspicions aroused but then deliberately omits to make further inquiries because he wishes to remain in ignorance, he is deemed to have knowledge."

The Treasury, in its Federal Register notice, warned "if a financial institution suspects a customer of structuring, perhaps because of repeated transactions just under $10,000, but refuses to investigate further because it wants to remain in ignorance, the financial institution may be deemed to have knowledge of structuring by virtue of its 'willful blindness'." Financial institutions should report suspicious transactions indicative of structuring to the Internal Revenue Service's Criminal Investigation Division, pursuant to Treasury instructions.

BUSINESSMEN BEWARE

One of the best kept secrets of the laws and regulations designed to thwart money laundering has been the requirement that businesses report currency transactions over $10,000 to the IRS.

The requirement was initially imposed in an obscure amendment to the IRS criminal statutes in 1984. The law required those engaged in a trade or business to file an IRS Form 8300 for currency in amounts over $10,000 received from a customer. There were rather light misdemeanor penalties for failure to file the 8300 report. Publicity about the law was minimal. Hardly anyone in the business community knew anything about it and compliance and enforcement activities were practically nonexistent between 1984 and 1988.

Things began to change with the passage of the Anti-Drug Abuse Act of 1988, however. That Act amended the Internal Revenue Code to increase from a misdemeanor to a felony violation failure to file Form 8300 or to fraudulently file such forms. In 1989, IRS began limited investigations of businesses that sold big ticket items to determine if they were accepting currency and not filing the forms.

In October 1989, IRS launched an effort to obtain better compliance from attorneys. Over 2400 certified letters were forwarded to attorneys who had filed Forms 8300 with incomplete, inaccurate, or illegible information. This action caused an immediate confrontation with the legal community, particularly the criminal defense bar. Attorneys claimed that providing all of the required information intruded into the attorney-client relationship and violated the Right to Counsel guarantees of the Sixth Amendment. Many defense attorneys refused to provide the identities of criminal defendants who paid them with currency in amounts over $10,000. In New York, the government filed a civil summons enforcement action against two law firms, in an effort to compel the firms to provide details required by Form 8300.

In March 1990, the government won the first round in its battle with the attorneys. Federal District Judge Vincent L. Broderick ruled that, "Neither the existence of an attorney-client relationship nor the payment of fees are protected by the attorney-client privilege." The law firms were ordered to provide all of the information required on Form 8300. The two law firms appealed the District Court Ruling. The government also won the second round, for in June 1991, the Second Circuit Court of Appeals upheld Judge Broderick's ruling. That decision was appealed to the U.S. Supreme Court and a decision was pending as of November 1991.

Even absent the debate with the legal community, compliance by the business community with the Form 8300 requirement was abysmal. A mere 22,000 Forms 8300 were filed by businesses in 1989, compared with over six million Forms 4789 filed by financial institutions. There were some sporadic enforcement efforts by IRS against businesses that did not file, but these efforts were not widespread and were not sustained. The IRS did not have sufficient enforcement personnel to conduct a major focus on the filing of Form 8300.

Then, in the summer of 1990, a significant watershed event occurred: The House Ways and Means Oversight Subcommittee asked the General Accounting Office (GAO) to investigate compliance by businesses with the reporting requirements. Two GAO investigators spent 39 days in nine cities during July and August, visiting 79 businesses to find out how many were willing to accept cash payments in excess of $10,000 and not report the transactions to the IRS on Form 8300. The results were shocking. Only three businesses resisted the investigators' overtures. Seventy-six businesses were more than willing to break the law by not filing the forms.

The businesses contacted were automobile dealers, jewelers, antique dealers, realtors, and Oriental rug dealers. Many of the people in the businesses suggested ways to evade report filing. A realtor suggested making payments with cashier's checks and money orders to circumvent the reporting requirements. An antique dealer said he did not have to report a cash sale to anyone and offered to give a blank receipt made out to cash for a $15,000 sale. An automobile dealer suggested putting a false name on the vehicle registration.

The Oversight Subcommittee held hearings and received detailed testimony from the two GAO investigators that indicated a complete disregard by businesses of the filing requirements, and that many businesses were encouraging customers to pay for big ticket items with monetary instruments like cashier's checks and money orders. Armed with this information and infuriated by the general lack of compliance, the Subcommittee Chairman, J.J. "Jake" Pickle of Texas, pushed through an amendment to legislation passed during the waning days of the 1990 Congress that included "monetary instruments" in the definition of "cash" transactions required to be reported on the Form 8300. The amendment also increased penalties up to $100,000 for noncompliance with the reporting rules.

In October 1990, a combined IRS and DEA undercover investigation added a new dimension to the amount of money that is being laundered with currency purchases of luxury cars. Agents purchased a total of 31 cars from five dealers, paying with currency. In each case, the undercover agents advised salespeople and management that the money came from drug dealing, and instead of rejecting the purchases, the auto dealers went out of their way to accommodate the buyers and ignore reporting requirements. The investigation ended with the arrest of 15 employees of the dealers and formal charges filed against the dealerships.

An analysis was conducted of Forms 8300 filed by the dealers from January 1, 1986 to October 1, 1990 and CTRs filed by the dealers' banks for currency transactions with them during the same period. The Form 8300 review showed that the five auto dealers filed a total of six Forms 8300 during the almost five-year period. The total amount of currency reported on the six forms was $212,000. During the same period, the auto dealers' banks filed 1,144 CTRs reporting over $18 million in currency transactions by them. One dealer alone made $5.4 million in currency deposits into its bank. During the period of the deposits, it did not file a single 8300 form.

NOT JUST CURRENCY

Money laundering activity almost always starts with currency payments for illegal goods and services. Drug dealers don't accept checks and credit cards; they get paid in cash. The bribe taker and the bribe payer do not want to leave a paper trail. Bribe payments are usually made in cash. The infusion of currency from illegal activity into financial institutions or into the retail economy is the first cycle in money laundering activity. It is known as "placement."

But there is a lot more to money laundering activity than the initial "placement" of currency into financial institutions. Once currency has been placed into a financial institution or into the retail economy, a second stage of laundering activity occurs. This stage is known as "layering," and it involves the movement of money by complex layers of financial transactions designed to disguise or confuse the audit trail. Most layering is carried out with monetary instruments and electronic funds transfers (EFT).

It is extremely important for financial institutions to keep in mind that money laundering activity involves more than currency transactions. Banks and other financial institutions are constantly being used by money launderers in situations where currency transactions are not involved. For the most part, noncurrency transactions associated with money laundering are unusual and suspicious in nature, and can be recognized by employees in financial institutions.

Take, for example, the "Papa Smurf" money laundering operation. The smurfs disposed of large quantities of currency by purchasing monetary instruments such as cashier's checks and money orders in amounts under $10,000 from banks throughout the United States. The monetary instruments were shipped to "Papa Smurf" in Miami, who deposited the instruments into one of several accounts at Miami banks. It was not uncommon for "Papa Smurf" to deposit as much as $400,000 in monetary instruments at a time into his accounts. These deposits were made regularly and frequently.

Banks must recognize that this type of activity is unusual and suspicious even though currency is not involved. A bank handling such transactions must be aware of the possibility that it is being used by its customer for money laundering activity.

Today, there is a very small step between a financial institution suspecting that it is being used by money launderers and the institution actually becoming criminally involved in the activity. Take a case similar to the "Papa Smurf" situation where a bank is regularly receiving large deposits of monetary instruments in amounts under $10,000. If it turns out that an employee of the bank, who is handling some of the transactions, has knowledge that the funds being deposited come from drug sales, both the bank and the employee could be charged with money laundering offenses.

Another type of transaction that money launderers use to move or "layer" funds once they have been "placed" in a financial institution involves Electronic Funds Transfers (EFT), more specifically, wire transfers. After "Papa Smurf" deposited monetary instruments into his Miami bank accounts, he wire transferred the funds to foreign bank accounts. In the Polar Cap case, once Ropex Corporation and Andonian Brothers had deposited currency into Los Angeles bank accounts, they wire transferred the funds to accounts in New York banks, ostensibly to pay for gold purchases. In the C Chase sting operation, BCCI was victimized by wire transfer money laundering activity without once accepting a currency payment from Customs undercover agents. There are lessons to be learned by financial institutions from all of these cases.

The vast majority of domestic and international financial transactions move by way of EFT. The amount of money moved through these transfers is mind boggling. Over 41,000 wire transfers are originated by banks in the United States every hour of every working day. This does not include thousands of transmissions initiated by nonbank transmitters. There are two principal wire transfer systems in the United States. Together, these networks handle more than 95 percent of all wire transfers received or sent, which total more than $174 billion every hour. One of the networks, the Clearing House Interbank Payments System (CHIPS), processed over 36 million wire transfers totaling more than $190 trillion in 1989. The average transfer amounted to approximately $5 million.

In the face of these staggering numbers, some bankers have suggested that government efforts to focus money laundering attention on wire transfer activity is a waste of time and is like looking for a needle in a haystack. Some bankers also have indicated that trying to identify suspicious wire transfer activity is an impossibility. In talking about activity at the wire network level or in the computer operations of large money center banks, it certainly is almost impossible to identify suspicious wire transfer activity. However, there are beginning and ending points to wire transfers and it is at these points that financial institutions should be able to recognize unusual and suspicious activity.

Let's examine some theoretical situations similar to those that existed in the "Papa Smurf" and BCCI situations. In the "Papa Smurf" case, the money laundering organization deposited monetary instruments into accounts of foreign banks at international banks based in Miami. This was done to facilitate the movement of the laundered funds to drug dealers in places such as Colombia and Panama. Similar situations have existed and continue to exist with domestic banks. Say a business account is opened at a bank for a management consulting firm, and some time after the account is opened, a large volume of cashier's checks, money orders, and traveler's checks start to be deposited to the account. Shortly after the deposits, instructions are received from the firm to wire transfer most of the funds to an account at a bank in the Cayman Islands, perhaps in the range of $400,000 to $500,000 weekly.

Taken separately, both the deposit and wire transfer transactions are unusual and suspicious. When put together, the activity becomes highly suspicious and is indicative of drug money laundering. In the case of the wire transfers, why would a legitimate management consulting firm want to wire $500,000 a week to an account in a Cayman Islands bank? The monetary instrument deposits are equally suspicious. There is no legitimate business reason for a management consulting firm to be taking in cashier's checks, money orders, or traveler's checks. The activity reeks of drug money laundering. Both kinds of transactions are easily recognizable.

In a situation similar to the BCCI case, let's suppose a domestic bank opens a business account for a financial consulting firm. The president of the firm states, at the time the account is opened, that his clients consist of a number of wealthy investors, most of whom are South Americans. The account is opened with the deposit of a $10,000 cashier's check issued by another bank in the same city. The account remains dormant for about six months, then suddenly there is a flurry of wire transfer activity. Over $3 million is wire transferred into the account in six transactions of about $500,000 each. The funds come from banks in two other cities. The president of the consulting firm then issues instructions for most of the funds to be transferred to an account in a Panamanian bank through a large New York bank. After a brief one-week respite, the wire transfer activity in the account resumes. This time there are six more transfers from banks in other cities, each in amounts of $1 million. Once again, most of the money is wire transferred to a large New York bank with instructions to move it into the same account in the same Panamanian bank where the initial funds were sent.

There is no question that when these transfers move through the New York bank they are a blur in the system. The New York bank would have no way of realizing that the transactions are unusual and suspicious in nature. It is quite a different story back at the bank where the financial consulting firm has an account. The sudden movement of over $9 million through a dormant account to a bank in Panama is highly unusual. BCCI had no trouble in recognizing the unusual nature of similar activity in Operation C Chase. No domestic bank should have any trouble in recognizing that this kind of activity represents a significant change in the relationship with the customer. It is unusual and suspicious. The bank should take action to determine the reason for the transfers and to protect itself from being used. Has the customer suddenly struck it rich with clients who want to make investments in Panama? If the customer's clients are mostly South Americans, why are funds coming from other U.S. cities and then being moved to Panama? These are questions that should be resolved before the business relationship is allowed to continue. The object of the inquiry with the customer should be to determine if the account activity is consistent with his legitimate normal business activity. The customer's responses and the result of other inquiries made by the bank might possibly provide a comfort level that the transactions represent legitimate new business generated by the customer. Most likely, the outcome will be a deepened suspicion that something highly unusual and irregular is taking place and that the funds probably originate from some form of illegal activity. The bank should then take action to terminate the account relationship and to notify an appropriate federal enforcement agency.

The consequences of not taking such action are potentially severe. At the very least there could be negative publicity that the bank was used by a major international drug money laundering operation when it should have known better. In a worst case scenario, the bank could face criminal money laundering charges. This is not so far fetched if a few facts are added to the hypothetical situation. Let's suppose that the financial consultant was, in fact, a money launderer and that the funds came from drug sales. Let's also suppose that it later turns out that the bank officer who opened the account knew the customer was a money launderer, knew that the account was being opened with drug money to facilitate the flow of that money to Colombia, and assisted the customer in getting the account opened and the wire-transfer transactions approved. Under these circumstances, the bank officer and the bank itself could face money laundering charges. The fact that the bank took no action to inquire about the highly unusual nature of the wire transfers and decided to remain "willfully blind" to the possibility that the funds were derived from criminal activity will not be helpful if criminal charges are filed.

Financial institutions must keep tabs on more than just currency trans-actions to avoid being used by money launderers. A range of monetary instruments are frequently used by money launderers. These include money orders, traveler's checks, cashier's checks, bank checks, and bank drafts. Personal and business account checks are also utilized, particularly in cases where money launderers have opened accounts in fictitious indi-vidual or business names.

Wire transfers are an important part of the "layering" phase of money laundering. Once currency from illegal activity has been "placed" into a financial institution, wire transfers are the quickest and most efficient means of moving it to other domestic banks or to offshore bank accounts to blur the paper trail so that it can be used by the kingpins of the criminal enterprise.

Financial institutions must be constantly vigilant to recognize unusual and suspicious activity other than currency transactions which may be in-dicative of a money laundering scheme.

LEGISLATIVE, REGULATORY, AND ENFORCEMENT TRENDS

The thrust of legislative, regulatory, and enforcement efforts against money laundering since 1985 has been to force financial institutions toward better compliance with the Bank Secrecy Act and to push these institutions to cooperate with enforcement agencies by reporting suspicious activity. These efforts have been accompanied by additional recordkeeping and re-porting requirements, tougher penalties for noncompliance with regula-tions, and laws which put financial institutions on the fringe of illegal activity when the source of funds in financial transactions is derived from that activity.

Additional Recordkeeping Requirements

A number of new recordkeeping requirements have been placed on finan-cial institutions and businesses in the last few years. These new require-ments were designed to deter money laundering and to provide better paper trails for the types of transactions most frequently used by launder-ers. At the same time, these measures have imposed a considerable burden of paperwork on financial institutions.

The Bank Secrecy Act was amended in 1988 to require that identifica-tion be obtained and records maintained for currency purchases of mone-tary instruments in amounts between $3,000 and $10,000. Regulations, which have come to be known as the "Monetary Instrument Log Regulations," now require all financial institutions to obtain identification and maintain detailed records of each transaction involving the purchase with currency of cashier's checks, bank checks or drafts, traveler's checks, and money orders in amounts between $3,000 and $10,000. The records must be obtained on a monthly basis on a monetary instrument log. This requirement was imposed both to deter "smurfing" and structured transaction activity and to establish a paper trail to help the government track down those individuals who purchase monetary instruments as a way of laundering money.

Another major recordkeeping requirement that has been proposed would require the maintenance of records on wire transfers. The proposed wire transfer regulations are very controversial. The most controversial elements focus on financial institutions that receive wire transfers. These institutions would be required to identify a foreign originator within 15 days of the time of payment. They would also have 15 days to get required information from a recipient accountholder if it is not available at the time of payment.

Identification requirements for the customers of non-bank money transmitters are somewhat more stringent.

Serious concerns have been expressed by money center banks and a number of major nonbank financial institutions that the proposed recordkeeping requirements will obstruct the payments system and the free flow of legitimate funds. The Federal Reserve has similar concerns, and, in the fall of 1991, was attempting to get Treasury to back off some of the requirements. The final wire transfer regulations will probably be issued in 1992.

A 1988 amendment to the Bank Secrecy Act gave the Treasury Department the authority to greatly expand its currency reporting requirements for limited periods of time in specific geographic areas where there is a severe money laundering problem. The Treasury issued a so-called Geographic Targeting Regulation in 1989. The regulation allows Treasury to require reports on Form 4789 for currency in any amount less than $10,000.01 from financial institutions in certain defined geographic areas for a period of up to 60 days. Theoretically, Treasury could direct several banks in the same vicinity to report all currency transactions above $50, or even less. The impact on targeted institutions could be Draconian. Despite the potential impact, there are strong indications that this tactic will rarely be used.

Geographic targeting orders were issued only twice in the first two years Treasury had such authority. In each case, the order was directed to nonbank financial institutions in locations involving a money laundering operation where currency was paid to money transmitters to be forwarded by wire transfer to other participants in the scheme. In one case the reporting threshold was $1,000 or more, and in the other case it was $100 or more.

In September 1990, the Treasury Department proposed a new regulation which would impose additional reporting requirements by requiring the aggregation of daily currency transactions at certain financial institutions. Banks with more than $100 million in deposits would have to implement systems and procedures to "track and capture, at a minimum, multiple currency transactions" of more than $10,000 "by or on behalf of the same accountholder that affect an account during one business day." Currency dealers and exchangers (including check cashers) and transmitters of funds, regardless of asset size, also would have to implement systems and procedures to aggregate currency transactions during one business day, if the rules are adopted as proposed.

There is no existing requirement that financial institutions aggregate multiple transactions. All that is required today is that an institution report aggregated same business day transactions over $10,000, if it has knowledge of the multiple nature of the transactions.

For years Treasury has been saying that it would not require financial institutions to develop aggregation systems. Obviously, Treasury has changed its mind.

There are estimates that this proposed regulation will force 1,000 banks and 14,000 nonbank financial institutions to install aggregation systems. It has also been estimated that the proposal will result in the annual filing of one million additional CTRs with the IRS. Financial industry sources estimate their cost for adopting aggregation systems at well over $100 million.

Impact of New Regulatory Tends

There can be little doubt from existing regulations and proposed regulations about the government's intention to impose additional recordkeeping requirements on the business and financial communities. These requirements are seen by the Congress and by the Executive Branch as partial solutions to the need to deter money laundering activity. They may or may not have this kind of impact. There are several potential effects, though, that are more certain.

One is the imposition of substantial burdens and costs on financial institutions that are already attempting to cut costs to bolster sagging earnings. Another is that the requirements and the proposals are bringing more and more officials in the financial community to question the wisdom and effectiveness of some of the measures.

Many knowledgeable individuals are questioning whether or not the government makes worthwhile use of the large volume of information which it collects and requires financial institutions to record. Questions are also being raised about the cost effectiveness of the regulatory initiatives. Does the cost match the benefits to be gained? There are pros and cons on both sides of the argument.

Forced Compliance

Both Congress and the Executive Branch of government have been working diligently to force financial institutions to comply with laws and regulations that deter money laundering activity. Criminal and civil penalties have been substantially increased. The Treasury Department has levied severe penalties against financial institutions. Some financial institutions have received substantial criminal fines. In a number of cases, employees of financial institutions have been given lengthy jail terms.

Until 1984, most Bank Secrecy Act offenses were misdemeanor offenses with relatively light maximum jail sentences and fines. BSA amendments in 1984, 1986, and 1988 changed all that and made all criminal violations felonies with maximum prison sentences up to 10 years and fines up to $10,000, and also substantially increased civil penalties. Civil penalties for willful failure to comply were raised from $1,000 to $25,000 per violation or the amount of the transaction not to exceed $100,000, which ever is greater. A civil penalty was created for negligent violations. Negligent errors can cost a financial institution $500 each.

The crime of money laundering was created in two statutes that were enacted in 1986. One carries a maximum prison sentence of 20 years and the other a maximum sentence of 10 years.

As of the fall of 1991, the Treasury Department had imposed over 50 civil penalties for BSA violations. Some have been substantial. Bank of America, for example, was fined $4,750,000 in 1986. Oscar's Money Exchange, a money exchanger in Texas, was penalized $3 million in 1988. The former Crocker National Bank was fined $2,250,000 in 1985. Texas Commerce Bancshares was fined $1,900,000 in 1986. Bank of Boston received a criminal fine of $500,000 in 1985. BCCI was fined over $14 million in 1990.

The government is sending a strong message to financial institutions: "comply with the Bank Secrecy Act and avoid involvement with money laundering activity or face stiff civil penalties, criminal prosecution, and large criminal fines."

Employees of financial institutions also must be made aware that they face harsh jail sentences for participation in money laundering schemes.

Financial Institutions on the Fringe

Two pieces of legislation were enacted in 1986 which put financial institutions and businesses on the fringe of criminal activity when they conduct financial transactions with money launderers. Both created new crimes, and both hold the possibility of creating severe problems for financial institutions.

One amended the Bank Secrecy Act to prohibit the structuring of currency transactions to evade the reporting requirements of the Act. The other incorporates two statutes that make the act of money laundering a crime.

Structuring

Ever since the Bank Secrecy Act went into effect, people have been figuring out ways to evade the reporting requirements by structuring transactions. Typical structuring schemes involved the splitting of a large sum of money, for example $15,000, into two smaller amounts of $8,000 and $7,000 to be deposited into a bank on separate business days; the regular deposit of amounts just under $10,000 on different business days; and currency purchases of monetary instruments in amounts under $10,000. There was a problem prior to 1986 in that there was no crime of structuring and it was very difficult to prosecute individuals involved in structuring operations.

The problem was remedied by an amendment to the Bank Secrecy Act in 1986 which created the criminal offense of structuring. That amendment prohibits one from "causing or attempting to cause a domestic financial institution to fail to file a report required" under the law, or causing or attempting to cause a domestic financial institution to file a report that "contains a material omission or misstatement of fact." It also prohibits the structuring or assisting in structuring, or attempting to structure any transaction with one or more domestic financial institutions.

In an effort to clarify the law, Treasury defined structuring in a new regulation issued in 1989. The definition made it clear that structuring includes breaking down a single sum of currency exceeding $10,000 into smaller sums, including sums at or below $10,000. It also includes conducting a transaction or a series of transactions in amounts at or below $10,000. The transaction or transactions need not exceed the $10,000 reporting threshold at any single financial institution on any single day in order to constitute structuring, the rule notes.

Because of language that prohibits assisting in structuring, financial institutions must train employees to exercise considerable caution when discussing large currency transactions with customers. Employees must avoid even the appearance of assisting customers in structuring currency transactions to evade the filing of a CTR. A distinction can be drawn between merely explaining the requirements of the law, which is permissible, and advising the customer how to evade the requirements, which would violate the law. Many banks and other financial institutions provide tellers

with pamphlets that explain the basics of large currency reporting requirements and the law that prohibits structuring. Employees are trained to give
a pamphlet to any customer who starts to discuss the breaking up of a
large currency transaction, and to avoid providing the customer with any
advice.

The Money Laundering Statutes

The United States was the first nation to establish the criminal offense of
money laundering. The offense was spelled out in two statutes that were
enacted into law as part of the Money Laundering Control Act of 1986.
Both statutes are part of Title 18 of the U.S. Code, which contains the basic
federal criminal laws.

One statute, Section 1956, is known as financial transaction money
laundering and carries penalties of up to 20 years in prison for each occurrence. The other, Section 1957, is known as financial institution money
laundering and has penalties of up to 10 years in prison for each offense.

The creation of the crime of money laundering has revolutionized federal law enforcement capabilities and policies and has substantially increased the exposure that financial institutions and businesses have when
dealing with people whose funds originate from criminal activity. The statutes are extremely broad and far-reaching. New applications are constantly
being developed by federal prosecutors against a wide variety of businesses in numerous different factual situations. The laws have extra- terri-
torial reach if the offense is conducted by a U.S. citizen or by a non-U.S.
citizen who conducts at least part of the offense in the United States.

In its simplest form, the crime of financial transaction money laundering occurs when property derived from specified unlawful activity is used
in financial transactions to accomplish one of the following purposes:

- To continue to further the criminal activity that generated the
  property; or

- To conceal or hide the ownership of the property obtained from
  the criminal activity; or

- To avoid a transaction reporting requirement under state or federal
  law.

To be found guilty of this type of money laundering, a person would
have to intend one of these purposes and have knowledge that the property involved in the transaction represents the proceeds of some form of
unlawful activity.

The word "property" in the context of this statute refers to real property and personal property, including money. The law covers nearly every

imaginable financial transaction. It is not restricted to currency transactions. It includes wire transfer, monetary instrument, and personal check transactions with financial institutions. It also includes purchase, sale, loan, and gift transactions.

The term "specified unlawful activity" refers to nearly every serious federal offense which generates money. These include virtually all narcotics offenses as well as securities fraud, bank fraud, espionage, kidnapping, government procurement fraud, counterfeiting, bribery, and a number of other crimes that are listed in the statute.

The concept of "some form of unlawful activity" as a knowledge element in the offense means that the parties conducting the transaction knew that the property involved represented proceeds from some form, although not necessarily which form, of activity that constitutes a felony under state or federal law, regardless of whether such activity is "specified unlawful activity." This is a very broad concept. Some legal observers have speculated that the definition of "some form of unlawful activity" may enable the government to satisfy the knowledge requirement by proving the existence of vast amounts of cash or valuable property being treated in a surreptitious manner. The fact is that this situation may constitute sufficient circumstantial evidence to demonstrate that the individual conducting transactions with the cash knew that it came from some kind of criminal activity, although not precisely what form of criminal activity.

The financial transaction money laundering statute also prohibits the transportation of criminally-derived property into or out of the United States, and relies on knowledge definitions similar to those involving financial transactions.

As written, the money laundering statutes have a very direct and far-reaching effect on financial institutions and employees. Indeed, if the structuring statute brings financial institutions to the fringe of illegal activity, then the money laundering statutes bring them to the brink.

Consider this hypothetical situation with a distinct real world potential. John Jones is a teller in a busy branch of the XYZ Bank located in the downtown area of a large city. He develops a romantic relationship with Mary Smith. Mary appears to have a lot of money and is very secretive about her background. Eventually she confides in John that she moves cash for a large gambling organization. She tells him that she needs new outlets to move currency so that it won't be traced back to her. Now Mary hasn't been completely truthful with John. She moves currency, all right, but it is for a drug trafficking ring and not for a gambling organization. In the course of their continuing relationship and discussions, John decides that he will try to help Mary with her currency problems. Mary has shown him several sets of identification in different names which she uses to help in moving cash without being identified. John suggests she open an account at the branch where he works in one of the fictitious names. They agree that she will make currency deposits several days each week in amounts under $10,000, and that on days when deposits are not made, she will purchase cashier's checks from him with currency in amounts under $10,000. He agrees to enter her false identification on the bank's monetary instrument log when the cashier's check purchases are $3,000 or more, and he agrees not to let on to his superiors about Mary's transactions.

The plan is carried out. Almost every business day for two months, Mary either makes currency deposits or purchases cashier's checks. She always conducts her transactions with John. At the end of two months she has laundered $205,000 at the XYZ Bank. Then the roof caves in. An accomplice in the drug trafficking ring is arrested and furnishes full details on the operation. He identifies Mary Smith as one of several money launderers and further indicates that she has a boyfriend at XYZ Bank who helps her move currency through the bank. Most members of the drug ring, including Mary Smith, are arrested. Mary cooperates and relates the full details of her money laundering activities, including her transactions at XYZ Bank under a fictitious name. She also reveals her relationship with John Jones and the scheme they worked out prior to the currency transactions. Subsequently, John Jones is arrested and indicted on money laundering and structuring charges.

In the scenario presented, Mary Smith and John Jones fulfilled just about every conceivable action and knowledge requirement of the financial transaction money laundering statute. The property or funds involved in the transaction came from "specified unlawful activity;" the money came from drug sales. Mary Smith and John Jones knew that the funds came from "some form of unlawful activity." Mary knew the true origin of the funds and John thought they came from an organized gambling operation. It didn't matter because organized gambling constituted a felony offense in the state where the bank was located. Mary and John also fulfilled three other intent requirements of the statute:

- They carried out the transactions for the purpose of furthering the criminal activity that produced the money;
- They conducted the transactions with the object of concealing the source and ownership of the funds; and
- Their purpose was clearly to conduct the transactions in a manner designed to avoid the reporting requirements of the Bank Secrecy Act.

In addition, Mary "structured" the transactions to evade the reporting requirements and John aided her in the structuring operation.

The XYZ Bank could be charged with money laundering violations. It is possible that the bank could be convicted if a jury were to find that John Jones' knowledge of the criminal nature of the transactions could be imputed to the bank. Whether or not the bank would be charged in the situation presented would be decided by the U.S. Attorney. The significant point of the scenario is that a bank, without any institutional intent, could face criminal charges on the basis of the actions of one of its employees, even though those actions go against every policy and procedure that the institution has set forth.

Financial Institution Money Laundering

The financial institution money laundering statute makes it a crime for anyone to knowingly engage in a "monetary transaction" with criminally-derived property of more than $10,000 with knowledge that the property came from unlawful activity.

The operative phrase here is "monetary transaction." It is defined in the statute as meaning the deposit, withdrawal, transfer, or exchange of funds or a monetary instrument by, through, or to a financial institution. To be guilty of this offense, the participants have to know that the criminally-derived property came from specified unlawful activity. The following scenario illustrates how a financial institution can become involved in this offense.

The example is akin to that which existed in the Polar Cap case. James Smith is the owner of the ABC Jewelry Exchange. He sells jewelry and deals in gold. He maintains a business checking account at DEF Bank. Smith is approached by a money launderer to move large amounts of currency through his business. He knows that the currency came from drug sales. He is to receive a percentage of all the currency that he moves through his business and places in banks. Smith agrees. He opens accounts at several other banks and begins to receive large cash shipments and deposits the money evenly in each of the accounts so that no single bank receives an unusually large amount of currency. Nevertheless, ABC Jewelry's currency deposits at DEF Bank begin to increase substantially, rising from an average of $40,000 a week to over $200,000 a week.

The head teller at DEF Bank advises the manager, Fred Johnson, of the unusual increase. Johnson, who knows Smith, advises the teller he will discuss the deposits with him, which he does. Initially, Smith explains that he has begun to sell large amounts of gold chains and that customers, particularly foreigners, are paying in cash. Johnson responds that he knows the jewelry business well enough to know that gold chain sales couldn't account for the amounts that Smith is depositing, and he indicates that he might have to close out the account. At this point, Smith confides in Johnson that the money is coming from drug traffickers and offers Johnson a one half of one percent cut on all currency deposits placed in the DEF Bank. Johnson agrees to the arrangement and ABC Jewelry Exchange's currency deposits at DEF increase to an average of $400,000 a week. Most of the funds in the account are quickly wire transferred to accounts in several New York banks. Johnson assures the head teller that he had spoken to Smith and is convinced the deposits are okay because Smith had expanded his business.

After six months of steady cash deposits of $400,000 a week at DEF Bank by ABC Jewelry, the drug trafficking ring and its money laundering operation are broken up by federal law enforcement officers, and a large number of arrests and currency seizures take place. Among the arrested are James Smith, who provides full details of the money laundering operation, including his arrangement with Fred Johnson. Subsequently, Fred Johnson and DEF Bank are indicted on money laundering charges.

The scenario represents a classic drug money laundering operation. All the knowledge and intent elements of both money laundering statutes were fulfilled. The government could have charged Johnson and the bank with violations under either statute. The scenario also illustrates several lessons for financial institutions. One lesson is how close a financial institution comes to criminal activity when transactions are conducted with funds derived from criminal activity. Another is that financial institutions need to be aware of transactions that indicate the possibility of money laundering, and must have controls in place to identify these transactions. The final lesson is that an institution must be prepared to take action once it suspects that it is being used by money launderers.

Suspicious Transaction Handling

For at least five years there have been a number of Congressional and Executive Branch actions pushing financial institutions to identify and report suspicious transactions to appropriate enforcement agencies. Congressional actions included the enactment of the money laundering and structuring statutes and an amendment to the Right to Financial Privacy Act that made it easier for financial institutions to report suspicious activity. Executive Branch actions included a regulatory announcement, two administrative rulings, and a new CTR form in 1990, all of which advise financial institutions how to report suspicious transactions.

The initial Executive Branch action came in Administrative Ruling 88-1 by the Treasury Department in June 1988. The ruling, which dealt with violations of the Bank Secrecy Act, stated that financial institutions should report information which may be relevant to a possible violation of the Act or its regulations to the local IRS, Criminal Investigations Division (CID) office, or to an 800 number staffed by IRS personnel. The ruling stated that all such disclosures should be made in accordance with the Right to Financial Privacy Act and it spelled out exactly what information could be provided.

This initial ruling was quickly followed by another Treasury Administrative Ruling, 88-2, on the filing of CMIRs in connection with the international transportation of monetary instruments. That ruling directed banks to report suspicious transactions involving the international transportation of monetary instruments to the U.S. Customs Service within the confines of the Right to Financial Privacy Act.

Yet another direction to financial institutions on how to handle suspicious transactions came in a January 1989 *Federal Register* notice in which Treasury set forth the regulatory definition of structuring. In the notice, Treasury stated that, if a financial institution suspects structuring is taking place, it should report its suspicion to the local office of IRS, Criminal Investigation.

In addition to the Treasury directives, all of the federal bank regulatory agencies have issued regulations requiring banks under their supervision to immediately report violations of the law or suspicious transactions to them on criminal referral forms and to also report this information to IRS-CID. Banks should note that suspicious transaction information reported to a bank regulator is not subject to the strictures of the Right to Financial Privacy Act.

The Treasury Department also makes its intentions known on suspicious transaction reporting on its current CTR form. The latest version of this form, issued on January 1, 1990, contains a box to be checked if the financial institution believes the transaction being reported is suspicious. In addition, the instructions state, "For a suspicious transaction, you should telephone as soon as possible the local office of the Internal Revenue Service, Criminal Investigation Division, in addition to submitting this form."

Despite these very clear and direct statements, some financial institutions have been slow learners. The nine out of ten banks in Los Angeles that did not report huge currency transactions in the Polar Cap case are a good example. They did what was technically required of them under the law. They filed CTRs for the currency transactions. Each of these institutions had to have been aware that there was no way that individual wholesale and retail jewelry businesses could have been legitimately generating millions of dollars in currency deposits on a regular basis.

Another indication that there are some slow learning banks is that the bank supervisory agencies, during the course of their examinations, are finding that some banking institutions have not been doing much about referring suspicious transaction information. In one instance during the past year, an examination showed that a sixty-branch bank in a major city had made only three suspicious transaction referrals during 1990. Despite these individual cases, the fact is that many banks do report suspicious financial transaction information to federal agencies with some regularity.

WHAT'S A FINANCIAL INSTITUTION TO DO?

How can a financial institution protect itself from the scourge of money laundering? It seems that problems are coming from all directions. The money launderers are pushing currency everywhere.

Launderers use currency deposits, monetary instrument purchases, fake businesses, and cash being run through otherwise legitimate businesses. By the time a financial institution gets squared away on the dangers of unusual currency transactions, it has to start worrying about transactions with monetary instruments, wire transfers, and unusual collateral and loan payments. New recordkeeping and reporting requirements are coming out all the time. Laws designed to combat money laundering are placing financial institutions in danger of prosecution if their employees become involved in the laundering activity. Bank regulators are pressing for strict compliance with recordkeeping and reporting requirements and suggesting that all employees be trained on recognizing suspicious transactions. On top of this, financial institutions feel the vast majority of the transactions they conduct represent legitimate business and banking activity. Add to all this the fact that bottom lines at many financial institutions are eroding and there is tremendous pressure on managers to get new business and drive up profits; indeed, the banking industry in many respects is in dire straights.

So, what can a financial institution do to cope with money laundering?

Perhaps the best answer comes from a set of principles adopted by the Committee on Banking Regulations and Supervisory Practices of the Group of 10 industrialized nations at a meeting in Basle, Switzerland in December 1988. The committee was formed by the central bank governors of Belgium, Canada, France, Germany, Italy, Japan, Netherlands, Sweden, Switzerland, and United States. The principles, which have come to be known as the Basle Principles, deal with the prevention of the criminal use of the banking system for the purpose of money laundering, and contain recommendations for banks and other financial institutions to follow in order to avoid being used as intermediaries for the transfer or deposit of money derived from criminal activity.

The principles set forth in this document suggest policies and procedures in four areas to assist in the suppression of money laundering: customer identification, compliance with laws, cooperation with law enforcement authorities, and policies which must be adopted to ensure adherence to the principles. The key recommendations in each of these areas are:

Customer Identification - Banks should make reasonable efforts to determine the true identities of all customers requesting the institution's services. All banks should institute effective procedures for obtaining identification from new customers. It should be an explicit policy that significant business transactions will not be conducted with customers who fail to provide evidence of their identity.

Compliance with Laws - Bank management should ensure that business is conducted in conformity with high ethical standards and that laws and regulations pertaining to financial transactions are adhered to. Banks should not offer services or provide active assistance in transactions which they have good reason to believe are associated with money laundering activities.

Cooperation with Law Enforcement Authorities - Banks should cooperate fully with national law enforcement authorities to the extent permitted by specific local regulations concerning customer confidentiality.

Adherence to the Statement - Banks should institute policies consistent with the Statement and communicate these policies to all employees. Staff training, specific procedures for customer identification, internal recordkeeping, and extended internal audit procedures are key elements in promoting adherence to the Statement of Principles.

The Basle Principles form an effective guideline for what financial institutions should do to cope with money laundering. Although intended for banks, the principles have application for all financial institutions. It is no accident that all federal bank regulatory agencies in the United States have enthusiastically adopted the Basle Principles and have instructed banks under their domain to incorporate these principles into their compliance policies and procedures.

MONEY LAUNDERING DETERRENCE PROGRAM

Financial institutions must develop deterrence programs to effectively deal with money laundering activities. To be effective, a deterrence program must contain a policy statement that commits the institution to high ethical principles, a strong "Know Your Customer" program, a money laundering awareness program that includes a commitment to and procedures for reporting suspicious transactions, and a strict Bank Secrecy Act compliance program.

All of these elements should be described in writing and incorporated into a comprehensive policies and procedures manual that deals with Bank Secrecy Act compliance and money laundering. It is important that the various elements of the money laundering deterrence program be directed and coordinated by one individual, and that all of the institution's employees receive training in the policies and procedures developed to deter money laundering.

Banks and most other financial institutions have had BSA compliance programs in effect for a number of years to deal with the requirements of the Bank Secrecy Act. For banks, these programs have been required by laws and regulations since 1987. It is no longer enough, however, for financial institutions simply to have good Bank Secrecy Act compliance programs in place. These programs must be expanded to include broader issues created by money laundering activity.

The fact is that a financial institution can have a good Bank Secrecy Act compliance program in place and still be severely damaged by money laundering activity. There must be an awareness on the part of the institution's employees of the kinds of transactions that indicate the possibility of money laundering and internal procedures for reporting suspicious transactions to federal authorities. Furthermore, a financial institution must have a strong "Know Your Customer" program to protect itself from money laundering activity.

Most financial institutions have an officer responsible for Bank Secrecy Act compliance. The duties of that individual and his or her staff could be expanded to include the coordination of the institution's "Know Your Customer" program and the coordination of procedures to collect, evaluate, and refer suspicious transaction information.

Policy Statement

Every financial institution should have a policy to avoid handling the proceeds of drug trafficking and other criminal activity and against being used by money launderers. This policy should be in writing and distributed to all employees. It also should be incorporated in the institution's Money Laundering Deterrence and Bank Secrecy Act Compliance Policies and Procedures Manual.

Financial institutions should take the high moral ground and dedicate themselves to operating within high ethical principles. These principles, with regard to money laundering, should include: refusing to do business with drug traffickers and their money launderers; a commitment to conduct business only with business organizations that appear to be involved in legitimate commercial enterprises; refusing to do business with individuals or organizations who will not properly identify themselves; a policy of referring all suspicious transaction information and criminal activity to the appropriate federal authorities within the confines of the Right to Financial Privacy Act; and a commitment to comply with the spirit and specific provisions of all laws and regulations of the Bank Secrecy Act.

Banks and other financial institutions should be in the forefront of efforts to assist the federal government in attempting to combat drug money laundering. They are really in the front lines of money laundering activity. In most cases, they are either the primary or secondary recipients of money from drug sales.

A financial institution's policy statement should also contain a firm statement about the adoption of a "Know Your Customer" program. Such a program is very important in properly identifying customers and in monitoring unusual account activity.

The most important thing about a good policy statement that is dedicated to ethical business principles and touches all the right bases is that it must be real. It must reflect the actual commitment of a financial institution's top management.

"Know Your Customer" Programs

Most financial institutions claim to have "Know Your Customer" (KYC) programs. It's a buzzword term in the banking business. In reality, though, most of these programs are not well defined and not enforced internally.

In an era when financial institutions cannot afford to be used or deceived by money launderers, an effective KYC program is very important. It should enable an institution to identify customers; provide some comfort level as to the legitimacy of funds from business customers; monitor accounts for unusual activity; and if properly administered, result in enhanced customer relationships.

Effective KYC programs usually have three phases. They involve customer identification, account monitoring, and appropriate action if there are significant and unusual changes in account activity. KYC programs should be reduced to writing and training should be provided to all employees who have responsibilities in the program. An institution's KYC program should be part of its Money Laundering Deterrence and Bank Secrecy Act Compliance Policies and Procedures Manual.

Customer Identification A key factor in any good KYC program is the identification of customers. This includes, for banks, nondeposit accountholders as well as accountholders. Proper customer identification can assist an institution in meeting BSA regulatory requirements, as well as help prevent it from being used by money launderers. Both the CTR reporting requirements and the monetary instrument recordkeeping requirements of the Bank Secrecy Act mandate the identification of customers using financial institution services. Wire transfer regulations that will be issued in 1992, will also mandate identification requirements for customers.

For banks, a key element in exempting business accounts from the CTR reporting requirements entails knowledge that the accountholders are engaged in legitimate businesses and that exemption limits are established in amounts commensurate with the customary conduct of the lawful domestic businesses of those customers. These regulatory requirements highlight the need for banks to know their customers quite well.

Financial institutions should make reasonable efforts to identify all new accountholders and loan customers and the persons on whose behalf they are establishing the relationship. If a customer refuses to provide required information, or any subsequent investigation raises suspicions about the proper identity or legitimacy of the customer, supervisory personnel must make a decision as to possible termination of the relationship. For banks, the amount of identification required and the nature of efforts to verify the identification should depend on whether the new account is an individual deposit, business, or loan relationship.

Individual Deposit Accounts Minimum identification standards should be established for all individuals who establish new account relationships. Typically, the information to be obtained should include the name, address, date of birth, social security number (or, for a non-U.S. citizen, a passport, visa, or alien registration number), current employer, business and residence telephone numbers. The information obtained, together with a description of the identification, should be recorded on the signature card and on the institution's customer file.

Financial institutions should not do business with individuals who provide false or misleading information about their identity or background. If there are any doubts or inconsistencies about information provided by a new customer, additional inquiries should be made to verify the information.

New Business Accounts Minimum identification standards for new business accounts should include the business name and street address, telephone number, taxpayer identification number, documents establishing the formation of the business entity (corporate resolution, partnership agreement, etc.), a full description of the operations of the business, credit and banking references, and the identity of the principal officers.

Business accounts usually generate more activity and more risk than individual accounts. Risks include the possibility of money laundering or new account fraud. In view of this fact, some inquiries should be conducted to verify information provided at the time the account was opened. These inquiries might include the following: checking credit and banking references; making a personal visit to the business during working hours; and checking with a reporting agency such as Dun & Bradstreet or conducting a business credit check.

It should be noted that a personal visit to a business by an officer of the institution can and should be a very positive customer relations effort. At the same time that officers are verifying the location and nature of businesses, they can be establishing personal relationships with principals, exhibiting an interest in the enterprise, and possibly offering additional financial services.

New Loan Relationships New loan accounts require considerable due diligence. There is a forfeiture risk for collateral pledged on loans. Real or personal property traceable to illegal drug sales or purchased with laundered money is subject to seizure and forfeiture. If collateral pledged on a loan is seized by the government, a financial institution must be able to prove it was an innocent owner or lien holder of the property. The institution would have to show that it had no knowledge of the illegal activity that led to the forfeiture.

Minimum standards for information to be obtained and verification procedures for establishing loan relationships should include:

- Reliable identifying information similar to that required for new deposit accounts;

- Reliable financial information such as financial statements, W-2s and/or copies of tax returns;

- The purpose of the loan, which must be established regardless of the value of any collateral;

- Credit and prior banking references should be checked;

- Establishing visible legitimate means of repayment; and

- An assurance that the loan amount is consistent with the purpose of the loan and the nature of the business.

Services for Nonaccountholders Banks and other financial institutions often provide services to nonaccountholders. These services most commonly include funds transfers, sales of cashier's checks, bank checks, traveler's checks or money orders, exchanges of foreign currency, and check cashing. Strict identification requirements should be established for all transactions by nonaccountholders. Bank Secrecy Act regulations require financial institutions to verify the identity of, and obtain additional information from, nonaccountholders who purchase monetary instruments with currency in amounts between $3,000 to $10,000 inclusive. Similar requirements will be imposed by wire transfer regulations for nonaccountholders who receive or initiate funds transfers. There are identification requirements in connection with CTR filing.

In view of these factors, and the risks entailed in dealing with nonaccountholders, some institutions may wish to limit the type and dollar amount of services provided nonaccountholders. Caution should be exercised to ensure that such limitations do not violate any law or regulation with regard to the needs of the local community.

Monitoring Account Relationships Some financial institutions concentrate KYC efforts on identification requirements in connection with new accounts and Bank Secrecy Act requirements. While this is necessary, it is even more important to monitor account activity during the course of a business relationship with a customer. A financial institution that fails to pay attention to unusual account activity is asking for trouble. If the unusual activity is due to money laundering, the institution could be putting itself in a vulnerable position. On the other hand, if the activity comes from legitimate business, it is possible that opportunities to sell additional services will be lost.

There should be a dual purpose in monitoring a customer's transaction activity. One is to identify unusual transactions that might not be consistent with the normal business of the customer. The other is to use the monitoring process to enhance business relationships. Account monitoring should not be restricted to currency activity. Unusual and dramatic changes in wire transfer, monetary instrument, and check transactions are just as important.

Financial institution officials should make periodic visits to the premises of active business accounts, both to verify the nature and volume of the customer's business and to enhance the business relationship by determining the customer's level of satisfaction with services and by being in a position to offer additional services. Periodic visits are particularly important for banks who have exempted retail business accounts from the reporting requirements of the Bank Secrecy Act. Such a bank cannot afford to be in a position where a very active exempted account is in the name of a business that has closed and vacated its premises.

Action on Significant Account Changes When monitoring shows signs of significant changes in account activity, a financial institution must take some action to protect itself. The action to be taken will depend on the facts of each case and how significant the changes are. In some situations, appropriate action may be to discuss the situation with the customer to find out the reason for the change. The discussion may lead to a finding that significant increases in account volume are due to increased sales coming from promotions and advertising. On the other hand, the discussion may lead to a conclusion that increased currency deposits are not consistent with the normal legitimate business of the customer and a suspicion that the currency comes from some form of criminal activity. Under these circumstances, appropriate action may be to report the suspicious activity to an appropriate government agency and terminate the business relationship.

In some cases, the nature of the change in account activity may be so dramatic as to lead to a strong suspicion that funds coming into the account are coming from drug sales. Inquiry with the accountholder may be inappropriate in this type of situation. A direct suspicious transaction referral to a law enforcement agency would appear to be the more appropriate course of action.

Money Laundering Awareness Program

An important part of any financial institution's efforts to cope with money laundering should be an awareness program for its employees. All employees must be made aware of the money laundering statutes and the serious implications they have for both the institution and individual employees. All employees must also be aware of suspicious transactions that might be indicative of money laundering activity. Finally, financial institutions must have policies and procedures in place to deal with suspicious activity and their employees must be aware of the policies and be active participants in the procedures.

Financial institutions should have a section on money laundering awareness in a prominent place in their Money Laundering Deterrence and Bank Secrecy Act Compliance Policies and Procedures manuals. This section ought to explain what money laundering is, the money laundering statutes, and the penalties involved in violating the law. It should also provide examples of the kinds of transactions that might indicate money laundering activity and detail the policies and procedures of the institution with regard to the collection, evaluation, and referral of suspicious transaction information.

Employee training is vital in the areas of money laundering awareness and suspicious transaction handling. All supervisors and managers, not just those involved in cash handling, should receive periodic training in these areas. If possible, the training ought to include information about situations that the institution has experienced with regard to money laundering problems. New employees need training in these areas.

Control of Suspicious Transaction Information It is absolutely essential that every financial institution maintain tight control over all criminal activity and suspicious transaction information that comes to the attention of its employees. If a financial institution has suspicious transaction information about a customer and continues to do business with him without reporting the information to a proper authority, the institution could possibly face criminal charges, civil penalties, bad publicity, and loss of its reputation as a good corporate citizen.

The most important factor in maintaining control over suspicious transactions and criminal activity information is for a financial institution to set up a central control point for all such information to be reported promptly for review and a decision as to appropriate action. An institution cannot tolerate a situation in which every branch and every employee can make disclosures of suspected criminal activity without management review and the availability of legal advice. This practice could lead to chaos and potential legal problems. Internal procedures and mechanisms should be set up so that all such information received by employees is reported to the central location as soon as possible through a supervisory chain of command. In large or midsized multibranch banking institutions, information about suspicious transactions comes to the attention of one or more employees frequently. The information can vary from a suspicious request for an exemption, a series of purchases of bank checks in amounts just under $3,000, to a series of unusually large currency deposits. Employees and supervisors must be trained to recognize suspicious transactions and to report them immediately to the central control point.

The location of the central control point depends upon the size and organizational structure of each institution. A logical place in one institution may be the office of the Bank Secrecy Act compliance officer. In another, it might be the office of the general counsel, and in still another it might be the security department. The location of the central control point is not important. What is important is that there be a central control point; that employees and supervisors know where it is; and that all suspicious transactions and criminal activity related to money laundering is referred to this control point on a timely basis.

Decision Process Once suspected money laundering information is received at the central control point, it must be evaluated as soon as possible and a decision made as to what action will be taken. Decisions will generally fall into three categories. One would be to decide that the activity is really not suspicious and not to take any action on a referral. The second would be to send the referral back to the originating branch or office for additional information, either from the customer or from the branch records. It should be noted that evaluations have to be made in the context of what is known about the customer's business. Suspicious activity for one customer may not be suspicious for another in a different type of business. This highlights the importance of a good KYC policy. The third decision would be that the referral constitutes suspicious activity that may indicate money laundering activity. When this decision is made, the information should be referred to an appropriate government agency within the confines of the Right to Financial Privacy Act.

Reporting Suspicious Transactions Financial institutions should report unusual transactions that may be related to money laundering activity to a government agency. First and foremost, it's the right thing to do. Ethically and morally, such reporting puts financial institutions in the position of good corporate citizens helping in the effort to combat drug trafficking and other illegal activity. Secondly, the government has clearly indicated, in several Treasury Department administrative rulings and in a regulatory pronouncement, that financial institutions should report suspicious transactions. Additionally, banking institutions supervised by the federal bank supervisory agencies are required by regulations to report the existence of suspicious money laundering activity to those agencies. The final reason is that suspicious transaction reporting shows a clear intention on the part of a financial institution not to be part of a money laundering scheme or conspiracy. Such reporting could help the institution to avoid prosecution, fines, and bad publicity.

Some legal observers suggest that such reporting poses serious legal dilemmas. They argue that reporting suspicious transactions can cause legal problems with customers who may complain on privacy grounds. They also claim that there is a "damned if you do, damned if you don't" problem with regard to a decision to stop doing business with a customer who appears to be involved in money laundering activities versus a decision to continue doing business and report the activity. On the one hand, the institution can face legal action by a customer whose account has been closed, while on the other hand, the financial institution could still face criminal charges for continuing to do business, even though a suspicious activity report was made. In the realm of legal theory, there is the possibility of these dilemmas. In the real world of banking, money laundering, and financial transactions, the problems cited are extremely remote.

First, let's look at the supposed dilemma with regard to the Right to Financial Privacy Act. There was always a provision in this law that appeared to allow financial institutions to notify government authorities of "information which may be relevant to a possible violation of any statute or regulation." In 1986, the law was amended to clearly delineate the kind of information that may be furnished. Treasury administrative ruling 88-1, issued in June 1988, lists exactly what kind of information can be provided without the customer's knowledge or consent.

This amendment to the law does not permit an institution to turn over its records to a federal enforcement agency or to give federal enforcement agents free access to its records. This should only be done pursuant to a judicial or administrative subpoena. It does, however, permit certain information to be furnished either verbally or in writing. The 1986 amendment to the Right to Financial Privacy Act provided that information could be furnished notwithstanding any state or local government law to the contrary. It also absolves any financial institution or employee who makes a disclosure pursuant to the law from any liability to the customer. It should be noted that banks can provide any information about customer records or accounts to their federal bank supervisory agencies without incurring liability under the right to Financial Privacy Act under an exception in the law.

The foregoing discussion of the Right to Financial Privacy Act illustrates how much leeway a financial institution has in reporting suspicious activity. Good faith referrals, within the confines of the law, do not pose legal problems for financial institutions. Civil suits based on privacy considerations for disclosures of suspicious activity related to Bank Secrecy Act or money laundering violations are extremely rare. There is certainly a more serious exposure from not reporting apparent criminal activity than there is from legal action by the customer involved in the activity.

The second alleged dilemma posed by some legal observers deals with the issue of whether to discontinue doing business with a customer involved in suspicious transactions or to continue to do business and report the activity to a law enforcement agency. Once again, the real world of financial transactions and banking experience makes this an easier problem to deal with than legal theory might indicate. In addressing this problem, a distinction should be drawn between clear and obvious criminal activity and activity which is suspicious and may indicate money laundering operations.

Let's look at some examples of clear and obvious criminal activity that have occurred in banks.

- A customer offers a bribe to a bank employee not to file CTRs or to file CTRs containing false information. The employee reports the bribe attempt to a superior.

- A customer makes a series of $9,000 currency deposits on different business days. When a teller asks the customer why the deposits are being made in this manner, the customers states that he is a cocaine dealer; that the cash comes from cocaine sales; and that he wants to keep his transactions under $10,000 so that the bank won't have to file a report. The customer then offers some cocaine to the teller. The teller reports this transaction to a bank officer.

- During an internal audit, some large currency transactions are uncovered for which no CTRs were filed. The employee who should have prepared the CTR is questioned. He admits that he has been receiving cash payments from the customer for not filing the CTRs.

In these examples, the banks have become aware of actual criminal conduct, not just a suspicion of possible criminal activity. They must be reported to appropriate federal enforcement agencies as soon as possible and to the bank's supervisory agency on a criminal referral form. Financial institutions are within their right to discontinue doing business with these customers. They have little or no concern about legal action by the customer. The institution should discontinue its business relationship unless requested not to do so by the enforcement agency to whom the violation has been reported. In some cases of ongoing criminal activity, enforcement agencies request financial institutions to continue the business relationship so that more evidence can be gathered and so that possible accomplices can be identified. In these situations, it is the financial institution's decision as to whether or not to cooperate. Many institutions have cooperated with very satisfactory results both for themselves and the federal enforcement agency.

The vast majority of unusual transactions that could involve money laundering may not appear to be criminal in nature. They are acts that give rise to suspicions. In most of these situations, a financial institution would be hard pressed to terminate the business relationship without exposing itself to the possibility of legal retribution from the customer. There is, however, a relatively simple solution to the problem and that is to report the suspicious activity to a federal enforcement agency and continue to do business with the customer. The reporting activity demonstrates the institution's good faith in cooperating; its recognition of a potential problem; and its intent not be used by money launderers. The activity now becomes a matter for the enforcement agency to evaluate and either disregard or pursue as the case may be.

This solution has worked successfully for many financial institutions who have made suspicious transaction referrals. In many instances, enforcement agencies have requested banks and other financial institutions to continue to do business with customers conducting unusual and suspicious transactions so that an investigation can be brought to a successful conclusion. This happened with the Wells Fargo Bank in the Polar Cap case. The bank decided to continue to do business until the investigation was concluded. The case was successfully prosecuted and the bank received reams of favorable publicity.

Some legal observers claim that an institution that continues to do business with a customer after reporting money laundering activity leaves itself open to the possibility of prosecution. If the reported suspicious activity is proven to be a money laundering violation, these observers claim the suspicious activity report indicates that the financial institution knew something was wrong and this knowledge could be used against the institution in a prosecution. Absent any evidence of collusion between the institution and the money launderers, the chances of such a prosecution are very remote, the key being the difference between suspecting and knowing.

Proponents of the "serious dilemma" theory go one step further by saying that a financial institution could be charged with money laundering offenses if, after notifying an enforcement agency of suspicious transactions, it was later determined that one or more of the institution's employees were criminally involved with the money launderers. Technically, this is an accurate statement. A decision to proceed with criminal charges is always a matter of prosecutorial discretion. The fact that a suspicious transaction report was made before the institution was aware that any of its employees were criminally involved would weigh very heavily against a prosecution of the institution.

In the final analysis, decisions as to whether to discontinue doing business with a customer involved in suspicious activity or to notify an enforcement agency and to continue to do business must be made by financial institutions based on the facts of every situation that arises. It is submitted that the decision is relatively easy to make in most cases and that it should be to report the activity and continue to do business.

The ability of a financial institution to recognize, evaluate, and refer suspicious activity is critical to the maintenance of its good name. Referring of suspicious transaction information to federal enforcement agencies is a strong affirmation of an institution's policy not to be used by money launderers or to do business with funds derived from criminal activity. Many bankers believe that the government is forcing them to become policemen by laws and regulations which require them to investigate money laundering. This is a considerable overstatement of the reality of the situation. The government is pushing financial institutions to identify and report more suspicious activity than they have in the past. It is still the federal enforcement agencies who have to investigate the activity reported.

Bank Secrecy Act Compliance Program

The cornerstone of any financial institution's money laundering deterrence program should be a comprehensive Bank Secrecy Act compliance program. It should be a major component of an institution's Money Laundering Deterrence and Bank Secrecy Act Compliance Policies and Procedures manual. Strict compliance to the program means a very determined effort to carry out all of the existing regulatory requirements because they have the full force of law.

Banks are required to have a Bank Secrecy Act Compliance program in place. Other financial institutions should also have similar compliance programs. In 1987, all of the federal bank supervisory agencies issued regulations requiring banks under their supervision to develop a written program designed to assure and monitor compliance with the recordkeeping and reporting requirements of the Bank Secrecy Act and its implementing regulations. The requirements of the compliance program are listed as follows:

1. Provide for a system of internal controls to control ongoing compliance.

2. Provide for independent testing for compliance to be conducted by bank personnel or by an outside party.

3. Designate an individual or individuals responsible for coordinating and monitoring day-to-day compliance.

4. Provide training for appropriate personnel.

After the compliance regulations were issued, banks scrambled to get written and actual programs in place. By mid-1987, most banks had developed fairly good programs. As noted earlier in this chapter, there have been many changes in Bank Secrecy Act laws and regulations since 1987. While most banks have adjusted their ongoing compliance programs to deal with these changes, many banking institutions have not updated their written policies and procedures manuals to reflect these changes. Banks and other financial institutions should review their Bank Secrecy Act compliance programs periodically to ensure that they have been adjusted to incorporate changes. The review should address the four primary areas addressed in the bank supervisory agency's regulatory requirements.

CONCLUSIONS

It cannot be emphasized enough that financial institutions must do more than be in strict compliance with the Bank Secrecy Act to avoid being victimized by money launderers. A strong KYC program is an essential ingredient of a good money laundering deterrence program. The KYC program should be utilized to enhance customer relations and increase business opportunities in addition to verifying the legitimacy of an accountholder's business. The more that an institution knows about customers and their businesses, the more likely that unusual account activity will be recognized.

Financial institutions must train their employees to recognize suspicious transaction activity and they must have internal mechanisms for collecting and evaluating suspicious transactions. Finally, it is recommended that suspicious transaction information be referred to federal enforcement agencies consistent with the restrictions of the Right to Financial Privacy Act. These referrals establish the intent of the financial institution to cooperate with the government and not to be used by money launderers.

It is submitted that institutions that follow the recommendations in this chapter will be able to cope with money laundering activity and the maze of burdensome, costly, and sometimes confusing regulations that come from Washington. Financial institutions that ignore these recommendations place themselves at great risk. Penalties are severe and an institution's reputation can be severely damaged. Some institutions have not been able to survive convictions for Bank Secrecy Act offenses.

In the milieu that exists, preventive measures can go a long way toward ensuring success and survivability.

INDEX

329

About the Publisher

PROBUS PUBLISHING COMPANY

Probus Publishing Company fills the informational needs of today's business professional by publishing authoritative, quality books on timely and relevant topics, including:

- Investing
- Futures/Options Trading
- Banking
- Finance
- Marketing and Sales
- Manufacturing and Project Management
- Personal Finance, Real Estate, Insurance and Estate Planning
- Entrepreneurship
- Management

Probus books are available at quantity discounts when purchased for business, educational or sales promotional use. For more information, please call the Director, Corporate/Institutional Sales at 1-800-PROBUS-1, or write:

Director, Corporate/Institutional Sales
Probus Publishing Company
1925 N. Clybourn Avenue
Chicago, Illinois 60614
FAX (312) 868-6250